Praise for *American Dreams* by H.W. Brands

"[A] clear, broad summary of events at home and abroad from the end of the Second World War to the election of Barack Obama. For anyone seeking a primer or refresher on America . . . this is a crisp, balanced, and easily digestible narrative." —*The Economist*

"*American Dreams: The United States Since 1945* belongs to a vanishing genre. In a partisan age dominated by 'people's history' and 'patriot's history,' Brands has taken on the formidable task of writing a concise, balanced account of America since World War II. And he has succeeded admirably."

—*San Francisco Chronicle*

"Fast-moving . . . comprehensive." —*Publishers Weekly*

"Elegantly written and sharp." —*Kirkus Reviews*

"[A] rich and incisive survey . . . in reader-friendly prose . . . An outstanding title for anyone who wants a solid introduction to the period." —*Bookpage*

"Readers of all stripes will appreciate this educational, easy to read history of themselves." —*The Past in Review*

"Brands delivers a history well modulated for readers seeking an introduction to American history of their living memory." —*Booklist*

"If you love history you will love this book. I did." —Alan Caruba, *Bookviews*

PENGUIN BOOKS

# AMERICAN DREAMS

Henry William Brands taught at Texas A&M University for sixteen years before joining the faculty at the University of Texas at Austin, where he is the Dickson Allen Anderson Centennial Professor of History. His books include *Traitor to His Class*, *Andrew Jackson*, *The Age of Gold*, *The First American*, and *TR*. *Traitor to His Class* and *The First American* were finalists for the Pulitzer Prize.

# AMERICAN DREAMS

## THE UNITED STATES SINCE 1945

H. W. BRANDS

PENGUIN BOOKS

PENGUIN BOOKS

Published by the Penguin Group

Penguin Group (USA) Inc., 375 Hudson Street, New York, New York 10014, U.S.A. · Penguin Group (Canada), 90 Eglinton Avenue East, Suite 700, Toronto, Ontario, Canada M4P 2Y3 (a division of Pearson Penguin Canada Inc.) · Penguin Books Ltd, 80 Strand, London WC2R 0RL, England · Penguin Ireland, 25 St. Stephen's Green, Dublin 2, Ireland (a division of Penguin Books Ltd) · Penguin Books Australia Ltd, 250 Camberwell Road, Camberwell, Victoria 3124, Australia (a division of Pearson Australia Group Pty Ltd) · Penguin Books India Pvt Ltd, 11 Community Centre, Panchsheel Park, New Delhi–110 017, India · Penguin Group (NZ), 67 Apollo Drive, Rosedale, North Shore 0632, New Zealand (a division of Pearson New Zealand Ltd) · Penguin Books (South Africa) (Pty) Ltd, 24 Sturdee Avenue, Rosebank, Johannesburg 2196, South Africa

Penguin Books Ltd, Registered Offices: 80 Strand, London WC2R 0RL, England

First published in the United States of America by
The Penguin Press, a member of Penguin Group (USA) Inc. 2010
Published in Penguin Books 2011

1 3 5 7 9 10 8 6 4 2



THE LIBRARY OF CONGRESS HAS CATALOGED THE HARDCOVER EDITION AS FOLLOWS:
Brands, H. W.
American dreams : the United States since 1945 / H.W. Brands.
p. cm.
Includes bibliographical references and index.
ISBN 978-1-59420-262-9 (hc.)
ISBN 978-0-14-311955-5 (hc.)
1. United States—History—1945– 2. United States—Social conditions—1945–
3. National characteristics, American. I. Title.
E741.B685 2010
973.9—dc22 2009046862

Printed in the United States of America
*Designed by Marysarah Quinn*

# CONTENTS

# PREFACE

AMERICANS HAVE BEEN DREAMING since our national birth. We dreamed of liberty, equality, and happiness. We dreamed of prosperity for ourselves and our children. We dreamed we would save our souls and save the world. We didn't all dream the same dream, or at the same time, for the American dream included the right of the individual dreamers to design their own. The dreams weren't always sunny and hopeful; some were darkly forbidding. But they drew America consistently forward, enticing us toward the horizon of the future.

Never were America's dreams more potent and beguiling than at the end of World War II. The country had vanquished the despair and poverty of the Great Depression; it had conquered the organized evil of militant fascism. The depression taught Americans of that generation resilience and fortitude; the war drew them together in a common purpose. Americans in 1945 stood united and confident at the apex of global power; before them lay more wealth and happiness than any large group had ever dared dream of in all human history.

But the dreams began to waver and lose focus almost at once. The unity of the war years diminished amid the distractions of a confusing peace; in politics and culture Americans drifted apart, often acrimoniously. The inner discipline of the depression slackened amid the comfort of prosperity; the postwar generations took material well-being for granted and demanded more. The capacity for selfless action wasn't lost: Americans challenged poverty, inequality, and prejudice and mitigated these historic scourges substantially. They battled for freedom abroad, and not without positive effect. But with every barrier that fell, others went up; with every measure that made Americans one, others made them many; with every effort that promoted democracy, others frustrated it—leaving Americans in the early twenty-first century to wonder who they were, where their country was going, and how it ought to get there.

Yet the dreaming persisted. If anything, there was more dreaming than ever. Three hundred million Americans harbored their individual dreams, some as old as the country, others of a sort unimaginable six decades before. Americans in 2010 were collectively less confident than their grandparents had been in 1945 that reality would favor their dreams; the world was catching up to America, and the bill for all the previous dreaming was coming due. But the moral foundation of America's dreams had always been the *right* to dream, and Americans weren't about to surrender that.

# I

# Visions of Omnipotence

1945–1965

# 1 | Last One Standing

## 1945–1946

### 1. SUNRISE AT ALAMOGORDO

Summer dawn in southern New Mexico comes slowly, with the eastern sky glowing gradually gray, then turning pink, orange, yellow, white, and finally blue as the sun clears the crest of the southern Rocky Mountains. Amid the white sands of the Tularosa Valley, in the part of the Chihuahuan Desert the Spanish called Jornada del Muerto, or Journey of Death, for its particular aridity and summer heat, the atmospheric palette can be especially subtle, with the pale ground reflecting the shifting hues of the sky.

All this changed one day in July 1945. Dawn came early, and it was a dawn unlike any New Mexico had ever seen. For weeks beforehand, a silent group of men in army trucks and unmarked cars had scurried about a ranch owned by David McDonald, who was strikingly absent. Some of the men dug bunkers; others erected a steel tower approximately two miles northwest of the unoccupied ranch house. Beside the tower was an industrial winch, designed to hoist heavy objects on thick steel cables. From the distance of the bunkers, seven miles from the tower in a semicircle arcing from north to west to south, the tower's details could be seen only with binoculars and spotting telescopes, but they appeared to include elaborate wiring, rigged as though for an electrical experiment. Suspended from the top of the tower, by those steel cables, was a nondescript round object that might, from its appearance, have been an oversize bowling ball. A close examination through the telescopes revealed that the electrical wires connected the round object to equipment on the ground.

In the bunkers on the night of July 15–16, the men who had been working on the tower gathered in small groups. A few of the men tried to sleep, but others paced anxiously, played cards, told stories, or sipped whiskey. Most smoked cigarettes, some lighting one after another throughout the night. Everyone glanced recurrently toward the tower—or where they knew the tower was, for in the darkness they couldn't distinguish it from the surrounding night.

July is the season of the monsoon in the Chihuahuan Desert, the sole time of year when rain isn't utterly unexpected. On this night a humid mass of air from the Pacific rolled up the ridges beside the Jornada del Muerto and in its rising cooled to the point of instability. Lightning flashed from the ridgetops, thunder rumbled through the canyons, sudden blasts of wind tore at the sagebrush and yuccas of the Tularosa Valley, and a year's worth of precipitation sheeted down from the sky. But the heavy rains stopped short of the steel tower, to the evident relief of the observers.

An hour before dawn the tension in the bunkers increased measurably. No one even tried to sleep anymore. The conversations grew quiet and terse; the men began to position themselves to have a clear line of sight toward the still-invisible tower. At 5:25 a signal rocket traced a ribbon of green across the blackness, riveting the attention of the observers on the point from which the rocket had been launched.

Five minutes later they saw what no one had ever seen before. "My first impression was of sudden brilliant lighting of the surrounding landscape, accompanied by a momentary flash of heat," one of them wrote. "I remember a feeling of surprise as the illumination, initially quite brilliant, continued to increase for a brief interval." Like most of the observers, this man had been provided with a filter to shield his eyes from a light whose searing intensity could only be guessed. He quickly raised the filter to his face, but soon lowered it.

> Within perhaps two seconds after the initial flash, it became possible to distinguish details of the explosion without the use of the filter. A ball of light about three or four hundred yards in diameter was clearly evident about a thousand feet above the ground. Beneath this ball there

> appeared to be a column of red flame about 150 or 200 yards in diameter. Flickering red reflections were distinctly seen on the clouds above the ball of light. As the intensity of light diminished, a smoky, grayish-brown ball took shape. . . . A fringe of violet light surrounded this ball, and that ball was rising rapidly, with some increase in diameter. The column beneath the ball darkened until it appeared to be a dense black pillar under the grayish brown ball. At about ten seconds after the detonation, the bottom of the ball seemed to flatten, and the ball and column of smoke took on the shape of a vast mushroom. Close to the ground and slowly spreading out on all sides from the point of detonation was a white cloud which looked much like ground fog. This cloud, I assumed, was composed of dust raised by the blast wave. The maximum diameter of this cloud I estimated to be about two miles.

After the fact, many of the observers were struck by the silence that surrounded the detonation. The astonishing display of light and color took place without a soundtrack—until the sonic waves reached the observation posts many seconds after the light waves. Various observers remembered the sound in different ways. Some likened it to thunder, others to artillery—"like the crack of a five-inch anti-aircraft gun at a hundred yards," according to an observer who watched and listened from a distance of twenty miles. "It bounced on the rocks," another hearer remembered. "And then it went—I don't know where else it bounced. But it never seemed to stop. Not like an ordinary echo with thunder. It just kept echoing back and forth in that Jornada del Muerto."

The interpretations of what they had seen varied even more. Everyone knew that the explosion represented the culmination of three years of frantic effort to build the most destructive weapon in human history. Until the moment of detonation, only the most confident of the physicists, engineers, and technicians didn't harbor doubts that the device at the top of the tower would actually work. Some were taking bets against success. When the device did go off, the initial reaction was relief: that all the effort and expense poured into the project hadn't been wasted, that all the professional reputation riding on it hadn't been squandered, that all the hopes for a weapon that might end the war hadn't been in vain. "Naturally, we were very jubilant over the outcome of the experiment," one of the scientists declared. "Our first feeling was one of elation," another remarked. Still another remembered sharing his relief with a colleague. "We just said, 'It worked.' . . . That's what we said, both of us: 'It worked.'"

But as the mushroom cloud ascended into the sky above the Jornada del Muerto, growing taller and taller and showing no sign of dissipating the way every other explosion any of the observers had ever witnessed had dissipated, the elation and relief gave way to other emotions. "There was a chill, which was not the morning cold," a physicist explained. "It was a chill that came to one when one thought, as for instance when I thought of my wooden home in Cambridge, and my laboratory in New York, and of the millions of people living around there, and this power of nature which we had first understood it to be—well, there it was." Another witness simply called the spectacle "very terrifying." A third remarked bluntly, "Now we are all sons of bitches." The director of the project, J. Robert Oppenheimer, seemed to some of the others present to be the picture of professional self-satisfaction. "His walk was like 'High Noon'—I think it's the best I could describe it," one of Oppenheimer's associates said. "This kind of strut. He'd done it."

Yet Oppenheimer himself later acknowledged serious reservations about what he had done. Oppenheimer mingled an Eastern aesthetic with his mastery of Western science, and he often read Indian poetry—even learning Sanskrit to appreciate the original. "We waited until the blast had passed, walked out of the shelter, and then it was extremely solemn," Oppenheimer recalled. "We knew the world would not be the same. . . . I remembered the line from the Hindu scripture, the Bhagavad Gita: Vishnu is trying to persuade the Prince that he should do his duty, and to impress him he takes on his multi-armed form and says, 'Now I am become Death, the destroyer of worlds.' I suppose we all thought that, one way or the other."

## 2. THE LOOMING SHADOW

Early morning in New Mexico was early evening in Berlin. At the long moment when the mushroom cloud of the world's first atomic explosion towered above the Jornada del Muerto, Harry Truman was touring the German capital. The American president had traveled to Germany, two months after the defeat of the Nazis and the death of Hitler, to survey the ruins of the Third Reich and meet with the leaders of Britain and the Soviet Union, America's partners in the Grand Alliance. Truman toured the suburbs and then the central streets of Hitler's imperial city, finally driving past the Reichstag, the Foreign Ministry, and the Sports Palace—or what remained of them. "They were nothing more than piles of stone and rubble," he later wrote. And this wasn't the worst of the destruction. "A more depressing sight than the ruined buildings was the long, never-ending procession of old men, women, and children wandering aimlessly along the autobahn and the country roads carrying, pushing, or pulling what was left of their belongings." Truman felt pity for their suffering, but it was pity mixed with bitterness. "It is a terrible thing," he said, "but they brought it on themselves. That's what happens when a man overreaches himself."

The displaced and destitute hardly had the capital to themselves. The American, Russian, and British troops that had fought their way into Berlin the previous spring still patrolled the city. Truman reviewed the American Second Armored Division. "We stopped, honors were rendered by a band and honor guard, and I left the sedan in which I had been riding and entered an open half-track reconnaissance car. In this I passed down the long line of men and vehicles, which comprised what was at that time the largest armored division in the world. Men and tanks were arrayed down the highway in front of me as far as the eye could see. The line was so long it took twenty-two minutes to ride from the beginning to the end of it."

The images of American power and the destruction of America's enemies remained with Truman when a cryptic message arrived from Washington. "Operated on this morning," the message read. "Diagnosis not yet complete, but results seem satisfactory and already exceed expectations."

The "operation," as Truman understood, was the atomic test in New Mexico, and the knowledge that it had exceeded expectations added to his impression of American power. American conventional forces—with the aid, to be sure, of the Russians and the British—had reduced Hitler's Reich to the rubble the president saw around him. America's atomic force, summoned into existence on the desert of the Jornada del Muerto, could wreak even greater destruction on any other enemy of the United States.

One such enemy remained. Though the war in Europe had ended in May, the war in the Pacific still raged. American military planners projected an invasion of Japan that would require many months and claim many thousands of American lives before the Japanese emperor and his generals surrendered. The atomic bomb held out the possibility of a swift end to the war. Truman and the other Allied leaders at Potsdam—Winston Churchill of Britain and Joseph Stalin of the Soviet Union—intended to issue a statement calling on Japan to surrender or be destroyed. Churchill was aware of the atom test, as the British had been partners in the development of the bomb. But Stalin was not, at least as far as Truman knew. And so Truman informed him. "I casually mentioned to Stalin that we had a new weapon of unusually destructive force," Truman wrote afterward. Stalin seemed unimpressed. "All he said was that he was glad to hear it and hoped we would make 'good use of it against the Japanese.'"

Truman had expected a stronger reaction—surprise, perhaps, or curiosity, or even envy. The bland response caused him to wonder if Stalin understood what the atomic bomb was all about. Churchill wondered the same thing. "If he had had the slightest idea of the revolution in world affairs which was in progress, his reactions would have been obvious," Churchill remarked afterward.

In fact Stalin knew perfectly well of the revolution that was afoot. Spies within the Manhattan Project had been informing Moscow of America's atomic progress; Stalin knew almost as much about America's new capabilities as Truman himself did. And he knew that the atomic bomb enhanced America's military advantage not simply against its current enemies but against every other country on earth, including the Soviet Union.

The wartime alliance between the United States and the Soviet Union was one based on common enemies, not common values. The principal enemy, Germany, had been defeated, and with its defeat the alliance was already beginning to fray. The reason for the conference at Potsdam was to keep the fraying within bounds, as long as possible. Yet Stalin understood that the United States and the Soviet Union would become rivals once again, as they had been rivals before the war. They might even become enemies.

And in that rivalry, or that enmity, America's atomic bomb would give Washington a huge advantage. Stalin's measured response to Truman's comment reflected no lack of appreciation for what the bomb portended, but rather the careful control of a poker player with a weak hand who can't let his face reveal his weakness.

## 3. THE DYNAMO OF AMBITION

Yet for those who knew what to look for, the real secret of America's strength was to be found neither in the desert of New Mexico nor in the ruins of Berlin but in the countryside of Michigan. Thirty miles southwest of Detroit, on a creek called Willow Run, in plain view of Soviet spies, inquisitive journalists, and casual passersby, lay the true engine of American victory. At the beginning of the war this part of Washtenaw County had been almost as bucolic as in the days when fur trappers and Indians swapped pelts for knives and pots; but within months the willow trees and prairie wildflowers gave way to a massive industrial plant unlike anything the world had ever seen. Built by Ford Motor Company for the federal government, the Willow Run plant sprawled across hundreds of acres. Its main building alone encompassed nearly seventy acres under a single roof. The facility employed forty thousand men and women and utilized the assembly-line techniques that had made Ford Motor the master of the automobile business early in the century. But instead of cars it produced airplanes, especially B-24 Liberators, the heavy bombers most responsible for the destruction rained down upon Germany and Japan. At peak production the B-24s rolled out of "the Run" at the rate of one per hour.

Visitors to the facility were astonished at its size, complexity, and productivity. Charles Lindbergh called it "a sort of Grand Canyon of the mechanized world." A usually gabby visitor confessed himself stunned into silence by "the roar of the machinery, the special din of the riveting gun absolutely deafening nearby, the throbbing crash of the giant metal presses." Still another guest came away shaking his head at the plant's "insane, overpowering immensity." The Run's production chief, Ford Motor's Charles Sorensen, reveled in the noise, scale, and ambition of the facility. "Bring the Germans and the Japs in to see it," he said. "Hell, they'll blow their brains out."

Willow Run was simply the largest of America's hundreds of war-production facilities. Plants in Wichita, San Diego, and Seattle contributed to the manufacture of warplanes; shipyards on the three American coasts built warships large and small, from aircraft carriers to landing craft, as well as the ubiquitous Liberty Ship transports that ferried troops and equipment across the Atlantic and Pacific. Smaller factories churned out fighter planes, trucks, tanks, jeeps, machine guns, grenades, bombs, torpedoes, and myriad other machines and instruments of war. The gross statistics were staggering. By the summer of 1945 America's war plants had manufactured 1,600 warships, 5,800 transport ships, 88,000 tanks, 300,000 airplanes, 635,000 jeeps, 2.4 million trucks, 6.5 million rifles, and 40 billion bullets. The United States outproduced all its enemies combined by a large margin; it also outproduced its allies, whose armies it equipped and regularly reprovisioned. Without American arms and ammunition—and food and fuel and clothing—the British might have collapsed amid the German bombing campaign of 1940; without American heavy equipment—including entire trains and thousands of miles of track—the Russians could easily have broken beneath the weight of the German blitzkrieg.

Churchill knew this. Stalin knew it. Truman knew it. At Potsdam the three men stood side by side as recent victors over Germany and prospective victors over Japan. But Churchill understood that the war had severely strained Britain, enervating its economy, unbalancing its finances, and weakening its grip on India and other parts of the British empire. Stalin realized that the Red Army was less impressive than it appeared—that without American aid, it would have difficulty simply maintaining itself in the field, let alone projecting Soviet power abroad.

It was a quirk of fate that the three Allied leaders were all short men. Stalin and Churchill were a bit less than five and a half feet tall; Truman was slightly more. Yet the American president towered over his Soviet and British counterparts at Potsdam by the yardstick that truly mattered: deliverable power. The war had devastated Germany; it was still devastating Japan. It badly weakened Britain and staggered Russia. Alone of the great powers of the world, the United States emerged from the war stronger than it entered.

Yet America's strength could hardly be taken for granted. Everyone involved in America's astonishing wartime production, from assembly-line workers to corporate executives, understood that it was *wartime* production. The war would end, and so would the orders for all the ships and planes and tanks and guns. The performance of the American economy in the decade before the war inspired feelings quite other than confidence. The stock market crash of 1929 had been followed by the most searing, mystifying, disheartening depression in American history. For ten years the economy floundered, casting every fourth worker out of a job at the worst of the crisis, throwing millions out of their homes and off their farms, setting hundreds of thousands of families on the road to destinations that were promising only by comparison with the desperation they were fleeing. Herbert Hoover tried to cure the depression from the top down, providing government aid to companies in the hope that they would rebuild production and inventories and reemploy workers. His prescription failed, and the economy slumped further

Franklin Roosevelt attempted a remedy from the bottom up, putting cash payments in the hands of the most destitute and placing millions of men and women in government jobs, in the hope that their revived incomes would stimulate demand that would in turn elicit new production and new hiring. Roosevelt's formula failed, too, and after some slight improvement between his 1933 inauguration and his 1936 reelection, a demoralizing recession in 1937 threw the economy almost back to where it had been when he took office. Certain of Roosevelt's New Deal reforms—preeminently Social Security—cushioned Americans from some of the pain previously associated with economic depressions, but not even the most devoted New Dealers honestly believed they had found the secret to ending or preventing depressions.

There were, moreover, reasons to believe that the conclusion of the war would erase the gains made during the fighting. The obvious one was that the war production would terminate. The war was a huge experiment in demand-side economics, although no one at the time called it that. The government guaranteed demand, by all its war orders, and the economy responded. Conceivably the government could continue to pump up demand, by ordering other items: roads, bridges, schools, housing, services of various kinds. Presumably this would stimulate a shift from war production to peace production. But such a course was politically infeasible. The opponents of the New Deal had grown in number and passion during Roosevelt's second term, and they consistently decried the high taxes and federal deficits the New Deal entailed. Most of them bit their tongues regarding the even higher taxes and deficits of the war years, on grounds that winning the war required sacrifice.

But as the end of the war drew near, their silence increasingly gave way to warnings that the federal government would have to be reined in. Taxes must be cut and spending slashed. The government's role in the economy must be curtailed dramatically.

Yet even as the demand for labor diminished, the supply of labor would soar. Some twelve million men and women were in the American armed services in the last year of the war. America's historic practice, from independence to the twentieth century, had been to demobilize its armies as rapidly as possible after every conflict. This habit reflected both a distrust of standing armies, which were blamed for the overthrow of popular governments in many countries where such overthrows had occurred, and a refusal to pay the upkeep of peacetime troops. Nearly all Americans anticipated a similar demobilization when the current war ended. Those millions of troops would require jobs—jobs America's peacetime economy had proven singularly unable to supply.

Dean Acheson would become secretary of state under Harry Truman, but in the war's final year he was Franklin Roosevelt's assistant secretary of state for economic affairs. Congress appointed a special committee to plan for the conversion of the wartime economy to the peace, and Acheson testified on how the conversion problem appeared to the administration. The essential task, Acheson said, was reabsorbing the million persons currently employed as soldiers and seamen back into the civilian labor force. "If we do not do that, it seems clear that we are in for a very bad time," Acheson told the committee. "We cannot go through another ten years like the ten years at the end of the twenties and the beginning of the thirties"—Acheson had his differences with Roosevelt, but he was a loyal enough Democrat to pin the blame for the depression on Hoover—"without having the most far-reaching consequences upon our economic and social system."

Reconverting the economy was a domestic matter, Acheson said, but also one of foreign policy. He pointed to the collapse of international trade during the Great Depression as a major cause of the prewar economic troubles; this must be remedied. "No group which has ever studied this problem, and there have been many, as you know," he told the committee, "has ever believed that our domestic markets could absorb the entire production under our present system. You must look to foreign markets." Acheson offered that a socialist system, like the Soviet Union's, might absorb its entire production domestically. But no one in America wanted that. "Therefore you must look to other markets, and those markets are abroad."

## 4. WHEN JOHNNY COMES MARCHING HOME

The transition to peace would be more than an economic problem. If the war was an (apparently irreproducible) economic experiment in demand management, it was simultaneously a sweeping sociological experiment in workplace relations. During the first phase of the war—after its outbreak in Europe but before the Japanese attack on Pearl Harbor—the conflict primarily drew unemployed men back into the labor force. Jobless rates fell without attracting large numbers of new participants to the workplace. But American entry into the fighting prompted the buildup of American armed forces, pulling those millions out of the civilian labor force, even as it heightened demands on America's farms, factories, and mines.

New workers took their places, and the most distinctive were women, who collectively acquired the nickname Rosie the Riveter. In certain respects the entry of women into the industrial workforce wasn't new at all. The early days of America's nineteenth-century industrial revolution had been characterized by New England textile mills in which young women—hardly more than girls, in many cases—operated the spindles and looms. The subsequent emergence of heavier industries—coal, iron, steel—shifted the gender balance in the male direction, although women continued to work in the garment and other trades, and in numerous services. But during World War II women took jobs in shipyards and drydocks, on truck and airplane assembly lines, on road and bridge construction crews, among the girders and scaffolding of building sites.

For some women the jobs were simply jobs, a means to put food on the table and a roof over the heads of themselves and their families. For others the new opportunities signaled an important advance toward gender equality. Women showed they could work, and work well, where men alone had worked before. The equality, however, was a double-edged sword. The new jobs typically paid better than those to which women had previously been confined, but they carried greater risk of injury and death. Different women assessed the trade-off differently. Some would be happy to relinquish the jobs upon the war's end; others would want to keep them.

No less dramatic than the movement in the workplace's gender line was the shift in the color line. In 1865 less than one African American in twelve had lived outside the South. Nearly all remained there early in the twentieth century, with the large majority working on farms as tenants, sharecroppers, or occasionally owners. World War I changed things, as wartime jobs in Northern factories drew blacks north in what came to be called the Great Migration, which for the first time populated Chicago, Detroit, and other industrial cities with large numbers of African Americans. Detroit, for example, began the war with fewer than ten thousand blacks; it ended the war with more than one hundred thousand. The migration slowed after the war ended, and in some locales it reversed during the Great Depression as jobless workers returned to their rural roots. But the migration resumed upon the outbreak of World War II. Some million black men and women moved out of the South during the conflict, for essentially the same reasons as during the previous war. This time, however, besides relocating to the cities of the North, they moved to Los Angeles, San Francisco, Portland, and Seattle, all of which had significant war-production facilities.

As during World War I, the movement of blacks triggered fear and sometimes hostility among their new neighbors. Blacks and whites competed for scarce housing and often irritated and angered each other. The summer of 1943 was hot throughout the Midwest but particularly in Detroit, where African Americans took every opportunity to escape the shacks of the ironically named Paradise Valley, the most overpopulated of the black neighborhoods. On one particularly oppressive day large crowds of people—whites and blacks—jammed an amusement park on Belle Isle in the Detroit River. Teenagers were the first to tangle, with groups of whites and blacks trading words and then blows. The fighting spread from the island and escalated onto the mainland. Several thousand whites rampaged through Paradise Valley and other black neighborhoods, beating and shooting residents and destroying property. The local authorities responded slowly, not wishing to acknowledge that they had lost control of the situation. President Roosevelt was finally compelled to send federal troops to restore order—and get workers back into the tank and truck plants. But by then nearly three dozen people, most of them black, had been killed, and seven hundred injured. An investigative commission appointed by Michigan's governor heard testimony from blacks describing the prejudice they daily encountered and the substandard conditions under which they lived, but the commission concluded that Detroit's blacks had brought the violence upon themselves.

While the rift between whites and blacks garnered the greatest attention during the war, other splits emerged as well. Latinos—of Mexican descent, for the most part—had lived along the U.S.-Mexican border for generations. In certain regions—South Texas, from the Rio Grande Valley to San Antonio, and parts of Southern California—the presence of Latinos antedated the arrival of Anglos. Elsewhere immigrants from Mexico, and their children, constituted the major portion of the Latino community. In both settings they often found life difficult. Many Latinos worked on commercial farms in grinding conditions and for low pay. In San Antonio and Los Angeles they inhabited barrios that operated under a variant of the Jim Crow system of racial segregation in the American South. The war provided Latinos certain new opportunities comparable to those experienced by African Americans, but it also created new tensions.

In June 1943—the same month as the Detroit riot—a series of confrontations between Anglo and Latino youths in Los Angeles grew larger and more violent. The Anglos were mostly military personnel from the army bases and navy yards of the city and its surroundings; in the nature of the military, most were from outside California and the Southwest, and most had never encountered Latinos. A clash of some kind was almost inevitable, for beyond such differences as existed in language and traditional values, the uniformed, closely shorn Anglo soldiers and sailors considered themselves paragons of patriotism, while the Latinos, who favored long hair swept back in ducktails and the oversize, extravagantly tailored coats and trousers known as "zoot suits," looked like rebels and considered the white boys racist thugs. The local press, seeking circulation, reported on the troubles between the two groups in lurid fashion, and the printed exaggerations contributed to real escalation, until a full-scale race riot convulsed the city. As in Detroit, local law enforcement proved unable to quell the violence; in this case military police from the nearby installations were called in. The extent of injury and destruction was less than in Detroit, but a similar sense of grievance, particularly among Latinos, who felt that the police favored their antagonists, persisted long after the fighting stopped.

Even as it jostled genders, races, and ethnic groups, the war disrupted old notions regarding the proper role of government in the lives of individuals. The Great Depression had seriously challenged the received version of the American dream: that men (mostly) and women who worked hard and saved for rainy days could expect a measure of material comfort and security in their golden years, without resort to government. Grover Cleveland had once said, in vetoing a bill that would have bailed out drought-stricken farmers, that the people should support the government, and not the other way around. Until the depression, most Americans endorsed Cleveland's view. But the depression, with its massive layoffs and ubiquitous bank failures, demonstrated how painfully exposed Americans could be to the caprice of a capitalist economy. Franklin Roosevelt failed to end the depression, but the programs he put into place went far toward dispelling the despair the depression evoked. Roosevelt accepted on behalf of the federal government greater responsibility for the welfare of the American people than any president before him. Many Republicans and conservatives resisted, but a majority of Americans greeted the new order with relief and gratitude, as evidenced by their thunderous reelection of Roosevelt in 1936.

During the war the welfare state—as it would come to be called—grew more permanent and elaborate. Very few people, as of 1940, received pensions from the Social Security system. But by 1945, as the system matured and the population aged, the number of recipients had grown dramatically, and it would continue to grow with each passing year. As a result, Americans built federal pensions into their mental landscapes, and what had seemed a novelty in 1935, when Social Security was established, came to be considered an entitlement.

The war expanded the federal role in other ways. To provide housing for workers in out-of-the-way war plants, the government built apartments and single-family homes. The precedent shaped expectations for the postwar period, with Washington becoming the landlord of last resort for the nation's struggling poor. The war diverted millions of young people from college; to compensate the colleges and especially the diverted, Congress passed the GI bill, which would provide funding for the soldiers' return to the ivy-covered walls. The GI bill also underwrote home mortgages for veterans after the war. The government mediated labor disputes, bringing management and labor together when economic self-interest threatened to drive the two groups apart. As owners and workers looked to the postwar period, many expected government to play a similarly constructive role.

Other expectations that emerged during the war weren't directly related to government but entailed a similarly diminished reliance on individual responsibility. A regime of wage and price controls constrained the ability of employers to compete for workers by the ordinary method of offering higher pay; instead the companies turned to fringe benefits, among which employer-funded medical insurance proved the most popular. No one deliberately designed this system of linking health care to the workplace; it was an accidental artifact of wartime policies targeting other goals. But the result was that individuals and families came to expect that someone else—employers—would fund all or a substantial part of their health care. Some conservatives lamented this development almost as much as they decried the growing reliance on government programs; both, they said, sapped the self-reliance that had made America what it was. But the larger number of pragmatists accepted it as part of the modern political economy.

## 5. WHAT (ELSE) ROOSEVELT HATH WROUGHT

In foreign relations no less than in domestic affairs, Americans in 1945 expected more of their government than they had a decade earlier. Roosevelt inherited a country almost incurably isolationist in its belief that America's fate depended little on the fate of other countries. Slowly, painstakingly, he turned this attitude around—too slowly to prevent the outbreak of World War II, which might have been averted, it seemed in hindsight, had the Western democracies stood up to Hitler at Munich in 1938, when the German dictator demanded the dismemberment of Czechoslovakia, or had they confronted the warlords of Japan when the latter invaded China in stages during the 1930s. The shift in popular thinking was completed only as Americans absorbed the significance of the Japanese attack on Pearl Harbor in December 1941. Besides the 2,400 Americans killed by the Japanese bombs and torpedoes, Pearl Harbor finished off American isolationism, convincing

Americans almost to a man and woman that the country could never again turn its back on the world.

Roosevelt attempted to institutionalize the new American thinking in a series of meetings during the last year of the war. At Bretton Woods, New Hampshire, in the summer of 1944, representatives of forty-five governments gathered at the historic Mount Washington Hotel to reconstruct the world economy. The irony of America's hosting the affair wasn't lost on many of the delegates, who recalled how Roosevelt had scuttled the most recent such effort, at London in 1933. At that time Roosevelt wasn't fully convinced that internationalism held the key to American economic recovery, and he *was* convinced that internationalism posed a threat to his reelection chances. But by 1944 isolationism was a spent force in American politics, and the American economy had so surpassed the economies of all other countries that such internationalist staples as free trade could only redound to America's benefit.

The Bretton Woods delegates began by pledging themselves to freer trade: not yet to free trade, which might jolt many economies excessively, but to a series of steps in that direction. The commitment to freer trade eventually took the form of the General Agreement on Tariffs and Trade, or GATT, which in rounds of negotiations over the following decades progressively reduced tariffs and other barriers to trade. The signatories believed that freer trade was in their economic interest, allowing each country to sell what it was most efficient at producing and purchase what other countries were good at. Most of them also believed that free trade calmed or prevented political and military rivalries—that where goods crossed borders, armies did not. This was partly a leap of faith but also a logical interpretation of the events of the 1930s, a decade that began with a trade war and ended with a shooting war.

Bretton Woods spawned two other institutions designed to improve the performance of the global economy. The International Bank for Reconstruction and Development, commonly called the World Bank, would coordinate and underwrite the efforts of the currently warring nations to rebuild their economies after the conflict. The International Monetary Fund, or IMF, would stabilize exchange rates and currency flows. Like the GATT, the World Bank and the IMF were at once altruistic and selfish. The altruism reflected the sincere desire of the sponsoring countries to alleviate world poverty; the selfishness, the recollection that the poverty and despair of the 1930s had contributed significantly to the rise of Hitler. Well-fed, fully employed people didn't heed the war cries of extremists, the Bretton Woods wisdom declared.

The most obvious manifestation of the Bretton Woods regime, on a day-to-day basis, was the monetary system it created. For centuries money had been whatever governments called it or individuals were willing to accept. In the United States money had consisted of gold and silver coins, notes circulated by banks, and "greenbacks" issued by the federal government, all competing in a welter of confusion and economic inefficiency. The latter half of the nineteenth century witnessed the emergence of an international gold standard, overseen by Britain, the leading commercial power of the time, and made possible by the gold dug from California and elsewhere after James Marshall's discovery on the American River in 1848. The United States joined the gold group informally at first and then, following a frenetic rearguard action by the advocates of silver, formally in 1900.

World War I disrupted the gold standard, along with most other aspects of the international economy, and it had been only shakily restored when the Great Depression shattered it again. The conferees at Bretton Woods made another try. They established a partial gold standard, pegging other currencies to the American dollar, and the dollar to gold (at $35 per ounce). The outstanding difference between this new system and the system of the period before World War I was the anchoring economy. Then it had been Britain's; now it was America's.

The United Nations Organization (so called briefly, to distinguish it from the formal name—United Nations—of the anti-Axis coalition) emerged from a different meeting, held at Dumbarton Oaks, an estate above Rock Creek in northwestern Washington, D.C. The participant list at the Dumbarton Oaks conference was shorter than that of the Bretton Woods meeting; representatives from the United States, Britain, the Soviet Union, and China—the Big Four of the antifascist front—laid the framework for the successor group to the League of Nations, which had been crippled at birth by America's refusal to join and mortally wounded by the league's failure to halt German and Japanese aggression during the 1930s.

The Dumbarton Oaks conference was followed by an April 1945 meeting at San Francisco, where the postwar United Nations was inaugurated. The United States, the Soviet Union, Britain, China, and liberated France took permanent seats on an inner group, the Security Council, in which each wielded a substantive veto; dozens of other countries (eventually nearly all the nations of the earth) became members of an outer group, the General Assembly. In the General Assembly the sovereign equality of nations was guaranteed; each member state could speak its mind and cast its vote like every other member.

Roosevelt didn't live to see the United Nations chartered; he died of a stroke two weeks before the San Francisco conference. But the United Nations, like the GATT, the World Bank, the IMF, and the Bretton Woods monetary system, reflected Roosevelt's determined belief that the nations of the world must cooperate economically and politically lest they return to blows militarily. This conclusion, like any forward-looking extrapolation from the past, came without guarantees. But the events of the 1930s made it appear quite plausible, and given the stakes—scarcely less than the survival of civilization—Roosevelt was willing to accept plausibility as a basis for action.

## 6. FLAMES AND A KISS

At two o'clock on the morning of August 6, 1945, Colonel Paul Tibbets and the crew of a specially modified B-29 bomber called the *Enola Gay* took off from Tinian in the northern Marianas and headed for Japan. The plane—named for Tibbets's mother—carried a single weapon, kin to the device tested at Alamogordo. Two observer planes accompanied it. The Japanese government had ignored the ultimatum delivered from Potsdam by the Allied leaders, and Truman ordered the new technology employed in battle. Four hours into the flight Tibbets directed the bombardier to arm the weapon, and he only then explained to the crew the historic nature of their mission. At seven o'clock the *Enola Gay* approached the Japanese coast and appeared for the first time on Japanese radar screens. Earlier in the war American bombers had encountered stiff resistance from Japanese fighter planes, but what remained of the imperial air force was on starvation rations of fuel and pilots, and no interceptors were scrambled against what seemed to be an insignificant raid. Japan's air defense issued warnings to civilians to take shelter, but the warnings were lifted when it became clear that the attacking force consisted of a mere three planes.

By eight o'clock the *Enola Gay* was at 32,000 feet above Hiroshima, a southern Japanese city of some quarter-million that had been spared the destruction inflicted on most other Japanese cities. Hiroshima had only modest military significance, which was one reason it hadn't been targeted. Another reason was that American scientists and military officers wanted to measure just how much damage their new weapon would accomplish, and they could do this better by bombing a fresh target.

At 8:15 the bomb—called "Little Boy," to distinguish it from another design in the small American atomic arsenal, "Fat Man"—was released from the *Enola Gay*. It fell for nearly a minute before detonating at 2,000 feet, an altitude chosen to maximize the effect of the blast. By far the largest in history, the equivalent of roughly 13,000 tons of TNT, the explosion leveled several square miles of central Hiroshima and set fires across a much broader area. "Where we had seen a clear city two minutes before, we could no longer see the city," Tibbets's copilot recalled. The tail gunner, who had the best view, observed, "The mushroom itself was a spectacular sight, a bubbling mass of purple-gray smoke. . . . You could see it had a red core in it and everything was burning inside. . . . I saw fires springing up in different places, like flames shooting up on a bed of coals. . . . It looked like lava or molasses covering the whole city."

Amid the inferno perhaps seventy thousand Japanese died. A roughly equal number died in the coming days, weeks, and months, many of radiation poisoning. The shock to Japan's sense of national self was enormous. American bombers had previously inflicted greater damage on Tokyo, but the destruction there had required hundreds of bombers and tens of thousands of bombs. This blow was the work of a solitary plane and a single bomb.

Absorbing the significance of the bomb took time, however, and as Tokyo continued to refuse to surrender, another American warplane dropped a second bomb—the Fat Man—on Nagasaki on August 9. The destruction was comparable to that at Hiroshima.

This time the lesson took hold. The Japanese emperor, explaining that "the enemy has begun to employ a new and most cruel bomb," declared that the war must cease. Some bitter-enders wanted to struggle on; a few attempted a mutiny against the emperor. But loyal forces quelled the uprising, and on August 14 (in America; August 15 in Japan) World War II ended with Japan's capitulation.

The news sent a thrill across America. Church bells rang; car horns and factory whistles blared; men and women crowded the streets of every city and most towns. Alfred Eisenstaedt, a Prussian Jew who had emigrated to America after Hitler's rise to power and become the lead photographer on the staff of *Life* magazine, captured the moment with an instantly famous image of a sailor kissing a nurse in Times Square.

Yet for all the same-day celebrating, the striking thing about the victory was how little lasting emotion it inspired in America. Compared to World War I, which had been sold to the American people as the war to end all wars and to make the world safe for democracy, and which had been followed by an angry backlash when the postwar settlement failed to yield the promised result, World War II was treated almost matter-of-factly. The American government encouraged patriotic thinking but declined to whip the public mood into the frenzy of the earlier conflict. A businesslike attitude marked the struggle against Germany and Japan; as a result, the war's end produced relief that the nasty job was finished, and a sober turning to whatever would be next.

Amid the turning, Americans considered what the war had taught them. A first lesson was that the United States could accomplish almost anything it set its mind to, within the limits of human nature. World War I had been, on the American side, an idealists' war, with Wilson leading the liberal charge for a fundamental change in human attitudes. Wilson really *did* believe war could be rendered obsolete and democracy could take hold in human hearts everywhere. Developments of the two decades that followed the war proved Wilson woefully wrong, or at least far ahead of the rest of humanity. In large part as a reaction to that disillusioning experience, World War II was a realists' war. Franklin Roosevelt did not promise to end all wars, and he did not promise to regenerate humanity. Evil would continue to exist in the postwar world, and the forces of good needed to be prepared to confront it.

A second lesson related to the first. As divided as Americans had been before Pearl Harbor, they united during the war in the conviction that their failure to confront aggression early had contributed to its rise and spread. Appeasement—a neutral word and concept before the war—became the worst form of condemnation, and Munich, the city where Hitler had duped the Western democracies, became the symbol of appeasement. Conventional wisdom coalesced in an anti-appeasement reflex, a ready response to anything that could be considered aggression.

A third lesson followed from the second and the first. Aware of their own power, primed to respond forcefully to aggression, Americans deemed themselves responsible for world order—not completely, but to a degree inconceivable less than a half-decade earlier. In 1940 the cautioning words of George Washington, warning Americans against involvement in the affairs of other countries, had evoked approving nods from a majority of the American population. In 1945 those words sounded archaic, even naïve. Isolationism had been respectable until the moment the Japanese bombs and torpedoes struck the American ships at Pearl Harbor; by the time the American atom bombs hit Hiroshima and Nagasaki, isolationism was the preserve of cranks. Americans would debate the appropriate alternative to isolationism, but the fulcrum of the debate had shifted so far toward continuing involvement in world affairs as to leave the few remaining isolationists without an audience.

# 2 | The War That Never Ended

## 1946–1948

### 1. MILD ABOUT HARRY

Few Americans expected much from Harry Truman at the time he took office. This son of small-town Missouri had spent a thoroughly lackluster youth and early manhood, tilling the soil for twelve years before joining the army during World War I. His artillery mates in Battery D liked him, but there weren't enough of them in Kansas City to keep the haberdashery he operated there after the war from failing. For want of better prospects, he turned to politics. He won election to local office and climbed through the ranks with the assistance of Kansas City boss Tom Pendergast, who expected and received consideration in return. After Pendergast delivered Kansas City for Franklin Roosevelt in 1932, Truman landed a federal appointment as a Missouri director of New Deal relief. Two years later Pendergast arranged Truman's nomination for U.S. senator. The Democratic landslide that year swept Truman to Washington as what his critics called the "senator from Pendergast."

Truman distinguished himself sufficiently to win reelection in 1940, and he made himself mildly notorious after the German invasion of the Soviet Union in 1941 by declaring a plague on both countries. "If we see that Germany is winning, we ought to help Russia," he declared, "and if Russia is winning we ought to help Germany, and that way let them kill as many as possible." He headed a Senate committee to investigate procurement practices; the committee publicized kickbacks and other malfeasances and inefficiencies in purchases by the War and Navy departments.

Yet this was hardly the stuff of a prospective president, and though Truman seemed a safe choice to replace Henry Wallace for vice president in 1944, almost no one at the Democratic convention seriously considered him a successor to Roosevelt. The president himself ignored Truman after the election, keeping him in the dark on such central matters as the Manhattan Project. Truman was as shocked as anyone on learning, on April 12, 1945, that Roosevelt had died. "Boys, if you ever pray, pray for me now," he beseeched reporters at his first press conference as president. "I don't know whether you fellows ever had a load of hay fall on you, but when they told me yesterday what had happened, I felt like the moon, the stars, and all the planets had fallen on me." A correspondent offered encouragement: "Good luck, Mr. President." Truman winced. "I wish you hadn't called me that," he said.

But Truman grew into the presidency, far more quickly than most people, including himself, had considered possible. He assumed the reins of foreign policy and guided the country through the final months of the war with Germany. He headed the American delegation to Potsdam for the conference with Stalin and Churchill. He acted decisively against Japan, ordering the use of the atom bomb despite the second thoughts of some of his scientific advisers.

On domestic matters he defended the New Deal against Republicans and Democratic conservatives, but with less enthusiasm than the left wing of the Democrats desired. Holding the middle proved a challenge. The honeymoon he enjoyed on account of the lingering respect for Roosevelt and of the country's satisfaction with the victory over fascism dissipated not long after the shooting stopped. Truman lifted the wartime wage and price controls too swiftly for some groups and too slowly for others. "Big money has too much power, and so have the big unions," Truman told his mother. "Both are riding to a fall because I like neither." He tangled with John L. Lewis in the spring of 1946 after the grandiloquent president of the United Mineworkers called a nationwide coal strike. "I have pleaded your case," Lewis told the miners, "not in the quavering tones of a mendicant asking alms but in the thundering voice of the captain of a mighty host, demanding the rights to which free men are entitled." Truman had disliked Lewis since the war years, when he thought the mine chief was putting his workers ahead of the nation. Lewis called strikes that, to Truman's way of thinking, were "worse than bullets in the back to our soldiers." Lewis was up to the same tricks again, Truman now thought.

Amid the coal strike another stoppage loomed, potentially even more damaging to the nation's welfare. At the middle of the twentieth century, America depended on railroads as never before or since. The trains transported the overwhelming majority of American cargo and logged the lion's share of long-distance passenger miles. Food, fuel, clothing, medicine—everything essential to human existence moved by rail, and almost nothing essential moved without it. To interrupt the trains was to jeopardize the American way of life—not only in the long term but immediately, within hours and days.

Precisely for this reason, the biggest rail unions supposed that merely threatening a walkout would force acceptance of their terms. Prices had risen faster of late than wages; the rail workers wanted to catch up. The rail unions had been a loyal Democratic constituency, and their leaders knew Truman personally; they hoped for sympathy from the White House. Truman talked them into postponing their strike, to allow time for further negotiations. But the railroad managers, complaining that they too were victims of higher prices, stood firm, and the rank-and-file workers grew increasingly militant.

In May 1946 they walked off the job. The nation's transportation system seized up at once. All but a handful of the 24,000 freight trains and 175,000 passenger trains sat idle on the tracks and sidings, the former full of freight, the latter empty of passengers. The effects began rippling outward at once. In tens of thousands of stores consumers stripped shelves of goods they knew wouldn't be replenished; in hundreds of cities and towns stranded travelers wondered how they would get home.

Truman was caught between his concern for labor and his care for the larger national welfare. "I am tired of the government's being flouted, vilified and misrepresented," he wrote to himself in a fit of exasperation. "Let us give the country back to the people. Let's put transportation and production back to work, hang a few traitors, make our own country safe for democracy." In public his language was more circumspect; he didn't threaten to hang the union leaders, but he did describe them as men "who place their private interests above the welfare of the nation." He gave the unions twenty-four hours to return to work; after that he would call out the army and take whatever steps were necessary to move the trains.

It was an audacious step. Truman's own attorney general doubted its constitutionality. But the president waved aside the objections, saying he'd "think about the law later." The next day, with the rail system still paralyzed, Truman went to Congress for authority to draft the strikers into the army, where they would be subject to his direct orders as commander-in-chief. Some of the lawmakers gasped; others applauded. But the most dramatic moment of the speech came after the secretary of the Senate, without interrupting Truman's remarks, slipped the president a note. Truman read the note and then announced proudly: "Word has just been received that the railroad strike has been settled, on terms proposed by the President!"

The coal miners settled shortly thereafter. Truman claimed a dual victory for decisive leadership. But the experience left a bad taste all around. Workers wondered what had happened to the support the Democratic party had long given labor. Consumers shuddered at the chaos that had threatened the country. Management imagined that Truman would cater to labor in the future to assuage the workers' hurt feelings.

Other issues crowded the president's agenda. The twelve million men and women under arms at the end of the war wanted to return home. They had agreed to serve, most quite willingly, for the duration of the conflict, but now that the conflict was over, they expected to get on with their lives. Demobilizing the millions, however, was a daunting task. Merely transporting them from Europe, from Africa, from the Pacific, and from Asia would take many months. Moreover, there would be good reasons for keeping some of the troops in place. Germany had been defeated, but no framework of peace had been erected; the American troops there couldn't simply leave without jeopardizing everything they had fought for. The situation in Japan was similar. Americans had thought winning the war was hard; gradually they came to realize that winning the peace would be no easier.

This realization meant little to many of the soldiers or to most of their relatives and friends at home. Riots broke out on military bases among troops demanding to be sent back to America; senators and congressmen in Washington received letters from soldiers' wives and children wanting to know when they would see their husbands and daddies. Baby boots and mittens arrived in the Capitol mail, emblems of infants who had never seen their fathers. One GI, who declined to affix his name, wrote the president in verse:

*Please Mr. Truman, won't you send us home?*
*We have captured Napoli and liberated Rome.*

*We have licked the master race,*
*Now there's lots of shipping space,*
*So won't you send us home?*

Added to Truman's other troubles, the slow demobilization put voters in a foul mood. If he had been up for reelection in 1946, he almost certainly would have lost. Polls registered a percentage approval rating in the low thirties, down fifty points from the year before. The future appeared grim for the president's party. "It's going to be a God-damned beefsteak election," Democrat Sam Rayburn of Texas predicted. "The ins are going out. . . . The outs are coming in."

Rayburn was right. The Republicans seized both the House and the Senate, making them the majority party in Congress for the first time since the onset of the Great Depression. The Republican leadership prepared to commence the demolition of the New Deal.

They aimed their first blows at the labor laws that had chafed employers for nearly a decade. The Taft-Hartley Act of 1947, named for Senator Robert Taft of Ohio and Representative Fred Hartley of New Jersey, rolled back some of the New Deal's most important guarantees to labor, including the closed shop—mandatory union membership. It also empowered the president to impose a no-strike cooling-off period when negotiations between management and labor failed.

Truman condemned the Taft-Hartley bill as unfair, unworkable, and a "clear threat to the successful working of our democratic society." He vetoed it. But the Republicans, with support from Southern Democrats, overrode the veto, and Truman appeared weaker than ever.

## 2. SOUNDING THE TOCSIN

On a visit to Washington during World War II, Winston Churchill mused to a joint session of Congress how his political career would have unfolded differently had he been born in America rather than in England. It wasn't an idle speculation. Churchill's father, son of the seventh duke of Marlborough, had married an American girl, Jennie Jerome, at a time when English aristocrats were seeking American wives from rich families such as Jennie's. Winston was born prematurely; had he been delivered on one of his mother's frequent visits home, he could have grown up an American citizen. As things happened, he had to settle for honorary citizenship, awarded in gratitude for Churchill's resolute defense of democracy against the Nazis during World War II. Americans thrilled to hear rebroadcasts of Churchill's speeches to the House of Commons, in which he promised: "We shall fight on the beaches. We shall fight on the landing grounds. We shall fight in the fields and in the streets. We shall fight in the hills. We shall never surrender." Churchill fell from power in the summer of 1945, replaced amid the Potsdam conference as a result of the first general election in Britain since 1935. This turn of events puzzled most Americans but didn't lessen their respect for Churchill.

Consequently, when the great man was invited to deliver an address at Fulton, Missouri, in March 1946, they crowded around their radios again. The several months since the war's end had been disappointing to those who hoped that the wartime camaraderie among the Grand Allies would persist. Roosevelt had been banking on some form of continued collaboration, as his acceptance of a Soviet veto in the UN Security Council made clear. FDR himself might have managed to keep Stalin cooperative, but Roosevelt's death left American foreign policy to a new president with little experience in foreign affairs, scant credibility with Stalin or Churchill, and numerous critics in Congress. Everyone wondered what Truman would do.

What he did was act—boldly and decisively. Truman's motto was "The buck stops here," and the buck screeched to a halt at once. Truman flabbergasted the British by canceling the Lend-Lease program just days after the Japanese surrender. The embargo made sense under the initial terms of the program, which had specified aid to those countries fighting the Axis. The Axis lay in ruins; the fight had ended in victory. Yet the British hoped that American assistance might continue after the war. Britain had given its all in the common cause; British leaders thought they deserved help getting their country back on its feet. Many of the British guessed that Roosevelt would never have acted so harshly, and said so. But Truman wasn't Roosevelt, and part of his purpose in stopping the aid so abruptly—some ships already en route to England were recalled to American ports—was to demonstrate this fact.

Truman moved no less decisively in dealing with Stalin and the Soviets.

Truman never disavowed what he had said early in the war about wanting the Germans to kill as many Russians as possible, and he never lost his distrust of Stalin. Truman treated Stalin like a Midwestern party boss, believing the dictator would respond more readily to toughness than to conciliation. Truman had another reason for adopting a hard line with the Kremlin: the new president lacked the confidence among the American people Roosevelt had enjoyed, a confidence that disposed most Americans to give Roosevelt the benefit of the doubt on issues relating to American security. Truman had to prove himself, and his scrappy personality was such as to make the proving more comfortable from a forward stance, with his chin out and fists up.

He seized an opportunity in a meeting with the Soviet foreign minister, V. M. Molotov. At a late-war conference at the Russian resort city of Yalta, Roosevelt, Stalin, and Churchill had reached an agreement on the future of Poland. Roosevelt and Churchill had acknowledged that the postwar government of Poland should be friendly to the Soviet Union; Stalin had consented to democratic elections to determine that government. Experienced observers noted at the time that the Yalta formula would be nearly impossible to fulfill, as the Polish distrust of the Russians was so deep that any democratically elected Polish government would almost certainly be *un*friendly to Moscow. Roosevelt had failed to obtain enforcement guarantees from Stalin at Yalta, believing he needed Stalin's cooperation against Japan and recognizing that, with the Soviet Red Army already occupying Poland, he had little leverage over his communist ally. The president settled for a paper promise. When Stalin broke that promise, many Americans—including virtually every American of Polish descent—accused Stalin of bad faith and malign intentions.

Truman took the Polish dispute as cause for confronting the Kremlin. In the bluntest language he told Molotov that Moscow had better do what it had promised. The Soviet foreign minister was shocked. "I have never been talked to like that in my life," he said, according to Truman's account. Truman retorted: "Carry out your agreements and you won't get talked to like that." Afterward, with some relish, Truman related how he had given Molotov a "straight one-two to the jaw."

The tension between the former allies increased during the following months. The peace conference everyone had anticipated as the means of charting Europe's future after the war never took place, as the diplomats of the two sides—meaning, increasingly the United States, Britain, and France, on one hand, and the Soviet Union, on the other—couldn't agree on the preliminaries to make a conference useful. Germany remained divided, with the American, British, and French armies cooperating among themselves in their western zones of occupation, and the Russian army having its way in the eastern zone. The two sides interpreted their occupation mandates differently. The Americans, British, and French thought in terms of reconstructing Germany, while the Russians looked to Germany to reconstruct their own country. The Red Army sent everything that was useful and wasn't bolted down to the Soviet Union, to remedy the devastation Hitler's forces had wreaked on Russia during the war. They likewise removed much that *was* bolted down, dismantling factories and sending them east as well.

There was nothing particularly invidious about the Russian policy, which was no harsher economically than the policies of Britain and France after World War I had been. But most Americans had hoped that the second great war would end more satisfactorily than the first, and the fact that it didn't, with the Russians violating the spirit of the wartime alliance most egregiously, caused them to remember why they had long distrusted communists.

Further friction accompanied Stalin's slowness in removing Soviet troops from Iran. That oil-rich country had been occupied by the Americans, British, and Russians during the war, to prevent the Germans from seizing its oil fields. The three allies agreed to withdraw their troops within six months of the war's end. The Americans and British beat the deadline, but the Soviets missed it. Some in Washington suspected Stalin of aiming to add Iran to Russia's empire, and Truman felt obliged to issue a stern reminder of what Stalin had agreed to regarding Iran. The Soviet troops eventually left, but the incident heightened American suspicions of the Kremlin.

Against this background of growing tension, Churchill arrived in America on a belated victory tour. He traveled with Truman to the president's home state of Missouri, and he agreed to deliver an address to the students and faculty of Fulton's Westminster College. Truman introduced Churchill to the academic audience and declared, "I know that he will have something constructive to say to the world."

"Constructive" wasn't the word; "combative" was much closer. Churchill had doubted Stalin's intentions even during the war, when Grand Alliance harmony required keeping his doubts to himself. With the war over, he felt free to speak his mind. "From Stettin in the Baltic to Trieste in the Adriatic," Churchill intoned, "an iron curtain has descended across the Continent." The Russians were crushing dissent and liquidating freedom behind this line, Churchill said, and the West must take a stand. "There is nothing they admire so much as strength, and there is nothing for which they have less respect than weakness, especially military weakness." The democracies had failed to act early against the Nazis, and the world had paid a terrible price. "There never was a war in history easier to prevent by timely action than the one which has just desolated such great areas of the globe. It could have been prevented, in my belief, without the firing of a single shot, and Germany might be powerful, prosperous and honored today. But no one would listen, and one by one we were all sucked into the awful whirlpool. We surely must not let that happen again."

## 3. A CONCEPT AND A DOCTRINE

Churchill's Iron Curtain speech evoked divergent reactions in America. Some listeners thought he exaggerated the similarities between the 1930s and the present. Stalin might be a bad man, the skeptics said, but he was no Hitler. Other listeners thought the former prime minister said only what needed saying. Aggression was aggression, and it must be resisted from the outset lest it grow larger and more lethal.

Truman adopted the latter view. Already disposed to think ill of Stalin, he took Churchill's warning as support for a hostile view of the Kremlin. But hostility wasn't a policy, and for the moment Truman's anti-Sovietism remained chiefly a state of mind.

Things changed during the following months. For millennia the eastern Mediterranean had been the gateway to the Middle East, and for decades the British had guarded the gate by supporting friendly regimes and resisting their enemies. But World War II had left Britain nearly bankrupt, and imperial retrenchment compelled a retreat in the Mediterranean. The British government invited the Truman administration to pick up where it was leaving off, especially in Greece and Turkey. Yet whether Washington accepted the invitation or not, London would relinquish the burden.

The announcement triggered a flurry of activity in Washington. The State

Department included a coterie of career officials who had learned their craft by observing Soviet affairs from consulates and embassies in Central Europe before American recognition of the Soviet government in 1933, and from Moscow afterward. Steeped in the anti-Bolshevism of their director, Robert Kelley, these pioneer American Kremlinologists took quite seriously Soviet assertions of a desire to conquer the world for communism. They had silenced their suspicions when World War II made allies of the United States and the Soviet Union, but no sooner had the war ended than they resumed their warnings about the world-dominating desires of Stalin and his henchmen.

The most influential member of this group was George Kennan, a Wisconsinite whose undistinguished looks and mild demeanor made him an unlikely candidate to be the guiding genius of four decades of American Cold War policy. But Kennan had a gift for words, and in a long telegram from Moscow in 1946 he described Soviet aims as implacably opposed to those of the West. Stalin and the current occupants of the Kremlin sat in a long line of Russian xenophobes, Kennan asserted. "They have learned to seek security only in patient but deadly struggle for the total destruction of rival power, never in compacts or compromises with it." Communist ideology reinforced the Russian drive for dominance. "We have here a political force committed fanatically to the belief that with the U.S. there can be no permanent modus vivendi." War might be averted, but only by American courage and resolve. "If the adversary has sufficient force and makes clear his readiness to use it, he rarely has to do so." The contest would be neither easy nor short. The Russian attitude toward the world had developed over centuries; dealing with the Soviets would take decades at least.

Kennan's telegram reached Washington at a moment when Truman and his advisers were trying to formulate an overall policy toward the Soviet Union. Hardliners pressed for strong action to roll back Russian power in Eastern Europe; accommodationists sought to recapture the spirit of wartime collaboration. Kennan's analysis offered a middle ground: the United States should resist Soviet expansion but patiently and persistently. In an article in the prestigious journal *Foreign Affairs*, Kennan made his views public (but only partly: he signed the article "X" rather than affixing his own name). And he furnished a label for the policy they implied. "Containment" would prevent the spread of Soviet power and would thereby "promote tendencies which must eventually find their outlet in either the breakup or the gradual mellowing of Soviet power," Kennan asserted. "For no mystical, Messianic movement—and particularly not that of the Kremlin—can face frustration indefinitely without eventually adjusting itself in one way or another to the logic of that state of affairs."

Containment took shape in American policy when Truman, in response to the British announcement of withdrawal from Greece and Turkey, went to Congress in March 1947 and requested $400 million in aid to the Greek and Turkish governments. Truman didn't mention Russia by name, but no one missed his meaning when he declared:

> At the present moment in world history nearly every nation must choose between alternative ways of life. . . . One way of life is based upon the will of the majority, and is distinguished by free institutions, representative government, free elections, guarantees of individual liberty, freedom of speech and religion, and freedom from political oppression. The second way of life is based upon the will of a minority forcibly imposed upon the majority. It relies upon terror and oppression, a controlled press and radio, fixed elections, and the suppression of personal freedoms.

The conclusion the president drew from this assessment was summarized in a sentence:

> It must be the policy of the United States to support free peoples who are resisting attempted subjugation by armed minorities or by outside pressures.

Almost everyone listening interpreted Truman's assertion as a turning point in American foreign policy. James Reston, who would anchor international-affairs reporting for the *New York Times* for decades, declared Truman's statement comparable to Lend-Lease or the Monroe Doctrine. "Like the Lend-Lease program, it proposed defending America by aiding those who are working for a free and non-communist world," Reston said. "Like the Monroe Doctrine, it warned that the United States would resist efforts to impose a political system or foreign domination on areas vital to our security."

Reston's latter analogy caught on, and the policy Truman described became known as the Truman Doctrine. Most Democrats fell in line with the president, as did some Republicans. Truman took particular comfort in the support of Republican Arthur Vandenberg, an erstwhile isolationist who until recently had been a skeptic regarding American commitments overseas. The Michigan senator now declared in favor of the aid. "The president's hands must be upheld," Vandenberg asserted. "The independence of Greece and Turkey must be preserved."

## 4. COLD WAR DISSENTERS

Robert Taft took a different view. William Howard Taft's son had sailed through Yale College and Harvard Law School at the head of his class before being rejected, on account of myopia exacerbated by excessive studying, for army duty in World War I. In lieu of assignment to the trenches of France, he served on the refugee relief staff of Herbert Hoover, who came to symbolize to Taft all that was right with politics and the philosophy of government. Taft decried the New Deal as corroding American individualism. "The measures undertaken by the Democratic administration are alarming," he declared during Roosevelt's first term. "Whatever may be said for them as emergency measures, their permanent incorporation into our system would practically abandon the whole theory of American government and inaugurate what is, in fact, socialism." Elected to the Senate from Ohio in 1938, Taft allied with conservative Southern Democrats who similarly rejected Roosevelt's domestic programs. Taft was persuasive within his circles, in a pedestrian way. "While I have no difficulty talking," he told a friend, "I don't know how to do any of the eloquence business."

Taft's opposition to big government at home was matched by his resistance to ambitious foreign policies. As a leader of the isolationists in Congress he attempted to thwart Roosevelt's efforts to draw the United States toward war with Germany and Japan, and even after Pearl Harbor he continued to blame the president for adventurism. "We need not have become involved in the present war," he declared in 1942. Taft rejected still more vigorously Roosevelt's efforts to construct a framework of world order centered upon the United States. He said he took his lessons in foreign policy from George Washington, Thomas Jefferson, and James Monroe; Washington and Jefferson guided him to eschew foreign entanglements, while Monroe's doctrine defined the Western Hemisphere as the appropriate realm of American action.

In 1947 he challenged Truman on the subject of military aid to Greece and Turkey. Taft didn't reject assistance aimed at the economic reconstruction of those countries, but he opposed underwriting their armies. Their generals, he predicted, would take American money, American arms, and American training for their troops, and then do whatever they chose. They were hardly paragons of democracy, and the United States would have little control over their actions.

There was a larger problem, Taft said. By dividing the world rhetorically into communist and non-communist spheres, Truman tended to confirm the actual division of the world. The United States had been trying to get the Russians out of Poland and the rest of Eastern Europe; Truman's policy would give them an excuse to stay. "If we assume a special position in Greece and Turkey," Taft said, "we can hardly longer reasonably object to the Russians' continuing their domination in Poland, Yugoslavia, Rumania and Bulgaria."

Taft eventually voted for Truman's aid package for Greece and Turkey, but only as a tactical matter—only because, as he put it, "the president's announcements have committed the United States to this policy in the eyes of the world, and to repudiate it now would destroy his prestige in the negotiations with the Russian government, on the success of which ultimate peace depends." Rejecting the philosophical heart of the Truman Doctrine, Taft declared, "I do not regard this as a commitment to any similar policy in any other section of the world, or to the continuation of the same policy in Greece or Turkey when peace negotiations are completed."

Walter Lippmann agreed with Taft that Truman was making too much of a pair of isolated cases. Lippmann had been the dean of American political journalists for decades, almost since he jumped ship from the Wilson administration before it sank beneath the waves of isolationism that swept America after World War I. Lippmann in 1947 gathered a number of his columns and published them under a title—*The Cold War*—that popularized this phrase as a label for the tension between the United States and the Soviet Union. Lippmann noted that containment would stand or fall on the ability of the

American people to persist for decades in their vigilance against Soviet expansion. Little in history suggested that they possessed such patience. "Americans would themselves probably be frustrated by Mr. X's policy long before the Russians were," Lippmann wrote.

Worse, the United States would have to rely on allies and proxies in containing Soviet power, as the Truman administration proposed to do in Greece and Turkey. Lippmann joined Taft in worrying about those persons who would be receiving American arms and money. "They will act for their reasons, and on their own judgment, presenting us with accomplished facts which we did not intend, and with crises for which we are unready," he wrote. "We shall have either to disown our puppets, which would be tantamount to appeasement and defeat and the loss of face, or must support them at an incalculable cost on an unintended, unforeseen and perhaps undesirable issue."

## 5. A MAN WITH A PLAN

The criticism didn't cause Truman to abandon or seriously modify the containment policy. The president got his money for Greece and Turkey, and notwithstanding the reservations of Taft and Lippmann, he construed the favorable vote in Congress as assent for his larger doctrine. Yet he was happy to change the subject when the opportunity arose, as it did almost at once.

Dean Acheson, as part of his fretting about the future of the American economy and his forecasting of its dependence on export markets, had joined others in Washington in wondering what might be done to rebuild Europe after the war. Reconstruction would have at least three purposes: humanitarian, in alleviating the distress of the European people; political, in securing the support of grateful recipients for the United States; and economic, in furnishing buying power that would purchase American exports and thereby prevent the United States from sinking back into depression. Partly because reconstruction had these multiple goals, partly because other issues seemed more immediately pressing, and partly because the Republican capture of Congress in the 1946 elections complicated the politics of just about anything the administration attempted, Truman and his advisers were slow to formalize their reconstruction plans. But the winter of 1946–47 happened to be one of the harshest in memory across much of Europe, and the newsreels and reports of hungry, shivering millions concentrated the mind of the American bureaucracy.

Truman sent Will Clayton, Acheson's successor as assistant secretary of state for economic affairs, to Europe to inspect the situation and make specific recommendations. Clayton reported that the social, economic, and political fabric of Europe was unraveling by the week. Without prompt American assistance, the countries there would soon be overwhelmed. "Aside from the awful implications which this would have for the future peace and security of the world," Clayton observed, "the immediate effects on our domestic economy would be disastrous: markets for our surplus production gone, unemployment, depression, a heavily unbalanced budget on the background of a mountainous war debt. *These things must not happen.*"

Clayton's recommendation furnished the basis for a speech given by George Marshall to a commencement crowd at Harvard in June 1947. The secretary of state skipped the usual counsel to the graduates in favor of advice to Congress and the American people. He called for an ambitious program of aid to Europe to stabilize and ameliorate the situation there, in the interests of the Europeans and of the world. "Our policy is directed not against any country or doctrine but against hunger, poverty, desperation, and chaos," Marshall asserted. "Its purpose should be the revival of a working economy in the world so as to permit the emergence of political and social conditions in which free institutions can exist." The aid should be allocated not piecemeal or country by country but rather continent-wide, or nearly so. The Europeans must cooperate with America and among themselves. "The program should be a joint one, agreed to by a number, if not all, European nations." And it should have the support of Americans of all political persuasions. "Political passion and prejudice should have no part."

What came to be called the Marshall Plan embodied the secretary's recommendations. The Europeans set to work establishing a framework of tariff reduction and joint economic planning, and Congress commenced hearings on the administration's proposal. Most of those who had supported the Truman Doctrine and the policy of containment found the European aid program comparatively easy to swallow; many of those who choked on the earlier initiatives gagged on this one too.

Robert Taft decried the "huge taxes" required to support the aid program. The Ohio senator didn't dispute that American aid might be necessary at particular times and in particular locations, but Truman made no distinctions among cases. "The administration can't get away from the New Deal principle that government spending is a good thing in itself," Taft said. He asserted that the aid program would increase taxes that were already too high. "Every man is working three days out of ten for the government and only seven for himself." The aid was offered as generosity, but it would elicit ill will. "We open ourselves to charges of interference and imperialism. . . . We give the Russians the basis for the charge that we are trying to dominate the countries of Western Europe." Nor could aid ever be decisive in the struggle against communism. "The people of France, for instance, are going to decide for themselves whether they go communist or not."

As in the earlier debates, Taft lost this one. Congress approved the Marshall Plan, which ultimately sent some $13 billion in aid to Europe (the equivalent of between $100 billion and $500 billion in 2010 dollars, depending on whether the conversion was in dollars or goods). The money came with strings; the longest and strongest required that the money had to be spent in the United States on American goods, which were then shipped to Europe in American vessels. In other words the Marshall Plan was, among other things, a huge make-work program for American farmers, manufacturers, and shippers. It set a pattern in this regard for most American aid afterward.

But it nonetheless served its humanitarian and political purposes as well. The hunger and homelessness in Europe diminished, and the recipient countries did indeed repay the United States with support for American policies. Nearly all of Western Europe participated. Briefly Truman and his advisers worried that the Soviets might horn in on the aid, taking Marshall at his word that the program wasn't directed against any country or doctrine. But the market-freeing conditions Marshall stipulated, and the American oversight they implied, put Stalin off, and he vetoed it for his own country and the Eastern European countries controlled by the Red Army. A few months after Marshall's speech the Kremlin announced the Molotov Plan, named for Marshall's Soviet counterpart and intended to accomplish for Eastern Europe, on socialist principles, what the Marshall Plan would do, on a capitalist basis, for the West.

## 6. ONE IF BY LAND, TWO IF BY AIR

The dueling aid packages additionally divided Europe. At the beginning of 1948 the fate of the continent remained in flux, with Germany at the heart of the matter. The occupation armies of the four great powers still held the positions they had taken in the spring of 1945, and none seemed in a hurry to leave. The Western powers continued to coordinate their German policies, giving the appearance of creating a new Germany out of their portion of the old one. In 1947 the Americans and British administratively merged their zones, and in early 1948 they issued a new currency, separate from that of the Soviet sector. A constitutional convention was called to draft a charter for a new West German state.

The Soviet government decried these developments. Having been overrun by German armies twice in little more than a generation, the Russians resisted anything that appeared likely to resurrect a strong German state. In March 1948 the Soviet army in eastern Germany began harassing ground traffic from the western zones to Berlin, the divided national capital, which lay more than a hundred miles inside the Soviet zone. In June the highways and rail lines were blocked entirely.

Whether the Soviet blockade of Berlin was an understandable protest against the Western policies regarding Germany or a provocation revealing Moscow's inherently aggressive designs was a matter of interpretation. Most American officials assumed the latter. Some urged vigorous countermeasures. General Lucius Clay, the military governor of the American zone, advocated sending an armed convoy down the autobahn toward Berlin. Clay was half-convinced the Soviets wanted war, and he was ready to give it to them. "If the Soviets go to war," he asserted, "it will not be because of the Berlin currency issue but only because they believe this is the right time." Clay and others thought that if war was inevitable, this was the right time for the United States, which alone possessed atomic weapons.

Truman was decisive, but he wasn't ready for war. He agreed with Clay and nearly everyone else that the United States must not be pushed out of Berlin by Soviet pressure. "We stay in Berlin, period," he declared shortly after the blockade began. But rather than challenge the blockade directly, he authorized an end run—or rather a leap over. He ordered an airlift of food, fuel, and everything else necessary to keep the West Berliners supplied. At the same time, as a signal of his willingness to match any Soviet escalation, he redeployed two squadrons of B-29 bombers to Britain. The B-29, as the Soviets knew, was the model that had dropped the atom bombs on Hiroshima and Nagasaki, and it possessed the range to hit targets deep inside the Soviet Union.

The Berlin airlift proved a miracle of transportation logistics. Hundreds of American and British cargo planes operated around the clock, landing and taking off as frequently as once per minute, carrying supplies for an urban population of more than two million. At the beginning everyone assumed the airlift would last days or perhaps weeks, until the crisis passed or escalated. Almost no one thought the pilots, navigators, cargo handlers, and air traffic controllers could maintain their exhausting pace. But the Soviets refused to lift the blockade—or to try to stop the planes—and the noisy, busy standoff persisted through the winter and into the spring of 1949.

Finally the Soviets, embarrassed by the bad light the situation cast on them, and unable to eliminate the smuggling that quietly but significantly assisted the Western airlift, canceled the blockade. The result of the whole affair was to transform Berlin from the bombed-out capital of a discredited regime to the most visible and potent symbol of the Cold War, which itself became more entrenched than ever in the heart of Europe.

## 7. DEWEY? OR DON'T WE?

The success of the Berlin airlift was a feather in Truman's cap, at the time when he needed every good thing that came his way. After their success in the congressional elections of 1946, the Republicans couldn't wait for a shot at the White House. Not for two decades had a Republican been elected president, and most historic and contemporary indicators pointed to a Republican victory. The nominee the party sent into battle was Thomas Dewey, the governor of New York and a former prosecutor of mob bosses, embezzlers, and stock market cheats. Dewey had run against Franklin Roosevelt in 1944 and finished respectably in what everyone understood was an impossible race against a revered wartime incumbent. Truman, who carried the baggage of the accumulated opposition to the New Deal but enjoyed little of the respect accorded Roosevelt, appeared an easy target. So confident, in fact, were the

Republicans that they declined to make an issue of foreign policy in the campaign. Dewey had supported the major initiatives of the Truman administration, including the Truman Doctrine, the Marshall Plan, and the Berlin airlift, and he didn't want to spoil his chances as president of continuing these and similar policies.

His prospects only improved with the emergence of a split—two splits, in fact—among the Democrats. Henry Wallace had been Roosevelt's secretary of agriculture before being tapped in 1940 for vice president, and he had hoped to climb the last rung to the presidency. But after Wallace demonstrated an inability to get along with others in the administration, Roosevelt replaced him on the 1944 ticket—with Truman. Wallace's personal belief system didn't help his chances. From the Presbyterianism of his youth he had wandered among several religions, including Catholicism, Judaism, Islam, Buddhism, and Zoroastrianism. He corresponded with a Russian mystic; the letters, leaked to the press, almost became a campaign issue in 1940 but were buried when the Democrats threatened to retaliate by revealing an extramarital affair of Wendell Willkie, the Republican presidential nominee. After Wallace was removed from the national ticket in 1944, Roosevelt consoled him with an appointment to the Commerce Department, from which he defended the New Deal against its Republican and conservative Democratic critics and positioned himself for the 1948 Democratic nomination for president.

Wallace taxed Truman for insufficient adherence to the liberal principles of the New Deal and for excessive truculence toward the Soviet Union. Wallace didn't go quite so far as to blame the American government for the Cold War, but he thought Truman's abrupt manner toward Moscow made a difficult situation worse. He left the Commerce Department to edit the liberal weekly *The New Republic*, in whose pages he charged Truman with conducting a foreign policy of fear. When it became clear that Truman would receive the Democratic nomination, Wallace jumped to the Progressive party, and he mounted a presidential campaign calling for an easing of international tensions and an elaboration of the New Deal, starting with the adoption of federally funded universal health care.

On Truman's right was Strom Thurmond, the governor of South Carolina and the nominee of a Democratic splinter group, the States' Rights Democratic party, more often called the Dixiecrats. Like their Confederate forebears, the Dixiecrats condemned the coercive power of the federal government; like the Confederates, too, the Dixiecrats most resented federal policies regarding race. Truman had recently issued an executive order to integrate the American military, which had been segregated for decades. Thurmond and the Dixiecrats opposed the order on its substance and for what it portended for the Jim Crow system in the South, and after the Democratic platform committee endorsed an antisegregationist plank, they walked out of the convention.

With his own party in shambles and the Republicans united behind Dewey, Truman appeared to lack even a prayer of victory. He nonetheless launched a vigorous campaign, including the last whistle-stop tour in American political history. At every railroad crossing and way station he assailed the "do-nothing" Republican Congress for failing to address the needs of the country. His scorching attacks struck a note among voters, who discovered more and more to like in the man from Independence. Audiences shouted "Give 'em hell, Harry!" at each rally, to which Truman responded, "I just tell the truth on the Republicans, and they think it's hell!"

Dewey nonetheless carried a lead into the final days of the campaign, and on election night the early returns indicated a Republican win. Several newspapers, including a gloating *Chicago Tribune*, printed editions proclaiming a Dewey triumph. But the voting in the West diminished Dewey's lead and eventually pushed Truman over the top in the most stunning upset in American political history. Truman finished with 24 million votes to Dewey's 22 million, and 303 electors to Dewey's 189. Dixiecrat Thurmond received 1 million votes and carried four Southern states. Progressive Wallace won almost the same number of votes as Thurmond, but because his support was scattered, he carried no states and received no electoral votes.

There were lessons all around from the election, although the different parties and groups interpreted them differently. The regional strength of the Dixiecrats indicated that civil rights reform wouldn't come easily to the South. The vote for Wallace suggested that while Americans might not want to relinquish Social Security and other parts of their welfare state bequest from Roosevelt, they weren't ready for anything like another New Deal. Truman, not surprisingly, interpreted the result as an endorsement of his administration and particularly its policies relating to the Cold War. He prepared to continue on the course he had already charted. The Republicans, shocked and embittered by their defeat, drew the opposite conclusion. Dewey hadn't convinced the foreign policy conservatives in the party so much as he had persuaded them to keep quiet. After his loss they screamed louder than ever, decrying bipartisanship as a sucker's game and vowing to have none of it in the future.

# 3 | Agnostics and Believers

## 1949–1954

### 1. INSTITUTIONALIZING THE REVOLUTION

Pearl Harbor commenced a revolution in American foreign policy, and the Truman Doctrine and the Marshall Plan continued it. The essence of the revolution was the belief that the United States could not afford to leave the world to its own devices, as it had done during the 1930s, and that disorder and aggression even in distant locales would eventually endanger the American way of life. Munich, the site of the sellout of Czechoslovakia to Hitler, became the symbol of the failed policy of appeasement, which itself became a label for all that must be avoided in American policy. Stalin and communism supplanted Hitler and fascism as the enemies of America, but their basic motives—the destruction of personal liberty, the imposition of one-party rule, the prospective domination of the world—were judged to be the same. The Cold War initiatives of the Truman administration were formulated with memories of Munich in the minds of American policymakers. The Truman Doctrine drew the line against aggression in Greece and Turkey in no small part because the Western democracies had not drawn the line against aggression in Czechoslovakia. The Marshall Plan sent aid to Europe to prevent the recurrence of the despair that had fertilized the soil of the continent for the evil flowering of Nazism.

Yet though Truman's measures received bipartisan support, that support wasn't unanimous. Henry Wallace and his associates on the Democratic and Progressive left pointed out that Stalin was *not* Hitler, nor communism fascism. Whether Stalin was directing or even supporting the insurgency in Greece was far from clear, the liberal critics said. And by treating the world as already divided into two camps, Truman encouraged that very division.

Robert Taft and the Republican right criticized Truman differently. The old isolationists viewed the world as a far darker place than Wallace and the liberals did, and darker than Truman and the Cold Warriors did. For precisely this reason they resisted Truman's efforts to link America's fate to that of the world. They wanted nothing to do with the United Nations, which symbolized a loss of American sovereignty. They rejected American responsibility for maintaining peace and order in Europe, arguing that such an effort would bankrupt the United States, would probably fail anyway, and would drag America into a third European conflict. In the meantime it would contribute to additional growth of the American government, which to the conservatives was a bad thing in itself. The conservatives urged a retreat to the Western Hemisphere, a return to the nineteenth-century principles of the Monroe Doctrine. By strengthening the United States at home and securing the hemisphere, they said, the American government would provide all the safety the American people required.

Consequently the Taftites protested loudly at the beginning of 1949 when Truman proposed to institutionalize the revolution in American foreign policy. The North Atlantic Treaty was the antidote to the Munich syndrome; by declaring in advance that an attack on any one of the member countries—the United States, Canada, Britain, France, and several other European states—would be considered an attack on the United States, Washington removed any doubts regarding America's commitment to Europe.

Taft led the opposition to the Atlantic pact in the Senate. "By executing a treaty of this kind, we put ourselves at the mercy of the foreign policies of eleven other nations," he declared. The policy of the United States didn't currently clash with those other policies, but none could say how long this consonance would persist. "The government of any one of these nations may be taken over by the Communist Party of that nation." What would that do to American security? Taft did not entirely reject a larger role for the United States in Europe, but any American initiative or declaration regarding European security should be unilateral. The Monroe Doctrine provided the model.

"The Monroe Doctrine was a unilateral declaration. We were free to modify it or withdraw from it at any moment." Under the Monroe Doctrine the United States government decided what to do in the event of conflict abroad. "We were free to fight the war in such a manner as we might determine, or not at all."

The Atlantic treaty was bad enough on its face, but Taft predicted that there was more to the pact than met the eye. The White House denied any intent to arm the Europeans or station American troops across the ocean. But such a consequence was nearly inevitable, given the nature of the treaty, the philosophy behind it, and the history of Democratic double-dealing. "I think the pact carries with it an obligation to assist in arming, at our expense, the nations of Western Europe," Taft said. This unavoidable policy would crush American taxpayers even as it provoked an arms race in Europe. "The history of these obligations has been that once begun, they cannot easily be brought to an end." Today Western Europe was the object of American attention and largesse; what country or region would be next? "If the Russian threat justifies arms for all of Western Europe, surely it justifies similar arms for Nationalist China, for Indochina, for India, and ultimately for Japan; and in the Near East for Iran, for Syria, and for Iraq. There is no limit to the burden of such a program or its dangerous implications."

Taft's speech against the North Atlantic Treaty was the greatest of his career, and it brought the entire Senate to its feet for a sustained ovation. Some of his colleagues sensed prescience in his remarks; others simply appreciated the seriousness with which he addressed this most crucial issue. The North Atlantic Treaty marked a fundamental departure in American foreign policy. Not since 1800 had the United States been party to a peacetime alliance, and never had it handed such control over its fate to other countries. Unilateralism—independence of action—had characterized America's foreign policy from the start; this now gave way to multilateralism—dependence on others in the making and implementation of policy. America might be more secure as a result; it might be less secure. But it would never be the same.

The North Atlantic Treaty, like all treaties, required a two-thirds majority in the Senate. It achieved that margin easily. For all the respect the Senate accorded Taft's words, only thirteen senators joined him in opposing the treaty when it came to a vote in July 1949. "This treaty is an historic step toward a world of peace, a free world, free from fear," Truman said, to the gratification of those who supported the pact. "But it is only one step," he added, to the further distrust of Taft and the opponents.

## 2. THE CHINA SYNDROME

Taft's dark forecast began to come true almost before the North Atlantic Treaty took effect in August 1949. For half a century China had occupied a peculiar place on the foreign policy horizon of the United States. Americans knew little about China except that it was large, heathen (that is, un-Bibled), and historically subject to depredations by outside imperialists. In the late 1890s the depredations intensified, to the point where it seemed likely that China would be carved into colonies, enclaves, or protectorates by some or all of Britain, France, Germany, Russia, and Japan. The McKinley administration circulated a pair of diplomatic documents called the Open Door notes defending China's territorial integrity and asserting equal opportunity for all comers to trade with China. The notes included neither threats nor mechanisms of enforcement, but they gave sufficient pause to the would-be dismemberers of China that the moment of crisis passed. China continued to disintegrate internally, till the emperor was forced to abdicate in 1911 in favor of a weak republican government, but Americans congratulated themselves—excessively—for having saved China from foreign aggression.

This flattering misconception gained credence from the small number and unusual circumstances of those Americans who could claim any expertise regarding China. For decades the foremost interpreters of China to America were Christian missionaries and their China-born children. The latter—the "mishkids"—spoke Chinese and understood Chinese culture and folkways far better than almost anyone else in America, but their Christian religious background tilted their interpretation of China in a distinctive direction. They unsurprisingly favored Chinese Christians, who formed a very small minority in the country, and they particularly detested Chinese communists, who like faithful communists elsewhere were officially godless.

The anticommunist angle grew particularly important during the 1930s, when a civil war raged between the Nationalist government of Chiang Kai-shek and a communist insurgency led by Mao Zedong. Chiang was a Christian who became a favorite of mishkid Henry Luce, the founder of the *Time-Life-Fortune* publishing empire in America, and of the Republican party. Chiang and Mao set aside their struggle during World War II, but no sooner had the war against Japan ended than they squared off for a final showdown over the future of China. The Truman administration backed Chiang but hesitated to be drawn too deeply into China's civil conflict. By the summer of 1949 Chiang's government, plagued by corruption and plummeting morale, was on the verge of defeat. His American partisans, mostly Republicans, demanded that Truman increase American aid to Chiang, but the president and his advisers, having concluded that Chiang was a lost cause, refused. Chiang fled with his government and eventually more than a million refugees to Taiwan, a hundred miles off mainland China's southeastern coast. In October 1949 Mao proclaimed the People's Republic of China, which most Americans and many others in the West promptly labeled Red China.

Truman and Dean Acheson, who had succeeded George Marshall as secretary of state, hoped that the end of China's civil war would put a stop to the demands for American intervention. In fact the shouting only intensified, especially on the Republican right. Many of the shouters were sincerely appalled that the world's most populous nation had fallen to communism. Others, still angry at the outcome of the 1948 presidential election, took the opportunity to beat Truman about the head with charges of "losing" China. Some spoke of rekindling the Chinese civil war, of "unleashing" Chiang so that he and the Nationalists might return to the Chinese mainland. Chiang himself spoke frequently of such an effort, and he sent his beautiful American-educated wife to Washington to lobby on his behalf.

Before long China became the hottest button in American politics. Truman found himself in an impossible position. Having proclaimed the two-world theory of international politics, he couldn't well say that China's choice of communism didn't matter. On the other hand, having prudentially declined to go to the rescue of Chiang, he couldn't concede that it mattered a great deal. He silently resolved that there should be no more Chinas, and he hoped the issue would gradually go away.

## 3. TAIL GUNNER JOE

Joseph McCarthy had no intention of letting it go away. McCarthy, a Wisconsin farm boy, had entered politics out of law school. He gained election to the state bench in 1939 but resigned his judgeship to enlist in the marines during World War II. He flew combat missions as a gunner-observer and unsuccessfully sought the Republican nomination for the Senate. After the war he tried again, won the nomination, and displayed a distinctive general-election style of hurling spurious accusations against his opponent—the Progressive hero Robert M. La Follette, Jr.—and hurling more while La Follette was still trying to refute the first salvo. McCarthy's victory won him emulators but less recognition in Washington than he thought he deserved. In 1950 he found a formula to fix the problem. He had been invited to address the Republican Women's Club of Wheeling, West Virginia; the occasion was Lincoln's birthday, and everyone expected a patriotic, if partisan, snoozer. Instead McCarthy produced a piece of paper, which he held up before his audience and described as a list of communists currently working in the State Department.

Communists in government had been on American minds since the onset of the Cold War. During the Great Depression, when capitalism appeared to be failing, if not to have failed altogether, many thousands of Americans sincerely looked to communism as an alternative. Membership in the American Communist party soared; party chief Earl Browder ran for president in 1936 and received 80,000 votes. Communists opposed fascism with greater conviction than members of America's major parties; until 1939 they could tell themselves and their compatriots that they were stauncher advocates of freedom than Republicans or Democrats. This interpretation suffered a blow when Stalin about-faced and signed a nonaggression pact with Hitler, which provided Germany the freedom to attack Poland and start World War II. Hitler's double-cross of Stalin in June 1941—the German invasion of Russia—and Pearl Harbor the following December made allies of American capitalists and Soviet communists and once more brought American communists back within the realm of respectability. But the postwar falling-out between Moscow and Washington and the congealing of the Cold War again cast the communists into suspicion.

In 1947 the House Un-American Activities Committee, under Republican leadership for the first time since its 1937 establishment, launched an investigation of communists in the United States. Chairman John Parnell Thomas had never forgiven Franklin Roosevelt for hiring leftist (and other) writers during the depression as part of the Federal Writers' Project; Thomas's revenge was to launch an investigation of Hollywood screenwriters for alleged subversive activities. The committee, commonly known as HUAC, had no powers of prosecution, and in any event few of those summoned before it were charged with any crime. But the glare of publicity, combined with the popular fears of communism, sufficed to damage or ruin the careers of many charged with communist sympathies.

Truman thought the country had worse to fear than red tendencies on the silver screen, but under the circumstances he felt obliged to demonstrate that the Republicans didn't have a monopoly on vigilance. As part of his political offensive on behalf of the Truman Doctrine he issued an executive order requiring investigations of employees of the executive branch of the federal government. "It is of vital importance that persons employed in the federal service be of complete and unswerving loyalty to the United States," the president explained. "The presence within the government service of any disloyal or subversive person constitutes a threat to our democratic processes. . . . Maximum protection must be afforded the United States against infiltration of disloyal persons into the ranks of its employees."

The concern regarding communists in government, in Hollywood, and in other allegedly sensitive positions in society intensified as the Cold War grew grimmer. The communist victory in China in 1949 prompted Republicans to hint or charge openly that communists within the Truman State Department had consciously or unwittingly contributed to the defeatist attitude that deprived Chiang Kai-shek of the eleventh-hour support that might have prevented his expulsion from the mainland.

Two additional elements raised the obsession with communists in government to the level of paranoia. Even as Mao and the Chinese communists were driving Chiang to Taiwan, the Soviet Union successfully tested an atomic bomb. The threat from Soviet communism had been nebulous till now, or confined to Europe. But a Russian bomb dramatically changed things. Soviet warplanes would threaten American cities soon if not immediately; a single Soviet bomb might vaporize New York or Washington the way America's bomb had vaporized Hiroshima.

If the existence of the Soviet bomb was alarming, the means by which the Russians attained the requisite technology was even scarier. Americans were sufficiently confident of capitalism's comparative prowess over socialism to believe that the Russians could not have built a bomb without stealing secrets from the West; Soviet spies must have infiltrated the atomic sanctum. In fact they had. For years American and British intelligence agencies had been tracking Soviet agents, and in January 1950 they got Klaus Fuchs, a German-born physicist who had worked on the Manhattan Project, to confess to espionage and transmitting atomic information to his Russian handlers.

It was into this atmosphere of escalating alarm that Joseph McCarthy made his dramatic entrance at Wheeling. Accounts differed as to how many communists he said were working in the State Department—57 by one version, 205 by another, no specific number by still others—and because no recording was made of his Wheeling speech, pinning the number down was impossible. But the Wheeling number didn't really matter, because after the press picked up on McCarthy's charges, he repeatedly raised the stakes and the numbers. "The government is full of Communists," he declared. To Republican friends he explained that the communists-in-government theme was the ideal weapon for pounding the Democrats. "We can hammer away at them," he said.

McCarthy became a virtuoso of the political attack. He waved papers he said documented the conspiracy; when reporters asked to examine the documents, he explained that he couldn't release them without revealing state secrets or spoiling his ongoing investigations. If Democrats demanded to see the evidence behind his allegations, he accused the demanders of being part of the conspiracy themselves. His choice of language guaranteed attention. His critics were "left-wing bleeding hearts" and "egg-sucking phony liberals." He impugned the masculinity of those not as devoted to rooting out communism as himself. He achieved a sort of bipartisan credibility by slashing moderate members of his own party. Ralph Flanders, a Republican septuagenarian from Vermont, had outlived his sanity, McCarthy said. "I think they should get a man with a net and take him to a good quiet place."

But when his fellow Republicans weren't worrying that he would turn on them, they loved McCarthy for the brutality with which he pummeled the Democrats. The two decades since the election of Franklin Roosevelt had been "twenty years of treason," McCarthy said. Things were worse now than ever. Dean Acheson, the "Red Dean," had made the State Department a nest of

"Communists and queers who have sold 400 million Asiatic people into atheistic slavery." Acheson's "primary loyalty in international affairs seems to run to the British Labor government, his secondary allegiance to the Kremlin"—although McCarthy allowed that the order might sometimes be reversed. Alger Hiss, a senior State Department official under Roosevelt and Truman and, in McCarthy's telling, a closeted communist, exercised a "Svengali-like influence" over his superiors and through them over American policy. Even George Marshall, the almost universally respected former secretary of state, now secretary of defense, was disloyal, McCarthy alleged. Marshall was part of "a conspiracy on a scale so immense as to dwarf any previous such venture in the history of man, a conspiracy of infamy so black that, when it is finally exposed, its principals shall be forever deserving of the maledictions of all honest men." Truman, of course, was beyond redemption. His daily decisions jeopardized American security; when the president crossed swords with Douglas MacArthur, the Republicans' favorite general, McCarthy angrily said of Truman, "The son of a bitch ought to be impeached."

How many people believed McCarthy is unclear. His allegations got him what he wanted most: attention. His words and photograph regularly appeared on the front pages of newspapers; *Time* and *Newsweek* made him their cover story. Polls revealed that nearly 85 percent of Americans had heard of his charges, and nearly 40 percent thought he was doing a service by airing them.

McCarthy clearly tapped into anxieties current in the American psyche. Some of the anxieties were perfectly rational. Soviet communism *was* a threat. Spies *did* exist—among them probably Alger Hiss, who was implicated many years after the fact by evidence from Soviet archives. Other emotions evoked by McCarthy were less directly connected to the communist question but no less effective in mobilizing political support. Catholics liked McCarthy as one of their own but also for harping on the atheism of communism, which many Catholics found especially disturbing. Conservatives from the heartland heard McCarthy saying what they had been feeling for years about the liberal elites of the East Coast. "I look at that fellow," Hugh Butler, a Republican senator from Nebraska, said of Acheson. "I watch his smart aleck manner and his British clothes and that New Dealism, everlasting New Dealism in everything he says and does, and I want to shout, Get out! Get out! You stand for everything that has been wrong with the United

States for years." When Democrats scoffed at McCarthy's charges and urged Wisconsinites to replace him, the local papers rallied to his defense in language that made plain that McCarthy wasn't the whole issue. "We don't want a group of New Yorkers and Easterners to tell us whom we are going to send to the Senate," one editor asserted. "That is our business, and it is none of theirs."

It was the Republican party's business, too, and for a time it was a very good business. McCarthy's charges, and those he inspired other Republicans to make, added to the burdens of incumbency for the Democrats, and in the 1950 congressional elections Truman's party lost significant ground. The Republicans picked up five seats in the Senate; one of their promising newcomers was Richard Nixon of California, whose red-baiting campaign script borrowed several pages from McCarthy. The Republicans gained twenty-eight seats in the House.

The lesson they learned was that hitting hard and low—McCarthy delighted in declaring he was going to kick some opponent in the groin—could be very effective. And it could be tremendously satisfying. For most conservatives and Republicans, the long period since 1932 had produced a dangerous detour from basic American values. They grudgingly credited Roosevelt with winning the war, but they still despised the New Deal, and Truman's Cold War was a constant source of frustration. McCarthy might be a demagogue; responsible Republicans were willing to admit that, among themselves. But even demagogues need an audience, and the size of McCarthy's audiences indicated he was onto something.

In time McCarthy overreached, to no one's great surprise. It was in the nature of his style that his allegations had to grow ever more outrageous, simply to retain the attention of the press and the public. Having impugned generals—after Marshall he took on Dwight Eisenhower, who responded with disdainful silence. "I just won't get into a pissing contest with that skunk," Eisenhower said privately—McCarthy eventually assaulted the U.S. Army as an institution. The army counterattacked, documenting that McCarthy had sought special favors for a friend. The Senate held hearings in the spring of 1954 to discover the truth of the matter, and on this televised stage McCarthy found himself outmaneuvered. At a critical moment his chief antagonist, Joseph Welch, chastised him for trying to slander a young lawyer who worked with Welch. "Let us not assassinate this lad further, Senator," Welch said. "You have done enough. Have you no sense of decency, sir, at long last? Have you left no sense of decency?"

The question hung over the hearing room, and it echoed via television and radio around the country. McCarthy had no answer. Americans asked themselves the same question, decided that they did have a sense of decency, and abandoned McCarthy. The Senate, catching the change of mood, censured McCarthy for past excesses. His personal life spiraled downward into an alcoholic haze. He died of liver failure in 1957, at the age of forty-eight.

## 4. REDEFINING THE PERIMETER

In January 1950, just before the McCarthy storm broke, Dean Acheson gave a speech to the National Press Club in Washington. Acheson attempted, in the wake of the communist victory in China, to explain how the Truman administration viewed the strategic situation in Asia. He described an American "defense perimeter" running from Japan to Taiwan and the Philippines. He failed to mention Korea and thereby implied that the United States did not consider that peninsula worth fighting for.

The omission was noticed by Stalin, Mao, and Kim Il Sung, the leader of Korea's communists. Korea had been divided at the end of World War II between a northern zone, above the 38th parallel, in which the Soviet Union oversaw the surrender of occupying Japanese troops, and a southern zone, where American troops did the honors. The division had been designed as temporary, but as the rift between the United States and the Soviet Union developed after the war, the division persisted. The Americans cultivated anticommunist elements in the south, led by Syngman Rhee, who had been educated in the United States before being imprisoned by the Japanese during the war. The Soviets looked to Kim and the communists in the north. Both Kim and Rhee hoped to reunite Korea, each under his own rule. Kim acted first, and in June 1950 he ordered his troops to cross the 38th parallel and attack Rhee's forces. Within days they captured Seoul, the South Korean capital, and compelled Rhee and his associates to flee for their lives. The North Koreans appeared likely, on momentum alone, to roll down the peninsula and impose their rule on the whole country.

The invasion caught Washington off guard, but the Truman administration responded swiftly. The president and his advisers interpreted the North Korean attack not simply as an assault on South Korea but as an "open, clear, direct challenge" to world order and free government, in Acheson's phrasing. Truman declared that "the attack upon Korea makes it plain beyond all doubt that communism has passed beyond the use of subversion to conquer independent nations and will now use armed invasion and war." Truman and Acheson dismissed the objection that Rhee was no democrat but a dictator himself. The point, they said, was that communism was on the march and the forces of freedom needed to stop it. Korea was a test; if the United States and its allies exhibited resolve, the fighting might go no farther. If the West retreated, the communist aggressors would attack elsewhere.

Truman's first step was to order American air and naval forces to the combat zone. These were followed by ground troops dispatched from Japan to South Korea. The president directed the U.S. Seventh Fleet to patrol the Taiwan Strait, lest the Chinese communists get ideas about attacking Chiang while the world was distracted by the events in Korea. (Although Truman didn't say so, the Seventh Fleet had orders to prevent *anyone* from crossing the strait, in either direction. The president worried that Chiang might attempt a return to the mainland, in the not-outlandish belief that the mood in Washington had shifted sufficiently that the administration would be compelled politically to come to his aid.) Truman ordered that American military and economic aid be sent to French forces fighting a communist insurgency in French Indochina.

Meanwhile Truman directed America's representative at the United Nations to put the Korean conflict before the Security Council, where it benefited from lucky timing. The UN had disappointed many of those who hoped it would prove more robust than the League of Nations, for the UN ran into the same problem that had vexed the league, namely the inability of the great powers to agree on what needed to be done. The United States and the Soviet Union, along with Britain, France, and China, each wielded a veto over substantive measures. As the Cold War drove a wedge between Washington and Moscow, the UN became paralyzed. By happenstance, however, the Soviet delegate in June 1950 was boycotting the deliberations of the Security Council, in protest of the refusal of the other members to oust Chiang's representative in favor of a representative from the new communist government of China. In the Soviet absence the Security Council voted to summon member states to the defense of South Korea. The Kremlin's man hurried back to UN headquarters, but by then the deed was done, and now the United States vetoed its undoing.

The defense of South Korea, consequently, was a UN operation. Several countries contributed troops. But the backbone of the operation was the American force, in conjunction with Rhee's own soldiers. The war went poorly at first, and the Americans and South Koreans were pushed to an enclave around the coastal city of Pusan. During the late summer of 1950, however, the American commander, Douglas MacArthur (who doubled as the UN commander), devised a daring amphibious landing far behind the North Korean lines, at Inchon, near Seoul. The landing was breathtakingly risky. The timing had to be perfect, as the extreme tides could easily leave the invaders wallowing in mud miles from shore, easy targets for North Korean gunners. But the difficulty contributed to the surprise, and the surprise allowed the success of the landing. Within hours the balance of the war shifted. The Americans and South Koreans recaptured Seoul and threatened to cut off the retreat of the North Koreans.

Kim's forces barely escaped, in such disarray that MacArthur determined to chase them north. At this point he ran up against the limits of the UN directive regarding the war. The Security Council had authorized the defense of South Korea, not an invasion of North Korea. MacArthur himself brushed aside the constraint, contending that as the battlefield commander he had a duty to win the war, which might be accomplished only by destroying the army that had started it. In Washington, Truman considered the matter more carefully but nonetheless agreed with MacArthur. The Republican charges of having lost China still stung; winning Korea would provide a satisfying riposte. The president told the general to go ahead.

For several weeks the invasion of North Korea proceeded promisingly. American units marched all the way to the Yalu River, the border with China. They could see Chinese troops resting on the other side and began to envision an imminent victory.

What they didn't detect were the Chinese troops that had slipped across the Yalu into North Korea. The Chinese government warned Washington about approaching too close to China. With much of America siding passionately with Chiang, and more than a few Americans calling for reopening the Chinese civil war, Mao and his generals didn't have difficulty believing that the American approach to the Yalu might foreshadow an American invasion of China. Yet the Chinese warning came indirectly, and American officials found it unconvincing.

They learned their mistake in late November when the Chinese troops attacked in massive force. They caught the Americans and South Koreans utterly unaware and inflicted heavy casualties, which the appallingly harsh conditions of the Korean winter made even more painful. The weight of the Chinese blow drove the Americans and South Koreans south, past the 38th parallel. Truman, frantic to do something to stem the collapse of the war effort, hinted at the use of atomic weapons against China. But the alarm of America's allies at the prospect of this kind of escalation caused him to drop the nuclear talk, which in any event was rendered unnecessary when the Americans and South Koreans dug in and finally halted the enemy advance.

The fighting continued, with no end in sight. As the casualties mounted, eventually reaching 35,000 Americans dead and 90,000 wounded, the war grew unpopular in the United States. MacArthur complained that he was being handcuffed by Truman's refusal to let him carry the war to the Chinese—in China. The president let the general complain, but after MacArthur's grumbling reached the level of insubordination, Truman fired him. MacArthur fully expected the American public to rally behind him and against the president. A congressional hearing into Truman's handling of the war gave MacArthur a platform for presenting his side of the story; he concluded his appearance by citing an old barracks song about how "old soldiers never die, they just fade away." Neither MacArthur nor his fans at the hearing expected him to fade away; many anticipated a run for the presidency. But the groundswell did not emerge, and MacArthur in fact slowly faded from view.

## 5. Liking Ike

One reason he did so was that Americans found a general they much preferred to MacArthur. Amid the finger-pointing mania of the early 1950s, Eisenhower emerged as a nearly ideal presidential candidate. A Kansas boy who grew up with six brothers and a pacifist mother, Eisenhower escaped Abilene for West Point, enrolling in the military academy on the recommendation of one of Kansas's senators and because the naval academy at Annapolis turned him down. As a cadet he made a good football player until a knee injury halted his playing career. He missed combat in World War I and spent the 1920s on a slow track to nowhere. An appointment as aide to Douglas MacArthur proved a mixed blessing. Eisenhower accompanied MacArthur in 1932 when the general violently dispersed the Bonus Army of war veterans who had come to Washington seeking relief from the depression. The incident embarrassed the War Department, alienated American public opinion from Herbert Hoover, and convinced Eisenhower that soldiering and politics didn't mix. "Most of the senior officers I had known always drew a clean-cut line between the military and the political," he wrote later. "Off duty, among themselves and close civilian friends, they might explosively denounce everything they thought was wrong in Washington and the world, and propose their own cure for its evils. On duty, nothing could induce them to cross the line they, and old Army tradition, had established. But if General MacArthur ever recognized the existence of that line, he usually chose to ignore it."

Eisenhower began World War II so far down the list of American officers that George Marshall, at that time chief of staff, required all the perspicacity for which he became famous to find him. Marshall made Eisenhower his assistant and then, despite Eisenhower's innocence of battlefield command, the officer in charge of the American invasion of North Africa in 1942. Eisenhower barely survived a controversial decision to collaborate with a Nazi-collaborating French admiral, but all was forgiven when that admiral was assassinated and the operation went on to success. Marshall appeared the obvious choice to command the Allied invasion of France in 1944, but Franklin Roosevelt wanted to keep him in Washington and tapped Eisenhower instead. When the invasion led to the liberation of France and, eight months later, the defeat of Germany, Eisenhower became the great American hero of the war.

He might have entered politics at once and in fact had to rebuff efforts by both parties to nominate him for president. Harry Truman offered to stand aside in 1948 if Eisenhower would accept the Democratic nomination. But Eisenhower was a Republican at heart, and he revealed his preference in 1952 when he declared his candidacy for the GOP nomination. The decision didn't come easily; the apolitical code of this soldier's lifetime couldn't be lightly overridden. But the recent events of the Cold War—the communist victory in China, the Soviet atomic bomb, the war in Korea—had made Truman so unpopular that he chose not to run again, and rendered the Republicans the presumptive favorites to win the White House. To Eisenhower's alarm, the leading Republican contender was Robert Taft, who remained as hostile to foreign commitments as ever.

Eisenhower had a special stake in the matter. As Taft had predicted, the signing of the North Atlantic Treaty led to demands that the United States put boots on the ground in Europe, to make the American commitment visible and palpable. In 1951, after further Senate debate in which Taft again took the losing side, the Truman administration deployed troops to Europe and directed the transformation of the North Atlantic alliance from a merely political grouping into a political and military organization with an integrated command structure. Eisenhower, as America's most popular general, Europe's most popular American, and an ardent believer in the American commitment to Europe, was the natural choice to be the first commander of the North Atlantic Treaty Organization's armed forces. Eisenhower might have been happy to conclude his public career in that position, but when Taft seemed poised to claim the Republican nomination and the White House, Eisenhower decided that American security required his entry into the political arena.

Americans in 1952 remained as susceptible to war-hero worship as they had often been in a history that included president-generals Washington, Jackson, Harrison, Taylor, and Grant, and never had they more craved the security assurance that only a general can provide. Eisenhower handily disposed of Taft in the Republican portion of the race, and then put Democratic nominee Adlai Stevenson at a disadvantage by promising to "go to Korea." Eisenhower didn't specify what he would do in Korea, but the simple fact that America's most celebrated general would take charge of the troublesome war reduced the anxiety of American voters.

Beyond his military experience, Eisenhower brought a charisma to the campaign that had been lacking in politics since Roosevelt died. Eisenhower would break into a broad, room-lighting smile at every opportunity, and he exuded an optimism wholly at odds with the gloom Americans felt from the combination of war abroad and communist-hunting at home. The most effective slogan of the campaign was "I Like Ike"; the phrase was printed under a photo of his famous grin.

Eisenhower swept to an easy victory. He garnered 55 percent of the popular vote and carried all but two states outside the traditionally Democratic South, while winning four states there.

Shortly after the election he redeemed his campaign promise and flew to Korea. His presence in the zone of operations did nothing by itself to break the stalemate, yet it signaled Eisenhower's seriousness about bringing the conflict to an end.

It may have been another transition, however, that mattered more. Only six weeks after Eisenhower took his oath of office, Stalin died. Sorting out the Kremlin succession took time, but the various contestants agreed that the post-Stalin era ought to begin with a liquidation of the Korean struggle, and they signaled their sentiment to China and North Korea.

After some stern language from Washington, interpreted in certain quarters as suggesting that Eisenhower was considering the use of nuclear weapons in Korea, negotiators from the warring countries cut a deal leaving the communists in power in the North, the anticommunists in the South, and the Korean peninsula divided more or less as it had been when the war began. Of some political significance was the fact that the deal was a truce rather than a peace treaty. Technically North Korea and South Korea would remain at war for half a century (and counting, as of 2010). This allowed the two sides to blast each other rhetorically and the North, in particular, to inflict enormous suffering on its own people in the name of the continuing war.

## 6. THE QUIET AMERICANS

Americans gave Eisenhower the credit he deserved for extricating the United States from Korea, but they gave him more credit than he deserved for keeping the United States out of Indochina. France had lost control of its Southeast Asian colony in 1940, when Japan exploited France's wartime distress to occupy it. The French tried to reassert their control after the war only to encounter the nationalist Viet Minh forces led by Ho Chi Minh. Americans might well have backed Ho and the Viet Minh had there been no Cold

War, as America had traditionally supported nationalists against imperialists. But Ho wasn't simply a nationalist; he was also a communist. Amid the political backlash following the communist takeover of China, Harry Truman wasn't willing to risk the loss of another country to the tenets of Marx and Lenin. He ordered American military aid to the French in Indochina.

The aid, however, failed to stem the insurgency, and in the spring of 1954 the French found themselves besieged at Dien Bien Phu, an outpost in the northern part of Vietnam, the most populous of the three Indochinese provinces (the other two being Laos and Cambodia). The French command sent envoys to Washington requesting an American rescue, potentially including the use of nuclear weapons. Eisenhower rejected the request. He had little desire to involve the United States in a war in Vietnam so soon after disengaging America from Korea. But no more than Truman did he wish that Vietnam follow China into the communist camp. And so after an accord negotiated at Geneva in the summer of 1954 resulted in a French withdrawal from Indochina and the temporary partition of the country at the 17th parallel, Eisenhower committed the United States to supporting an anticommunist regime that took shape in Saigon, under the leadership of Ngo Dinh Diem. The Geneva accord called for countrywide elections in 1956, but when Ho Chi Minh appeared to be far more popular than Diem, Eisenhower supported Diem's boycott of the elections. The temporary division of Vietnam grew increasingly permanent, and the United States found itself responsible for maintaining that division against the efforts of Ho to erase it.

Other efforts by Eisenhower to forestall the spread of communism were arguably more successful, although the arguments were muted by the covert nature of the American forestalling. In 1951 the nationalist regime of Mohammed Mossadegh in Iran expropriated the Anglo-Iranian Oil Company, of which the British government was principal owner. The British were understandably upset, and they approached the Truman administration about clandestine measures to reverse the seizure. Truman distrusted British motives in the affair, and he had hardly more confidence in his own Central Intelligence Agency, the spy service created in 1947 (by the same act that established the National Security Council and combined the War and Navy departments into a unified Defense Department). Truman referred to the CIA as an "American Gestapo," and he confined it to bit parts in the making and implementing of foreign policy.

Eisenhower, by contrast, put great confidence in the CIA. He had worked with its forerunner, the Office of Strategic Services, during World War II and been mightily pleased at the performance of the secret agents. He concluded that they could do similar service in the Cold War.

Eisenhower unleashed the CIA against Mossadegh in Iran. American operatives, working closely with their British counterparts, encouraged and armed Mossadegh's enemies, who drove the nationalist prime minister from power in favor of the country's young monarch, Shah Pahlevi. In appreciation for the American assistance, the shah cut American oil companies into the consortium that succeeded the restored Anglo-Iranian Oil Company (which was renamed as British Petroleum).

Closer to home, Eisenhower employed the CIA in Guatemala, where another nationalist regime, under Jacobo Árbenz Guzmán, engaged in a similar expropriation. To be sure, the bananas of the American-owned United Fruit Company were less obviously related to American security than Iranian oil was, but Eisenhower and particularly his secretary of state, John Foster Dulles, believed that expropriation was a leading indicator of communism. Árbenz denied being a communist—but who could believe a communist? The State Department's Richard Patterson delineated Washington's thinking on identifying communists:

> Many times it is impossible to prove legally that a certain individual is a communist, but for cases of this sort I recommend a practical method of detection—the "duck test." The duck test works this way: suppose you see a bird walking around in a farm yard. This bird wears no label that says "duck." But the bird certainly looks like a duck. Also, he goes to the pond, and you notice he swims like a duck. Then he opens his beak and quacks like a duck. Well, by this time you have probably reached the conclusion that the bird is a duck, whether he's wearing a label or not.

The outcome of the covert operation in Guatemala was the overthrow of Árbenz and the installation of a military regime in Guatemala City. The latter proved murderously determined to crush all kinds of Guatemalan dissent. During the following decades more than a hundred thousand people would be killed in a brutal campaign that wiped out not just the few communists in the country but most persons who questioned the regime on any account and many who simply got in the way.

Eisenhower and others aware of the covert operations sometimes acknowledged, among themselves, the dirty nature of clandestine warfare. But they accepted it as part of the Cold War. In 1954 Eisenhower commissioned a top-secret examination of the role of covert operations in American foreign policy. General James Doolittle, who had led a daring raid against Japan during the early part of World War II, headed the committee that produced the report. "It is now clear that we are facing an implacable enemy whose avowed objective is world domination by whatever means and at whatever cost," Doolittle wrote in summarizing the committee's findings.

> There are no rules in such a game. Hitherto acceptable norms of human conduct do not apply. If the United States is to survive, long-standing American concepts of "fair play" must be reconsidered. We must develop effective espionage and counterespionage services and must learn to subvert, sabotage and destroy our enemies by more clever, more sophisticated and more effective methods than those used against us. It may become necessary that the American people be made acquainted with, understand and support this fundamentally repugnant philosophy.

Eisenhower was a better general and a better politician than Doolittle. While accepting the advice about subverting, sabotaging, and destroying America's enemies, the president declined to acquaint the American people with what he was up to. American morale during the Cold War depended heavily on the belief that the United States held the moral high ground in the struggle with communism. Eisenhower as general knew that morale was critical to success in any battle; Eisenhower as president understood that voters would never forgive him for tearing away the veil of their innocence.

## 7. THE SHADOW LENGTHENS

No small part of the appeal of the covert operations was that they reduced the political risk to the United States of failure. Should things go wrong in a country where America was acting clandestinely, Washington could plausibly deny involvement. Another advantage of operating covertly was that such an approach diminished the danger of direct confrontation with the Soviet Union.

This danger imposed caution on every aspect of America's Cold War policy. As soon as the Soviets acquired the atomic bomb in 1949, Harry Truman was faced with two alternatives: to accept parity in weapons of mass destruction or to push on to bigger bombs. Some of Truman's advisers, unnerved at the annihilation already unleashed upon Hiroshima and Nagasaki and at the greater destruction threatened by the Soviet bomb, urged diplomatic efforts to control the existing technology. This route had been tested before, without success. In 1946 the United States proposed a plan, drafted by Bernard Baruch, for handing control of atomic energy and atomic weapons to the United Nations. The Soviet Union rejected the Baruch plan, asserting that it didn't sufficiently constrain America, that it demanded too much of Russia, and that anyway the UN was in the pocket of the West. The skeptics of diplomacy among Truman's advisers pointed to the Baruch plan as evidence that arms control couldn't work, and after the Soviet acquisition of the bomb, they insisted on a crash effort to move from fission weapons, the first-generation devices, to fusion weapons. The latter, also called hydrogen or thermonuclear bombs, would be to the former nearly as the former were to the conventional explosives of the pre-Alamogordo era.

The debate went on within the administration for months. The arguing got ugly; the advocates of the "superbomb" called the opponents weak and irresponsible, while the opponents accused the advocates of gambling with the future of humanity. A top panel of scientists explained that there was "no limit to the explosive power of the bomb itself except that imposed by requirements of delivery." The president must consider what this meant. "It is not a weapon which can be used exclusively for the destruction of material installations of military or semi-military purposes. Its use therefore carries much further than the atomic bomb itself the policy of exterminating civilian populations." The panel advised against the new bomb.

Atomic energy commissioner Lewis Strauss took the opposite view. "I believe that the United States must be as completely armed as any possible enemy," Strauss said. "From this, it follows that I believe it unwise to renounce, unilaterally, any weapon which an enemy can reasonably be expected to possess."

The Joint Chiefs of Staff sided with Strauss. "The United States would be in an intolerable position if a possible enemy possessed the bomb and the United States did not," the chiefs told Truman.

The debate was supposed to be secret, but the contending parties leaked information to the press, which ran articles on the devastation the fusion bombs could wreak upon New York or Chicago. Experts were summoned to speculate on how America might defend itself against such weapons. The prospect was grim. Ralph Lapp, the head of the nuclear physics branch of the Office of Naval Research, said that building the hydrogen bomb was a bad idea because it wouldn't kill *enough* Russians. By Lapp's reckoning, of Russian cities only Moscow was big enough to warrant attack by a hydrogen bomb; every other city could be annihilated by existing atomic weapons. America, however, possessed several such targets, including New York, Chicago, Philadelphia, Detroit, and Los Angeles, which among them contained twenty million people. For America to build the bomb would be like "the man who lives in a tar paper shack and develops a flame thrower to protect himself."

Truman listened to all the arguing and considered the matter carefully. He ultimately decided that the issue came down to a single question. "Can the Russians do it?" he asked at the climactic session of the debate. Even the opponents agreed that they could. "In that case," the president said, "we have no choice. We'll go ahead."

The United States had beaten the Soviet Union to the fission bomb by four years; the race for fusion weapons was far closer. In fact, although America's scientists and engineers in November 1952 detonated the first successful fusion device, it was an unwieldy contraption far too big and touchy to have been dropped from a plane. Before the Americans could weaponize their device, the Soviets in August 1953 tested a fusion device that, while less sophisticated than the American design, had the advantage of being deliverable.

At this point the weapons race ramified from the explosives themselves to their means of delivery. The United States and the Soviet Union each built new long-range bombers, designed to carry the nuclear weapons into the airspace of the other. The Americans enjoyed a major advantage over the Soviets in possessing allies not far from Soviet borders. When Turkey joined NATO in 1952, many observers thought the "North Atlantic" concept was being stretched considerably; but they missed the point, which wasn't broadly publicized: that Turkey offered airfields from which American bombers might be launched against Soviet targets.

America's edge in airfields provided a modicum of reassurance to American leaders and to those ordinary Americans who studied such matters. Yet the reassurance could be no more than fleeting, for the nuclear arms race continued, and the shadow across the American future—and the future of the world—grew ever longer.

# 4 | The Golden Age of the Middle Class
## 1955–1960

### 1. Boom!

In 1950 the population of the United States was a little over 151 million. This was 18 million more than in 1930, and by the standards of many countries such growth would have been impressive. But by American historical standards it was downright anemic. Benjamin Franklin had noted in the eighteenth century the habit of America's population to double every twenty-five years, and so it had done throughout the nineteenth and early twentieth centuries. The growth tailed off considerably after the 1920s, however, for three reasons. The first was self-inflicted, or at least deliberate: the quotas on immigration established by the 1924 National Origins Act, America's first comprehensive immigration measure. Besides giving preference to natives of the countries of northern and western Europe, over southern and eastern Europe and all of Asia, the 1924 act capped immigration far below the numbers that had been arriving during previous decades.

The second cause of the slowdown in population growth might have been considered self-inflicted, but only in an accidental sense. The Great Depression, by throwing millions of people out of work and putting their futures in doubt, caused Americans to postpone marriage and delay starting families. The delay inevitably resulted in fewer children. The depression also discouraged immigration among those groups legally allowed to enter the country. The primary attraction of America had always been economic opportunity, which by the 1930s meant jobs—except that in the 1930s there weren't many jobs. So many would-be immigrants stayed put.

The third reason for the lagging population growth was World War II. Even more effectively than the depression, the war suppressed immigration. Crossing an ocean in wartime was dangerous and expensive; even more difficult was getting to the ports of embarkation. The war utterly disrupted travel across Europe; only the most desperate dared the military checkpoints, active battlefields, and ruined roads. The war simultaneously suppressed the natural increase among native-born Americans. The sixteen million persons who served in the American military during the war were nearly all of prime procreative age. Far from home, they might dream romantically of spouses and prospective spouses, but their dreams didn't register in the statistics of births.

At the war's end, the restrictions on immigration remained largely in place, but the two other deterrents to population growth disappeared. The war years left most Americans with money burning holes in their pockets. Not only had incomes increased during the war, but the opportunities for spending had decreased. Americans were flush with funds for buying houses and otherwise establishing families. And after the four years of war-imposed separation, they were more than eager to get together and start those families.

What demographers later called the Baby Boom began after the war and lasted into the 1960s. The national birth rate jumped and stayed high for nearly two decades. During the depression the birth rate had hovered around 19 live births per thousand of population per year; in 1947 the rate reached nearly 27, and it remained above 24 till the end of the 1950s. A total of seventy-six million babies were born between 1946 and 1964; in 1964 this bulging cohort accounted for four of every ten Americans alive that year.

All the babies and young children prompted a reorientation of American culture. For much of American history children had been thought of as small adults. They started work—on the family farms, in their fathers' shops, by their mothers' sides—at whatever time they became physically able. As the country industrialized, the worlds of children and of adults began to diverge, but only slowly. Child labor was a common practice into the early twentieth century, which was why social reformers had to pass laws against it. The decline in birth rates during the Great Depression might have made parents unusually solicitous of the welfare of their fewer children, but many of those parents lacked the time and resources to lavish on their little ones.

After World War II the combination of more time, more resources, and more kids created a child-based culture unlike anything previous in American history. The eight-hour day and forty-hour week became standard during the depression, partly as a way of rationing the available work; they remained standard after the war, allowing working parents greater opportunity to attend or join in their children's activities. Rising postwar incomes enabled families to thrive with single breadwinners. These were typically the husbands; their wives could devote themselves to caring for the children. Nearly all the parents and grandparents of the postwar generation recalled the depression; many wanted their children to have what they had been compelled to do without.

As long as the Baby Boomers were children, they didn't realize they were different from previous generations. Their world, like the world of all children, was the only one they knew. But they grew up with a sense of entitlement, a feeling that the world existed for their benefit, that was more pronounced than the comparable sentiments of any generation before them. This sentiment served them well at certain times and poorly at other times. Their elders had to deal with it, and their children would have to as well.

## 2. GENERAL EISENHOWER, MEET GENERAL MOTORS

Central to the experience of the Baby Boomers was the strong performance of the American economy. The worries of the war years regarding the ability of the economy to weather the reduction of military spending and absorb the return of the soldiers to the civilian workforce proved to have been overblown. So great was the pent-up demand for the houses, cars, washing machines, sofas, radios, sinks, and myriad other items large and small that had been unpurchased during the depression and unpurchasable during the war, and so great was the pent-up purchasing power from all the unspent war wages, that the economy shifted from war production to peace production without losing appreciable momentum. The strikes and other difficulties of the immediate postwar period gradually diminished as wage and price controls were dismantled. National income rose by more than a third during the 1950s. Home ownership, for many Americans the hallmark of prosperity, soared till six of ten homes were owned by their occupants. Unemployment, while higher than during the war years, was far lower than during the depression. Typically nineteen out of twenty Americans who wanted to work for wages were able to do so.

Much of the economic activity revolved around the physical needs and wants of the Baby Boomers and their families. Home construction was up; auto manufacturing was up; appliances and furniture and clothing and recreational equipment were up; food and pharmaceuticals were up. New industries blossomed in areas little known before the war. Electronics emerged as a growth leader, based on the recently invented transistor, which powered computers used by businesses but not yet by individuals. Television, first demonstrated before the war, entered homes by the hundreds, then thousands, then millions. Plastics replaced metal, wood, paper, and other natural materials in toys and tools, necessities, and knickknacks. The aircraft industry filled the sky with planes and factories with workers; in 1957 airplanes for the first time carried more passengers than trains.

The 1950s were the heyday of the modern corporation. Detroit's Big Three—General Motors, Ford, and Chrysler—were models of stability and steady growth. Factory workers in proverbial blue collars typically joined GM or one of the other companies right out of high school and spent entire careers there, enjoying company-sponsored health care and generous vacations before retiring on company pensions. White-collar workers staffed company headquarters, designing new models, marketing and financing them, and managing the workforce. In other industries other corporations set the pace. U.S. Steel remained the giant of ferrous metal. Boeing was the best of the aircraft makers. IBM built the computers that handled more and more of the data that increasingly moved the economy. General Electric lit the darkness and lightened the workloads of Americans at home, office, and factory.

So widely respected were the big corporations that few people took it amiss when Dwight Eisenhower looked to General Motors to head one of his most important cabinet departments. The president nominated Charles E. Wilson, the chief executive of GM, to be secretary of defense. Wilson answered a question at his confirmation hearing regarding potential conflicts of interest by declaring, "For years I thought what was good for our country was good for General Motors, and vice versa." Had he left out the "vice versa," his remark would have been considered patriotic and unexceptionable, but that tag allowed his statement to be interpreted as saying that what suited GM ought to suit the country. Even so, he sailed through the confirmation process. (Wilson's critics—and many others—sometimes confused him with another Charles E. Wilson, who likewise crossed the border between the corporate world and government. This second Charles Wilson had headed General Electric and Truman's Office of Defense Mobilization. Pundits took to calling the two men "Engine Charlie" and "Electric Charlie.")

The counterparts to the great corporations were the big unions. Although the Taft-Hartley Act reduced the leverage of the unions compared to what it had been during the 1930s, unions remained a fundamental part of the economy. The solid pay, job security, and generous benefits the industrial workers enjoyed came not from the generosity of GM and the other companies but from the determination of the leadership of the United Auto Workers and other unions that their members receive a fair share of the companies' profits. Many companies had bitterly resisted the unionization of their workers, but by the 1950s they came to accept the unions as de facto partners. As long as demand for their products remained strong—as it did throughout the decade—the companies could meet the unions' demands and pass the higher costs on to their customers.

Manufacturing, having supplanted farming as the signature occupation of the American people around the turn of the century, remained the beating heart of the economy, but a growing segment of the workforce provided services. Americans ate more meals in restaurants than ever, and for the first time they had prepared food—preeminently pizza, Chinese food, and a few other favorites—delivered to their doors. They read more advertisements in newspapers and magazines, drafted by a growing phalanx of copy writers, and for the first time encountered television commercials, produced by an entirely new sector of the advertising industry. Thousands of new schools, staffed by tens of thousands of new teachers, educated the Baby Boomers. Colleges and universities expanded to accommodate the students the GI bill funded. More doctors and nurses were required to treat the Boomers when they were ill, and for the first time provided vaccines against such ancient scourges as polio. Psychologists and counselors of various sorts tended to their emotional state. A new publishing genre, the child-rearing book, led by Benjamin

Spock's enormous bestseller, *The Common Sense Book of Baby and Child Care*, crowded the shelves of bookstores, blazing the trail for the hundreds of self-help bestsellers that would guide the Boomers throughout their lives.

## 3. THE MAGIC KINGDOM AND THE KING

A particular segment of the service industry—entertainment, in its numerous forms—grew into a powerhouse of its own. Hollywood churned out movies by the hundreds, with an increasing portion of them aimed at children and families. Walt Disney, whose animated pictures had charmed America during the 1930s, now moved into live-action films, with *Treasure Island* and *20,000 Leagues under the Sea* packing the theaters. Disney branched out into television, creating the weekday favorite *Mickey Mouse Club* and the Sunday staple *Walt Disney Presents* (later *Walt Disney's Wonderful World of Color*, after the country began switching from black-and-white television to color). Other programs with faithful followings included *The Lone Ranger, The Adventures of Ozzie and Harriet, Dragnet*, and *The Honeymooners*.

Disney diversified still more when he built the first modern amusement park. Disneyland opened in Anaheim, California, in the summer of 1955. Previous parks had featured roller coasters, Ferris wheels, and other rides in eclectic combinations; Disney wrapped the whole package in themes—Adventureland, Frontierland, Fantasyland, Tomorrowland—keyed to Disney movies and the Disney television show. The park got off to a slow start; on opening day everything that could possibly go wrong did so at once. The mercury topped 100 degrees, softening the fresh asphalt in the parking lots and making visitors think they had taken a wrong turn and wound up at the La Brea Tar Pits. The local chapter of the plumbers' union went on strike, leaving many of the water fountains unconnected and the toilets unmentionable. A gas leak forced the evacuation of large sections of the park. So disastrous was the unveiling that Disney decided to try again the next day. The reopening fared better, and for years the company pretended that the second opening was the real one and the first only a rehearsal.

One secret of Disneyland's success was the consistent pleasure it provided patrons (after the initial false start). A company survey in 1959 found that 99 percent of visitors believed they got their money's worth, and 83 percent planned to return. Another secret was the seamless integration of the various aspects of the Disney experience. The opening of the park had been preceded by a television contract between Disney and the ABC network for a weekly hour-long show called *Disneyland*. The show became a nonstop advertisement for the park, and the park for the show. (Disney's embarrassment at the opening-day fiasco was compounded by the fact that ABC covered the opening on live television.) And both the park and the show became advertisements for the *Mickey Mouse Club* and the Disney movies.

At times it seemed there was no niche of popular culture that hadn't been invaded by the Disney combine. "It is Mickey Mouse's day," a journalist covering the company asserted.

> Shoppers carry Mickey Mouse satchels and briefcases bursting with Mickey Mouse soap, candy, playing cards, bridge favors, hairbrushes, chinaware, alarm clocks and hot-water bottles, wrapped in Mickey Mouse paper, tied with Mickey Mouse ribbon, and paid for out of Mickey Mouse purses with savings hoarded in Mickey Mouse banks. . . . The children live in a Mickey Mouse world. . . . They sup from Mickey Mouse cups, porringers and baby plates and lie down to sleep in Mickey Mouse pajamas between Mickey Mouse crib sheets.

Yet one area of the popular psyche was largely unprobed by Disney: popular music. Part of the explanation was that Disney had his hands full with all his other endeavors. The larger reason was that tastes in music were moving in directions that didn't enhance the family atmosphere Disney wanted to foster. The hero of rock and roll, the emerging hot genre of the 1950s, was Elvis Presley, whose suggestive gyrations scandalized parents even as they delighted teenagers and young adults. Presley burst out of Memphis in 1956; his single "Heartbreak Hotel" sold a million copies and topped the sales charts. An appearance on the *Ed Sullivan Show* attracted more than fifty million viewers. Elvis soon went into movies, and though he was never mistaken for an actor, he filled tens of millions of seats. The younger generation suffered collective withdrawal when Elvis was drafted into the army in 1958, but the two-year hiatus in his career simply intensified his popularity when he returned.

Spectator sports became an American obsession during the 1950s. Baseball was the national pastime, as it had been for decades, and the boys of summer enthralled the country each year as the races wound to the finish. The major leagues were small then, consisting of eight teams each. The sport's epicenter lay in the Northeast; St. Louis, home of the Cardinals, was at once the far western and far southern outpost. Baseball wasn't the strictly day game it had been; night baseball began in 1935 when Franklin Roosevelt threw a switch in Washington to light Crosley Field in Cincinnati. Most other teams installed lights by the 1950s, but baseball's soul still longed for the sunlight. Not till the 1970s would the first World Series game be played after dark.

Driving the move to the night was the emergence of the factor that would transform sports almost beyond recognition during the coming decades. Television carried its first major league game in 1939, but merely as a demonstration. Not until the 1950s, when a critical mass of households first owned televisions, did TV games become a regular thing. Once they did, advertisers began paying for commercials to be shown on the broadcasts, and the ad money launched baseball on a meteoric rise that would continue into the twenty-first century.

New racial attitudes changed baseball in other ways. For decades African American players had been restricted to the Negro Leagues, which featured some of the finest athletes in the country. Branch Rickey, the general manager of the Brooklyn Dodgers, realized what his team and its fans were missing, and in 1947 he signed Jackie Robinson to play second base and break the color line. (Later Rickey would sign the man who became American baseball's first Hispanic star, Roberto Clemente.) Robinson's presence on the Dodgers would have posed even greater problems had there been any major league franchises in the Deep South; all the same, Robinson and the black players who followed him encountered considerable hostility before eventually being accepted simply as ballplayers.

Tight pennant races galvanized the nation. In 1951 the New York Giants battled from thirteen games back to tie their hated crosstown rivals, the Dodgers, and force a three-game playoff. The Dodgers and the Giants split the first two, and when New York's Bobby Thomson hit a home run in the bottom of the ninth inning of the third game, it was promptly labeled "the shot heard round the world." A worse blow befell Dodger fans in 1958, when team owner Walter O'Malley moved the franchise to Los Angeles.

Many Brooklynites had come to think of their beloved "Bums" as a civic institution; Ebbets Field without the Dodgers would be like the Lincoln Memorial without Abe. But the lure of California, which was about to pass New York as the most populous state in the Union, was too great. Nor was O'Malley alone. The Boston Braves moved to Milwaukee; the New York Giants to San Francisco.

When fall nipped the leaves across the heartland, America's attention turned to football. Professional football had nothing like the following of professional baseball; the colleges generated most of the autumn excitement. The Big Ten—the public universities of the Midwest, primarily—were the powerhouses, although Notre Dame, Army, Navy, and certain schools of the Southwest, including Texas and Oklahoma, fielded formidable teams. The college bowl games on New Year's Day—the Rose Bowl, Cotton Bowl, Orange Bowl, Sugar Bowl—were the highlight of the college season, surrounded by pageantry, parades, and hundreds of thousands of fans who traveled south from colder climates to party and cheer their alma maters to victory in Pasadena, Dallas, Miami, and New Orleans.

By the end of the 1950s nearly all the major sporting events were televised, although radio remained the favored medium among those many who preferred to conjure private mental images of their heroes in action. Every major newspaper had a sports section, to which millions of readers turned first in the morning. Fans who needed a further fix could subscribe to *Sports Illustrated*, launched in 1954 by Henry Luce, the magazine mogul responsible for *Life* and *Fortune*, to great and enduring success.

## 4. OUR TOWN, YOUR TOWN

"On 1,200 flat acres of potato farmland near Hicksville, Long Island, an army of trucks sped over new-laid roads," a cover story in *Time* (another Luce magazine) explained.

> Every 100 feet, the trucks stopped and dumped identical bundles of lumber, pipes, bricks, shingles and copper tubing—all as neatly packaged as loaves from a bakery. Near the bundles, giant machines with an

> endless chain of buckets ate into the earth, taking just 13 minutes to dig a narrow, four-foot trench around a 25-by-32 ft. rectangle. Then came more trucks, loaded with cement, and laid a four-inch foundation for a house in the rectangle.
>
> After the machines came the men. On nearby slabs already dry, they worked in crews of two and three, laying bricks, raising studs, nailing lath, painting, sheathing, shingling. Each crew did its special job, then hurried on to the next site. Under the skilled combination of men & machines, new houses rose faster than Jack ever built them; a new one was finished every 15 minutes.

The face on the *Time* cover belonged to William Levitt, the choreographer of the largest residential construction project in American history. Levitt was forty-three years old and as cocky as a man that age could be. He was five feet eight inches tall but described himself as "nearly six feet"; by his own avowal his construction company was "the General Motors of the housing industry." The General Motors reference involved not merely size; Levitt's genius was to apply the principles of the assembly line to home construction. Levittown, as the former potato patch was called, served as his proving ground and shop floor. He expected to complete construction on nearly six thousand new homes in the current year and many thousands more in the years to come.

One secret of Levitt's success was the same kind of standardization that had driven down the price of automobiles. The basic Levitt model had two bedrooms, one bathroom, a living room, and a kitchen. The living room had a fireplace, a picture window, and a built-in television set; the kitchen had a refrigerator, a stove, and a clothes washer. Radiant heating in the floor saved on ductwork. The attic allowed space for expansion; two more bedrooms and another bath might be built without raising the roof. The finished product sold for $7,990.

A second secret of Levitt's success was the federal policy of supporting home ownership. Levitt was the most visible of the big home builders of the 1950s, but he wasn't the only one. In every large city construction companies applied assembly-line principles to homes, with the result that Levittown knockoffs appeared throughout the country. A San Francisco builder was proud of his role in the expansion but nonetheless explained, "If it weren't for the government, the boom would end overnight." For all the efficiency of Levitt's crews and those of the other builders, the price of a home remained beyond the unassisted reach of most people. The median family income in America in the mid-1950s was less than $4,000; to buy a Levitt home or one of the others required borrowing money. The federal government didn't lend much money directly, yet it did the next best thing: it insured the loans extended by private banks and savings-and-loan companies. The typical loan insured by the Federal Housing Administration required the buyer to pay as little as 5 percent of the sale price in cash, with the rest spread over thirty years. The federal guarantee to the lender kept interest rates down, and for military veterans even the 5 percent down payment was waived. A former GI could buy a home in Levittown for nothing down and $56 per month, which often made buying a new home easier than buying a new car.

Small armies of veterans and their young families moved into Levittown and its counterparts. These communities weren't the first American suburbs, which had sprung up along commuter rail lines outside major cities during the late nineteenth and early twentieth centuries. But the new communities were suburbs on a mass scale, and they were characterized by a sameness unprecedented in American history. The requirements of efficient production dictated architectural uniformity; the financing arrangements facilitated sociological uniformity; and the conventional wisdom produced functional uniformity.

The suburbs were designed as bedroom communities, havens of rest from the workaday world. No industry and not much commerce intruded upon them; the residents had to leave their neighborhoods for work, for serious shopping, or for an evening out. In the suburbs women stayed home with their children; the sights, sounds, and rhythms of suburban life reflected the era's emphasis on domesticity. "In front of almost every house along Levittown's 100 miles of winding streets sits a tricycle or a baby carriage," a visiting reporter observed. "In Levittown, all activity stops from 12 to 2 in the afternoon; that is nap time." The suburbs featured schools, parks, playgrounds, and swimming pools; they lacked activity centers for old people, not least because they lacked old people. The domestic routine of the suburbs tended to block out the rest of the world. "It's not a community that thinks much about what's going on outside," one Levittown woman conceded.

## 5. MEN IN GRAY FLANNEL SUITS

The great significance of Levittown and its imitators was that it put millions of Americans on the road to full membership in the middle class. For generations Americans had boasted that theirs was a country without classes, and by the standards of Europe they weren't far wrong. Southern planters, of course, had occupied a different stratum than their slaves, but the Emancipation Proclamation and the Thirteenth Amendment eliminated this egregious anomaly. In the rest of the country the absence of titled nobility, combined with the reality of widespread access to land, had fostered a social egalitarianism that at once supported and was supported by the political egalitarianism of democracy. The industrial revolution of the late nineteenth century produced a very wealthy stratum at the top of the socioeconomic order, but the wealth of the Gilded Age never translated into an accepted ideology of difference. The rich were rich and the poor poor, but the poor didn't expect to stay that way, and rather than resent the rich, they strove to emulate them.

One result of this was that socialism never caught on in America, and even labor unions, whose lasting success required a conviction in workers that they would always be workers—and not eventually their own or someone else's bosses—encountered chronic skepticism among many workers. Another result was that most Americans came to consider themselves middle class. Some distinguished between the blue collars of the factory floors and the white collars of the office suites, but equally often the former were thought of as lower middle class and the best-compensated of the latter as upper middle class.

Part of this perception was delusional; fivefold differences in pay did translate into different life experiences. Vice presidents joined country clubs and sent their children to private schools and Ivy League colleges; pipe fitters grilled hamburgers in the park and were happy if their kids completed public high school and perhaps attended state universities.

Yet there was substantial reality behind the belief. Starting around the beginning of World War II the disparity between the wealthy and the rest of America diminished drastically. Wartime taxes took much of the income of the really rich, and jobs in war industries boosted incomes of wage workers. The trend continued after the war, with the result that from the early

1940s through the 1950s (and all the way into the 1980s, in fact), the share of national income claimed by the top 10 percent of Americans hovered between 30 and 35 percent, having been over 45 percent as recently as the 1920s. (It would reach that high figure again in the early 2000s.) As a result, Americans thought they were equal because they *were* equal—at least much more equal than they had been in their recent history.

The egalitarianism revealed itself in numerous ways. Men tipped their hats to women but not to other men, regardless of the disparity in wealth. The rich often pushed their own shopping carts through grocery stores like everyone else. The rich might drive Cadillacs, General Motors' top-of-the-line model, rather than Chevrolets, the entry-level version, but the Chevy owners could aspire to move up the ladder: to Pontiacs, Oldsmobiles, Buicks, and finally to Cadillacs (with GM furnishing the financing at each step of the way).

In the 1950s factory workers and office workers alike earned enough money to support a thoroughly respectable middle-class lifestyle. The workers were mostly men, except for the secretaries in the offices, and their wives typically did not work outside the home. (The secretaries were usually unmarried.) The families of the middle class owned their own houses and furnished them with the accepted necessities of middle-class life. Many middle-class women hired domestic help for a morning or two a week. The milkman delivered fresh milk to the doorstep every few days. Both blue-collar and white-collar families replaced their cars every few years, if only because American cars—essentially the only kind Americans bought—weren't built to last more than a few years.

Families of the broad middle class took vacations, usually by car. They stayed at motor hotels—"motels"—located on highways rather than near downtown rail depots. Air travel was exotic and too expensive for most families, although businessmen increasingly chose planes over trains for long trips. Ordinary people traveled more than they had in previous decades (but far less than they soon would).

The existence of the large middle class triggered the emergence of a new mass culture. Economies of scale—the cost savings that result from making many of a few items rather than a few of many items—applied to nearly all the goods and services the middle class consumed. Movies and television shows could be distributed to audiences throughout the land. Books, magazines, and newspapers could be printed for hundreds of thousands or millions of readers. Fashions in clothing and music spread rapidly from coast to coast, crowding out the regional distinctiveness that had marked America in earlier decades.

No one contributed more to the creation of a single popular culture than Ray Kroc. The Chicago native got his first jobs playing piano in Prohibition-era speakeasies frequented by the likes of Al Capone. Eventually he decided there were safer gigs, and he relocated to Florida to promote real estate. This didn't work out, either, so he switched to selling paper cups to the beverage and restaurant industry. After World War II he moved upscale to milk-shake mixers. One of his accounts, in San Bernardino, California, intrigued him with an order for eight of the five-shake machines, which gave them twice the milk-shaking capacity of anyone else in the area. Investigating, Kroc discovered in 1954 that the McDonald brothers, Dick and Mac, had perfected a formula for fast food—hamburgers, French fries, and milk shakes—that won them a loyal following throughout Southern California.

Kroc cut a deal with the McDonalds that allowed him to franchise their system and spread it across the country. Within half a decade hundreds of McDonald's dotted the American landscape. Kroc and the McDonald brothers eventually had a falling-out, and the brothers left the company, but by then the Golden Arches were an established feature of American life. What made them so successful was the consistency of their product. Travelers on the nation's highways or arriving in new cities had always wondered where to eat; how was a stranger to choose between Mom's Cafe and Joe's Diner? McDonald's cuisine was hardly haute—although millions of customers swore the French fries were the best available anywhere—but it was reliable. When the kids were getting cranky after a long day on the road, the Golden Arches could seem a welcome lighthouse guiding the weary travelers to a safe culinary harbor.

More than a few observers, and some participants, found the emergence of a mass middle class stultifying. Where was the charm, the interest value, in a society in which everyone was growing more alike? Sloan Wilson's 1955 novel, *The Man in the Gray Flannel Suit,* which Hollywood made into a film the following year, captured some of the striving and discontent of the middle class. The title alone suggested the blandness that many saw as afflicting American life in the age of the middle class. Neither the novel nor the film was particularly distinguished—a negative fact the culture critics took as proving their point.

## 6. ON THE ROAD

It only enhanced the prospects of McDonald's that the mid-1950s marked the dawn of a new era of American highway construction. Eisenhower, although a Republican, respected government's ability to get things done; after all, the federal government had guided the country to victory during the war. He remembered a journey he had made at the head of a military convoy in 1919 that took two months to traverse the country, and he reflected on that endless trek when he got to Germany at the close of World War II and experienced Germany's marvelous system of autobahns. More to the immediate point in the 1950s—although Eisenhower didn't dwell on it in public lest Americans become unduly alarmed—he recognized that American cities were sitting ducks for Soviet air strikes. Given the patchwork of roads left over from early in the century, clogged with stop lights and cross traffic, it would take days to evacuate New York or Chicago or Philadelphia should war loom.

Numerous groups had been lobbying for better roads for years. City planners wanted to ease congestion and pollution. Concrete-makers and general contractors dreamed of the work they might land if the federal government started paying for highways, which heretofore had been primarily a state and local responsibility. Unions applauded the solid, well-paying jobs road construction would bring. Truckers appreciated that better highways would speed their cargoes and boost their profits.

But not till Eisenhower came on board did the crews get moving. The Federal Aid Highway Act of 1956—commonly called the National Interstate and Defense Highways Act—revealed an emerging secret of American politics during the Cold War: that wrapping almost any measure in the language of national defense enhanced its viability in Congress, in some cases decisively. Even leftover defenders of states' rights, who would have complained and perhaps blocked this astonishing extension of federal authority—the American interstate highway system turned out to be the largest public works project in the history of the world—fell into line when the program was presented as vital to defense.

The interstate system absorbed some existing highways and constructed others from scratch. It established a grid of divided, limited-access roads, with the major north-south thoroughfares receiving numbers ending in 5 (from Interstate 5, which connected Seattle to San Diego; to Interstate 95, running from Maine to Miami) and the east-west routes ending in 0 (from Interstate 10, linking Jacksonville to Los Angeles; to Interstate 90, joining Boston to Seattle).

The construction of the tens of thousands of miles of interstate highways signaled the passing of the age of railroads in American history. Railroads had been America's first big businesses, and they had made possible the industrialization of a country that spanned the continent. In the 1950s railroads continued to be cost-effective for certain kinds of freight carried over particular routes. But the flexibility of the interstate system allowed shippers to send freight in smaller lots than railcars, and the trucks transporting the freight could drive directly to the loading docks of companies on any road or street in America.

Air travel was already eating into the railroads' long-distance passenger traffic; now the interstate highway system made most shorter trips more convenient by car than by train. Car travelers left home when it suited their schedules, rather than the railroads' timetables, and they often arrived sooner than they would by train. For the growing families of the Baby Boom era, autos had the additional advantage of carrying four or five people—to Grandma's house, to Disneyland—at no greater expense than carrying one person.

The interstate highways facilitated the emergence of the mass culture of the middle class. McDonald's and other chain restaurants sprang up along the interstates, making every city and town look—and taste—increasingly like every other. Inexpensive interstate transport facilitated the spread of chain stores, including Wal-Mart, the general retailer that would become the largest corporation in America, and the dozens of specialty brands that populated the strip malls of the American suburbs.

At the same time, and paradoxically, the interstates contributed to a kind of atomization of American life. The interstates were no less important for travel in and around cities than for journeys between states; the new roads made the daily journey from suburban home to urban workplace and back swifter and more convenient. In the process they took tens of millions of Americans out of commuter trains and buses and put them into cars. The typical rush hour featured single drivers in separate cars, inhabiting separate small worlds, thinking separate thoughts. (Not for decades would mobile telephones allow them to communicate while driving.) In all but a few cities mass transit atrophied, left to those comparative few who couldn't afford to drive or who, for reasons mysterious to most of their contemporaries, chose not to.

## 7. FROM THE BACK OF THE BUS

African Americans were overrepresented among those who couldn't afford to drive. Blacks numbered some seventeen million in the mid-1950s, or about 10 percent of the population, and despite the migrations to the North during the two world wars, most still lived in the South, where the Jim Crow system of racial segregation remained much as it had existed since the late nineteenth century. Black children attended black schools; black worshippers filled black churches; black moviegoers frequented black theaters; black drinkers tippled at black bars; black shoppers patronized black stores. Blacks and whites met one another on the streets and in the workplace, but their encounters were carefully scripted by the prevailing social mores. When blacks deliberately or inadvertently crossed the color line, the response could be swift and brutal. Lynching no longer enjoyed the popular sanction it had sometimes elicited in the decades after the Civil War, when the seizure and execution of prisoners accused of rape—the crime that triggered the deepest, most violent passions—could attract approving crowds of thousands. But lynchings did occur, often enough to remind African Americans that they couldn't count on the laws to protect them if, for whatever reason, they aroused the ire of the white majority. In 1955 fourteen-year-old Emmett Till, visiting Mississippi from Chicago, was brutally murdered after whistling at a white woman. The murderers were never convicted, though they later boasted of their deed.

Yet attitudes were changing. In 1948 the Democratic party's national platform declared that "racial and religious minorities must have the right to live, the right to work, the right to vote, the full and equal protection of the laws, on a basis of equality with all citizens as guaranteed by the Constitution." This was quite a statement for the party that for decades had relied on its white Southern base, and it was what prompted the walkout of Strom

Thurmond and the Dixiecrats. An executive order that same year from the Truman White House mandating the desegregation of the military stirred the Pentagon to action, if slowly. The officers corps contained a large number of Southerners who shared the prejudices of their region, and even many of the non-Southerners resented the idea that the military be made the instrument of a giant social experiment. For two years almost nothing happened by way of implementing the president's order. But under the duress of the Korean War, when the army was desperate to find warm bodies of any description or color to fill gaps in the ranks, the order finally achieved its desired effect. Blacks and whites shared foxholes and barracks, with very few of the ugly incidents the opponents of integration had predicted.

Yet integrating the military, important though it was, was simple and straightforward compared with integrating other areas of American life. In the end, the orders of the commander-in-chief had to be obeyed. But the president wasn't commander-in-chief of the nation's schools, for example, which answered to local superintendents and school boards. Not even Congress, had it been so inclined—which, with Southern legislators controlling important committees, it wasn't—could tell the nation's schools what to do. Only the Supreme Court, interpreting the Constitution, wielded that authority.

The high court took a bite of the apple in the 1950 case of *Sweatt v. Painter.* Heman Marion Sweatt lived in Houston, Texas, where he made his living carrying the mail. But he dreamed of becoming a lawyer. He applied to the state law school at the University of Texas in Austin and was denied admission because it was segregated and he was black. He turned for help to the National Association for the Advancement of Colored People, whose chief counsel, Thurgood Marshall, was looking for test cases to challenge the Jim Crow system. While Sweatt and Marshall prepared their challenge, the University of Texas beat a tactical retreat, hastily creating a law school for blacks. Yet the jerry-rigged institution was in no way comparable to the existing law school—not in facilities, library holdings, professors, or prestige. The Supreme Court ruled, in a unanimous decision, that the Texas policy violated the equal protection clause of the Fourteenth Amendment. Under the standard of "separate but equal," first articulated in the 1896 *Plessy* case and never reversed, the Texas policy failed in that the separate accommodations made for Sweatt and other African Americans were not equal.

The separate-but-equal standard still stood, until Marshall brought another case before the court. Linda Brown attended third grade in Topeka, Kansas—not in the school closest to her home, but in a black school farther away. Her father, Oliver Brown, consulted the local office of the NAACP, which referred his and his daughter's case, and those of twelve other black families similarly excluded from Topeka's white schools, to Marshall at national headquarters. The cases went forward as a single suit, with Oliver Brown as the lead plaintiff. When it reached the Supreme Court, it was linked to several cases from other states. Key to Marshall's argument in what became known as the *Brown* case was that the schools in question were *not* clearly inferior, as had been true in the *Sweatt* case. Marshall wanted the separate-but-equal standard struck down on the principle that mere separation of the races violated the Constitution.

The Supreme Court, under new chief justice Earl Warren, accepted Marshall's argument. By another unanimous verdict, the court ruled in favor of Brown and the other plaintiffs. "In the field of public education," Warren declared, "separate but equal has no place." Jim Crow schools were unconstitutional.

Yet the ruling, while momentous, fell short in two regards. The court recognized that revamping school systems would require time and money, and in a follow-up decision it instructed the schools to desegregate with "all deliberate speed." To many observers this formula appeared to invite foot-dragging, and in fact the heels soon began digging in all over the South.

The second shortcoming of the *Brown* decision was that it applied only to schools, and public schools at that. Segregated public schools were an important pillar of the Jim Crow system, yet the edifice could survive without them. The much larger realm of segregation remained untouched.

But not for long. Six months after the court unveiled its "deliberate speed" formula, Rosa Parks was arrested in Montgomery, Alabama. Parks had been born in 1913 into the fully matured Jim Crow system of the South. She remembered her grandfather, in the 1920s, standing at the door of her home with a shotgun, guarding his family as the local chapter of the Ku Klux Klan marched past. She completed high school in an era when very few blacks, and even fewer black girls, did so. She surmounted still greater odds and successfully registered to vote, even though the Southern political system placed hurdle after barrier in her way. Not surprisingly, given the devotion to equality she had already displayed, she joined the NAACP, and in the summer of 1955 she attended a session of the Highlander Folk School, a depression-born educational center for labor activism and civil rights in Tennessee.

Her Highlander experience, coming just after the second of the *Brown* decisions, prompted Parks to consider how she might challenge the Jim Crow system. Some of the first Jim Crow laws had involved transportation; the *Plessy* case was originally about Louisiana railroads. Every day Parks rode the Montgomery bus system to and from her downtown department store job; the buses were segregated by race, with blacks required to sit in the rear. On December 1, 1955, Parks refused to heed a driver's order to move to the back. She was arrested, booked, and scheduled for trial.

The head of the local chapter of the NAACP was E. D. Nixon, who had been looking for an opportunity to challenge the Montgomery bus law. Parks made an ideal defendant. She was a slight woman of pleasing appearance and unthreatening demeanor. Nixon knew, as other civil rights leaders were beginning to understand, that the emergence of television made a plaintiff's appearance and public persona more important than ever. If something came of the Parks case, television crews would be all over Montgomery. Audiences around the country would quickly recognize her face. Earlier that year a black teenage girl had been arrested for doing what Rosa Parks did. Nixon had considered pressing her case forward, but when he discovered that the unmarried girl was pregnant, he dropped the idea, knowing that her morals would be called into question and the segregation issue blurred.

Nixon mobilized the NAACP's resources behind Parks. Defending her in court was but a small part of the strategy. Nixon aimed to bring the national spotlight upon Jim Crow, believing—accurately, as events proved—that a system that had grown up in the regional shadows of Southern life couldn't long survive the glare of national television cameras. He also intended to mobilize the Montgomery black community against Jim Crow, to demonstrate that Rosa Parks wasn't alone. He proposed an African American boycott of the bus system. In his mind's eye he could already see the televised images: black men and women trudging miles to work, in silent, civilized protest, while half-empty buses drove uncaringly by. The boycott began, and it unfolded much as Nixon had imagined it would.

Nixon needed someone to head the boycott. He guessed that Martin Luther King, Jr., might be suitable, in that King was a minister, which counted for much in both the black and white communities; he was well educated and well spoken, which would appeal to news reporters and interviewers; he was telegenically handsome, which would move those Northern audiences Nixon wanted to reach; and he had arrived in Montgomery only two years before and hadn't made enemies in the community.

King's gifts grew evident at once. "You know, my friends, there comes a time when people get tired of being trampled over by the iron feet of oppression," he declared. "There comes a time, my friends, when people get tired of being plunged across the abyss of humiliation." King cast the Montgomery boycott in the tradition of American protest.

> The great glory of American democracy is the right to protest for right. . . . We only assemble here because of our desire to see right exist. . . . We're going to work with grim and bold determination to gain justice on the buses in this city. And we are not wrong. We are not wrong in what we are doing. If we are wrong, the Supreme Court of this nation is wrong. If we are wrong, the Constitution of the United States is wrong. If we are wrong, God Almighty is wrong.

The boycott lasted much longer than almost anyone had guessed. Rosa Parks was convicted at trial of violating the city bus law and was fined ten dollars plus four dollars court costs. She refused to pay and was jailed. While her case was being appealed, the blacks of Montgomery remained off the buses. They walked; they hitchhiked; they carpooled. They suffered taunts, slurs, threats, and actual violence. Many lost their jobs—some for their visibility in the boycott, others for missing work. The city refused to relent, and the impasse stretched into the spring and then summer of 1956. Only after the Supreme Court intervened, ruling in November that the Montgomery ordinance violated the equal protection clause of the Fourteenth Amendment, were King and the boycotters able to declare victory. The city acted vindictively petty in defeat, fining King $85 for violating a special antiboycott measure. On principle he refused to pay and kept the boycott going. The city backed down, and in December 1956, more than a year after it began, the Montgomery boycott ended.

## 8. BEFORE THE EYES OF THE WORLD

By then the emphasis in the civil rights movement was shifting back to education. No one knew what "deliberate speed" meant, and the result of the confusion was that segregated school districts moved at different rates to comply with the Supreme Court's order. In early 1956 nearly a hundred members of Congress from the South signed the "Southern Manifesto," a statement condemning the Supreme Court for overreaching in the *Brown* case. "The original Constitution does not mention education," the manifesto asserted. "Neither does the Fourteenth Amendment nor any other amendment. The debates preceding the submission of the Fourteenth Amendment clearly show that there was no intent that it should affect the system of education maintained by the states." The activism of the court was destabilizing Southern society, the manifesto said. "This unwarranted exercise of power by the Court, contrary to the Constitution, is creating chaos and confusion in the States principally affected. It is destroying the amicable relations between the white and Negro races that have been created through ninety years of patient effort by the good people of both races. It has planted hatred and suspicion where there has been heretofore friendship and understanding."

With such encouragement from Washington, many Southern school districts simply refused to integrate. Often this flouting went unchallenged; in small, country districts with neither an active NAACP chapter nor access to national media, a person had to be extremely bold to take on the white power structure.

In Little Rock, Arkansas, the outcome was different. Little Rock wasn't exactly New York City, but it was the capital of its state, and when the Arkansas governor, Orval Faubus, in 1957 decided to demagogue the integration issue, he made national headlines. Little Rock's school authorities appeared willing to bend to the Supreme Court mandate, but Faubus, who was up for reelection the following year, refused. He melodramatically deployed hundreds of troops of the Arkansas national guard to the campus of Little Rock's Central High School to guard against violence he said he feared in the event black parents tried to enroll their sons and daughters there.

Nine African American children arrived peacefully, accompanied by an integrated escort of ministers. They walked past an angry crowd of whites, incited by Faubus's words and actions. The children reached the cordon of guardsmen, who had orders not to let them pass. In the view of national television they turned away and went home. Faubus celebrated a triumph but wondered if it came too easily.

Dwight Eisenhower had not intended to get involved in the integration issue. Eisenhower's social conservatism reflected his Texas birth, his Kansas upbringing, and his military career. He had no desire to become a crusader for civil rights. He sympathized with Southern whites who distrusted the intrusion of the courts into their schools. "These are not bad people," he said privately. "All they are concerned about is to see that their sweet little girls are not required to sit in school alongside some big overgrown Negroes." Yet Eisenhower recognized his obligation as president to uphold the Constitution. "There must be respect for the Constitution—which means the Supreme Court's interpretation of the Constitution—or we shall have chaos," he wrote an old friend. "This I believe with all of my heart, and shall always act accordingly."

Governor Faubus, by stirring such a furor over the rules of a single high school, forced Eisenhower's hand. The president said he would act as necessary: "The federal Constitution will be upheld by me by every legal means at my command." Faubus employed the president's warning to agitate things further in Little Rock. By late September 1957 angry whites roamed the streets of the city vowing to prevent the destruction of the Southern way of life at the hands of either uppity Negroes or a fascist federal government. Faubus applauded their devotion to Arkansas values and promised to stand beside them, or perhaps ahead of them.

Eisenhower let the situation simmer, hoping Arkansas moderates would talk sense into Faubus. If they tried, they failed, and the governor held his ground. Accordingly Eisenhower, with great reluctance, took a step fraught with symbolism. On September 24 he ordered units of the U.S. Army's 101st Airborne Division to seize Central High School in Little Rock. Not since Reconstruction had federal troops been used to impose racial equality on the South, and neither Faubus nor other segregationists let the region forget it.

Eisenhower could have accompanied the order with a ringing affirmation of racial equality, but he didn't. Instead he spoke of his obligation to uphold the law. "Mob rule cannot be allowed to override the decisions of our courts," he said. The federal government was not going to run Little

Rock's schools, and the troops were not going to be hall monitors. "The troops are there, pursuant to law, solely for the purpose of preventing interference with the orders of the Court." But they would accomplish that sole objective, come what might. Eisenhower asked Americans to note that the world was watching.

> At a time when we face grave situations abroad because of the hatred that Communism bears toward a system of government based on human rights, it would be difficult to exaggerate the harm that is being done to the prestige and influence, and indeed to the safety, of our nation and the world. Our enemies are gloating over this incident and using it everywhere to misrepresent our whole nation. We are portrayed as a violator of those standards of conduct which the peoples of the world united to proclaim in the Charter of the United Nations.

Conceivably Eisenhower hoped to shame Faubus for bringing America into disrepute. But the governor was beyond shame, at least on racial issues. He yielded but made clear that he was giving way only to force. Central High was integrated, with the paratroopers ensuring the safety of the black schoolchildren. By the following spring the issue had moved into the political arena, where Faubus had intended it to be all along. His reelection campaign celebrated him as the defender of the rights of the Arkansas majority, and he won handily. Meanwhile the Arkansas legislature closed the state's public schools, draining Eisenhower's reluctant victory of much of its meaning for Arkansas schoolchildren.

## 9. REHEATING THE COLD WAR

Eisenhower's concern at the damage the Little Rock imbroglio was having on America's reputation reflected a fundamental fact of Cold War life. By the mid-1950s the most hotly contested battlegrounds in the struggle between the United States and its communist rivals had shifted to what was coming to be called the "Third World"—the large swath of Asia, Africa, and eventually Latin America that lay outside the alliance systems of the superpowers. Europe, where the Cold War began, had been divided and was comparatively stable. The anomalous condition of Berlin still caused tension, but for the most part NATO secured the western half of the continent to the American side, while the Warsaw Pact, an alliance established by Moscow as a riposte to NATO, held down the eastern half. Large parts of East Asia were similarly spoken for. American forces had occupied Japan until 1951, when a peace treaty returned control of the country to the Japanese. But Japan's new constitution, largely drafted by Douglas MacArthur and his assistants, forbade Japan from having an army, and American troops remained in the country as guarantors against external aggression. American troops similarly garrisoned South Korea, an obvious flashpoint, and the Philippines, independent from the United States since 1946 but still under the American umbrella. Soviet influence was predominant in China, with which Moscow had signed a mutual security treaty in 1950, and North Korea.

As ambitious as the designs of the superpowers were, most of the world remained uncommitted. Americans naturally considered the Cold War the crucial feature of international life during the period after 1945, but for much of humanity the bigger story was the dissolution of European empires. The British empire broke up first and fastest. In 1947 London let go of India, which split into independent India and Pakistan upon the release. (Pakistan itself would split in 1971, with the eastern half becoming Bangladesh.) In 1948 the British pulled out of Palestine, leaving the Holy Land—holy to Jews, Christians, and Muslims—to an independent Israel and a nearly stillborn Palestinian proto-state. The British empire in Africa began to unravel in 1955, when the British Gold Coast became independent Ghana, and the unraveling continued for another decade. The Dutch empire lost its crown jewel in 1949, when the Netherlands East Indies became Indonesia. The French got the boot from Indochina in the mid-1950s, leaving behind Vietnam, Laos, and Cambodia.

All the new countries faced a choice: to ally with the United States, the Soviet Union, or neither. Most chose the third route, and hence the sobriquet Third World. But their eschewal of alliances didn't prevent the superpowers from competing for their favor. Sometimes the competition involved burnishing the image of one or the other superpower, or at least limiting damage to the image. The latter was what Eisenhower was doing in Little Rock. Often the competition entailed foreign aid. During the 1950s India was the big fish in the Third World pool. Democratic in politics but mildly socialist in economics, India deliberately played the United States and the Soviet Union against each other. Both superpowers furnished economic and technical aid, both wooed Indian prime minister Jawaharlal Nehru, and neither succeeded in winning his allegiance.

Sometimes the competition for the Third World got rough. Egypt was never part of the formal British empire, but since the 1880s British troops had occupied parts of the country, ostensibly to guard the Suez Canal, Britain's lifeline to India, but also to influence the policies of the Egyptian government. In 1952 a revolt of colonels in the Egyptian army led to the emergence of Gamal Abdel Nasser, who expelled the British troops and charted a nonaligned path for Egypt. The United States and the Soviet Union offered aid for the construction of a giant dam on the Nile River at Aswan, but Nasser played too hard to get for the tastes of the Eisenhower administration, which withdrew its offer. Nasser thereupon seized the Suez Canal and announced that the tolls would be applied to the dam construction. This outraged the British government, the principal owner of the company that operated the canal, and prompted London to conspire with the governments of France and Israel, which had their own reasons for disliking Nasser. The three parties launched a war against Egypt, under the pretext of protecting the canal but with the larger aim of overthrowing Nasser.

They kept their conspiracy from Eisenhower, suspecting he might not approve. Nor did he, and when he learned what the three governments were up to, he could scarcely believe their folly. The imperialist days were over, Eisenhower judged, and this sort of action risked turning the entire Third World against the West. He responded at once with an ultimatum that stopped the Suez War in its tracks, humiliated the British, and made the American president a (momentary) hero in the Third World. Eisenhower wielded two of the most potent levers of power in the postwar world against London: oil and the dollar. He threatened to cut off American oil exports to Britain, and he refused to support the British currency, the pound, when it began to plummet against the dollar. His actions had the desired effect: within days the Suez War was over. So too were the days when the British could imagine themselves a great power. Henceforth in the English-speaking world there was but one country that mattered: the United States.

Eisenhower's use of American power against Britain was the exception; customarily he wielded it against America's enemies. During the mid-1950s the communist government of China regularly threatened to invade Taiwan and finish off Chiang Kai-shek once and for all. Eisenhower countered the Chinese threats with threats of America's own, at times suggesting that the United States might employ nuclear weapons in Chiang's defense. Whether he was serious—whether he really would have gone nuclear against a conventionally armed Chinese attack on Taiwan—was impossible to say. The Chinese chose not to test him, and the crisis passed. But the Taiwan Strait remained tense.

In 1958 it was Nikita Khrushchev's turn to provoke a crisis. Khrushchev was the heir to Stalin, having made himself first among equals in the Kremlin after Stalin's death, and then simply first. In part to demonstrate his preeminence, Khrushchev pressed the Western powers on Berlin. For several years Berlin had served as an escape valve for refugees fleeing East Germany; they entered East Berlin from East Germany, crossed the city to West Berlin, and then exited West Berlin to West Germany. The flow had always been embarrassing to the communist regimes of the Soviet Union and East Germany, but it became economically threatening when it began to include large numbers of talented young people who took their talents to the West, where greater opportunity beckoned. To stem the flow, Khrushchev announced in late 1958 that the Western powers must leave Berlin within six months and thereafter deal with the East German government regarding access to the city.

Eisenhower immediately and categorically rejected the Soviet ultimatum. America had fought its way to Berlin, he said, and it would remain in Berlin pending a comprehensive settlement acceptable to all parties.

For months the world wondered if the Cold War would turn hot. Khrushchev blustered; Eisenhower stood firm. Eventually Khrushchev decided to let the six-month deadline pass, but he continued to assert that something must be done about the anomalous position of Berlin.

## 10. THE HEAVENS ABOVE

Adding bite to the Berlin crisis was a new development in military technology. Khrushchev pressed the German issue in part because the superpower arms race was moving into outer space, and the Soviet Union seemed to be leading.

During World War II, Hitler's scientists and engineers had built rockets that rained destruction down upon Britain. At the end of the war American and British troops spirited away as many of Hitler's rocketeers as they could lay hands on. Wernher von Braun headed the American rocket program, which nonetheless lagged behind that of the Soviets, who, lacking bomber bases close to America, concentrated on intercontinental missiles. The programs on both sides were cloaked in the deepest secrecy, but the world got a view of Russia's rocket technology in October 1957 when Moscow's scientists announced the successful launch of the first artificial earth satellite, called Sputnik.

The news astonished Americans, who had believed that their country led the world in all important aspects of science and technology. The Soviets had been making assertions about testing long-range military missiles, but few in the West believed them. Moscow's announcement of Sputnik, which was quickly confirmed by Western telemetry—as well as by short-wave radio operators in America and other countries, who could easily hear the satellite's beeping signal—made the Soviet assertions suddenly plausible. "The Soviet announcement inevitably was a sobering one for the West, particularly the United States," the *New York Times* editorialized. "It tended to confirm the claim by Moscow six weeks ago of the first successful test of an intercontinental ballistic missile, and indicated that the U.S.S.R. was, for the moment at least, ahead of the U.S. in the crucial rocket race." The fact of Sputnik's launch and orbit was only part of the story; the size of the satellite was no less remarkable. American scientists were preparing a satellite of their own, but it was barely a tenth as heavy as Sputnik. "If they can launch one that heavy," the head of an American scientific board said, "they can put up much heavier ones."

They soon did. A month after Sputnik, Moscow's scientists placed Sputnik II in orbit. The new satellite weighed half a ton; moreover it carried a passenger, a dog named Laika. Shortly thereafter America's rocket team, desperate not to fall farther behind, pushed forward the launch of an American satellite, a three-pound pipsqueak mounted on a Vanguard rocket. Television crews trained their cameras on the launch pad; Americans held their breath as the rocket engine ignited. The first few feet of the flight went well, but then the engine inexplicably lost thrust, the missile fell back onto the launch pad, and the fuel tank exploded, destroying the missile, the satellite, and much of America's self-esteem. "Since military rocketry was not involved, we feel that this incident has no bearing on the programs for the development of intercontinental range and intermediate ballistic missiles," Donald Quarles, the acting secretary of defense, declared, to general incredulity.

Yet Quarles was more right than wrong. The Sputnik scare caused the federal government to earmark hundreds of millions of dollars for scientific and technical education, through the National Defense Education Act. It prompted the creation of the National Aeronautics and Space Administration, or NASA, to coordinate American space efforts. It made things easier for advocates of increased defense, who pleaded their case with Congress more successfully than before.

Meanwhile, beyond the view of the Sputnik-Vanguard audience, America's military missile program made steady progress. By the end of the 1950s the United States began to deploy nuclear-tipped missiles; these included intermediate missiles based in Turkey and intercontinental missiles siloed in the United States. Either version could hit targets in the Soviet Union within fifteen to forty minutes of launch. The Soviet Union countered with intercontinental missiles of its own.

The paradoxical effect of the arms race was that the more weapons the two sides deployed, the less secure they were. Until the nuclear age, killing large numbers of an enemy took time and a great deal of effort. Offensive weaponry sometimes outstripped defenses, but with rare exceptions—poison gas, for example—the defense soon caught up. Nuclear weapons were different. Bombers carrying nuclear devices might be intercepted and perhaps shot down, but if even one bomber got through, it could kill millions at a single blow. Nuclear missiles made matters worse. No defense whatsoever existed against intercontinental missiles, and none appeared feasible or likely. (Nor would any defenses have emerged fifty years later.)

The only defense against nuclear missiles was psychological: the knowledge in each side's leaders that if they launched a nuclear attack upon the other side, they could expect a comparable retaliatory attack. The resulting standoff eventually acquired a name, "mutual assured destruction," and a fitting acronym, MAD. For decades nuclear strategists on the two sides wrestled with questions of the usability of nuclear weapons, the durability of the deterrence MAD provided, and the credibility of warnings by the possessors of the weapons. At times the theorizing would echo medieval theology, with assertions about how many people would survive first and second nuclear strikes sounding like the much-earlier arguments about how many angels could dance on the head of a pin.

Whether or not the theorizing had any actual effect, the standoff persisted. As it did, it intensified the anxiety ordinary Americans—and presumably their Soviet counterparts—felt regarding the state of international affairs. For the first time in history, humans possessed the capacity to destroy a large part of their species (and other species as well). Some people felt the anxiety acutely and consciously; others managed to relegate it to the unconscious. Schools conducted air raid drills for students, who eventually thought as little about them as they did about fire drills. Food and water were stockpiled in underground bomb shelters but in time grew musty and stale. And then something would happen between Washington and Moscow to heighten tensions, and the specter of annihilation would loom large and dire once more.

## 11. A COLD WAR COMPLEX

When George Washington prepared to leave the presidency after two terms, he bade farewell to the American people with a message that, among other things, warned against foreign entanglements. Andrew Jackson followed Washington's adieu-bidding example at the end of his own second term, but the farewell address never caught on as presidential practice. Eisenhower, another famous general before becoming president, decided to try his hand at the genre.

Three days before leaving office he went on television to address the American people. He focused on international affairs, particularly the Cold War. "It commands our whole attention, absorbs our very beings," Eisenhower said. "We face a hostile ideology—global in scope, atheistic in character, ruthless in purpose, and insidious in method. Unhappily the danger it poses promises to be of indefinite duration." But precisely because of the struggle's expected duration, Americans needed to keep a firm grip on their own values. Every new challenge provoked demands for greater spending on arms; these demands ought to be treated skeptically. "Each proposal must be weighed in the light of a broader consideration: the need to maintain balance in and among national programs—balance between the private and the public economy, balance between cost and hoped for advantage."

Eisenhower worried in particular about the enormous growth of the military establishment and its civilian adjuncts.

> Our military organization today bears little relation to that known by any of my predecessors in peacetime, or indeed by the fighting men of World War II or Korea. Until the latest of our world conflicts, the United States had no armaments industry. American makers of plowshares could, with time and as required, make swords as well. But now we can no longer risk emergency improvisation of national defense; we have been compelled to create a permanent armaments industry of vast proportions. Added to this, three and a half million men and women are directly engaged in the defense establishment. We annually spend on military security more than the net income of all United States corporations.

The conjoining of a huge military establishment with a massive arms industry was novel in American life. Its influence—"economic, political, even spiritual"—was felt from the bottom to the top of American society. It was necessary, but it was no less dangerous for its necessity.

> We must not fail to comprehend its grave implications. Our toil, resources and livelihood are all involved; so is the very structure of our society. In the councils of government, we must guard against the acquisition of unwarranted influence, whether sought or unsought, by the military-industrial complex. The potential for the disastrous rise of misplaced power exists and will persist.

These were sobering words—the more sobering for coming from the person perhaps best positioned to know what American defense required. Eisenhower's phrase "military-industrial complex" became his legacy to the

American lexicon. Critics of the Cold War seized the phrase, acronymed it (MIC), and made it the subject of countless disquisitions on where America was going wrong. Surviving supporters of Henry Wallace and Robert Taft found common ground in saying we told you so; their only surprise was that Eisenhower said it better than they ever could.

# 5 | Abraham Lincoln Walks at Midnight

## 1961–1965

### 1. THE NEW FRONTIERSMEN

Eisenhower's words, like good wine, required aging before they were fully appreciated. At the time he wrote them, the country was less interested in a septuagenarian general (Ike turned seventy the month before the 1960 election) and his dowdy wife (Mamie's minimal glamour wasn't enhanced by her maiden name, Dowd) than in the youngest and arguably the handsomest and most charming man ever elected president, and in his even younger, more photogenic, and more charming wife. John Kennedy came to politics from an overachieving family of Irish immigrants and their offspring. His father, Joseph Kennedy, had made a fortune on Wall Street during the Roaring Twenties and had managed to hold on to his fortune through the Great Crash. He was linked to bootleggers during the Great Depression, and though nothing criminal was ever proved against him, the link seemed a plausible explanation of why he continued to do so well when so many people were doing so poorly. Franklin Roosevelt appointed Joe Kennedy as the first director of the Securities and Exchange Commission. Critics complained that this was like putting the fox to guard the henhouse, but Roosevelt, a bit of a fox himself, replied that only a fox knew the tricks of his kin.

As Kennedy aged and his offspring matured—his wife, Rose, bore nine children—he devoted his wealth to acquiring respectability. He bought, in effect, the American ambassadorship to Britain by making large donations to Roosevelt's reelection campaign, and he educated his sons at the best schools in America and Europe. His eldest son, Joseph Jr., appeared the most promising, and when young Joe joined the army during World War II, he seemed likely to add a distinguished war record to the visibility his father's money could supply. But Joe was killed in 1944, at which point the mantle passed to the second son, John, called Jack by friends and family.

Jack Kennedy possessed, or at least exhibited, a wilder streak than Joe, having assumed that he would be the family playboy. But now their father insisted he straighten up. Jack himself compiled a record of wartime gallantry. Despite chronic poor health he had enlisted in the navy, and when the PT boat he commanded was sliced in two by a Japanese destroyer (an incident that raised questions about Kennedy's command skills, in that PT boats were faster than destroyers and almost always managed to get out of their way), Kennedy inspired, guided, and in one case dragged the crew members from the wreckage through miles of open water to safety.

Kennedy returned to America to a hero's welcome. With his father's contacts and cash, he won election to the House of Representatives from Massachusetts in 1946 and was elevated to the Senate in 1952. Yet he lacked an agenda and showed little enthusiasm for the work he had been elected to do. He kept clear of the McCarthyist attacks and counterattacks, although his family, even more than most Catholics, generally applauded the Wisconsin senator's search for godless communists. (Kennedy's younger brother Robert served on the staff of McCarthy's committee.) Kennedy garnered a Pulitzer Prize for *Profiles in Courage*, which documented conspicuous instances of high-minded political risk-taking; reviewers assumed it must represent Kennedy's aspirations since it had little to do with his accomplishments. At the 1956 Democratic convention Kennedy came close to receiving the vice-presidential nomination. Getting close, in this case, proved better than getting there, as the Democratic ticket, headed by Adlai Stevenson again, lost again to Eisenhower and Richard Nixon. A largely unscathed Kennedy looked forward to 1960.

As the end of Eisenhower's second term approached, Senate Democrats lined up to replace him. Kennedy lacked the heft of Lyndon Johnson, the majority leader from Texas, or the experience of Stuart Symington of Missouri, but he had panache. Bestselling novelist Norman Mailer, who was simultaneously breaking ground for the era's "new journalism," a genre that dressed reality in the impressions and constructions of fiction, covered

Kennedy at the Democratic national convention for *Esquire* magazine. "His style in the press conferences was interesting," Mailer wrote.

> Not terribly popular with the reporters . . . he carried himself nonetheless with a cool grace which seemed indifferent to applause, his manner somehow similar to the poise of a fine boxer, quick with his hands, neat in his timing, and two feet away from his corner when the bell ended the round. There was a good lithe wit to his responses, a dry Harvard wit, a keen sense of proportion in disposing of difficult questions—invariably he gave enough of an answer to be formally satisfactory without ever opening himself to a new question which might go further than the first. . . . There was an elusive detachment to everything he did.

Mailer followed Kennedy after one of the press conferences.

> His personal quality had a subtle, not quite describable intensity, a suggestion of dry pent heat perhaps, his eyes large, the pupils grey, the whites prominent, almost shocking, his most forceful feature: he had the eyes of a mountaineer. His appearance changed with his mood, strikingly so, and this made him always more interesting than what he was saying. He would seem at one moment older than his age, forty-eight or fifty, a tall, slim, sunburned professor with a pleasant weathered face, not even particularly handsome; five minutes later, talking to a press conference on his lawn, three microphones before him, a television camera turning, his appearance would have gone through a metamorphosis, he would look again like a movie star, his coloring vivid, his manner rich, his gestures strong and quick, alive with that concentration of vitality a successful actor always seems to radiate.

Kennedy's style charmed the Democratic convention, and it charmed the country after he landed the nomination. His Republican opponent, Nixon, knew far more about government and policies than Kennedy; as vice president for eight years he had sat at the right hand of power (although he hadn't tremendously impressed his boss: Eisenhower, asked during the campaign what important ideas Nixon had brought to the administration during those eight years, responded, "If you give me a week, I might think of one"). Yet

Nixon seemed part of the tired status quo, while Kennedy cast himself as the vigorous exemplar of the new generation.

There was real irony here, as Kennedy, unbeknownst to all but his inner circle, suffered from various chronic and degenerative diseases. But Kennedy pulled off his role, and in a decisive debate with Nixon—the first presidential debate carried on live national television—he appeared tanned, fit, and rested, while Nixon looked harried and worn. Radio listeners and newspaper readers gave Nixon the nod for the substance of his debate remarks, but among the seventy million television viewers a sizable majority found Kennedy the more impressive.

On election day the results were agonizingly close. Kennedy won the popular vote by two-tenths of a percent. Rumors of ballot-box stuffing and other irregularities surrounded the tallies from Illinois and Texas, which together narrowly put Kennedy over the top in the electoral college. But Nixon accepted the verdict, and Kennedy became president.

His inaugural address was immediately accounted one of the most stirring in American history. "Let the word go forth from this time and place, to friend and foe alike, that the torch has been passed to a new generation of Americans," he said. "Let every nation know, whether it wishes us well or ill, that we shall pay any price, bear any burden, meet any hardship, support any friend, oppose any foe to assure the survival and the success of liberty." He challenged his compatriots: "Ask not what your country can do for you; ask what you can do for your country." And he challenged the world: "Ask not what America will do for you, but what together we can do for the freedom of man."

## 2. TO THE BRINK

Kennedy's twin challenge soon rattled the planet. In the last months of the Eisenhower administration, Soviet anti-aircraft defenses had shot down an American U-2 spy plane over Russia. The American government was caught in a clumsy cover-up, which angered Nikita Khrushchev even as it caused him to think the Americans were weak. The Soviet leader determined to test the inexperienced Kennedy.

At a summit meeting in Vienna a few months after Kennedy's inauguration,

Khrushchev pushed the American president hard. He lectured Kennedy on the merits of communism versus capitalism. Kennedy declined to be provoked. "Look, Mr. Chairman," he said, "you aren't going to make [a] communist out of me, and I'm not going to make a capitalist out of you. So let's get down to business." Khrushchev demanded that Berlin be restored to the control of East Germany. Kennedy rejected this as stoutly as Eisenhower had: "We are in Berlin not because of someone's sufferance. We fought our way there." Khrushchev asserted that the United States was trying to humiliate the Soviet Union over Berlin; America's policies were tantamount to aggression. The Soviet Union would meet force with force, Khrushchev said. "It is up to the United States to decide if there will be war or peace." Kennedy replied grimly: "Then, Mr. Chairman, there will be war. It will be a cold winter."

The cold winter came after a hot summer. Khrushchev and the East Germans solved their Berlin problem by the surprisingly simple—and simply surprising—device of a wall separating West Berlin from East Berlin. Erected almost overnight during the late summer of 1961, the Berlin Wall stanched the hemorrhage of population and talent from the East. In one respect it signaled an admission of Soviet and East German defeat. So oppressive was communism that people had to be walled in to prevent their choosing capitalism and democracy. Kennedy visited West Berlin after the wall was completed and vowed solidarity with the people of the city. "As a free man," he declared, "I take pride in the words, '*Ich bin ein Berliner!*'" (I am a Berliner).

At the same time the wall represented the final settlement of World War II in Europe—which, for Germany, was no settlement at all. Divided and occupied in 1945, Germany remained divided and occupied and appeared likely to continue in that state for decades.

The Berlin settlement, such as it was, might have let both sides in the Cold War catch their breath if not for troubles elsewhere. Even as the status quo in Europe was congealing, the rest of the world was in a state of upheaval. Nowhere was the turbulence more unnerving to Americans than in the Caribbean.

Since the beginning of the twentieth century the United States had exercised a protectorate over Cuba, formal at first, informal thereafter. In the 1950s Washington backed Cuban strongman Fulgencio Batista, who did business with the American Mafia and other unsavory characters and ran

Cuba like his own racket. Various Cuban dissidents opposed Batista; the most successful—eventually—was a firebrand law-student-turned-guerrilla named Fidel Castro. Castro first achieved notoriety as the leader of an amateurish attack against a Cuban army barracks that ended in the death or capture of nearly all the attackers. Castro himself spent two years in prison, terminating in exile to Mexico. But he returned to Cuba and in early 1959 led his insurgent army to victory. The United States government didn't take long to conclude that Castro was trouble, nor he to appreciate that Washington made a wonderful villain against which to mobilize the Cuban people and, in the process, consolidate his rule.

The enmity escalated when Eisenhower declared an economic embargo against Cuba and employed the CIA to destabilize Castro's regime. The intelligence agency went so far as to try to kill Castro; when this failed, it raised an army of anti-Castro exiles who trained for an invasion of their homeland. By the time the army appeared ready, Eisenhower had left office and Kennedy had become president. With some misgivings Kennedy approved the invasion.

He almost immediately wished he hadn't, for everything went wrong. Castro, it turned out, had infiltrated the exile army and knew the attack was coming. He and his own army and small air force were waiting when the exiles' landing craft approached the beach at the Bay of Pigs. The invaders were quickly captured, and the American role in the affair, which was supposed to have been hidden, became embarrassingly public.

For Kennedy the Bay of Pigs was a tremendous setback. The world couldn't decide whether his greater failing was to be malign, in having attacked a country with which the United States was not at war, or to be inept, in not succeeding in the attack, against a country one-fiftieth as strong as the United States.

Castro trumpeted the Bay of Pigs as a triumph for the Cuban revolution, but he feared that the Americans might come again, this time with decisive force. The Cuban dictator appealed to the Soviet Union for protection. Khrushchev saw a chance to steal a march on Kennedy and perhaps alter the balance of strategic power. Khrushchev and Castro agreed that the Soviet Union would secretly install nuclear-tipped missiles in Cuba. Once operational, these would deter another American attack on Cuba, and they would counter nuclear missiles that the United States had installed in Turkey, aimed at the Soviet Union.

The Soviet-Cuban plan went forward in secrecy. Soviet ships had been arriving in Cuba for some while, carrying food, machinery, and other signs of socialist solidarity. Soviet technicians had been bustling about the island showing their Cuban comrades how to put the equipment to use. This much was known to American intelligence analysts, who scanned pictures taken of Cuba and the surrounding waters by reconnaissance satellites. The satellites were the successor technology to the U-2 spy plane, and they had the advantage over the spy planes in that the satellites soared in outer space, beyond the reach of anti-aircraft missiles. (For this reason both the United States and the Soviet Union tacitly accepted the principle that a country's national airspace didn't extend above the national air: that satellites could fly freely over anyone's country, snapping their pictures and relaying them back to earth.) But the satellites didn't have the proven record of the planes, and once the pictures showed signs of the construction of something more serious than schools and sewer lines, American intelligence officials ordered closer flights by the spy planes. What the new photographs revealed was unarguable and shocking: the Soviet crews were constructing bases that looked nearly identical to nuclear-missile installations in the Soviet Union.

Kennedy could have dealt with the matter quietly, through a firm but private ultimatum to Khrushchev to reverse course. But the missile story was already leaking to the press, Kennedy was being criticized in Congress and elsewhere for weakness in handling the Soviet Union and Cuba, and elections to Congress were only weeks away. So he went public with what he knew about the recent events in Cuba. "Within the past week, unmistakable evidence has established the fact that a series of offensive missile sites is now in preparation on that imprisoned island," Kennedy told a national—and world—television audience on October 22, 1962. "The purpose of these bases can be none other than to provide a nuclear strike capability against the Western Hemisphere." The United States had no alternative to strong action. "The 1930s taught us a clear lesson: aggressive conduct, if allowed to go unchecked and unchallenged, ultimately leads to war. . . . Our unswerving objective, therefore, must be to prevent the use of these missiles against this or any other country, and to secure their withdrawal or elimination from the Western Hemisphere." To this end the president had ordered a "quarantine" of Cuba. "All ships of any kind bound for Cuba from whatever nation or port will, if found to contain cargoes of offensive weapons, be turned back." Kennedy had placed America's own nuclear weapons on high alert, and now he threatened to use them. "It shall be the policy of this nation to regard any nuclear missile launched from Cuba against any nation in the Western Hemisphere as an attack by the Soviet Union on the United States, requiring a full retaliatory response upon the Soviet Union."

No president had ever spoken like this, nor had the head of any other country. Diplomats rarely talk of war directly; circumlocution is their stock in trade. For Kennedy to blockade Cuba was in itself an act of war, which was why he employed the term "quarantine" instead. For him to brandish American nuclear weapons so openly was unheard of. It put Khrushchev in a nearly impossible position. To accept Kennedy's demand would make Khrushchev and the Soviet Union appear submissive; to reject it would be to risk nuclear war.

The world held its breath awaiting the Kremlin's response. Everyone realized that, seventeen years into the nuclear age, humanity had never been so close to the brink of the nightmare implicit in the test at Alamogordo.

The fate of the world hung on the answers to two questions. The first was whether Khrushchev would challenge the American blockade. He chose not to, directing the Soviet ships to stop short of the line Kennedy had drawn. The second question, the really big one, was whether Khrushchev would heed Kennedy's ultimatum and withdraw the Soviet missiles from Cuba.

The answer to this one came harder. Even less than Kennedy did Khrushchev want a nuclear war. He knew something Kennedy knew but what neither man—Khrushchev for reasons of diplomacy and national pride, Kennedy to protect American intelligence sources—was willing to admit: that the United States held a decisive lead over the Soviet Union in nuclear missiles. If a war broke out and the missiles started flying, both sides would lose, but Russia would suffer far greater destruction than America.

There were political considerations as well. While Kennedy had to worry about American congressional elections, Khrushchev had to worry about the balance of power in the Soviet politburo. Khrushchev also had to worry about Moscow's leadership of the world communist movement. Mao Zedong and the Chinese were already berating the Kremlin for "revisionism"; to lose face in Cuba might mean losing influence throughout the Third World.

Khrushchev tried to squirm his way through the tight spot in which he found himself. He sent Kennedy a letter offering to trade the Soviet missiles in Cuba for an American promise not to invade Cuba. Before Kennedy could answer, Khrushchev added a condition: that the United States remove its nuclear missiles from Turkey.

Now Kennedy started sweating. On its face—which was to say, to most of the world—Khrushchev's offer appeared reasonable. The United States shouldn't be invading Cuba anyway, and if Washington insisted that Moscow not have missiles next door to America in Cuba, it could hardly object when Moscow demanded that American missiles be removed from Russia's neighbor Turkey. Besides, though this wasn't common knowledge, the American missiles in Turkey were outdated and had already been scheduled for removal.

But the point of Kennedy's performance had been to appear tough. To be seen bargaining away the missiles in Turkey would anger the Turks and perhaps unnerve other American allies, who relied on America's steadfastness against communism. It would also invite political attacks from the same Republicans who had been on Kennedy's mind from the start.

So Kennedy in public offered Khrushchev half a loaf. He would promise not to invade Cuba if Khrushchev would remove the missiles. In private he offered the other half. He sent assurances through back channels that the American missiles would come out of Turkey.

Khrushchev accepted the bargain, on the calculation that two half-loaves were better than a nuclear war. The world sighed with relief. Kennedy turned from the brink a hero in America for having boldly rebuffed the Soviet threat. Khrushchev cast himself, less successfully, as the apostle of peace and reason.

The world escaped a nuclear war, but neither side in the Cold War truly came out ahead. Khrushchev never recovered from his Cuban misstep, and he fell from power in Moscow eighteen months later. Yet the Soviet government took the lesson from the affair that it couldn't afford to be caught short in nuclear weaponry again. It began a decade-long buildup that erased the American arms lead and left both sides more vulnerable than ever.

## 3. DREAMS OF A BETTER DAY

As nerve-wracking as the Cuban missile crisis proved to be, Kennedy found foreign affairs more congenial than domestic politics. The most contentious issues in American life continued to center on race. The victory of Martin Luther King and the Montgomery bus boycotters had prompted other African Americans to adopt the strategy of peaceful protest King espoused. On a February day in 1960 a small group of students from North Carolina A&T College, an all-black school in Greensboro, entered the local Woolworth's department store and took seats at the lunch counter. The store accepted blacks as customers but reserved the lunch counter to whites, as similar establishments across the South often did. The presence of the students—four young men—at the lunch counter flummoxed the employees of the store. A black woman working in the kitchen fretted that she'd lose her job. A white security guard, who had no desire to be caught in the middle of a ruckus, awaited orders from management. The manager on the premises, not sure what the policy of the corporation was, adopted the expedient of closing the store early. Everyone—white and black—had to leave.

This didn't solve his problem, for the next day the four silent protesters became more than twenty. The number quadrupled again the next day and included some white students from the Women's College of the University of North Carolina. The mode of protest caught on and spread across the state and then into neighboring states. Within weeks dozens of sit-ins, as they were called, occurred across the segregated South.

White authorities, initially taken aback, responded as most people expected. The protesters were arrested and carted away. Nearly all responded politely, accepting arrest as the price of their civil disobedience. The white crowds that gathered around the protesters were less restrained. Many of their members shouted at, spat on, and threatened the protesters; in some cases the protesters were physically assaulted. But the movement accomplished its immediate purpose: to bring the spotlight of national publicity upon the Jim Crow system. The protesters were counting on the conscience of America, believing that sooner or later Congress would compel a rewriting of the South's segregationist laws.

The sit-ins got the attention of John Kennedy, at that time still a senator and candidate for president. Kennedy met with Martin Luther King and declared his support for the protesters. "It is in the American tradition to stand up for one's rights," Kennedy said, "even if the new way to stand up for one's rights is to sit down."

Kennedy soon became the political hope of the civil rights activists. A

Northern liberal nominated for president on a platform endorsing racial equality, Kennedy seemed just the person to press for positive change. During the 1960 campaign he made a point of calling King's wife after King was jailed for his integrationist activities in Georgia, and offering to help in any way he could.

But after his election he put civil rights on hold. He couldn't have been elected without Southern support, and he couldn't govern without the support of the white Southerners in Congress. And precisely because he was a Northern liberal, he knew that those Southerners weren't likely to heed to his advice on race. A disappointed Bayard Rustin, an African American leader of the Congress of Racial Equality, or CORE, remarked of Kennedy's refusal to make civil rights a priority: "This is the way all presidents behave. They give you as little as they can. And one of the reasons for that is they're president of all the people and they have to accommodate all segments. . . . So they are constantly weighing where is the weight of the problem for me if I don't act?"

Rustin and others attempted to shift the balance of Kennedy's problems. During the spring of 1961 CORE sponsored a "freedom ride," a rolling demonstration designed to test compliance with a recent Supreme Court ruling banning segregation on interstate buses and trains. At Birmingham, Alabama, a white mob attacked the biracial buses. Kennedy allowed his attorney general and brother, Robert Kennedy, to send federal marshals to protect the freedom riders, but he considered the whole affair an unnecessary distraction. "Can't you get your goddamned friends off those buses?" he demanded of Harris Wofford, his special assistant on civil rights. "Stop them!"

The activists refused to get off the buses until they achieved their goal: actual equality in interstate travel, which came after an order by the Interstate Commerce Commission a few months later. By then the civil rights movement had opened a new front. In September 1962 James Meredith, a black man, sought to enroll in the University of Mississippi. "Ole Miss," the pride of the state, had always been all white, and the governor of Mississippi, Ross Barnett, was determined that it always would be. Meredith, an air force veteran, was equally determined that it would not be, starting now with him. The NAACP backed Meredith and won a Supreme Court order mandating his admission to the university. Barnett had seen how Orval Faubus's defiance of Eisenhower had redounded to the Arkansas governor's political benefit, and he adopted a similarly stubborn posture. "We must either submit to the unlawful dictates of the federal government," he told his Mississippi constituents, "or stand up like men and tell them '*Never.*'"

Kennedy tried to talk Barnett into stepping back, to no avail. The governor wanted a clash. And he got it. A noisy, bloody-minded crowd of more than two thousand whites invaded the campus on the day Meredith, accompanied by a phalanx of federal marshals reinforced by national guard troops, arrived to register. Meredith succeeded in registering, but not before a riot broke out in which two people were killed and more than three hundred wounded.

The Mississippi mayhem raised the stakes in the civil rights struggle, as nearly all participants and observers had guessed it would. Martin Luther King capitalized on the broad revulsion to the events in Mississippi and during the spring of 1963 led a protest in Birmingham designed to force the integration of public offices, public places, and public employment. He wasn't surprised that the authorities in the city, which had a reputation for a particularly ugly form of racism, tried to halt the protest, although the degree of the violence unleashed by Eugene "Bull" Connor, the police commissioner, momentarily shocked him. With flailing nightsticks, ferocious dogs, and torrents of water from high-pressure hoses, Connor's men assaulted the marchers, who included thousands of children.

The brutality was captured on television and broadcast around the country. Kennedy, watching from Washington, acknowledged that one image in particular, of a police dog viciously biting a boy in the stomach, made him physically ill.

The words of King hit him nearly as hard. "I have almost reached the regrettable conclusion," King said, "that the Negro's great stumbling block in his stride toward freedom is not the White Citizen's Councilor or the Ku Klux Klanner, but the white moderate, who is more devoted to 'order' than to justice."

Kennedy himself muttered privately against the white South. "The people in the South haven't done anything about integration for a hundred years, and when an outsider intervenes they tell him to get out—they'll take care of it themselves, which they won't."

In public, in a nationally televised address on June 11, 1963, the president finally called for new civil rights legislation. "We are confronted primarily with a moral issue," he said.

> It is as old as the scriptures and is as clear as the American Constitution. The heart of the question is whether all Americans are to be afforded equal rights and equal opportunities, whether we are going to treat our fellow Americans as we want to be treated. If an American, because his skin is dark, cannot eat lunch in a restaurant open to the public, if he cannot send his children to the best public school available, if he cannot vote for the public officials who represent him, if, in short, he cannot enjoy the full and free life which all of us want, then who among us would be content to have the color of his skin changed and stand in his place? Who among us would then be content with the counsels of patience and delay?

A century had passed since Lincoln freed the slaves, and since the Fourteenth Amendment promised equality to the freedmen. "The time has come for this nation to fulfill its promise," Kennedy said. "The events in Birmingham and elsewhere have so increased the cries for equality that no city or state or legislative body can prudently choose to ignore them."

Yet Kennedy understood that any civil rights bill would face strong opposition in Congress, especially in the Senate, where the peculiar rules of that body allowed a minority to block action. He hoped the leaders of the civil rights movement would let things calm down awhile. "We have a right to expect that the Negro community will be responsible," he said.

King interpreted responsibility differently. More than twenty years earlier Franklin Roosevelt had sweet-talked A. Philip Randolph out of leading a march on Washington to protest racial discrimination. No similar march had taken place since, and African Americans had never achieved their rights. They remained, in some ways, more vulnerable than ever. Just hours after Kennedy's civil rights speech, Medgar Evers, an African American activist in Mississippi, was gunned down in the driveway of his home. The murder was appalling even by the violent standards of that time and place, and it reinforced an idea King had been developing: to resurrect Randolph's march on Washington. "We are on a breakthrough," he told friends. "We need a mass protest." King envisioned a hundred thousand people gathered before the great shrines of American democracy; in the face of such pressure, Congress would have to act.

King got more than his hundred thousand. Perhaps twice that number gathered on August 28, 1963, for the largest civil rights demonstration in American history until then. The crowd came from all over the country, traveling by bus, train, car, air, and foot. An octogenarian pedaled to Washington from Ohio on his bicycle; a younger cyclist wheeled in from South Dakota. A black roller skater arrived from Chicago wearing a sash demanding "Freedom." On the National Mall between the Washington Monument and the Lincoln Memorial, blacks and whites, laborers and intellectuals, students and teachers, celebrities and nobodies mingled and mixed. Joan Baez opened the show—for it seemed as much a performance as a protest—by singing "Oh Freedom." Odetta, the black blues singer, rocked the crowd with "I'm on My Way." Peter, Paul and Mary performed their cover of Bob Dylan's "Blowin' in the Wind," prompting Dylan himself to take the stage with some fresh material. Other musicians followed, all celebrating the promise of American equality with such devotion that it was difficult to imagine anyone registering skepticism, let alone opposition. Norman Thomas, the patriarch of American socialism, wiped a tear from his eye and declared, like Moses sighting the Promised Land, "I'm glad I lived long enough to see this day."

Speeches followed the music, and the event began to drag as the speakers droned on. Bayard Rustin, the principal organizer, urged the speakers to hurry lest the crowd wander away before the climax. He succeeded so well that the program was running ahead of schedule when Martin Luther King's turn arrived. CBS television had covered the event from the start; now ABC and NBC, aware that something huge was happening, shifted from their regular programming to join the live feed. Philip Randolph introduced King to the crowd, calling him the "moral leader of our nation." The applause rolled down the mall and echoed off the marble of the Lincoln Memorial.

When it fell silent, King read from a written text. The audience listened quietly till near the end, when a riff on the Prophet Amos—"We will not be satisfied until justice runs down like waters and righteousness like a mighty stream"—elicited the sort of response King encountered every Sunday at church. From there he left off the lecturing and adopted the preaching mode in which he was more comfortable and more compelling.

> I have a dream that one day this nation will rise up and live out the true meaning of its creed: "We hold these truths to be self-evident: that all men are created equal."

> I have a dream that one day on the red hills of Georgia the sons of former slaves and the sons of former slave owners will be able to sit down together at the table of brotherhood.
>
> I have a dream that one day even the state of Mississippi, a state sweltering with the heat of injustice, sweltering with the heat of oppression, will be transformed into an oasis of freedom and justice.
>
> I have a dream that my four little children will one day live in a nation where they will not be judged by the color of their skin but by the content of their character.
>
> I have a dream today.

The crowd, packed close below where King stood on the steps of the memorial but stretching far back along the reflecting pool, swayed and shouted to the rhythms of King's words. The crowd became his chorus as he neared the end.

> Let freedom ring from the prodigious hilltops of New Hampshire.
>
> Let freedom ring from the mighty mountains of New York.
>
> Let freedom ring from the heightening Alleghenies of Pennsylvania! . . .
>
> But not only that; let freedom ring from Stone Mountain of Georgia!
>
> Let freedom ring from Lookout Mountain of Tennessee!
>
> Let freedom ring from every hill and molehill of Mississippi.
>
> From every mountainside, let freedom ring.

They knew he was almost there. They fell silent so as not to miss a word.

> And when this happens, When we allow freedom to ring, when we let it ring from every village and every hamlet, from every state and every city, we will be able to speed up that day when all God's children, black men and white men, Jews and Gentiles, Protestants and Catholics, will be able to join hands and sing, in the words of the old Negro spiritual, "Free at last! free at last! Thank God Almighty, we are free at last!"

## 4. LYNDON JOHNSON'S STETSON

The Jim Crow system had peculiar effects on the politics of the nation, beyond its obvious impact on the lives of Southern blacks. To climb their career ladder, Southern politicians had to give hostages to the white supremacists who dominated local and state politics in the South. At certain times and in particular districts this could dictate joining the Ku Klux Klan; in other cases it simply required currying the favor of Klan leaders and members and people who thought like them. Liberals on the subject of race existed in the white South, but they rarely swung elections, and they were hardly a constituency an ambitious young politician could build a career on.

This state of affairs might have been merely a Southern problem, and for most Dixie politicians it was no more than that. Occasionally, however, the old Confederacy sent an especially able young man to Washington, where he mastered the arts of congressional politics and dreamed of advancing still farther, to the presidency. Yet despite the storied tradition of Southerners in the White House—starting even before there was a White House, with George Washington—the Southern aspirant was well advised to abandon his dreams. In the century between 1860 and 1960, the two major parties between them nominated precisely one Southerner for president, and he had lived nearly all his adult life outside the South. Even then, Woodrow Wilson slipped into the presidency only because of the 1912 split in the Republican party. The parties knew better than to waste nominations on Southerners, for by the time a Southerner achieved the prominence necessary to stand out in his region, those hostages he had given to white supremacy made him unelectable in the nation at large. On the evidence of their historic unwillingness to do anything to change it, Northerners didn't feel strongly about the Jim Crow system in the South; but they didn't want to be reminded of it.

The result was a kind of catch-22 in the American politics of race. John Kennedy's initial reluctance to launch a crusade for civil rights was well founded; white Southerners almost certainly wouldn't stand being lectured to by a Northerner. They would say, and doubtless would believe, that a Northerner simply couldn't understand Southern life. And the politics of the Senate would allow them to block any measure they objected to. The only way the Southern embargo could be broken was for a Southern president to take up the cause and speak to the Southerners on their own terms and in their own language. But until the embargo was broken and the Jim Crow system dismantled, there could be no Southern presidents. It was an apparently insoluble problem.

Lyndon Johnson understood the situation. Johnson understood nearly everything about American politics. No keener student of politics strode the corridors of power during the quarter-century that followed World War II. Born in the Texas Hill Country, a land of limestone terraces and cedar canyons, Johnson came of age after the industrial revolution transformed urban life in America yet before it reached the rural districts. The Hill Country defeated the irresolute but rewarded the striving, and none strove more diligently, at times ferociously, than Lyndon Johnson. He attended the state teachers college at San Marcos, the first town below his part of the Hill Country, and he spent a year as principal and classroom instructor in Cotulla, Texas, where he witnessed at close proximity the trials of the Mexican community in the state. He took a job as assistant to his congressman, who introduced him to politics in Washington and let him find his life's calling. In 1935 Franklin Roosevelt tapped Johnson to head the Texas division of the National Youth Administration. Johnson silently integrated parts of the Texas NYA, so as to spread the New Deal's benefits more equitably but without creating a fuss. The death of the congressman from Austin afforded an opening to an elective post, and Johnson, with the help of his wife, Claudia, universally called Lady Bird, and her family's money, made a successful race. He hewed close to Roosevelt and the New Deal and became a protégé of Sam Rayburn, the East Texan who led the Democrats in the House.

In 1948, following wartime service in the navy, Johnson ran for the Senate. One feature of the politics of the "Solid South"—a sometimes overstated but nonetheless real condition characterized by the exclusion of blacks and the marginalization of Republicans—was that such political battles as occurred took place within the Democratic party. Johnson's opponent in the Democratic primary was Coke Stevenson, a crusty former governor who remained quite popular. Johnson conducted what was literally a whirlwind tour of the state, renting a helicopter to cover the long distances campaigning in Texas required and to generate excitement among that large majority of Texans who had never seen a helicopter. Johnson added a twist to each noisy airborne arrival. Just before landing he would have the pilot hover the aircraft above the crowd, and then, leaning far out the open door, Johnson would take off his hat and toss it down to the crowd below. With practice he got the hat to circle slowly on its earthward course, and the children in the crowd would scramble to see who could catch it. (Johnson's campaign assistant, J. J. Pickle, who would grow up to hold Johnson's former congressional seat, spent that season fetching Johnson's hat from whichever quick-footed and sure-handed child caught it.)

The hat trick was an act of political theater with particular symbolism. Texas has always existed on the border between the American South and the American West. Parts of East Texas, where cotton traditionally was king, are as Southern as the Georgia pine woods and the Mississippi Delta. West Texas, where cattle ranching was the chief occupation, is as Western as America gets. Already Johnson was thinking beyond the Senate; already he realized how the South's racial baggage limited a Southern politician's options. So he campaigned not as a Southerner but as a Westerner. His hat, of which he made such a show, was a Stetson, the classic hat of the West. He wore the hat everywhere, and when propriety made him doff it, he held the hat for photographs that carried his image far beyond Texas.

The primary election was close and almost certainly fraudulent. Johnson won, but only after the late arrival of some malodorous returns from South Texas, where many voters' signatures strangely seemed to have been written by the same hand. Johnson acquired the mocking nickname "Landslide Lyndon" for his paper-thin margin of victory, but a win was a win, and he determined to make the most of it. After voters in the general election duly ratified the primary wisdom of the Democrats, he raced to Washington and began building a reputation as a political genius. His Democratic colleagues made him the party whip and then their Senate leader. The Democrats' recapture of the upper house in the 1954 elections lifted Johnson to majority leader, his party's closest counterpart to Dwight Eisenhower. He and Ike and Sam Rayburn, by then the speaker of the House, formed a bipartisan troika that spearheaded the most significant legislation of the 1950s. The Civil Rights Act of 1957, the first federal civil rights measure since Reconstruction, was less significant as a matter of substance than of symbolism, but it rubbed a bit more of the Southern patina off Johnson's Western hat and boots.

Johnson considered himself the best qualified of the Democrats entering the race for the party's presidential nomination in 1960. A story, perhaps apocryphal, captured Johnson's sense of himself. Johnson, John Kennedy, and Stuart Symington were waiting for one of their joint appearances to begin. Kennedy, the youngest of the three, turned to his elders and said, "Lyndon, Stu—I've got to tell you about a remarkable dream I had last night. God reached down from heaven, tapped me on the shoulder, and said, 'Jack, you're my boy. You'll win this year.'" Symington, exhibiting surprise, rubbed his hand through his silvering hair. "That's strange," the Missouri senator asserted. "*I* had a dream last night, and God touched *me* on the shoulder. He said, 'Fear not, Stuart. *You* are the one.'" Johnson shook his big head slowly as he looked from Kennedy to Symington and back. "That's *very* strange," Johnson said. "*I* had a dream last night. And I don't remember tapping *either one* of you on the shoulder."

But the old anti-Southern feeling in the national party prevented Johnson from gaining the nomination, which went to Kennedy. The Massachusetts senator then offered the number two spot on the ticket to Johnson, evidently thinking to win credit in the South for the gesture while assuming Johnson would consider the office of vice president beneath him and accordingly decline the offer. Johnson fooled Kennedy by accepting, and Kennedy was stuck. Yet Johnson's presence helped deliver most of the South, and in the agonizingly close general contest every vote counted.

Johnson bided his time, presumably calculating that four or eight years as vice president would dilute his Southernism further and make him more eligible for the presidency. Things might have worked out that way, or they might not have. But they weren't given a chance. On November 22, 1963, an assassin named Lee Harvey Oswald fatally shot Kennedy, and Johnson became president five years sooner than his most optimistic timetable had indicated. (Nearly all the evidence indicated that Oswald acted alone, rather than as part of a multiperson plot. But conspiracy theorists, including some who perceived a dark hand of Johnson in the murder that vaulted him into the White House, refused to accept this conclusion, either then or half a century later.)

## 5. FREE AT LAST?

Where Kennedy had thrived on foreign policy and turned to domestic affairs only grudgingly, Johnson reversed the priorities. Johnson couldn't avoid the world, if only because he inherited so many commitments and obligations from Kennedy, Eisenhower, and Truman; but his heart belonged to the American people. At some point in his youth or early adulthood, Johnson came to identify with the downtrodden in American society. Johnson's family had never been poor, but Johnson knew lots of poor people. His family had never suffered racial discrimination, but he knew many people, black and brown, who had. And he made it his mission to end that discrimination and improve the lives of the poor.

Johnson was blessed with astonishing gifts of intelligence and energy. "I can't stand the bastard," Robert Kennedy once commented. "But he's the most formidable human being I've ever met." Eric Goldman, a Princeton professor on leave to the Johnson administration, said he had never encountered anyone with more intellectual firepower. Johnson's ability to fill a space with his physical presence was legendary. "I'm not frightened of him," David Bruce, the U.S. ambassador to Britain, remarked. "But I must say that when he entered a room, particularly if you were going to be the only person in it, somehow the room seemed to contract—this huge thing, it's almost like releasing a djinn from one of those Arabian Nights bottles. . . . Extraordinary thing." John McCloy, who had been American high commissioner for Germany after the war, described the "Johnson treatment" in action. The president wanted McCloy to accept the ambassadorship in Saigon.

> Talk about twisting your arm! I will never forget it. It was not in the big oval room but in that little room at the side there. And he was quite insistent. He's a pretty tall man, and he leaned over me and he said, "We're organizing for victory there, McCloy, and I want you to go out there and help in the organization." He rang all the changes. He went from appealing to my patriotism and shaming me with my lack of it, or lack of willingness to take on a tough job. . . . He said to me, "I want you to go out there, McCloy, because you're the finest"—or greatest or something. I forget what the adjective was but the indication was that I was a pretty successful proconsul, having in mind my German experience. And he said to me—these may not have been his exact words but they were close to it—"You're the greatest proconsul the Republic has ever had." I saw myself with a Roman toga and a laurel wreath around my head.

McCloy escaped Johnson's clutches this time, and he managed to refuse the Saigon job. But it was part of Johnson's strategy to wear his targets down with guilt. "I came out of there limp and feeling a bit ashamed of myself because I hadn't agreed to it," McCloy admitted. Johnson soon returned with another, even more important request, and McCloy couldn't refuse.

There was something else driving Johnson. He came of political age under Franklin Roosevelt, and Roosevelt served as Johnson's model for everything a president could be. Yet the farther Johnson advanced in politics, the more he wanted not simply to emulate Roosevelt but to surpass Roosevelt. Roosevelt had woven America's first social safety net, with sturdy strands of unemployment relief, government jobs, farm-support payments, bank-deposit insurance, and pensions for the elderly. But the strands of the net were fairly widely spaced, and deserving people fell through. Johnson vowed to finish the job Roosevelt had started. He would complete and perfect the New Deal.

He started with race. Roosevelt hadn't touched the subject, at first from fear of alienating the Democrats' Southern wing and then, after the Southerners had gone into opposition for other reasons, from a knowledge that their hostility doomed any effort at race reform. Johnson guessed that what was impossible for Roosevelt might be possible for him. Kennedy's death, coming after King's great speech, allowed Johnson to portray the civil rights bill, which had languished in committee while Kennedy lived, as the nation's way of honoring its martyred president. More to the point, Johnson could speak to Southerners as a Southerner—however much he had tried to portray himself as a Westerner en route to the White House.

Only days after Kennedy's death, Johnson called Richard Russell into the Oval Office. The Georgia Democrat had been one of Johnson's mentors in the Senate; he remained an ally and a friend. He also remained what he had always been: a diehard segregationist. Johnson pulled a wing chair close to where Russell was sitting on a small sofa. Their knees brushed one another, and Johnson leaned into Russell's face. Intensity oozed from Johnson's pores as he explained his utter determination to pass a civil rights bill. "Dick, you've got to get out of my way," Johnson said. "I'm going to run over you. I don't intend to cavil or compromise."

"You may do that," Russell replied. "But by God, it's going to cost you the South and cost you the election."

"If that's the price I've got to pay," Johnson said, "I'll pay it gladly."

The following days and weeks saw Johnson pressing every influential group he could think of on civil rights. Labor leaders were mostly white and socially conservative; many distrusted civil rights as a distraction from issues closer to the wallets of union members. Johnson invited them in. "We have talked too long," he said. "We have done too little. And all of it has come too late. You must help me make civil rights in America a reality." To emphasize his point about the basic unfairness of Jim Crow, Johnson told the story of Zephyr Wright, his cook. She was a college graduate—an intelligent, well-informed woman whose only sin, in the eyes of the South, was being black. When Johnson was vice president, he had asked her and her husband to drive his vice-presidential car back to Washington from Texas. All across the South, when they would stop for gas, the stations wouldn't allow them to use the restrooms. "Zephyr Wright, the cook of the vice president of the United States, would squat in the road to pee," Johnson told John Stennis, Democratic senator from Mississippi. "That's wrong. And there ought to be something to change that. And it seems to me that if people in Mississippi don't change it voluntarily, it's just going to be necessary to change it by law."

Certain African American leaders were skeptical. Johnson was a Southerner, just like Orval Faubus and Ross Barnett and all the others who had created the Jim Crow system. Why should African Americans trust him? Why had he not adopted civil rights as a priority before now?

Johnson explained to Roy Wilkins of the NAACP and other black leaders that he had been working toward the presidency for decades. He had sometimes made compromises to achieve his long-term goal, but he had finally attained it. "You will recognize the words I'm about to repeat," he told Wilkins. "Free at last, free at last. Thank God Almighty, I'm free at last."

So he was: free to pursue his long-standing, if previously soft-spoken, goal of racial equality. He twisted arms and bent ears; he promised favors and threatened sanctions. Under the Senate rules then in effect, a mere third of the membership could filibuster a bill to death; Johnson needed many Republican votes in addition to those of Democrats. He identified members of the upper house whose support would be essential. Everett Dirksen took himself very seriously; the conservative Illinois Republican was the self-appointed historical conscience of the Senate, besides being minority leader. Johnson promised Dirksen a place in the pantheon of the GOP, next to his fellow Illinoisan, Lincoln, if he would bring a critical mass of Republicans to the side of civil rights.

Johnson generally worked behind the scenes. He knew that a vote in favor of the civil rights bill would be painful for every Southerner, and the more he focused the spotlight on the measure, the more painful the voting would become. But after his cajoling and threatening paid off, and the House and Senate sent him the Civil Rights Act of 1964, which mandated an end to Jim Crow in nearly all areas of public life, he allowed himself a heartfelt, nationally televised statement. "We believe that all men are created equal, yet many are denied equal treatment," Johnson said. "We believe that all men have certain unalienable rights, yet many Americans do not enjoy those rights. We believe that all men are entitled to the blessings of liberty, yet millions are being deprived of those blessings—not because of their own failures, but because of the color of their skin." The reasons for the denial were rooted in history and in human nature, but the reasons had lost force and the denial could not continue. "Our Constitution, the foundation of our Republic, forbids it. The principles of our freedom forbid it. Morality forbids it. And the law I will sign tonight forbids it."

It was a moment of triumph, yet Johnson didn't feel triumphant. Bill Moyers, his young press secretary, caught him after the signing ceremony and asked why he didn't seem happier. Johnson explained: "I think we just delivered the South to the Republican party for a long time to come."

## 6. A GREATER SOCIETY

Amid the campaign for the Civil Rights Act, Johnson asked Moyers and Richard Goodwin, a speechwriter he inherited from Kennedy, to come to the White House swimming pool. Swimming was the sole form of exercise Johnson allowed himself, and only on doctor's orders after a 1955 heart attack that nearly killed him. But he didn't cease working while he paddled back and forth in the White House basement, and on this day he wanted to talk with Moyers and Goodwin about an ambitious antipoverty program he had in mind. "We entered the pool area," Goodwin recalled later, "to see the massive presidential flesh, a sun bleached atoll breaching the placid sea, passing gently, sidestroke, the deep-cleft buttocks"—Johnson swam naked—"moving slowly past our unstartled gaze. Moby Dick, I thought." Johnson invited Moyers and Goodwin to join him. They stripped off their business clothes and hopped in. Johnson continued to swim while he sketched for them a bold but inchoate plan to end poverty in America. Kennedy had spoken of something similar, but Johnson wanted, as Goodwin remembered, a "Johnson program, different in tone, fighting and aggressive." He told the two to get to work, to come up with a speech, a label, and a package of legislation.

They gave him all three. "For a century we labored to settle and to subdue a continent," Johnson told the graduating class of the University of Michigan at Ann Arbor in May 1964. "For half a century we called upon unbounded invention and untiring industry to create an order of plenty for all of our people." The challenge of the decades to come was to use that wealth to lift the quality of American life and advance the condition of American culture. "Your imagination, your initiative, and your indignation will determine whether we build a society where progress is the servant of our needs, or a society where old values and new visions are buried under unbridled growth. For in your time we have the opportunity to move not only toward the rich society and the powerful society, but upward to the Great Society."

This label—the Great Society—became Johnson's answer to Franklin Roosevelt's New Deal. He proceeded to describe it. "The Great Society rests on abundance and liberty for all. It demands an end to poverty and racial injustice, to which we are totally committed in our time. . . . The Great Society is a place where every child can find knowledge to enrich his mind and to enlarge his talents. . . . It is a place where the city of man serves not only the needs of the body and the demands of commerce but the desire for beauty and the hunger for community." Above all the Great Society was a work in progress. "It is a challenge constantly renewed, beckoning us toward a destiny where the meaning of our lives matches the marvelous products of our labor."

Johnson proposed to renew America's cities. "Our society will never be great until our cities are great," he said. He promised to protect the nation's natural resources. "The water we drink, the food we eat, the very air that we breathe, are threatened with pollution. Our parks are overcrowded, our seashores overburdened." The Great Society would curb pollution and end overdevelopment. Johnson vowed to strengthen American education. "Our society will not be great until every young mind is set free to scan the farthest reaches of thought and imagination." Johnson spoke directly to the Michigan graduates but indirectly to the American people: "Will you join in the battle to give every citizen an escape from the crushing weight of poverty? Will you join in the battle to build the Great Society?"

What Johnson meant, at this early stage of the campaign for the Great Society, was, would the American people return him to office? The president knew perfectly well that though his personal persuasiveness—and the moral imperative of the issue—might get a civil rights law through Congress, for the more sweeping program he was calling the Great Society he required an electoral mandate. He received the Democratic nomination without difficulty, although not without reservations on the part of certain Democrats who wondered whether a single civil rights act could, should, or would lift the de facto embargo against Southern presidential candidates.

His Republican opponent was Barry Goldwater. The Arizona senator was the harbinger of a new wave within the Republican party: as skeptical of government as Robert Taft on economic and social questions, as ardently anticommunist as Joseph McCarthy or Richard Nixon in matters of foreign policy. The Southwest, a region that combined the historic mythology of rugged individualism with the postwar reality of the military-industrial complex, seemed a breeding ground for such opinions, and Goldwater became their champion.

But the country as a whole wasn't ready for Goldwater's views, and it definitely wasn't ready for him. When he told the Republican convention that "extremism in the defense of liberty is no vice," he sounded scary to many Americans who were still shuddering from the close brush with nuclear war during the Cuban missile crisis. Johnson's campaign succeeded in amplifying Americans' fears about Goldwater. In one of the most incendiary advertisements in the history of American politics, the Democrats aired a television commercial showing a small girl plucking the petals off a daisy. As she imperfectly counts them, another voice, male and ominous, joins hers, and then takes over in a countdown to zero, at which the screen dissolves into the mushroom cloud of a thermonuclear explosion. Johnson's voice is heard: "These are the stakes! To make a world in which all of God's children can live, or to go into the dark. We must either love each other, or we must die." An announcer closes: "Vote for President Johnson on November 3. The stakes are too high for you to stay home."

The commercial evoked howls of protest from the Goldwater camp, and the Johnson side pulled it after one airing—although it was replayed endlessly on news programs reporting the controversy. Whether the commercial shaped the public mind, or merely articulated preexisting fears, Goldwater never recovered. In the November balloting he suffered the worst drubbing of any Republican in decades. Johnson won 61 percent of the popular vote, and 486 electors, to Goldwater's 39 percent and 52 electors. (Yet Johnson's prediction to Bill Moyers about the South's Republican future was beginning to come true. The six states Goldwater carried consisted of Arizona, his home state, and South Carolina, Georgia, Alabama, Mississippi, and Louisiana.) Johnson's coattails pulled large numbers of Democrats into Congress with him. The president's party wound up holding two-thirds of the seats in both the Senate and the House.

This result was precisely the mandate Johnson had been seeking. His advisers told him he could now accomplish whatever he wanted. Adviser Clark Clifford ticked off the reasons: "1. You have been elected by the largest majority in modern political history. 2. You carried into office with you senators, congressmen, and governors who would not have made it without you. 3. You wear no man's collar. You have come through without any restricting commitments to any individual or group. This gives you complete freedom of decision."

Johnson had been in politics long enough to know that honeymoons end and pluralities dwindle. His sixteen-million-vote margin over Goldwater was impressive, but he reckoned to friends that he had already lost three million since the election, after Goldwater exited the national stage and took the nuclear nightmare with him. As soon as Congress convened, the lawmakers would find something to argue with him about. "I'll lose another couple of million. I could be down to eight million in a couple of months." He explained to Eric Goldman: "I've watched the Congress from either the inside or the outside, man and boy, for more than forty years, and I've never seen a Congress that didn't eventually take the measure of the president it was dealing with."

This concern was all the more reason for Johnson to strike while his majority lasted. In his State of the Union address in January 1965, he laid out a breathtaking agenda: a coordinated attack on major diseases, a massive program of urban renewal, clean-air and clean-water legislation, an anticrime campaign, a federal right-to-vote law, federal subsidies for art, extension of the minimum wage, modernization of the unemployment insurance program, high-speed trains between major cities, medical care for the elderly, new antipoverty funding, a federally underwritten preschool program, aid to elementary and secondary schools, low-interest college loans, research money for universities, community centers for the handicapped and mentally ill, a highway beautification initiative.

Johnson didn't get everything he asked for. But he got a great deal—more than any president in history, including FDR. Medicare, the first venture of the federal government into the field of health care, guaranteed medical treatment to Americans aged sixty-five and over. Medicaid did the same for low-income families. Head Start furnished preschool education to poor children, with the goal of preparing them to enter first grade on par with their more affluent contemporaries. The Elementary and Secondary Education Act put major federal money into schools for the first time. The Higher Education Act underwrote college scholarships and student loans. The National Endowment for the Arts and the National Endowment for the Humanities sponsored projects and performances by artists, authors, and other creative types.

Most of the Great Society programs were designed for the long haul and would take years or decades to evaluate fully. Medicare proved the most popular. Despite being attacked as "socialized medicine" by opponents, including the influential and well-funded American Medical Association, Medicare joined Social Security as a mainstay of elderly life in America. Soon it, like Social Security, couldn't be politically touched, except to expand coverage. Head Start was almost as popular. Children who participated in the preschool program showed substantially increased readiness by the time they reached the age for regular school, although the degree to which this readiness translated into better performance at school—the staying power of Head Start, so to speak—was harder to document. The National Endowment for the Arts elicited squawking when the artists it funded produced controversial works. Proponents said art was supposed to be controversial; critics said the controversy shouldn't come at taxpayer expense.

This last complaint underscored the big question about the Great Society. Some libertarian types objected on philosophical grounds to any growth of government; most Americans were more pragmatic and asked simply whether the benefit justified the cost. In the flush times of the 1960s, with the economy chugging forward as powerfully as ever, the Great Society seemed to most Americans something they could afford. In subsequent years and decades, however, as the economy slowed and money grew tighter, many would wonder if Johnson and the Democrats hadn't promised more than America could pay for.

## 7. CROSSING THE BRIDGE

The Voting Rights Act of 1965 was passed amid the legislation of the Great Society, but it reflected the culmination—for the time being—of other, larger forces. The Civil Rights Act of the previous year had opened many doors, literally, to African Americans, but one door remained stubbornly closed. White authorities in the South continued to employ various methods to prevent most African Americans from voting. Literacy tests were administered by white registrars in a manner that made it almost impossible for black applicants to pass. Intimidation, ranging from threats to murder, compelled many African Americans to choose between their personal safety and their right to vote. The effectiveness of the methods appeared in the statistics. In Selma, Alabama, for instance, fewer than four hundred African Americans had managed to register out of a voting-age population of fifteen thousand.

Martin Luther King and other civil rights leaders recognized that until blacks could vote, whatever other gains they made would be insecure. The federal Civil Rights Act was a big step in the right direction, but the federal government might lose interest in the South in the future, as it had in the past. Only if Southern blacks exercised independent voting power would they have a chance to defend themselves.

In the spring of 1965 King and others organized a protest march at Selma. They chose the town partly because its treatment of blacks was so unfair but also because the local authorities were known for their lack of patience with challenges to the status quo. King admitted to associates that he was looking for a confrontation. The formula was fairly perfected by now: Black marchers would move peacefully, demanding nothing more than what the Constitution supposedly guaranteed. A white mob and perhaps the white sheriff and other white officers would set violently upon the marchers. Television cameras would capture the violence, and the conscience of America would feel another twinge.

But the violence at Selma on Sunday, March 7, shocked even King. John Lewis and Hosea Williams led six hundred marchers to the Edmund Pettus Bridge, where the sheriff warned them to turn back. When the marchers stood their ground, the sheriff ordered his men forward. They attacked the marchers with batons, tear gas, bull whips, and rubber hoses. They didn't distinguish women and the elderly from young men; the most appalling news photographs and television footage showed burly, helmeted white troopers bludgeoning black women already on the ground. Seventy marchers were hospitalized for their injuries.

"Bloody Sunday," as the incident was instantly called, echoed across the nation. Papers and pundits demanded that this species of Southern barbarism be brought to an end. Johnson seized the opportunity to establish voting rights as a central part of the Great Society. He called Alabama governor George Wallace to Washington. Wallace was the hardest of the die-hard segregationists, proclaiming, "Segregation now, segregation tomorrow, segregation forever!" in his inaugural address as governor. He had opposed the integration of the University of Alabama, making a melodramatic (and temporary) "stand in the schoolhouse door" against federal marshals; he had opposed the Selma march, branding King and the other protesters communists. And he opposed the expansion of black voting.

Johnson gave him the full treatment. He knew that Wallace was thinking about his next governor's race. The president asked him to think farther—not about 1968 but about 1988. "You and me, we'll be dead and gone then, George. Now, you've got a lot of poor people down there in Alabama, a lot of ignorant people. You can do a lot for them, George. Your president will help you. What do you want left after you die? Do you want a great big marble monument that reads, 'George Wallace—He Built'? Or do you want a little piece of scrawny pine board lying across that harsh caliche soil that reads, 'George Wallace—He Hated'?" Wallace left the White House as quickly as he could. "Hell, if I'd stayed in there much longer, he'd have had me coming out for civil rights."

Johnson went before a joint session of Congress to deliver what many observers judged the most personal and moving speech of his entire career.

He explained that he was preparing a comprehensive voting rights bill. To those Southerners who opposed such federal action, he offered a simple, voluntary alternative: "Open your polling places to all your people. Allow men and women to register and vote whatever the color of their skin. Extend the rights of citizenship to every citizen of this land." Johnson understood how Southerners felt. "As a man whose roots go deeply into Southern soil I know how agonizing racial feelings are. I know how difficult it is to reshape the attitudes and the structure of our society." But the time had come.

> A century has passed, more than a hundred years, since the Negro was freed. And he is not fully free tonight. It was more than a hundred years ago that Abraham Lincoln, a great president of another party, signed the Emancipation Proclamation, but emancipation is a proclamation and not a fact. A century has passed, more than a hundred years, since equality was promised. And yet the Negro is not equal. A century has passed since the day of promise. And the promise is unkept.

Johnson told of teaching in Cotulla, Texas. "My students were poor and they often came to class without breakfast, hungry. They knew even in their youth the pain of prejudice. They never seemed to know why people disliked them. But they knew it was so, because I saw it in their eyes." Johnson said he had often wished he could do more for those children. "I never thought then, in 1928, that I would be standing here in 1965. It never even occurred to me in my fondest dreams that I might have the chance to help the sons and daughters of those students and to help people like them all over this country. But now I do have that chance—and I'll let you in on a secret—I mean to use it. And I hope that you will use it with me."

Johnson reminded the legislators of the motto on the great seal of the United States: "God has favored our undertaking." Johnson acknowledged that it would be presumptuous to claim that God favored everything they did. "But I cannot help believing that He truly understands and that He really favors the undertaking that we begin here tonight."

There was hardly a dry eye among the lawmakers by the time Johnson finished. Southern members composed themselves quickly enough to claim that Johnson's voting bill would trample states' rights. But they were badly outnumbered in the House, where the measure passed easily, and they were eventually outmaneuvered in the Senate, where a broken filibuster ended three weeks of debate. Johnson signed the measure, which put federal muscle behind ensuring that blacks be able to register and vote in the South, on August 6. It was a day of accomplishment, he explained, and a day of challenge. Congress had opened the doors. "But only the individual Negro, and all others who have been denied the right to vote, can really walk through those doors, and can use that right, and can transform the vote into an instrument of justice and fulfillment. So, let me now say to every Negro in this country: You must register. You must vote. . . . Your future, and your children's future, depend upon it."

He needn't have worried. The Voting Rights Act proved to be one of the most effective laws in American history. Blacks did register, and they did vote. And they began electing black candidates to office across the South. In the decades after 1965 black sheriffs starting patrolling Southern towns, black mayors led Southern cities, black legislators wrote laws in Southern statehouses, and black representatives promoted Southern interests in Congress. They didn't eliminate every vestige of inequality, but neither Lyndon Johnson nor Martin Luther King had ever claimed such powers for the vote. Yet they did remake the politics of the South, which was a revolution in itself.

# II

# The Twilight of Liberalism

1965–1986

# 6 | Paved with Good Intentions

## 1965–1968

### 1. WHAT ASIAN BOYS OUGHT TO BE DOING

"I knew from the start that I was bound to be crucified either way I moved," Johnson told an interviewer after he left the presidency.

> If I left the woman I really loved—the Great Society—in order to get involved with that bitch of a war on the other side of the world, then I would lose everything at home. All my programs. All my hopes to feed the hungry and shelter the homeless. All my dreams to provide education and medical care to the browns and the blacks and the lame and the poor. But if I left that war and let the Communists take over South Vietnam, then I would be seen as a coward and my nation would be seen as an appeaser, and we would both find it impossible to accomplish anything for anybody anywhere on the entire globe. Oh, I could see it coming all right.

Johnson would have ignored foreign policy if the decision had been entirely up to him. Where Truman revolutionized America's relationship with the world by embracing containment and creating NATO, where Eisenhower engaged in covert operations around the world and ambivalently built the military-industrial complex, and where Kennedy carried America and the world to the brink of nuclear war, Johnson simply wanted the rest of the planet to leave America alone so he could pursue his domestic vision of a Great Society.

It was not to be. Johnson inherited his predecessors' commitments when he inherited the presidency. The most pressing of these was the American pledge to defend South Vietnam. By the time Johnson became president, the threat to South Vietnam was twofold. Ho Chi Minh had consolidated his communist regime in North Vietnam, and Ho remained as determined as ever to reunite Vietnam, under his control. Within South Vietnam itself, dissidents increasingly objected to Ngo Dinh Diem's government. Diem was a Catholic, in a predominantly Buddhist country; he was an authoritarian, at a time when ordinary South Vietnamese sought greater political participation; and he was a protégé of the United States, in an age of assertive nationalism throughout Asia and the Third World. Eisenhower had propped up Diem with economic and military aid and covert operations against Diem's opponents. Kennedy added American troops to the mix.

None of this succeeded in suppressing the opposition, which increasingly took the form of a military insurgency. The insurgents named themselves the National Liberation Front, or NLF; Diem called them Viet Cong, for Vietnamese communists. Diem's efforts weren't simply ineffectual; they were counterproductive, or so it seemed to American officials in Saigon, who began seeking a replacement. When a group of generals stepped forward, the Kennedy administration quietly signaled its willingness to countenance a coup against Diem. The coup went forward, perhaps more violently than the president and his advisers had expected: Diem was assassinated in the overthrow, along with his brother.

Three weeks later Kennedy was assassinated in Dallas, and Vietnam became Johnson's problem. Johnson quickly discovered that the coup and murders had made the bad situation in Saigon worse. The insurgency intensified and the ruling clique couldn't handle it. "We went in there and killed them off," Johnson lamented to an aide, regarding Diem and his brother, "and now you see what shape we're in." The inept generals were themselves ousted three months later, but the regime that followed them appeared hardly more permanent. "On the contrary, it is likely to be only the second in a series, as military leaders, released from all civilian restraint, jockey for control," Mike Mansfield, the Senate majority leader, warned Johnson. "This process of coup upon coup may be expected to become increasingly divorced from any real concern with the needs of the Vietnamese people. If the people do not go over actively to the Viet Cong, they will at best care very little about resisting them."

Johnson didn't exactly disagree with Mansfield, but he couldn't figure out how to act on the insight they shared. As Kennedy's heir—at least until the 1964 election—he couldn't afford to appear less determined than JFK to halt the spread of communism. He summoned his top foreign policy advisers and ordered them to find a policy they could agree on. Given that Johnson's advisers were, at this point, nearly all former Kennedy men, few observers were surprised that the policy they recommended to Johnson was more of what they had recommended to Kennedy. Nor was it surprising that Johnson accepted the recommendation. Johnson knew Congress and the American people well enough to couch his request for new aid to Saigon in terms of ensuring that the sixteen thousand American troops currently in Vietnam had the tools they needed to do their job. "Duty requires, and the American people demand, that we give them the fullest measure of support," Johnson said.

Johnson didn't mention it, in this or any other public statement, but what he most wanted from Vietnam was sufficient stability for that country not to derail his domestic plans. He trod a narrow path between too little support of Saigon, which would risk a South Vietnamese collapse, and too much support, which would appear alarmist and would distract Congress and the American people from issues on the home front.

The narrow path could be treacherous and deceptive. At the beginning of August an American destroyer in the Gulf of Tonkin off North Vietnam reported receiving North Vietnamese fire. Johnson ordered American vigilance intensified. Three days later another American vessel reported a second hostile engagement.

Johnson's White House was primed for action. The president summoned the National Security Council. Dean Rusk, the secretary of state, called the latest attack an instance of unprovoked aggression. "An immediate and direct reaction is necessary," Rusk asserted. Others at the session were less certain. The commander of the ship reporting the attack had begun to question his own report, suggesting that his men might have overresponded to some questionable evidence. "Do we know for a fact that the provocation took place?" Carl Rowan, the director of the United States Information Agency, asked. "We must be prepared to be accused of fabricating the incident." Robert McNamara, the secretary of defense, recommended awaiting follow-up reports. "We will know definitely in the morning," McNamara said.

McNamara was wrong. The administration knew nothing more in the morning. But Johnson was eager to act: to demonstrate that if the North Vietnamese communists thought they could pull a fast one on Lyndon Johnson, they misread their man. Johnson ordered air strikes against North Vietnamese naval bases on the Gulf of Tonkin, and he had congressional allies propose a resolution authorizing the president to employ "all necessary measures to repel any armed attack against the forces of the United States and to prevent further aggression" in Southeast Asia.

The Gulf of Tonkin Resolution, as the measure was called, found Congress as determined to demonstrate American resolve as Johnson was. Whether the lawmakers would have voted differently had they known of the doubts regarding the triggering incident—an incident that seems, after much subsequent examination, to have been nothing more than a misinterpretation of innocuous natural phenomena—is impossible to know. Johnson kept the doubts within the administration, and Congress approved the resolution overwhelmingly. The vote was unanimous in the House; in the Senate only Wayne Morse of Oregon and Ernest Gruening of Alaska dissented. The courage of Morse and Gruening might have been reinforced by the fact that they would not face reelection till 1968.

The Tonkin resolution accomplished precisely what Johnson hoped it would. It deflected the charges of Barry Goldwater and the Republicans that Johnson wasn't taking the communist challenge seriously enough. It demonstrated that the president had the overwhelming support of Congress. And it gave sufficient pause to the North Vietnamese and the Viet Cong that they didn't mount any major offensives before the November election.

Johnson's landslide victory over Goldwater afforded him a mandate to chart a course of his own, independent of what he had inherited from Kennedy. Had he chosen to disengage from Vietnam, he might have done so. It would not have been easy, and it would have consumed a large part of his political capital. But he might have explained that American aid was contingent on acceptable performance by the recipients, and that Saigon hadn't measured up. "We are not about to send American boys nine or ten thousand miles away from home to do what Asian boys ought to be doing for themselves," Johnson had said during the campaign. The Asian boys weren't doing it, and neither, Johnson might have explained, should the Americans.

Yet Johnson didn't disengage. In the first place, he believed in what he was doing. Johnson yielded nothing to Truman or Eisenhower or Kennedy in his distaste for communism. He didn't doubt for a minute that a communist victory in Vietnam would bode ill for the United States and worse for the Vietnamese people. General Earle Wheeler, the chairman of the Joint Chiefs of Staff, was speaking for the president as well as the service chiefs when he said, "If we should lose in South Vietnam, we would lose Southeast Asia. Country after country on the periphery"—of the American alliance system—"would give way and look toward Communist China as the rising power of the area." Wheeler was citing the conventional wisdom of the so-called domino theory. Johnson was an innovator domestically, but no one was more conventional in matters of foreign policy.

In the second place, Johnson didn't think winning in Vietnam would be inordinately difficult. The United States was the greatest military power in world history. North Vietnam hardly registered by comparison. In every category of firepower and logistics, the United States outclassed North Vietnam; in war games exploring the possible courses of the war in Vietnam, the American side always prevailed.

In the third place, Johnson believed that a commitment given had to be honored. Johnson's political enemies accused him of many things during his long career, but they rarely said he reneged on a promise. What he wouldn't do as Lyndon Johnson, still less would he do as president of the United States. Johnson had a respect for the office that bordered on reverence. His predecessors in the White House had pledged to defend South Vietnam; he could do no less. "Stable government or no stable government," he declared, "we'll do what we ought to do."

Finally, Johnson refused to spend the political capital that withdrawing from Vietnam would cost him. He had played the political game too long to think that the lopsided vote in favor of the Tonkin resolution represented anything more than the legislators' fear of looking weak or unpatriotic. As fast as they had rallied to his side, with equal speed they would abandon him if their political self-interest so dictated. The purpose of Johnson's election victory, as he interpreted it, was to build the Great Society. If staying the course—Truman's course, Eisenhower's course, Kennedy's course—in Vietnam was the price of the Great Society, he would pay it.

## 2. A NEW WAR

The problem was that staying the course wouldn't keep the communists from winning. The NLF continued to sap the strength of the regime in Saigon, which had troubles enough of its own. Corruption permeated the government, demoralizing the citizenry and legitimizing the insurgency. The government reacted viciously to political demonstrations, adding further to the ranks of the rebels. The generals spent more time fighting among themselves than fighting the Viet Cong, and the enlisted men responded by refusing to put their lives on the line. Johnson wondered how things had gone so wrong. "We could have kept Diem," he told a group of his closest advisers. "Should we get another one?"

No Diems appeared, and Johnson confronted the sobering prospect of losing South Vietnam to the communists even before the groundwork of the Great Society was finished. In February 1965 the Viet Cong attacked an American base at Pleiku in the central highlands of Vietnam. Several Americans were killed and more than a hundred wounded. Johnson ordered limited air strikes in reprisal while he gathered his foreign policy team to formulate a larger response. Earle Wheeler and the Joint Chiefs advocated a bombing campaign against North Vietnam. For Johnson to accept this recommendation required a modest but not insignificant leap of faith: that North Vietnam controlled the actions of the Viet Cong. George Ball, the undersecretary of state, urged Johnson to take the leap. "We must make clear that the North Vietnamese and the Vietcong are the same," Ball said. "We retaliate against North Vietnam because Hanoi directs the Vietcong, supplies arms, and infiltrates men."

McGeorge Bundy, Johnson's national security adviser, thought the administration had no choice. "The prospect in Vietnam is grim," Bundy told the president. "The energy and persistence of the Viet Cong are astonishing. They can appear anywhere, and at almost any time. They have accepted extraordinary losses and they come back for more." Bundy acknowledged the weakness and instability of the government in South Vietnam, and he said there was little the administration could do about that. But it *could* demonstrate America's resolve. "There is one grave weakness in our posture in Vietnam which is within our own power to fix, and this is the widespread belief that we do not have the will and force and patience and determination to take the necessary action and stay the course." A bombing campaign would show precisely that will, force, patience, and determination.

Johnson accepted the bombing recommendation, but he declined to announce it in public. The president was busy unveiling his Great Society agenda, and he had no intention, amid his effort to rally support for the war on poverty and inequality, to make a major issue of the war in Vietnam.

Yet he did bring the congressional leadership to the White House to explain the administration's understanding of the events at Pleiku and to justify the actions already taken. "We had to respond," Johnson told the legislators. "If we had failed to respond we would have conveyed to Hanoi, Peking, and Moscow our lack of interest in the South Vietnamese government. . . . The South Vietnamese would have thought we had abandoned them." Johnson hinted at further measures, saying he would not limit American actions to reprisals against Viet Cong attacks. He explained that he would be guided by what Hanoi did. "If the response to our action is larger than we expect, we will then of course make a request for a larger amount of U.S. military assistance and will need additional personnel."

Operation Rolling Thunder, as the bombing campaign against North Vietnam was called, began in early March 1965. American planes flying from bases in Thailand and from aircraft carriers off the North Vietnamese coast bombed military and naval bases, ammunition dumps, and transport facilities. Johnson's purpose was to demonstrate America's steadfastness. The president acknowledged that the communists were tenacious; he intended to show them that he was no less tenacious.

An unrelated incident the following month distracted Johnson. An insurrection in the Dominican Republic against a comparatively pro-American regime threatened to reprise the Castro revolution in neighboring Cuba. Or so Johnson interpreted events. If another communist country in Asia would be a blow to American prestige—and his own political fortunes—another communist country in the Caribbean would be a disaster. Johnson responded by dispatching twenty thousand American troops to Santo Domingo. Johnson's critics contended that he overreacted; they pointed out that lists of alleged communists circulated by the White House were rife with inaccuracies. The troops stabilized the situation and departed, having done little damage to Dominican society or politics. But the incident spawned a term—"credibility gap"—that would haunt Johnson when applied to Vietnam.

The Dominican scare redoubled Johnson's determination not to be defeated in Vietnam. The bombing of North Vietnam may or may not have gotten Johnson's message of determination across to Hanoi, but it didn't halt the erosion of security in South Vietnam. The Viet Cong launched additional attacks on American bases even while they continued to sabotage, ambush, and blow up South Vietnamese activities, personnel, and facilities. William Westmoreland, the general commanding American forces in South Vietnam, requested the dispatch of two U.S. marine battalions to Da Nang, on the coast of South Vietnam, where American forces were expanding an air base. Johnson approved the request, and in March 1965 the marines landed at Da Nang. Until this point American troops in Vietnam had functioned chiefly as advisers; the arrival of the marines signaled a shift in the American mission. The marines were combat forces, trained and equipped to fight on their own.

The shift in American policy continued during the summer of 1965. Neither the bombing of the North nor the arrival of American combat troops in the South persuaded the communists to diminish their attacks. If anything, the larger American role prompted the Viet Cong to strike harder. The insurgents inflicted serious damage on the South Vietnamese army in a coordinated series of assaults. Meanwhile North Vietnam infiltrated regular army units into South Vietnam along the Ho Chi Minh Trail, the main north-south artery. By June 1965 Westmoreland warned that unless Johnson approved a major increase in American troop strength in South Vietnam, the country might soon be lost to the communists.

Johnson reluctantly turned from the Great Society, which was gaining momentum with each month, to a fundamental reconsideration of his Vietnam policy. In July he convened a series of meetings to examine the alternatives before the administration. Defense secretary McNamara and the Joint

Chiefs called for sending 100,000 new troops to Vietnam, to make a total of 180,000. Only in this manner, McNamara said, could the United States prevent the collapse of Saigon.

Johnson listened carefully. "We must make no snap judgments," he said. "We must consider all our options." He asked whether anyone objected to the Pentagon proposal.

George Ball did. The recent events had caused the undersecretary to change his mind about South Vietnam, which he now considered a lost cause. "We can't win," Ball said. "The most we can hope for is a messy conclusion." The United States was already bogged down, and things would simply get worse. "Every great captain in history is not afraid to make a tactical withdrawal if conditions are unfavorable."

Johnson was hardly more hopeful than Ball, but he feared a fatal loss of American prestige in Southeast Asia and beyond. "Wouldn't all these countries say Uncle Sam is a paper tiger?" the president asked Ball. "Wouldn't we lose credibility, breaking the word of three presidents? . . . It would seem an irreparable blow."

"The worse blow," Ball countered, "would be that the mightiest power in the world is unable to defeat guerrillas."

"You're not troubled by what the world would say about us pulling out?" Johnson demanded.

"If we were actively helping a country with a stable, viable government, it would be a vastly different story," Ball said. The United States must cut its losses in Vietnam, to avoid larger losses elsewhere.

Most of Johnson's other advisers rejected Ball's defeatism, or at least his advice about withdrawing. "The world, the country, and the Vietnamese would have alarming reactions if we got out," McGeorge Bundy predicted. "It goes in the face of all we have said and done." Dean Rusk cited the domino theory. "If the communist world finds out that we will not pursue our commitments to the end, I don't know where they will stay their hand." Henry Cabot Lodge, who had previously been the U.S. ambassador to South Vietnam and was about to resume that post, reminded Johnson and the others of the lesson of Munich. To fail in Vietnam would invite larger challenges in the future. "There is a greater threat of World War III if we don't go in," Lodge said.

Clark Clifford, who had been one of Harry Truman's close advisers, sided with George Ball. The United States could never win a war in Southeast Asia, Clifford said. The numbers were against it. "If we send in 100,000 more, the North Vietnamese will meet us. If the North Vietnamese run out of men, the Chinese will send in volunteers." Even if America possessed the manpower to prevail in Vietnam, it lacked the willpower. The American people would not accept the losses a victory in Vietnam would require. "If we lose 50,000 plus, it will ruin us. Five years, billions of dollars, 50,000 men; it is not for us." If Johnson Americanized the war—which was what the Pentagon plan entailed—he would rue the day. "I can't see anything but catastrophe for my country," Clifford said.

Johnson respected Clifford's judgment, and he acknowledged the dangers of escalation. "Doesn't it really mean we are in a new war?" he demanded of the advocates of the Pentagon plan.

McNamara conceded that it did. Until now the United States had depended on South Vietnam to bear the heaviest burden of fighting the communists. "Now we would be responsible," the defense secretary said.

Yet Johnson couldn't bring himself to withdraw. He remembered Munich, and he took its lesson most seriously. Assaults on international peace must be countered at once; if they weren't, the assaults would continue and grow more dangerous. Appeasement had failed in the past; it would fail now. Johnson cursed fortune for making him responsible for South Vietnam, which was as unpromising a protégé as America ever took on; he told the group at the White House meeting, "We did not choose to be guardians at the gate." But they couldn't shirk their duty.

To the extent Johnson was referring to himself and his Vietnam policy when he talked about reluctant guardians, he was correct. He had no enthusiasm whatsoever for the war in Vietnam. But to the extent he was speaking of the United States and the defense of Third World regimes, he was quite wrong. America had chosen the path of Cold War containment with open eyes. Clark Clifford, who had helped formulate the Truman Doctrine, could have told him as much. But Clifford didn't contradict the president on this point. Neither did Ball or the others.

"There is no one else," Johnson concluded, and he approved the Pentagon's escalation plan.

## 3. INTO THE JUNGLE

"P.J., that was Lemmon. He's OD today and he just got the word. We're going South."

P.J. was Marine Corps second lieutenant Philip Caputo. Glen Lemmon was the officer of the day, and South was South Vietnam.

"What?" Caputo asked.

"We're going to war!"

Caputo had been training for this moment for many months and expecting it for many weeks. But the military moves at its own pace, and the moment had been postponed several times. Caputo and his fellow junior officers frequented the Officers' Club in Okinawa, waiting and doing what off-duty officers do while waiting: drinking. Caputo called Lemmon himself to make sure the report was true. Lemmon reiterated: Caputo's unit would fly out that night and land at Da Nang the next morning.

*"Danang tomorrow morning!"* Caputo wrote in his memoir of his Vietnam service. "The words yanked me out of the sluggishness induced by the hot weather and six beers. I felt an adrenal surge, a tingling in my hands, and an empty sensation in my stomach, as if I were in an elevator that was descending too fast."

The landing at Da Nang was unopposed and uneventful. Caputo's unit, C Company, spent the day digging foxholes, securing the perimeter of the base, and settling in for the night. They remained wary—against the wrong foe. "Our toughest battle that night was waged against Vietnam's insect life," he remembered. "Mosquito netting and repellents proved ineffective against the horde of flying, creeping, crawling, buzzing, biting things that descended on us. From every hooch came the sound of slaps and cries of 'goddam little bastards, get outta here.'"

For seven weeks Caputo's battalion saw no action. "We waited and waited for an attack that never came. Finally, in the latter half of the month"—April 1965—"someone decided that since the Viet Cong would not come to us, we would go to them." Caputo and his comrades heard the news with satisfaction. "Since the landing, we had acquired the conviction that we could win this brushfire war, and win it quickly, if we were only turned loose to fight. By 'we' I do not mean the United States, but our brigade alone; and by 'quickly' I mean very quickly. 'I think we'll have this cleaned up in a few months,' a staff major told me at the time."

A few days later C Company conducted its first "search and destroy" operation. The men boarded helicopters that carried them into battle. "I felt happy," Caputo remembered. "The nervousness had left me the moment I got into the helicopter, and I felt happier than I ever had."

The good feeling dissipated as the helicopters descended below the tree line and the forest closed in around the company. "The landing zone was just ahead, coming up fast, a circle of brightness in the gloom of the jungle," Caputo recalled. The helicopter crew chief fired a machine gun into the trees around the landing zone to clear away any Viet Cong. "The rotors made a *wap-wap-wap* noise, the aircraft settled against the earth, and we were out and running in a skirmish line through the wind-flattened grass."

Once more they met no resistance. But Caputo and the others felt danger all around, just beyond their field of view. In the helicopters in the air, they were in the American zone of the war; on their feet on the ground, they were in the enemy's zone. The helicopters flew off. "A feeling of abandonment came over us," Caputo wrote.

They marched from the landing zone toward a village a few miles away. Caputo later recalled the disorientation he and the others felt. "The trail looped and twisted and led nowhere. The company seemed to be marching into a vacuum, haunted by a presence intangible yet real, a sense of being surrounded by something we could not see. It was the inability to see that vexed us most. In that lies the jungle's power to cause fear: it blinds." Caputo noticed that those soldiers fared best who lacked lively imaginations—who didn't constantly wonder what was behind this tree and around that bend. "The rest of us suffered from a constant expectancy, feeling that something was about to happen, waiting for it to happen, wishing it would happen just so the tension would be relieved."

A sudden burst of rifle fire from the trees shattered the silence. Caputo and the others flattened upon the ground. The commander of another platoon, closer to the fire, ordered his men to return the fire, without knowing just where it came from, and called in an air strike. Within minutes two A-4 Skyhawks roared low above the forest canopy, strafing the zone with rockets that punished the ears of the marines but calmed their nerves. "That may have been the real reason for the air strike and the blind firing into the underbrush," Caputo reflected afterward. "They made noise, and noise made us feel less afraid. It was as though rockets and machine guns were merely the technological equivalents of the gourds and rattles natives use to chase away evil spirits."

Covering the three miles to the village took four hours. "It was the land that resisted us, the land, the jungle, the sun," Caputo remembered. He was soon exhausted and sweating so heavily he could hardly see. "It was as though I was looking at the world through a translucent curtain." In his half-blindness he wandered off the trail and felt the earth give way beneath his feet. He helplessly plunged into a pangee trap, with sharpened stakes that pointed upward, designed to wound or kill anyone who fell into it. Luckily this one was old, and the stakes were rotten. They broke without impaling him.

At the village the marines searched for evidence of Viet Cong activity. They entered the bamboo and thatch huts and rummaged through the villagers' belongings. Nearly all the villagers had fled at their approach. A young mother with an infant whose head was covered with sores nursed her child and stared blankly at the American soldiers. An ancient woman squatted by a fire, hardening the sharpened tips of wooden stakes like those that might have skewered Caputo. The response these villagers elicited from Caputo's fellows seemed to him to capture the paradoxical nature of the war, as he was already coming to understand it. "One of our corpsmen was treating the infant with the skin ulcers, daubing salve on the sores while other marines entertained the baby to keep it from crying. At the same time, and only a few yards away, our interpreter, a Vietnamese marine lieutenant, roughly interrogated the woman who had been tending the fire. The lieutenant was yelling at her and waving a pistol in front of her ravaged face. I could not understand a word, but I did not have to be a linguist to guess that he was threatening to blow her head off." An American officer stepped in. He said the stakes would be destroyed, but he was not going to allow the cold-blooded killing of an old woman, Viet Cong or not. The South Vietnamese lieutenant stormed off, "warning us that we would learn how things were done around here," Caputo recalled. "The old woman shuffled away, a sack of bones covered by a thin layer of shriveled flesh. The Enemy."

## 4. SUMMER OF LOVE

"One sociologist calls them 'the Freudian proletariat,'" a journalist wrote of an emerging subculture in July 1967.

> Another observer sees them as "expatriates living on our shores but beyond our society." Historian Arnold Toynbee describes them as "a red warning light for the American way of life." For California's Bishop James Pike, they evoke the early Christians: "There is something about the temper and quality of these people, a gentleness, a quietness, an interest—something good. To their deeply worried parents throughout the country, they seem more like dangerously deluded dropouts, candidates for a very sound spanking and a cram course in civics—if only they would return home to receive either."

The writer was characterizing a small but highly visible population of late teenagers and young adults who gathered in the seedier parts of New York, Boston, Chicago, Seattle, and especially San Francisco during the second half of the 1960s. The "hippies," as they were universally known, embraced a lifestyle as far at odds with the prevailing middle-class culture as they could make it. They wore castoff clothes retrieved from thrift stores or garbage cans, or shirts and dresses tie-dyed in rainbow colors. The women grew their hair long and let it hang straight or wavy or curly, as it chose. The men grew their hair long and their beards long or short but generally unkempt. They ate plain, organic, or natural foods when they could, and they consumed drugs of all kinds at every opportunity. Marijuana was for socializing, methamphetamines and cocaine for partying, LSD for probing the mysteries of the psyche. Their music matched their taste in drugs. The Grateful Dead, the Jefferson Airplane, and other new bands sang of getting high and staying high. They read informal newspapers and listened to poets recite experimental, obscene, and otherwise provocative verse and nonverse. They practiced "free love," which was made somewhat less consequential by the ready availability of oral contraceptives.

They weren't threatening in any but a symbolic and exemplary sense. Yet that was threat enough for many representatives of what the hippies called the "Establishment." The federal government belatedly banned LSD, and the feds and state authorities cracked down on users of marijuana and other drugs. Editors and pundits furrowed their brows over the hippie lifestyle. Parents fretted at the promiscuity. Local officials employed antiloitering laws against young people who congregated in public places; regular sweeps of parks broke up campsites where they stayed in nice weather.

But the counterculture, as the phenomenon was also called, wouldn't have been much of a counterculture if it meekly bowed to the opposition. The Establishment measures simply pushed the hippies even further into their own world. In January 1967 they moved from the Haight-Ashbury neighborhood of San Francisco a few blocks to Golden Gate Park, where they staged "the first human be-in." Allen Ginsberg, the poet laureate of the counterculture, read and chanted; Timothy Leary, a former Harvard psychologist, extolled the virtues of LSD. "Turn on, tune in, drop out," Leary preached. Numerous speakers praised peace and condemned war. Musicians, professional and amateur, strummed, drummed, blew, and sang beneath the eucalyptus trees. Tens of thousands of people arrayed in beads, robes, and every kind of attire the human mind—sobered or drug-assisted—could imagine flowed through the park, which itself was shrouded in marijuana smoke.

The event seemed such a success that the participants decided to do it again on a much larger scale. The summer of 1967 was promoted in advance as the "summer of love," and San Francisco's Haight was declared the place to be. The city's elected officials would have ordered the organizers of the event to desist, but there weren't any organizers. In true countercultural fashion, the affair evolved on its own. As it was, the mayor and the city council warned out-of-town hippies to stay away, but their warnings merely served as corroboration of the reports that something really good was going to happen in San Francisco.

En route to the city, many thousands of visitors swung south to Monterey, which for years had hosted a jazz festival and which this season branched into pop music. The pop festival roughly coincided with the release of the Beatles' new album in praise of psychedelic drugs, *Sgt. Pepper's Lonely Hearts Club Band.* The Beatles didn't play at Monterey, but band member Paul McCartney helped land an invitation for Jimi Hendrix, whose guitar pyrotechnics proved one of the sensations of the festival. Janis Joplin transfixed the audience with soulful vocals that slid into screams. The Who's Pete Townshend astonished his first big American audience by building to a crescendo that culminated in his smashing his guitar. The list of acts became a lineup of many of the most successful bands of the next decade, even as the Monterey festival became the model of the modern rock festival.

The summer of love that followed proved to be a letdown, as was probably inevitable. The Haight grew overcrowded and the drugs overpriced. The hippies might have been peaceful, but their suppliers weren't always so, and after a business dispute left two dealers dead, even persons who were deeply into the movement began wondering what was happening. "Acid dealers *killing* each other?" one old-school hippie mused. "This was what the New Age promised?" The most lasting memory of the summer was a song by Scott McKenzie offering advice: "If you're going to San Francisco / Be sure to wear some flowers in your hair." Most of the hippies hated the song, which they considered sappily commercial. If *this* was what the New Age promised, they wanted nothing to do with it.

## 5. SUMMERS OF VIOLENCE

It wasn't just the fallout among the drug dealers or the hijacking of the music by the record labels that took the bloom off the rose of the summer of 1967. Elsewhere in the country that summer visitors were advised to wear not flowers but helmets. The nonviolence preached and practiced by Martin Luther King caught on with many African Americans but left others dissatisfied. In the crumbling inner cities of America, blacks lived in substandard housing, attended substandard schools, and worked at substandard wages, if they worked at all. The promise of the Civil Rights Act of 1964, of the Voting Rights Act of 1965, and of the rest of Johnson's Great Society seemed distant and often irrelevant to the trials of everyday life on the streets. Black residents expected to be harassed by white police officers; if arrested, they expected to receive harsher treatment than whites.

On August 11, 1965, Marquette Frye, an unemployed black man, was stopped while driving down one of the main streets of Watts, the largest black neighborhood in Los Angeles. The stop was legitimate: Frye had been drinking. In part because he *had* been drinking, he resisted arrest. And in part because unemployment was rampant in Watts, there were plenty of young men on the street to cheer Frye's resistance. The officers who made the stop called for backup, and as the additional units arrived, the incident assumed ominous overtones. The weather was hot, and few homes in the neighborhood had air conditioning; many residents were happy for any excuse to be outside. Before long a thousand people were on the street, shouting at the police, throwing stones and bottles, rocking cars, and shouting "Burn, baby, burn!" the catchphrase of a local disc jockey.

The words became reality as the rioting spread during the following days. The outnumbered police struggled to restore order as looters broke the windows of shops and storefronts and left with what they could carry. Those persons who arrived after the best items had been taken vented their anger by setting the buildings alight. One by one the fires sent plumes of smoke into the already polluted air above the city till Watts glowed dull red, as seen from the Hollywood hills and other high spots in the area.

Outsiders puzzled at the logic of the destruction; why would the residents of Watts burn down their own neighborhood? The answer, to the extent there was one, seemed to be that the violence sent a long-suppressed message of anger and defiance.

Troops of the California national guard eventually arrived and by sheer numbers brought the situation under control. As the smoke cleared and the embers cooled, the authorities tallied up the damage: thirty-four persons killed, more than a thousand injured, four thousand arrested, a thousand buildings partly or totally destroyed.

To the dismay of millions of Americans of all races, Watts became a perverse symbol of black empowerment, and the riot there furnished a model for riots in other cities during the following years. Local and state officials dreaded the approach of each "long, hot summer," as the rioting season became known. Riots broke out in dozens of cities in 1966, and in more than a hundred in 1967. Riots in Newark and Detroit in the latter year provided a grim counterpoint to the summer of love in San Francisco.

The Newark riot looked more like urban warfare than an ordinary riot. Looters marched down the streets robbing and vandalizing white-owned businesses but leaving black property alone. Snipers, presumably black, targeted the mostly white emergency and police personnel, provoking the police and their national guard reinforcements, also predominantly white, to fire almost indiscriminately on looters, suspected looters, and anyone who looked suspicious. By the time the shooting ended, nearly two dozen people had been killed and seven hundred injured.

The Detroit riot followed a police raid on a nightclub open after legal hours. The raid prompted a protest among the patrons and attracted a large crowd. Looting and arson erupted and quickly spread. These looters and arsonists took no apparent notice of race in their choice of targets; black businesses went up in flames beside those of whites. The Detroit media tried to calm matters by underreporting the violence, to no avail. Looters stole thousands of rifles and handguns from stores; with the rifles, snipers shot at firemen and police. The governor of Michigan, George Romney, sent in eight thousand troops of the Michigan national guard, backed by tanks. Hundreds of arrests were made.

But the violence continued unabated, and Romney appealed to the federal government. Johnson, who was loath to escalate a conflict at home while the war in Vietnam was raging abroad, reluctantly ordered the airlift of five thousand paratroops. "We will not tolerate lawlessness," the president said. "We will not endure violence. . . . This nation will do whatever it is necessary to do to suppress and to punish those who engage in it."

Yet the violence continued to intensify. Snipers increased their fire on the police and the guardsmen. The police and guardsmen fired back, the former with high-powered rifles, the latter with automatic weapons and tank-mounted machine guns. "It looks like Berlin in 1945," Detroit's mayor, Jerome Cavanagh, declared. A guardsman admitted, "If we see anyone move, we shoot and ask questions later." The death toll rose to twenty, then thirty, then forty. Four prominent civil rights leaders—Martin Luther King, Philip Randolph, Roy Wilkins, and Whitney Young—issued a joint appeal to all parties for calm. "Killing, arson, looting are criminal acts and should be dealt with as such," they said. "There is no justice which justifies the present destruction of the Negro community and its people. . . . Who are the dead, the injured, and the imprisoned?"

Eventually the weight and firepower of the troops took hold and the violence diminished. The last major blaze was extinguished on the sixth day, and the troops were withdrawn the day after that. Forty-three people had been killed, more than a thousand injured, and seven thousand arrested. Property damage ran to the hundreds of millions of dollars.

Not surprisingly, elected officials and other observers wondered what all the violence meant. Congress conducted hearings; editors and pundits opined. Police brutality—white policemen bashing black heads—was commonly cited. Substandard housing—black families crowded into reeking, decaying, soul-crushing apartment blocks—seemed another logical cause. Paradoxically, urban renewal—the renovation of inner-city neighborhoods—seemed a contributor, for the first step in the renovation was the razing of thousands of African American homes. "White flight"—the habit of whites to leave a neighborhood when blacks began to move in—was alleged to cause city governments to lose interest in the neighborhoods the whites left; it also deprived cities of crucial tax revenues.

An undeniable element in the militancy of African Americans was the emergence of the "black power" movement. Even as King and the other civil rights leaders were advocating nonviolence and urging blacks to work within the existing political system, Stokely Carmichael, H. Rap Brown, and a cadre of militants declared the system incurably corrupt and told African Americans to take their grievances to the streets. The Oakland-based Black Panther party, organized by Huey Newton and Bobby Seale in 1966, called for armed resistance to white oppression and rejected racial integration in favor of strengthening the black community on its own.

Separate from the Black Panthers but part of the same rejectionist milieu were the Black Muslims, formally the Nation of Islam. The Muslims' most visible spokesman was Malcolm X, who had stopped using his last name—Little—as a reminder that African American slaves typically had not had last names. Malcolm derided Martin Luther King's nonviolent strategy. "Who ever heard of angry revolutionists all harmonizing 'We shall overcome' . . . while tripping and swaying along arm-in-arm with the very people they were supposed to be angrily revolting against?" Malcolm demanded. "Who ever heard of angry revolutionists swinging their bare feet together with their oppressor in lily-pad park pools, with gospels and guitars and 'I have a dream' speeches?"

Some of the black power advocates excused the black violence. "Violence is as American as cherry pie," Rap Brown asserted. Others forthrightly encouraged it. Black Panther leaders frequently carried weapons in public and brandished them as political props. On one occasion two dozen Panthers stormed into the California state capitol waving their weapons (and were immediately arrested). Panther leaders engaged the police in shootouts. In

Oakland in 1968 Bobby Hutton, the Panthers' "minister of defense," was killed and Eldridge Cleaver, the "minister of education," was wounded in a gun battle in which two policemen were also shot. Cleaver jumped bail after his arrest and fled to Cuba and later Algeria, where he continued to preach the black revolution.

But the action that garnered the greatest attention for the black power movement was nonviolent—and silent. At the 1968 Olympics in Mexico City, Tommie Smith won the gold medal in the 200-meter sprint, and John Carlos won the bronze. The two men mounted the medal stand before a packed stadium and a worldwide television audience of hundreds of millions. Champions in each event were honored by having their country's national anthem played and its flag raised; while the "Star-Spangled Banner" rang out across the stadium and the airwaves, and the Stars and Stripes climbed the stadium flagpole, Smith and Carlos bowed their heads and each thrust a fist enclosed in a black glove to the sky.

They had hoped to attract notice; they got far more than they ever dreamed of. They were denounced for insulting the American flag and impugning the Olympic movement; even many persons sympathetic to their cause felt compelled to state that an international forum like the Olympics wasn't the place to protest America's domestic policies. The two were suspended from the American team and banished from the athletes' Olympic Village. In time the gesture would be seen for what it was: a symbolic action that was innocuous next to the burning of cities and the murder of police and firefighters. But such perspective was hard to attain at the time.

## 6. HEY, HEY, LBJ . . .

A concurrent form of protest dealt not with an abiding issue like race but with a recent and temporary provocation—or at any rate a provocation the protesters hoped to make temporary. Some Americans had objected to the war in Vietnam from the outset. They asked whether the status of a small country far away justified the expenditure of American blood and treasure. But not till Johnson escalated the war in 1965 and Americans started dying in large numbers did the antiwar movement broaden and deepen.

Some of the protests took place within the walls of the American establishment. Democratic senator J. William Fulbright of Arkansas had long been skeptical of the American venture in Vietnam. He voted for the Tonkin Gulf resolution out of party loyalty, but he soon concluded that the war was a bad idea. "We just don't belong there," he said. "We are alien to their culture, and where the French failed, we will fail." Fulbright could be self-righteous; in a series of lectures that became a book entitled *The Arrogance of Power*, he suggested that Johnson and his advisers were manifesting just such arrogance in Vietnam. Johnson complained and Fulbright retreated. "Never at *any* time have I spoken, or even thought, of *you* in connection with arrogance," he wrote the president. But Johnson didn't believe him, and his disbelief intensified with the war. During the spring of 1966 Fulbright, in his capacity as chairman of the Senate Foreign Relations Committee, conducted televised hearings on the Vietnam War. Fulbright summoned administration officials to defend their policies, which they did with varying degrees of success. Yet the mere holding of the hearings legitimized dissent, even within the president's own party, and it augured ill for Johnson's ability to conduct the war as he saw fit.

Outside the walls of power, the opposition to the war built on previous forms of political dissent. The Students for a Democratic Society was founded in either 1959 or 1960, depending on who was claiming credit, but it didn't make an impression until 1962, when the SDS issued a manifesto of its aims. *The Port Huron Statement* was at once lullingly vague ("We would replace power rooted in possession, privilege, or circumstance by power and uniqueness rooted in love, reflectiveness, reason, and creativity"), earnestly provocative ("A new left must start controversy across the land, if national policies and national apathy are to be reversed"), and clumsily oratorical ("If we appear to seek the unattainable . . . then let it be known that we do so to avoid the unimaginable"). But it did serve the purpose of introducing Tom Hayden, its principal drafter, to the world. Hayden was a better organizer than wordsmith—more Sam Adams than Thomas Jefferson—and the SDS gradually spread across the country.

Yet Lyndon Johnson did more for the SDS than Hayden or anyone else, and the escalation of the war caused membership to mushroom. In time the growth proved unmanageable, and the SDS splintered into moderate and radical wings, with the latter in turn spawning a faction that called itself the Weathermen (after a song by Bob Dylan asserting that "you don't need a weatherman to know which way the wind blows"). The Weathermen and similar groups espoused violence in America as a way to end the violence in Vietnam, and members bombed college ROTC buildings, draft board headquarters, army induction facilities, and research laboratories conducting defense-related work. By 1970 the target list had expanded to include corporate headquarters. In February of that year bombs went off at the New York offices of Socony Mobil (a major oil company), IBM (the computer giant), and General Telephone and Electronics.

Most members of the antiwar movement, however, confined themselves to peaceful protest. "Teach-ins" took place at colleges and universities; antiwar marchers crowded the Mall in Washington, occupied the plaza of the United Nations in Manhattan, and laid symbolic siege to military bases. As the war grew larger, so did the antiwar demonstrations. A march in New York during the spring of 1967 drew an estimated two hundred thousand people. A march on the Pentagon that autumn was smaller but included the broadest spectrum of American life thus far. Student radicals rubbed shoulders with clergymen; counterculturists shared leaflets with white-collar managers; celebrity authors shook hands with military veterans of the Vietnam War itself. The event produced dozens of sober speeches and numerous unsober—in both the literal and the figurative senses—statements and actions. Hippies approached the scowling troops deployed by the Defense Department to guard its headquarters and stuck flowers in the muzzles of their rifles. A contingent of the marchers, having levitated themselves with marijuana and other illicit substances, assumed the yoga lotus position and chanted "om, om, om" in a self-described effort to levitate the Pentagon.

Norman Mailer was one of the celebrity authors; he participated both to protest the war and to gather material for his next book, *The Armies of the Night*. Mailer described what happened when the troops moved to break up the demonstration. A military policeman with a raised baton approached Mailer, who worried for his safety, only to discover that he wasn't the only one sweating.

> The MP was trembling. He was a young Negro, part white, who looked to have come from some small town where perhaps there were not many other Negroes; he had at any rate no Harlem smoke, no devil swish, no black power for him, just a simple boy in an Army suit with a look of horror in his eye. . . . "Go back," he said hoarsely to Mailer. . . .

> As the MP spoke, the raised club quivered. He [Mailer] did not know if it quivered from the desire of the MP to strike him or—secret military wonder—was he now possessed of a moral force which implanted terror in the arms of young soldiers?

If moral force, it didn't prevent the soldiers from whacking heads that night as the marchers tried to force their way through the cordon around the Pentagon. Mailer escaped injury but not arrest; he joined several hundred others in detention. David Dellinger, an organizer of the march and one of those arrested, declared the protest a "tremendous victory."

Not everyone agreed. The war was growing more controversial, but the ranks of the Establishment weren't exactly collapsing. Ronald Reagan, then running for California governor, dismissed the antiwar protests in three words—"sex, drugs, and treason"—and while he was a bit to the right of the American mainstream, the fact that he won his election (and won again in 1970) indicated he wasn't out of touch with American thinking.

Still, each defection from the Establishment mattered. About the time of the march on the Pentagon, Johnson read in the newspapers that Congressman Thomas O'Neill, a Democratic loyalist from Massachusetts, was changing his mind about the war. Johnson summoned him to the White House. "Tip, what kind of a son of a bitch are you?" he demanded. "I expect something like this from those assholes like Bill Ryan"—a liberal New Yorker. "But you, you're one of my own!" O'Neill explained that he hadn't joined the opposition lightly, and he wasn't angling for political gain. The war, he said, had become a matter of conscience. Johnson generally respected a person's political conscience, and he didn't try to change O'Neill's mind. But he didn't want the congressman's example to catch on. "Don't go running to the press or telling everybody your views on the war," Johnson said. "You're the first member of the Democratic establishment to oppose me on this, and I don't want you to start the snowball rolling."

## 7. THE HANDWRITING ON THE EMBASSY WALL

The avalanche came soon enough. Between the beginning of the escalation in 1965 and the final months of 1967, American troop levels rose to nearly half a million. The need for the troops suggested that the war wasn't going well, as indeed it was not. Administration officials admitted as much to one another in private. But in public they put on a brave face. Ellsworth Bunker, the American ambassador to South Vietnam, in November 1967 praised the "steady progress" the United States was achieving in Southeast Asia. William Westmoreland made a special trip to Washington that same month to describe the situation in Vietnam as "very, very encouraging." The general elaborated: "We have got our opponent almost on the ropes. We are confident that we are winning the war. . . . We are grinding this enemy down. And at the same time, we are building up the South Vietnamese to the point where they will be able to progressively take over the greater part of the load." Westmoreland concluded, "I have never been more encouraged in my four years in Vietnam."

Consequently the American public was shocked and the administration rendered speechless when the Viet Cong and North Vietnamese launched a major offensive at the end of January 1968. The Tet offensive, named for the lunar new year holiday on which it began, commenced with communist assaults on thirty-six of the forty-four South Vietnamese provincial capitals and dozens of other cities, and attacks on nearly every South Vietnamese and American military base or airfield. Viet Cong commandos blasted their way into the American embassy compound in central Saigon, where they exchanged fire with American troops for several hours.

The breadth of the offensive gave the lie to Westmoreland's boast about having the enemy on the ropes; its coordination revealed a capacity for command and control among the communists that American officers and civilian officials hadn't suspected.

The fighting raged fiercely for weeks. The communists overextended themselves; town by town and village by village the Americans and South Vietnamese forced the Viet Cong and North Vietnamese to yield the positions they had seized. By early March the Tet offensive had turned out to be a military failure. The communists retained no territory, and their losses were substantially greater than those of the Americans and South Vietnamese.

But the operation proved a moral and psychological triumph. Americans who had been willing to accept the assurances of Westmoreland and the others who spoke for the Johnson administration began to think they had been played for suckers. "What the hell is going on?" Walter Cronkite reportedly demanded. "I thought we were winning the war!" Cronkite, the anchor of the CBS evening news program, had taken pains to give the administration its due. But now he decided to dig deeper. He traveled to Vietnam, with cameras in tow, and concluded grimly for his viewers: "It seems more certain than ever that the bloody experience in Vietnam is to end in a stalemate." Public approval of Johnson's handling of the war, a dubious 40 percent before Tet, plunged to an unsustainable 26 percent.

American military leaders were honestly puzzled at the public reaction. "The enemy exposed himself by virtue of his strategy, and he suffered heavy casualties," Westmoreland declared, accurately enough. The general thought the United States should turn the screws even tighter. He and Joint Chiefs chairman Earle Wheeler asked Johnson for two hundred thousand more troops.

Until now the president had given the generals most of what they wanted, recognizing his own limitations on matters of military strategy. But Johnson belatedly recognized that the war in Vietnam was chiefly a political contest. It had always been a political contest in Vietnam, with the communists and the anticommunists struggling for the support of the people of South Vietnam. (The communists had already won the struggle for the people of North Vietnam, which they governed with an iron hand.) But now the Vietnam War had become a political struggle in the United States as well. The fundamental question of the war was whether the determination of the American people to defend South Vietnam would outlast the determination of the communists in Vietnam—the North Vietnamese and the Viet Cong—to impose their will on South Vietnam. The American response to the Tet offensive suggested that it might not.

The generals' request for more troops prompted Johnson to conduct the first fundamental reconsideration of American policy toward Vietnam in nearly three years. The Pentagon had a new boss by the end of the Tet offensive; Robert McNamara, having grown discouraged at the prospects of winning in Vietnam, accepted an offer to head up the World Bank—an offer Johnson had arranged to rid himself of the increasingly pessimistic Pentagon chief. But McNamara's successor was no more upbeat. Clark Clifford told Johnson and the president's top advisers that Vietnam had become a "sinkhole." The United States could never win a war of attrition against the North Vietnamese, the new defense secretary said. "We put in more; they match it. We put in more; they match it." If the administration didn't change course, nothing but tragedy would follow. "I see more and more fighting with more and more casualties on the U.S. side, and no end in sight."

McGeorge Bundy had left the administration but now returned as a member of the informal council the press dubbed the "wise men." The former national security adviser had supported the initial buildup in Vietnam, and he had continued to back the American commitment to South Vietnam as recently as the previous autumn. But the Tet offensive caused him to reconsider. And he had plenty of company, he told Johnson. "A great many people, even very determined and loyal people, have begun to think that Vietnam really is a bottomless pit."

Dean Acheson, the most senior of the wise men, held the most dismal view. "We can no longer do the job we set out to do in the time we have left," Acheson said. The American people had run out of patience. "We must begin to disengage." Johnson reluctantly agreed.

The president received a shock almost as great as from the Tet offensive when Democratic voters in New Hampshire cast their ballots in that state's season-starting primary. As a White House incumbent, Johnson ordinarily would not have had any competition, but Eugene McCarthy, an antiwar senator from Minnesota, decided to challenge him. McCarthy didn't defeat Johnson, yet his 42 percent of the vote came alarmingly close to Johnson's 49 percent. Conservative New Hampshire was hardly a hotbed of pacifism; Johnson could imagine greater shocks ahead.

To forestall them, he delivered a shock of his own. On March 31 the president addressed the American people. Not even his close advisers knew what he was going to say. Johnson reiterated his desire for peace, and toward that objective he announced a halt to most of the bombing of North Vietnam. He offered to open truce negotiations with Hanoi. "The United States is ready to send its representatives to any forum, at any time, to discuss the means of bringing this ugly war to an end." Johnson saved the biggest surprise for his conclusion. The search for peace, he said, would require his undivided energy and attention. "Accordingly, I shall not seek, and I will not accept, the nomination of my party for another term as your president."

# 7 | The Triumph of Cynicism

## 1968–1974

### 1. The Cruelest Season

In the weeks after Johnson's announcement, Americans received two further shocks, of a different, deeper nature. The riots in Watts and Detroit and other cities had profoundly dismayed Martin Luther King, for they suggested that his advocacy of nonviolence had been lost on the younger generation of African Americans, who appeared to prefer the language of black power and the actions of black rage. He wasn't yet forty years old, but he sometimes felt like a relic of an era gone by.

Even so, he waged the good fight. In early April 1968 he traveled to Memphis to support a strike of African American sanitation workers—garbagemen. His arrival prompted the usual complaints of outside agitation that had been a staple of resistance to civil rights reform since Reconstruction. Death threats were made against King—something else he had learned to live with. "I don't know what will happen now," he told a rally of strikers and their supporters on the night of April 3.

> We've got some difficult days ahead. But it really doesn't matter with me now. Because I've been to the mountain top. I won't mind. Like anybody, I would like to live a long life. Longevity has its place. But I'm not concerned about that now. I just want to do God's will. And He's allowed me to go up to the mountain. And I've looked over, and I've seen the promised land.

The next evening, while standing on the second-floor balcony of his Memphis motel, King was struck in the head by a rifle bullet fired from cover some distance away. Rushed to the hospital, he was pronounced dead an hour later. The gunman remained a mystery—he was later identified as James Earl Ray, a white man of limited education and a minor criminal record—but news of the assassination flashed across the continent and triggered the largest wave of riots to date. Johnson pleaded for calm and declared a national day of mourning in King's honor. Opening day games in major league baseball were postponed out of respect; businesses, schools, and government offices were closed. Four thousand mourners crammed the National Cathedral in Washington for a memorial service; fifty thousand joined the funeral procession in Atlanta; a hundred million watched the event on television.

Robert Kennedy hurried to the funeral from Indiana. Kennedy, then the junior senator from New York, was campaigning for president when he learned of King's killing. His handlers urged him to stick to the countryside, safely away from Indianapolis, Gary, and other cities with black communities that appeared about to explode. But Kennedy ignored the advice and ventured to the heart of the largest black neighborhood in Indianapolis. Under the glare of searchlights, Kennedy addressed a restive crowd. "Those of you who are black can be filled with bitterness, with hatred and a desire for revenge," he said. "We can move in that direction as a country, in great polarization—black people amongst black, white people amongst white, filled with hatred toward one another. Or we can make an effort, as Martin Luther King did, to understand and to comprehend, and to replace that violence with an effort to understand, with compassion and with love." Kennedy reminded his listeners that he had lost a brother to an assassin. He appreciated what the King family must be feeling. "I ask you now to return home to say a prayer for the family of Martin Luther King . . . but more important to say a prayer for our country."

Few of those who had watched Bobby Kennedy had thought him capable of such eloquence. Best known as the combative younger brother of the charming president, Bobby Kennedy had apprenticed with Joseph McCarthy before taking over the Justice Department for his brother. John Kennedy brushed off the charges of nepotism and the complaint that Bobby lacked the usual credentials for the post by joking that it would give him valuable experience. The younger Kennedy did a creditable job at Justice, and after John Kennedy's assassination Lyndon Johnson kept him on.

But bad blood developed almost at once between the Texan and the Yankee. Johnson suspected Kennedy of wanting the presidency for himself, which Kennedy did. Kennedy considered himself the rightful heir to his martyred brother, and he judged Johnson a usurper. Kennedy remained in Johnson's cabinet just long enough to avoid charges of abandoning the ship, but he soon began building a political base of his own. He moved to New York and ran successfully for the Senate, and from his new position he challenged Johnson's conduct of the war in Vietnam. He called for peace talks rather than further escalation, and on his return from a visit to Paris in 1967 he was reported to have brought home a peace overture from Hanoi. Johnson didn't believe the report, which in fact was not true, but he thought Kennedy had planted the story to make himself look good and the president bad. Johnson called Kennedy to the White House and vented his anger at the ploy. "If you keep talking like this," the president said, "you won't have a political future in this country within six months. . . . The blood of American boys will be on your hands." Kennedy responded, "I don't have to sit here and take that shit." He called Johnson a son of a bitch and stalked out.

From that point it was open warfare between Johnson and Kennedy. After Eugene McCarthy revealed Johnson's post-Tet vulnerability, Kennedy declared his candidacy for the Democratic nomination, and party liberals began flocking to his banner. Johnson feared Kennedy far more than McCarthy—to the point of having nightmares about him. In retirement Johnson recalled a dream he had during this period. A great mob was driving him toward a cliff. "I was being forced over the edge by rioting blacks, demonstrating students, marching welfare mothers, squawking professors, and hysterical reporters. And then the final straw. The thing I feared from the first day of my presidency was actually coming true. Robert Kennedy had openly announced his intention to reclaim the throne in the memory of his brother. And the American people, swayed by the magic of the name, were dancing in the streets."

Johnson's nightmare helped persuade him to drop out of the race, and his departure made Kennedy the popular favorite for the nomination. In early June he won the crucial California primary. But at the celebration afterward, at the Ambassador Hotel in Los Angeles, a young man bearing a pistol shot him at close range. He died the next day.

The assassination of Robert Kennedy, coming two months after the assassination of Martin Luther King and five years after the assassination of John Kennedy, killed that part of the liberal vision the war in Vietnam and the riots in the cities hadn't already destroyed. Essential to American liberalism had always been the hope that people can resolve their problems peacefully. The blood of the two Kennedys and King, the blood on the streets of America's cities, and the blood in Vietnam made that hope almost impossible to maintain.

## 2. THE RISE OF RICHARD NIXON

If anyone stood to benefit from the demise of liberalism, it should have been Richard Nixon. When Johnson told Bill Moyers on the night of signing the Civil Rights Act that he had delivered the South to the Republicans for a generation, he was thinking about people like Nixon. The former vice president had hit a fallow patch after his eight years as Eisenhower's second; following his 1960 defeat by John Kennedy for president he lost the 1962 California governor's race. He blamed the press, and he appeared to be leaving politics. "Just think how much you're going to be missing," he told reporters. "You won't have Nixon to kick around any more because, gentlemen, this is my last press conference."

But Johnson wasn't fooled. He knew Nixon from the 1940s, when the two had clawed their way into national politics simultaneously. Nixon hit low and hard. He won election to Congress in 1946 after alleging that the Democratic incumbent was soft on communism, and advanced to the Senate in 1950 by a similar strategy. He branded his opponent in the latter contest, Helen Gahagan Douglas, the "pink lady" (she returned the favor with a label that lasted longer: "Tricky Dick"). Nixon's reputation as a street fighter recommended him in 1952 to Eisenhower, who intended to remain above the McCarthyist fray. The discovery of a campaign slush fund nearly compelled Eisenhower to throw Nixon off the campaign train, but he let Nixon defend himself, which the vice-presidential candidate did in a maudlin but effective takeoff on one of Franklin Roosevelt's most famous speeches. Roosevelt had defended the honor of his dog, Fala, against the attacks of his enemies; Nixon said he would return any money donated on dubious terms, but he wouldn't return a cocker spaniel, Checkers, that a supporter in Texas had given his daughters. "You know, the kids, like all kids, love the dog, and I just want to say this, right now, that regardless of what they say about it, we're going to keep it."

During his eight years as vice president, Nixon strove to appear more presidential; he convinced the Republican party he had what it took but not voters at large, and after his 1960 and 1962 losses he retired to the practice of law. It was a politically active retirement, though: he traveled the country doing favors for Republicans and collecting chits in return, and by the time Johnson announced his own retirement in March 1968, Nixon was a leading candidate for the Republican nomination, which suddenly seemed more valuable than it had only several months earlier. And it grew more valuable still upon the murder of Bobby Kennedy, which deprived the Democrats of their most charismatic candidate.

Nixon wasn't charismatic, but he was calculating. And he reckoned that America was ready for a president who promised law and order as a remedy to the chaos afflicting the nation's cities. "As we look at America, we see cities enveloped in smoke and flame," he told the Republican national convention, which nominated him after primary voters rejected Nelson Rockefeller as too liberal, Ronald Reagan as too conservative, and George Romney as too unstable (he said he had been "brainwashed" regarding the Vietnam War) and too Mormon. "We hear sirens in the night," Nixon said. "We see Americans hating each other, fighting each other, killing each other." The nominee appealed to the silent majority who constituted the backbone of the nation. "They work in American factories. They run American businesses. They serve in government. They provide most of the soldiers who die to keep it free. . . . This great group of Americans—the forgotten Americans and others—know that the great question Americans must answer by their votes in November is this: Whether we shall continue for four more years the policies of the last five years."

Nixon received a gift when the Democrats met at Chicago a few weeks later. The disillusionment of the Democrats' liberal center guaranteed that the convention would become a battleground between its reactionary right and its radical left. The lefties arrived in force and camped outside the convention hall, intending to make the war the issue that determined the choice of the party's nominee—and, with luck, the issue that decided the election. A hard core of the reactionaries didn't have to travel to attend the convention; Richard Daley and his henchmen lived in Chicago, where Mayor Daley operated the last of the powerful political machines. Daley deemed the antiwar protesters the scum of the earth and refused to let them soil his city with their presence. He mobilized twelve thousand Chicago police and gave them orders to defend their home.

Tom Hayden, the SDS leader, had been hoping and working for a huge turnout, a hundred thousand at least. Perhaps a tenth that many showed up. "My God," Hayden moaned, "there's nobody here!" But there were enough to provoke the police with taunts of "Pigs, pigs, fascist pigs," and "Pigs eat shit." The police and the protesters skirmished until the evening of August 28, when the police decided they'd had enough of the lefties. Pocketing their badges so they couldn't be identified, they laid into the protesters with nightsticks, fists, and chemicals.

Norman Mailer, still looking for material for his writing but sufficiently chastened by his experience the previous year at the Pentagon to watch the contest from his hotel room, described the initial assault. "The police attacked with tear gas, with Mace, and with clubs, they attacked like a chain saw cutting into wood, the teeth of the saw the edge of their clubs, they attacked like a scythe through grass, lines of twenty and thirty policemen striking out in an arc, their clubs beating demonstrators fleeing. Seen from overhead, from the nineteenth floor, it was like wind blowing dust, or the edge of waves riding foam on the shore."

Television cameramen captured the violence until the police cracked the cameramen with their batons. The nation, hardened by this time to scenes of poor black people rioting, watched in horror as the national meeting of one of the country's two major parties dissolved in anarchy.

(The horror turned into black comedy when the leaders of the protests were brought to trial for conspiracy and incitement to riot. The Chicago Eight, as the defendants were called, were reduced to the Chicago Seven after Judge Julius Hoffman severed Black Panther Bobby Seale from the case. Hoffman refused to let Seale represent himself, whereupon Seale repeatedly denounced Hoffman as a racist and a fascist. Hoffman ordered Seale bound and gagged; ultimately he jailed Seale for contempt. Meanwhile the other defendants brought forward witnesses who explained that the group could never have committed conspiracy. "Left-wingers are incapable of conspiracy," Norman Mailer testified, "because they're all egomaniacs." Defendant Abbie Hoffman was asked whether he had entered into any agreement with the other defendants for the purpose of promoting violence. "Agreement?" Hoffman retorted. "We couldn't agree on lunch.")

Hubert Humphrey, Johnson's vice president, ended the week with the nomination, but it was a dubious prize. "The Democrats are finished," veteran journalist Theodore White predicted. How finished they were became clear in the denouement. Alabama's George Wallace imitated Strom Thurmond from twenty years before and led a defection of the party's Southern wing. The central issue behind the defection—race—was the same as then, and this time it possessed the added salience of black power, black rioting, and black voting. But times had changed, and Wallace avoided the explicit race-baiting that had marked Thurmond's campaign. "I've never made a racist speech in my life," he declared, hoping listeners lacked access to newspaper files. He ranted against hippies, against "pointy-headed intellectuals," and against antiwar protesters, as well as against rioting blacks. "When we get to be president and some anarchist lies down in front of our car," he liked to say, "it will be the *last* car he ever lies down in front of."

Oddly, the issue that loomed over everything else—the war—played a relatively small role in the three-way campaign. None of the three candidates opposed the war; none called for a pull-out. Nixon gained an edge on the war question by hinting at a new strategy, which he declined to detail on grounds that it would unpatriotically undercut the president, but it neither contemplated nor suggested abandoning the South Vietnamese.

Nixon led by a large margin in the immediate aftermath of the Democrats' Chicago debacle, but the race tightened, as presidential races typically do. Humphrey was by far the best campaigner, being unsinkably ebullient if notoriously long-winded. Nixon had never been a natural politician, and Humphrey's sheer joy on the stump made Nixon's unnaturalness appear even more pronounced. George Wallace stole some of Nixon's law-and-order thunder, especially in the South but among blue-collar Northerners as well.

The election day margin was narrow. Nixon beat Humphrey by barely half a million votes, of more than sixty million cast. Nixon's electoral edge was larger: 301 to 191. Wallace didn't come close to matching Nixon or Humphrey, but his ten million popular votes constituted more than an eighth of the total, and his 46 electoral votes (from five Southern states and a slice of North Carolina) made him the strongest third-party candidate in half a century.

The Wallace vote, together with the five Southern states carried by Nixon, boded ill for the Democratic party. The shift away from the Democrats that Johnson had predicted was well begun. The Wallaceites and the Southerners who voted for Nixon still mostly called themselves Democrats, but they weren't voting like Democrats. From their current rejection of the candidate of the Democrats to a positive affiliation with the Republicans didn't seem a large step.

## 3. THE HIGHEST GROUND

In July 1969 Americans and people all around the world huddled close to their television sets to witness what many supposed would be the dawn of a new era in human history. A quarter of a million miles away, an American astronaut, Neil Armstrong, descended the ladder from a spacecraft that had deposited him and Buzz Aldrin on the surface of the moon. As Armstrong stepped off the ladder onto the moon's powdery soil, he blew one of the biggest lines every spoken: "That's one small step for man, one giant leap for mankind." (Armstrong meant to say, "One small step for *a* man . . .") But the world forgave his minor slip in recognition of his major accomplishment. Humans, after hundreds of millennia of gazing up at the moon, had finally reached it. They had left the only home the human species—or any other species, as far as they could tell—had ever inhabited, and visited another celestial body.

The moon had been an American objective since the early 1960s. John Kennedy, trying to dislodge the inferiority complex Americans had labored under since Sputnik, proclaimed in May 1961 that America should commit itself to putting a man on the moon by the end of the decade. The Cold War motivated Kennedy's challenge to his compatriots, as he made clear in the address to Congress in which he laid it down. Six weeks earlier Soviet cosmonaut Yuri Gagarin had become the first human to venture into space;

American Alan Shepard matched the feat three weeks later, and the space race was on. Kennedy contended that the fate of freedom hung, in large measure, on an American victory. "If we are to win the battle that is now going on around the world between freedom and tyranny, the dramatic achievements in space which occurred in recent weeks should have made clear to us all, as did the Sputnik in 1957, the impact of this adventure on the minds of men everywhere, who are attempting to make a determination of which road they should take." The Russians had been the first into space, but Americans would be the first to the moon. "No single space project in this period will be more impressive to mankind. . . . None will be so difficult or expensive to accomplish." Kennedy reemphasized this latter point in a subsequent speech. "Why, some say, the moon? Why choose this as our goal? And they may well ask why climb the highest mountain. Why, thirty-five years ago, fly the Atlantic? Why does Rice play Texas?" (The president was speaking at Houston's Rice University, which typically lost to much larger Texas.) "We choose to go to the moon in this decade and do the other things, not because they are easy, but because they are hard, because that goal will serve to organize and measure the best of our energies and skills."

The American space program proceeded through Project Mercury, which sent astronauts one by one into space; Project Gemini, which put pairs of astronauts into orbit around the earth; and Project Apollo, which launched trios toward the moon. Each launch, from Cape Canaveral in Florida (later renamed Cape Kennedy, and still later renamed back again to Cape Canaveral), riveted the attention of American television audiences who held their collective breath as the countdown neared zero, which signaled the ignition of the rocket engines in a breathtaking burst of flame, smoke, and sound, followed by liftoff as the mighty vehicle rose slowly, then faster and faster until it curved out of sight over the Atlantic. Equally nerve-wracking, though less telegenic, was the concluding phase of each flight, in which the space capsule reentered the atmosphere and grew hotter and hotter from the air friction. The slightest miscue, viewers were told, could result in the capsule and the astronauts being incinerated. Viewers had to be told this, as no television cameras recorded the reentry phase; the first sight the cameras caught was the capsule drifting down to the ocean beneath its parachute.

Most of the missions went well; a few did not. In January 1967 a fire flashed through an Apollo capsule undergoing launch pad tests; three astronauts were killed. The tragedy delayed the program and necessitated changes in design and procedure.

But two and a half years later Apollo 11 lifted off from Florida, orbited the earth once, and headed for the moon. On the third day out the spacecraft entered lunar orbit. A small landing vehicle, called Eagle, separated from the larger craft and descended to the surface, touching down in the dry Sea of Tranquility. "Houston, Tranquility Base here," mission commander Armstrong radioed home. "The Eagle has landed."

Six hours later, at almost eleven p.m. Eastern time on July 20, 1969, Armstrong took the small step that marked the giant leap. A television camera mounted on the side of the Eagle captured his movements and sent them the hundreds of thousands of miles to the hundreds of millions of earthlings watching the event. Twenty minutes later Buzz Aldrin joined Armstrong on the lunar surface. The two men planted an American flag, set up some scientific experiments, gathered rock and soil samples, and skipped about like schoolboys, enjoying the moon's weak gravity. They took a call from Richard Nixon—"the most historic telephone call ever made," the president said. "Because of what you have done," Nixon asserted, "the heavens have become a part of man's world."

## 4. MEANS AND ENDS

Nixon's call to the moon was expected; some of Nixon's other actions were a surprise. After campaigning as a conservative, Nixon adopted certain characteristics of his liberal predecessors. "I wanted to be an activist president in domestic policy," he explained in his memoirs. He would keep a closer watch on spending than Johnson, and he would diminish expectations, but he wouldn't necessarily reduce outcomes. "I wanted to be certain that the things we did had a chance of working. 'Don't promise more than we can do,' I told the Cabinet. 'But do more than we can promise.'"

What Nixon called the "new federalism" envisioned returning authority in some realms of government—education, for instance—to the states. But the federalism in the new federalism remained crucial. Washington would fund the programs and deliver the money to the states in blocks. Moreover, because the bureaucracy that currently directed the programs could be expected to resist the devolution, Nixon would center its control in the White House. Leonard Garment, Nixon's lawyer, acknowledged what he called "the central paradox of the Nixon administration," namely "that in order to reduce *federal* power it was first necessary to increase *presidential* power."

The new federalism aside, Nixon pursued various policies that looked a lot like the old federalism. The Clean Air Act of 1970 did more for the environment than anything Lyndon Johnson had accomplished or even envisioned. From the moment railroads had begun belching black smoke into the comparatively pristine atmosphere of preindustrial America, through the emergence of the automobile as the foremost threat to the country's lungs, air quality had relentlessly declined. But as the measures stipulated by Nixon's Clean Air Act and its successors took hold, the skies began to clear. The Environmental Protection Agency was another product of the Nixon presidency. Created by executive order in July 1970, the EPA assumed oversight of the American environment and commenced addressing long-delayed concerns in the relation of Americans to the air, water, and land around them.

Nixon's environmentalism, for all its importance, was tactical rather than philosophical. If the president had read Rachel Carson's 1962 *Silent Spring*, the book widely credited with awakening Americans to the degradation of their environment, he showed no sign of having been moved by its message. "In a flat choice between smoke and jobs," he asserted privately, "we're for jobs." Nixon judged the most devoted environmentalists to be dangerous radicals. If the environmentalists had their way, he told automakers Lee Iacocca and Henry Ford II, Americans would have to "go back and live like a bunch of damned animals. . . . They're a group of people that aren't one really damn bit interested in safety or clean air. What they're interested in is destroying the system."

To a large degree, Nixon supported environmental issues—and such other progressive causes as affirmative action and workplace safety—to get the liberals off his back and let him focus on the issues that really mattered to him. Most pressing was Vietnam. Nixon could read public opinion as well as Johnson could, and he could tell that the American electorate wouldn't support the war much longer. As a first step away from Saigon, Nixon announced a policy of "Vietnamization," the essence of which was the reduction of the American troop presence in South Vietnam, with the deficit to be filled by newly trained, newly armed, and presumably newly motivated South Vietnamese troops.

The training and the arming were easy; the motivating was hard. As American troops gradually withdrew from South Vietnam, Washington increased military aid to Saigon. And lest the North Vietnamese—or the Chinese or the Soviets—infer that the American withdrawal represented a loss of interest in the affairs of Southeast Asia, Nixon widened the war into Laos and Cambodia. For years the North Vietnamese had taken refuge from the fighting in South Vietnam by slipping over the border into Laos and Cambodia, which also provided supply routes to South Vietnam. Nixon ordered the bombing of Laos and, in the spring of 1970, the invasion of Cambodia.

Whether or not these efforts conveyed to the communists the message Nixon intended, they got the attention of the antiwar movement in America. The Cambodian invasion sparked the largest protests of the war. On hundreds of campuses across the country students boycotted classes and faculty suspended teaching in favor of discussions—which was to say, condemnation—of the war. A new wave of arson and sabotage destroyed defense laboratories and ROTC offices. At Kent State University in Ohio, protesters clashed with national guard troops, who fired on the crowd and killed four students. Days later a similar tragedy occurred at Jackson State in Mississippi, where two students were killed by police fire.

Among American troops, the policy of Vietnamization had paradoxical effects. The war had always been difficult; the troubles Philip Caputo encountered on his first patrol—of distinguishing enemies from allies—only intensified with the American escalation. Caputo himself was court-martialed after marines under his command killed a noncombatant they claimed was Viet Cong; Caputo escaped with a plea bargain but lost any illusions that the war was just or reasonable.

He was one of the lucky officers. Many troops interpreted Vietnamization as a phased abandonment of the American mission in Vietnam, and few wanted to die for a cause Washington apparently considered lost. Morale plummeted; soldiers turned to drugs to ease the boredom and uncertainty of their position. It hardly helped matters that the world's most prolific poppy fields were nearby; in 1971 an estimated forty thousand American troops—or one-sixth of the American force in Vietnam—were addicted to heroin. Soldiers routinely refused orders to engage in dangerous patrols; when their commanding officers insisted, some troops "fragged" the officers—led them into traps, ambushed them at night, or tossed grenades into their tents.

## 5. FROM BEIJING TO MOSCOW . . .

"We've got those liberal bastards on the run," Nixon asserted hopefully in November 1969. Not much at the time indicated that this was true, but he was thinking ahead, to a thorough recasting of American foreign policy. By the late 1960s an essential premise of America's Cold War policy had been proven wrong. The communist world, conceived in monolithic terms by Truman and Eisenhower, had fractured, with the deepest fault running between the Soviet Union and China. Mao and his Chinese colleagues condemned Moscow more vociferously than ever for revisionism, and as the European empires continued to crumble, the Chinese asserted their right to lead the Third World. The dispute between the Forbidden City and the Kremlin escalated from words to weapons when troops of the Chinese People's Liberation Army skirmished with soldiers of the Soviet Red Army along their countries' common border in 1969.

Nixon watched and calculated. He judged that if the communist world was no longer a monolith, the separate parts might be played against one another to America's benefit. Thus was born the idea of détente, an unwinding of the ideological Cold War. The bipolar basis of American containment policy—the two worlds of the Truman Doctrine—would yield to a tripolar scheme. Washington would treat Moscow and Beijing not as existential enemies but as manageable rivals.

In the summer of 1971 Nixon unveiled his grand diplomatic scheme. His partner in détente was Henry Kissinger, a German Jew driven from home by the Nazis in the 1930s. Kissinger served in the U.S. Army during World War II and subsequently attended Harvard for college and graduate school. His doctoral thesis examined the restructuring of Europe following the Napoleonic wars; he became intrigued, and then persuaded, by the hard-eyed realism of Castlereagh and Metternich, the British and Austrian architects of the Concert of Europe. He taught at Harvard while ingratiating himself to the American Cold War establishment. He attached himself to Nelson Rockefeller, but when Rockefeller's star faded Kissinger made himself indispensable to Richard Nixon. He briefed Nixon on foreign policy during the 1968 campaign; Nixon returned the favor after his election by naming Kissinger his national security adviser.

In this capacity Kissinger traveled to Pakistan in July 1971. He engaged in talks with Pakistani officials before begging off with complaints of gastro-intestinal trouble of the sort that has long afflicted Westerners in South Asia. His press man told the reporters covering his visit that they might amuse themselves until Dr. Kissinger recovered. They went sightseeing, only to be surprised—and embarrassed—when Kissinger turned up in Beijing the next day. The stomachache had been a cover for a secret flight over the Himalayas, after which Kissinger met with Mao Zedong and Zhou Enlai. In light of the fact that the United States still clung to the fiction that Taiwan was China, Kissinger's visit represented a major concession—if only to reality—by the Nixon administration.

This didn't prevent Nixon from claiming a great victory. The opening to China, he said, constituted "the most significant foreign policy achievement in this century." Kissinger declared that his meetings with the Chinese leadership had prepared the way for a momentous presidential visit to Beijing. "We have laid the groundwork for you and Mao to turn a page in history," Kissinger told Nixon. "The process we have now started will send enormous shock waves around the world."

Kissinger was right about the shock waves. A spokesman for the Soviet government warned darkly of "secret collusion" between Washington and Beijing. "This is a matter of grave consequence for the Soviet people, for world socialism, for the entire international situation, for world peace," the Kremlin's man asserted. Japan's government, which had faithfully toed America's anti-Chinese line, was flummoxed by the "Nixon shokku."

The jolt was hardly gentler in America. The Republican party had made a postwar career of condemning the Democrats for anything construable as being soft on communism or insufficiently harsh on China. Nixon himself had climbed to the pinnacle of American politics on the backs of those he trampled for fellow-traveling. And now he was going to China. The Republicans didn't know what to say. Democrats, too, were tongue-tied, in their case by Nixon's embrace of a policy many of them had silently espoused for years.

The presidential visit took place with suitable fanfare in February 1972. Nixon drank tea with Mao and climbed the Great Wall with reporters. "It exceeds all expectations," he said of the wall. "I think you would have to conclude that this is a great wall and that it had to be built by a great people." He and Zhou toasted a new day in Sino-American relations. "Seize the day, seize the hour," Nixon quoted Mao. "This is the day, this is the hour for our two peoples to rise to the heights of greatness which can build a new and better world."

Nixon wasn't immune to political theater, but the real purpose of going to Beijing was to prepare a visit to Moscow. By opening to China, Nixon aimed to entice the Soviet Union, which presumably would feel compelled to court the Americans lest they fall in too closely with the Chinese.

His aims were partly realized when he traveled to Moscow in May 1972. Soviet general secretary Leonid Brezhnev was neither as legendary as Mao nor as urbane as Zhou, but he did control thousands of nuclear missiles aimed at the United States. He might have built thousands more had he and Nixon not signed the first important arms control agreements of the Cold War. The Strategic Arms Limitation Treaty (SALT—which would be called SALT I after SALT II came along) banned comprehensive antimissile defense systems. Each side could construct one antimissile installation near the national capital and one near a missile field of its choosing. But anything more was out. As a result of this agreement, the world was spared an arms race in defensive technology. SALT I also capped offensive missiles, putting a limit on that side of the arms race as well.

Nixon and Brezhnev simultaneously inked an accord defining the principles of détente. The first principle was ideological nonaggression: a live-and-let-live affirmation that capitalism and socialism could coexist and even establish productive relations. Other principles—the forswearing of force and the promise to dampen rather than exacerbate regional conflicts—followed from this.

It was a remarkable set of accords. If the two sides actually delivered on what they promised as part of détente, the Cold War was over. The United States and the Soviet Union would treat each other as normal great powers, with interests that might clash but would not threaten the existence of the other.

## 6. . . . TO PARIS

Détente had another appeal to Nixon, apart from easing tension with the Soviet Union and China. The president expected the new policy to cover America's exit from Vietnam. The peace talks that commenced during Johnson's last months in office went nowhere slowly. The North Vietnamese could see that American interest in the fate of South Vietnam was diminishing; with American troop levels falling from 550,000 in 1969 to 400,000 in 1970 to 300,000 in 1971, Hanoi had little reason to do anything but procrastinate at Paris.

By the spring of 1972 the North Vietnamese were convinced that the South had become fatally weakened. They launched a major offensive—only to be beaten back by a surprisingly resilient South Vietnamese army supported by American air power. The battle inflicted heavy casualties on the communist side and seemed to confirm the strategic basis of Nixon's Vietnamization policy. The North Vietnamese licked their wounds and returned to the peace talks.

Nixon grew hopeful regarding a settlement. With détente putting the Soviets and Chinese in a cooperative mood, he indicated to the two great communist powers that he would consider it a sign of good faith if they pressured Hanoi to step back in South Vietnam. He couldn't expect the North Vietnamese to abandon their dream of reunifying Vietnam, but if they accepted a ceasefire that allowed the United States to withdraw in good order, their gesture would be appreciated. The alternative was a continued war. To remind Hanoi that the United States would be able to inflict pain even without troops on the ground, Nixon ordered the most intense bombing of the entire conflict, the so-called Christmas bombing of 1972.

Shortly thereafter Hanoi came to terms. In January 1973 Henry Kissinger and Le Duc Tho signed an agreement in Paris that specified a ceasefire in exchange for the withdrawal of the last American troops from South Vietnam. The most important provision, from the perspective of Hanoi—and of the government in Saigon, which observed the American withdrawal with trepidation—was an article allowing North Vietnamese troops to remain in place in South Vietnam.

The Paris pact gave Nixon the breathing space he desired. For two years after the American departure the North Vietnamese essentially honored the ceasefire. Then, following a continued erosion of American support for South Vietnam, Hanoi in the spring of 1975 launched another final offensive, which this time succeeded. At the end of April the communists captured Saigon and renamed it Ho Chi Minh City, for their now-departed leader, whose lifelong ambition—of uniting Vietnam under communist rule—they quickly fulfilled.

The communist conquest completed America's Vietnam debacle. Sixty thousand Americans had died in the vain struggle to apply the containment policy—fashioned a quarter-century earlier in response to events half a world away—to Southeast Asia. The experience seared itself on the American mind, replacing the Munich syndrome with a Vietnam syndrome. The former had said that when in doubt, America must fight. The latter asserted that when in doubt, America mustn't. Neither did much to diminish the doubt, the source of all the trouble.

## 7. NOW OR NEVER

"The problem lay buried, unspoken, for many years in the minds of American women," Betty Friedan wrote.

> It was a strange stirring, a sense of dissatisfaction, a yearning that women suffered in the middle of the twentieth century in the United States. Each suburban wife struggled with it alone. As she made the beds, shopped for groceries, matched slipcover material, ate peanut butter sandwiches with her children, chauffeured Cub Scouts and Brownies, lay beside her husband at night—she was afraid to ask even of herself the silent question—"Is this all?"

Friedan was a 1942 summa cum laude graduate of Smith College, and after Smith she accepted a fellowship to the University of California at Berkeley, where she started to study for a doctorate in psychology. But a young man she was dating convinced her that graduate school wasn't for women, and she dropped out. She married, had children, and spent the 1950s tending them, her husband, and their suburban home. On the side she wrote free-lance articles for magazines. She considered herself happy, and she assumed that others of her age and educational cohort were happy too.

As her fifteenth reunion at Smith approached, she conducted an informal survey of her former classmates, intending to discredit a common contention of those days, that higher education unsuited women for domestic happiness. The response she received caused her to send similar questionnaires to graduates of Radcliffe and other women's colleges, and to conduct face-to-face interviews with several dozen women. What they told her confirmed not her own experience but the conventional wisdom. Well-educated women chronically yearned for more than their domestic lives afforded them. And almost to a woman they felt that no one understood their plight.

> For over fifteen years there was no word of this yearning in the millions of words written about women, for women, in all the columns, books and articles by experts telling women their role was to seek fulfillment as wives and mothers. Over and over women heard in voices of tradition and of Freudian sophistication that they could desire no greater destiny than to glory in their own femininity. Experts told them how to catch a man and keep him; how to breastfeed children and handle their toilet training; how to cope with sibling rivalry and adolescent rebellion; how to buy a dishwasher, bake bread, cook gourmet snails, and build a swimming pool with their own hands; how to dress, look, and act more feminine and make marriage more exciting; how to keep their husbands from dying young and their sons from growing into delinquents. In the fifteen years after World War II, this mystique of feminine fulfillment became the cherished and self-perpetuating core of contemporary American culture.

The "feminine mystique," Friedan asserted in a 1963 book with that title, was a fraud and a trap. Millions of women must have agreed, for the book became a huge bestseller and catapulted Friedan to the front ranks of advocates of equal rights for women.

In an age of movements, she decided that women needed their own equivalent of the National Association for the Advancement of Colored People, and in 1966 she helped found the National Organization for Women, of which she served as president. NOW organized conferences and symposia but truly came to the attention of the country in 1970, when it sponsored the Women's Strike for Equality, an effort to get American women to leave their kitchens and laundries for the streets and to stay there until they achieved equal pay, equal respect, and equal rights. To underscore the parallel with the civil rights movement, Friedan kicked off a march down Manhattan's Fifth Avenue by sitting in at Whyte's, a New York restaurant that barred women.

The marchers chanted, sang, and carried banners that read "Don't Cook—Starve a Rat Tonight!" and "Don't Iron While the Strike is Hot." Most of the marchers were women, but some men joined in. The march snarled traffic as it wound through midtown to Bryant Park, where Friedan, Bella Abzug, Gloria Steinem, and other noted feminists fired the crowd with calls for equality.

The strike and similar activities rekindled interest in an equal rights amendment for women. Such an amendment had been on the congressional agenda since 1923, when it was introduced as a way of honoring the seventy-fifth anniversary of the historic Seneca Falls Convention. The equal rights amendment was introduced at every subsequent session of Congress, but not until the 1960s did it gain anything close to the two-thirds majority in each house required for it to be sent to the states for ratification.

The egalitarian ethos of that decade improved the amendment's chances, yet resistance remained. Many women distrusted what they perceived as the elitism of NOW and other feminist organizations, and they resented the message the feminists often appeared to be sending: that motherhood mattered less than careers.

But during the late 1960s and early 1970s the feminist wave continued to rise. Dozens of new organizations joined NOW and broadened the struggle for equality. Admission and hiring practices in education, business, industry, and government came under severe scrutiny and often shriveled beneath the attention. *Ms.* magazine, founded in 1972 by Gloria Steinem, sold a quarter-million copies of the first issue in little over a week. Organized labor, long a conservative bastion of opposition to women's rights, swung around in support of the equal rights amendment.

Congress got the message. In the autumn of 1971 the House approved the amendment, which declared that "equality of rights under the law shall not be denied or abridged by the United States or by any state on account of sex." The Senate seconded the measure the next spring, and the amendment was referred to the states.

Thirty-eight states—three-quarters of the fifty—had to ratify the amendment for it to become law. Twenty-two states signed on within a year. "Ratification by mid-1973 looks probable," *Ms.* magazine happily asserted. The pace subsequently slowed, compelling *Ms.* to postpone the party, but eight more states approved it in the next several months.

Yet the very success of the feminist movement provoked an antifeminist backlash. The growth of political consciousness in some women had been accompanied by an increase in sexual assertiveness in others—and in many of the same women. Friedan's *Feminine Mystique* had to fight for bookshelf space with Helen Gurley Brown's 1962 *Sex and the Single Girl*, which celebrated a lifestyle that could scarcely have been mentioned in public a decade earlier. Certainly single girls had been having sex before the 1960s, although the availability of oral contraceptives now made the practice less chancy and likely more prevalent. (Accurate statistics on sexual behavior have always been hard to come by.) But in the 1960s they—and others, like the married Mrs. Brown—definitely *talked* about sex more than they ever had. Brown's success with *Sex and the Single Girl* won her the editor's job at *Cosmopolitan* magazine, in which she proclaimed that women could have sex and love and material success without bothering about marriage. The "Cosmo girl," the summary of the Brown philosophy, became a subcultural icon, challenging in her own saucy way everything her mother had taught her about women's place in society.

The sudden openness about sex spread into other genres and media. William Masters and Virginia Johnson in 1966 summarized their clinical research on sexuality in *Human Sexual Response*, which became a bestseller despite a scientifically dry style. David Reuben's 1969 *Everything You Always Wanted to Know about Sex (But Were Afraid to Ask)* and Alex Comfort's 1972 *The Joy of Sex* spiced the subject up considerably. Movies portrayed sexuality with far greater candor than before. Where films of the 1940s and 1950s had simply suggested sex, cutting discreetly away at the bedroom door, those of the 1960s and 1970s followed their characters clear into bed. The 1969 *Midnight Cowboy*, starring Jon Voight and Dustin Hoffman, earned an X rating for its explicit portrayal of the misadventures of a male prostitute, and then an Academy Award for best picture.

It also earned the wrath of women—and men—who thought feminism and the new openness about sex had gone entirely too far. Some picketed movies and boycotted bookstores; others mobilized against the equal rights amendment. Phyllis Schlafly's conservative Eagle Forum added STOP ERA to its name, and its spokespersons argued that the equal rights amendment would deprive women of traditional distinctive rights, such as the right to be supported by their husbands and the right to be exempt from military service—besides being an affront to states' rights. The amendment was "a big grab for vast federal power," Schlafly said. "It will take out of the hands of the state legislatures and transfer to Washington the last remaining piece of jurisdiction that the national politicians and bureaucrats haven't yet put their meddling fingers into." Christian conservatives contended that the Bible mandated women's subservience to their husbands and fathers. The religious right also worried that the equal rights amendment would open the door to demands by homosexuals for equal treatment, perhaps including gay marriage.

The Supreme Court unintentionally added a powerful argument—or perhaps just powerful emotions—to the anti-amendment cause. During the nineteenth century most states had adopted laws sharply restricting abortion. Women continued to get pregnant inadvertently (or forcibly, in the case of rape), and they continued to seek abortions, but they had to dodge the law in doing so. The introduction of oral contraceptives in the 1950s fostered greater openness about sexual practices and issues and led to demands for reconsideration of the anti-abortion regime. At the same time, the discovery that thalidomide, a drug widely prescribed to treat the symptoms of morning sickness during pregnancy, could cause severe birth defects prompted women and their partners to seek ways to terminate high-risk pregnancies.

Some states rewrote their laws, allowing abortions in certain instances. Texas was not among them, and in 1970 Norma McCorvey, represented in court under the pseudonym Jane Roe, sued Henry Wade, the district attorney of Dallas County, for the right to have an abortion. McCorvey/Roe claimed to have been gang-raped (years later she changed her story, saying that the pregnancy commenced during a consensual relationship that subsequently failed), and her attorneys asserted that by preventing her from having an abortion, the state of Texas curtailed her constitutional rights. The district court agreed, but Texas appealed and the case went to the Supreme Court.

In 1973 the court ruled, in *Roe v. Wade*, in favor of the plaintiff. The seven-to-two vote struck down the most restrictive laws against abortion. The court declared that during the first trimester of pregnancy a woman might have an abortion for any cause and without any hindrance. States might regulate abortion during the second trimester, while safeguarding the mother's health. They might forbid abortion during the third trimester unless it was necessary to protect the life or health of the mother.

Women's rights advocates hailed the *Roe* decision as a breakthrough for female equality. Women had finally won control of their bodies in the crucial realm of reproduction, they said. But religious and other conservatives condemned the decision as allowing infanticide: the murder of millions of unborn children.

The *Roe* decision would remain controversial well into the twenty-first century, but its immediate impact was to mobilize conservatives against the equal rights amendment. States stopped adding their names to the ranks of the ratifiers, and some previous ratifiers voted to rescind their support. The legality of the rescissions was never tested, for the amendment stalled three states shy of the required thirty-eight. Subsequent efforts to revive it failed.

## 8. IT'S NOT THE CRIME, IT'S THE COVER-UP

The final chapter of the Vietnam War might have played out differently had Richard Nixon been available to direct America's part in it. That he wasn't available owed to his hubris and to the truism that good help is hard to find. The local newspaper of Nixon's adopted hometown carried a story on June 18, 1972, that hinted at the latter problem:

> Five men, one of whom said he is a former employee of the Central Intelligence Agency, were arrested at 2:30 a.m. yesterday in what authorities described as an elaborate plot to bug the offices of the Democratic National Committee here. Three of the men were native-born Cubans and another was said to have trained Cuban exiles for guerrilla

> activity after the 1961 Bay of Pigs invasion. They were surprised at gunpoint by three plain-clothes officers of the metropolitan police department in a sixth-floor office at the plush Watergate, 2600 Virginia Ave., N.W. . . . There was no immediate explanation as to why the five suspects would want to bug the Democratic National Committee offices or whether or not they were working for any other individuals or organizations.

Several reporters were identified as contributing to this *Washington Post* story; two junior staffers—Bob Woodward and Carl Bernstein—would spend the rest of the summer, then the rest of the year, and then the year and a half after that, pursuing those concluding questions: why were the burglars bugging the Watergate, and who were they working for?

What they discovered was a sordid tale that had started in an understandable concern by the Nixon White House regarding leaks of information connected to arms control negotiations with the Soviets. In June 1971 the *New York Times* began publishing parts of a classified Pentagon retrospective on the war in Vietnam. The Pentagon Papers, as the collection came to be called, included nothing that embarrassed Nixon personally; the misjudgments and dissimulations the documents revealed involved the Kennedy and Johnson administrations. But the leak occurred at precisely the moment when Nixon was arranging his China spectacular, which might have been halted in its tracks had any of the parties with reason to object learned about it before Kissinger showed up in Beijing. Nixon ordered an embargo on interviews with the offending newspaper. "Under *no circumstances* is anyone connected with the White House to give any interview to a member of the staff of the *New York Times* without my express permission," the president told chief of staff H. R. Haldeman.

The embargo failed to prevent the continuing publication of the Pentagon Papers, and, more infuriating to Nixon, it failed to prevent a leak of the secret the president was most concerned about: his bottom-line position in the SALT talks with the Soviets. Nixon consequently intensified his counterleak offensive. He gave orders to find, at all costs, the sources of the leaks and to plug them. Nixon's aides established the Special Investigative Unit—affectionately called the Plumbers—which shortly went after Daniel Ellsberg, the former Pentagon official thought to be behind the release of the Pentagon

Papers. "I did not care about any reasons or excuses," Nixon later explained, without remorse. "I wanted someone to light a fire under the FBI in its investigation of Ellsberg. . . . I felt that his views had to be discredited. I urged that we find out everything we could about his background, his motives, and his co-conspirators, if they existed."

The Plumbers burgled the office of Ellsberg's psychiatrist, hoping to find the discrediting dirt the president demanded. They didn't find any dirt, but neither did they get caught, and their ability to manage the caper encouraged them to expand their activities. Nixon, to an even greater degree than most ambitious public figures, divided the world into friends and enemies. His latter category was capacious, and again exaggerating a common failing among political leaders, he treated his political enemies as enemies of the state. Accordingly the Plumbers, as the election year 1972 unfolded, went to work against the president's Democratic rivals, seeking information not about security leaks but about Democratic strategy. It was on one such job that the five men were arrested at the Democratic National Committee headquarters at the Watergate in June 1972.

Had Nixon stepped forthrightly in front of the *Washington Post* story, accepted responsibility for the actions of the Plumbers, and lopped off a few heads among the White House staff, the Watergate tale might have been a one-week wonder. But forthrightness wasn't in Nixon's nature, and rather than revealing information, he did his best to cover it up. Oddly, he knew better. "If you cover up, you're going to get caught," he told aide John Ehrlichman. Yet he couldn't help himself. Even while warning Ehrlichman about the dangers of a cover-up, he told Haldeman to keep a lid on things. "Play it tough," he said. "That's the way they play it, and that's the way we're going to play it." White House spokesman Ron Ziegler publicly dismissed the Watergate break-in as a "third-rate burglary attempt" that had nothing to do with the president.

The dike held long enough for Nixon to be reelected. The Democrats were only marginally more organized in 1972 than they had been in 1968, and in one crucial respect they were less organized. The Democrats had written new rules in the wake of the 1968 fiasco that were designed to make the party more accommodating of women, minorities, and youth. The aim was to bring the dissidents inside the convention hall so they wouldn't be demonstrating outside. The strategy worked too well. The dissidents came in, and in doing so they guaranteed the nomination of a candidate who hadn't a prayer of carrying the country. George McGovern was a decorated bomber pilot from World War II; he had earned a doctorate in American history before representing South Dakota in the House and, since 1963, the Senate. He had opposed the Vietnam War early and still did. Had the election been about the war, he might have stood a chance. But Nixon's Vietnamization strategy, while doing little for South Vietnam, worked much better in America; most Americans believed the war was ending, and their belief appeared confirmed when Kissinger announced, just days before the election: "Peace is at hand."

McGovern's other baggage guaranteed not simply defeat but a Democratic disaster. The liberals who nominated him hadn't noticed that the 1960s were over, and they placed the candidate on a platform celebrating "the right to be different" and detailing demands on behalf of women, children, poor people, American Indians, the physically disabled, the mentally retarded, and the elderly. All this suited the rainbow coalition that now controlled the party, but it said little—at least, little that was intelligible or appealing—to the broad mass of American voters. Republicans tagged McGovern as the candidate of "acid, amnesty, and abortion," and the label stuck. Blue-collar workers defected from the Democrats by the millions; Southern whites continued their migration to the Republicans. The result on election day was the worst shellacking in Democratic history. McGovern received a pitiful 37 percent of the vote and carried a single state, Massachusetts, along with the unshakably Democratic enclave of Washington, D.C.

Nixon didn't enjoy the victory for long. In January 1973 the Watergate burglars were convicted. The judge in the case, John Sirica, had become convinced there was more to their story than they were telling, and he threatened to sentence them to the maximum time allowable under the law. One of the five, James McCord, started to talk. As he did, the cover-up began to unravel. A grand jury was empaneled, and the Democratic-controlled Senate commenced an investigation. White House counsel John Dean was implicated and fired. Nixon next threw Haldeman and Ehrlichman overboard. Nixon's attorney general, Richard Kleindienst, resigned under pressure.

The Senate committee, headed by Sam Ervin of North Carolina, conducted hearings that lasted into the summer of 1973. Televised testimony by McCord, Dean, and other witnesses riveted national audiences. But the biggest bombshell was a July remark by Alexander Butterfield, an erstwhile assistant to Haldeman, that Nixon had taped the conversations of visitors to the Oval Office. "The president is very history-oriented and history-conscious," Butterfield explained; the tapes were to help him write his memoirs.

The Senate committee naturally sought to acquire the tapes, which became the focus of bitter wrangling with the White House. Nixon clung to the recordings, claiming executive privilege—the right of the executive branch, under America's system of separated powers, to be free from legislative oversight. The wrangling laid waste to the Justice Department when Nixon ordered Elliot Richardson, the attorney general who replaced Kleindienst, to fire Archibald Cox, the special prosecutor Nixon had reluctantly named to probe the administration's wrongdoings. Cox wanted the tapes, too, and Nixon decided he had to go. But Richardson refused to fire Cox, and Nixon forced him out. Then Richardson's deputy, William Ruckelshaus, likewise refused to fire Cox, and he too quit. Robert Bork, the next in line, followed Nixon's order and fired Cox, but the "Saturday Night Massacre," as the affair came to be called, created such a stir that Nixon felt obliged to turn over some of the tapes.

One tape, of a conversation between Nixon and Haldeman only days after the Watergate break-in, contained a mysterious eighteen-minute gap. Rose Mary Woods, Nixon's secretary, loyally asserted that she must have inadvertently erased that portion of the tape while transcribing it. Curious reporters asked her to reproduce the motions required to effect the erasure; the contortions she demonstrated cast serious doubt over any accidental explanation.

The rising waters grew murkier in the autumn of 1973 amid allegations that Spiro Agnew, Nixon's vice president, had taken bribes from contractors while governor of Maryland and perhaps even while vice president. The case was strong enough that Agnew pleaded no contest and resigned the vice presidency. Nixon's own finances, newly scrutinized, displayed irregularities involving tax returns and payments. Nixon defended himself vigorously but ineptly. "I am not a crook," he declared, making people think maybe he was.

By early 1974 the battle over Watergate was all about the tapes. Nixon conducted a fighting retreat, surrendering transcripts while holding on to the remaining tapes more stubbornly than ever. The transcripts revealed a president with an extremely foul mouth. The phrase "expletive deleted" appeared thousands of times, where four-letter words had been. "The president has nothing to hide," Nixon said, after it had become obvious he had a great deal to hide.

During the summer of 1974 the Supreme Court stepped in. The justices unanimously ruled that in a criminal matter such as Watergate had patently become, executive privilege did not apply. The president must hand over the tapes.

On the same day the House Judiciary Committee stepped up proceedings pointing toward impeachment. Obstruction of justice was the central charge; the committee had approved one article of impeachment and was weighing four more. Once the committee completed its work, the impeachment article or articles would go to the full House for a vote. If the House approved, the Senate would hold a trial of the president.

Between the unanimous decision of the Supreme Court and the impending impeachment, Nixon was cornered. The tapes he was required to release made his participation in the cover-up undeniable. A recording from June 23, 1972—soon called the "smoking gun" tape—caught Nixon ordering the CIA to block the FBI's investigation of the Watergate affair. Now even Nixon's supporters realized the game was up. "I just don't see how we can survive this one," Alexander Haig, Haldeman's replacement as chief of staff, told Nixon. Barry Goldwater had stuck by the president this far; the Arizona Republican suddenly felt a fool. "The best thing he can do for the country is to get the hell out of the White House, and get out this afternoon," Goldwater told colleagues in the Senate.

Nixon finally understood. On August 9, 1974, he resigned. "I have never been a quitter," he declared in his final address to the nation. "To leave office before my term is completed is abhorrent to every instinct in my body." But having lost the support a president required to govern, he must resign. He offered no apology and scant explanation. "If some of my judgments were wrong—and some were wrong—they were made in what I believed at the time to be the best interest of the nation."

As Nixon stepped off the stage, Gerald Ford, Spiro Agnew's appointed replacement, stepped on. "My fellow Americans," Ford proclaimed in his first address as president, "our long national nightmare is over." Perhaps Ford knew more than he was willing to share at that moment, for many people thought the nightmare was merely shifting jurisdictions. Nixon's resignation precluded impeachment, but it didn't bar indictment. Obstruction of justice was obstruction of justice, whether committed by a president or by a private citizen. John Dean had just been sentenced to one to four years in prison for his role in the cover-up; several lesser figures were already behind bars. Simple fairness suggested that the head of the cabal should do time too.

Jerry Ford thought otherwise. The prospect of a pardon had come up before, and Ford had been quick to shoot it down, saying he didn't think the public would tolerate such a short-circuiting of the legal process. But that was before he became president. His thinking apparently changed, for on September 8 he surprised the country by granting a "full, free, and absolute pardon" to Nixon for anything the former president might have done wrong.

The honeymoon Ford had enjoyed since taking office ended that day. His approval ratings plunged by a third; an avalanche of angry letters buried the White House mail room. Editors thundered against the pardon. People who didn't know Ford alleged a backroom deal: Nixon had let Ford into the Oval Office, and Ford kept Nixon out of prison.

Most of those who did know Ford took him at his word. Any Nixon prosecution would take years, Ford said. "During this long period of delay and potential litigation, ugly passions would again be aroused. . . . Our people would again be polarized in their opinions. . . . The credibility of our free institutions of government would again be challenged at home and abroad." A pardon would prevent such an outcome and allow the country to move forward. Ford understood the political costs of his decision, but he was willing to accept them. "I cannot rely upon public opinion polls to tell me what is right," he said. "Right makes might."

# 8 | Days of Malaise

## 1974–1979

### 1. DIRTY LAUNDRY AND FAMILY JEWELS

Ford's pardon of Nixon spared the country the sight of a former president in the dock, but it left many questions unanswered. Foremost was: What *else* had Nixon and his henchmen been up to? Quite a lot, as it turned out, including use of the Internal Revenue Service to harass enemies, of the CIA to destabilize governments abroad, and of the FBI to spy on and intimidate domestic dissidents. But it also turned out that Nixon didn't invent most of the shenanigans the government committed during his tenure. The agencies involved had been crossing the line for years.

Though much of the investigation of Nixon was partisan, some was principled, and the principled part produced an unflattering portrait of the presidents as far back as Eisenhower. The Pentagon Papers, which had prompted the measures that led to Nixon's downfall, described a Vietnam policy that had been rife with deception from the beginning. American troops had been engaged in combat operations while American voters were being assured that they were simply advisers. The Tonkin Gulf incident was not what Congress had been told it was. Plans to escalate the war long antedated what Johnson admitted. The president knew considerably before Tet that things weren't going well.

The Pentagon Papers revealed merely the narrow opening of the credibility gap. Congressional investigators subpoenaed witnesses who testified that the CIA had been engaged in all sorts of unsavory activities abroad. The most shocking involved efforts to assassinate foreign leaders. In 1959 Allen Dulles, Eisenhower's intelligence director, ordered operatives to examine how Fidel Castro might be eliminated. Dulles's people initially expressed skepticism, contending that Castro's death might simply hand control of Cuba to Fidel's brother Raul and Che Guevara, who were likely to be even more radical than Fidel. But after the Bay of Pigs fiasco embarrassed Kennedy, the White House insisted that the assassination planning resume. Apparently on the assumption that nobody does contract killing like the Mafia, CIA agents met with mobsters to set up a hit on Castro. Meanwhile agency chemists concocted devices worthy of James Bond: exploding seashells to be planted on reefs where Castro liked to scuba dive, powders that would cause his famous beard to fall out.

Nothing came of the assassination efforts against Castro—except confirmation, in the hyperactive minds of the conspiracy theorists who refused to believe that Lee Harvey Oswald acted alone, of a Cuban connection to the shooting of Kennedy. Similar efforts in other countries ended better, so to speak. When Belgium granted independence to the Congo in 1960, various locals struggled for primacy. One of the contenders was Patrice Lumumba, a charismatic firebrand with a soft spot for communism. Eisenhower tacitly ordered the CIA to take action against Lumumba. The agency's scientists went to work again, devising biological weapons that would incapacitate or kill him. The agency's station chief in Leopoldville (later Kinshasa) kept a close watch on Lumumba's home, with an eye toward when he might simply be shot. But Lumumba never went out. "Target has not left building in several weeks," the station chief reported back to headquarters.

Lying low didn't save Lumumba. He did leave the building a short while later and was kidnapped by his Congolese enemies, who killed him on their own near Elisabethville (Lubumbashi), without explicit American help. The CIA's man in Elisabethville expressed satisfaction at the result but regret that he hadn't participated. "Thanks for Patrice," he wired Washington. "If we had known he was coming we would have baked a snake."

The CIA wasn't the only agency chagrined by the release of its backstory. (Not all of which, in fact, was released. Agency officials clung tightly to what they called the "family jewels": details of operations that were even more sensitive than those revealed. These would be released decades later, by which time the news was so old—and Americans so jaded regarding their government's motives—that the release prompted little finger-pointing or soul-searching.) The FBI proved to have similar dark secrets in its past. During the 1950s the bureau infiltrated the American Communist party so thoroughly that it might have staged a takeover of the party had J. Edgar Hoover, the bureau's director, given the word. During the 1960s the FBI focused its surveillance and harassment on American civil rights leaders and antiwar activists. Hoover became convinced that the civil rights movement was aided and abetted by communists, if it wasn't an outright communist plot. William Sullivan, Hoover's assistant director, aimed to please his chief when he described Martin Luther King as "the most dangerous Negro of the future in this Nation from the standpoint of communism, the Negro, and national security." The communists had their eye not only on King but on the whole race, Sullivan said. "Nineteen million Negroes constitute the greatest single racial target of the Communist Party U.S.A. This is a somber reality we must never lose sight of."

The bureau never lost sight of King. Agents tapped his phone, trailed him physically, investigated his associates, and compiled a massive dossier that detailed all they found. "Martin Luther King is growing in stature daily and is the leader among leaders of the Negro movement," an FBI report asserted, accurately. The report continued, more tendentiously: "Communist party officials visualize the possibility of creating a situation whereby it could be said that, as the Communist party goes, so goes Martin Luther King, and so also goes the Negro movement in the United States."

To avert this outcome, the bureau embarked on an effort to destroy King. FBI wiretaps revealed that King had strayed from strict observance of his marital vows. Bureau officials suggested employing his indiscretions against him. "Although King is a minister, we have already developed information concerning weaknesses in his character which are of such a nature as to make him unfit to serve as a minister of the gospel," an FBI memo explained. A six-point program targeting King concluded: "We will, at the proper time when it can be done without embarrassment to the Bureau, expose King as an immoral opportunist who is not a sincere person but is exploiting the racial situation for personal gain." William Sullivan emphasized this objective in his notes of the meeting at which the anti-King agenda was presented:

"We will continue to give this case priority attention at both the Seat of Government"—Washington—"and in the field and will expose King for the clerical fraud and Marxist he is at the first opportunity."

The campaign took more concrete form when the bureau transcribed the wiretap tapes of King's conversations and anonymously sent him an edited version as a warning. "King, look into your heart," the unsigned cover letter commanded. "You know you are a complete fraud and a great liability to all of us Negroes. White people in this country have enough frauds of their own, but I am sure they don't have one at this time that is anywhere near your equal. . . . King, like all frauds, your end is approaching. . . . There is only one thing left for you to do. You know what it is. . . . There is but one way out for you. You better take it before your filthy, abnormal, fraudulent self is bared to the nation."

When the FBI's campaign against King became known in the mid-1970s, questions immediately arose as to whether the bureau had anything to do with his assassination. No direct evidence was adduced that it did, but suspicions lingered that the bureau at least contributed to the climate that pushed James Earl Ray from bigotry to murder.

The FBI's anti-King campaign was part of a larger program called COINTELPRO (Counter Intelligence Program) that dated from the 1950s and targeted perceived agitators of all kinds. The Socialist Workers party loomed large on the COINTELPRO radar screen, as did the SDS, the Black Panthers, the Nation of Islam, the Ku Klux Klan, and the American Indian Movement. At one time or another almost every important antiwar leader was considered a legitimate target for investigation and harassment.

The CIA got in on the domestic disruption as well. Something called CHAOS was the CIA's counterpart to the FBI's COINTELPRO, but it differed in having primarily outward-looking motivations—in determining the extent to which foreign intelligence services might have infiltrated domestic dissident groups—and in being illegal in substance and not merely in tactics. The CIA's charter explicitly forbade domestic intelligence operations. Director Richard Helms was fully aware that the agency had overstepped. "This is an area not within the charter of this Agency," Helms wrote confidentially, regarding an agency examination of America's "restless youth." Helms continued: "I need not emphasize how extremely sensitive this makes this paper.

Should anyone learn of its existence, it would prove most embarrassing for all concerned."

Lots of people learned of the paper's existence when the Senate committee investigating the domestic intelligence operations published its final report in 1976. And it indeed proved most embarrassing. The Church committee, as the Senate group was called, after chairman Frank Church of Idaho, issued a scathing summary of what the FBI, CIA, and other federal agencies had been up to. "The Government has often undertaken the secret surveillance of citizens on the basis of their political beliefs, even when those beliefs posed no threat of violence or illegal acts on behalf of a hostile foreign power," the committee asserted.

> The Government, operating primarily through secret informants, but also using other intrusive techniques such as wiretaps, microphone "bugs," surreptitious mail openings, and break-ins, has swept in vast amounts of information about the personal lives, views, and associations of American citizens. . . . Groups and individuals have been harassed and disrupted because of their political views and their lifestyles. . . . Unsavory and vicious tactics have been employed—including anonymous attempts to break up marriages, disrupt meetings, ostracize persons from their professions, and provoke target groups into rivalries that might result in deaths.

By this time such revelations no longer possessed the ability to shock. After Vietnam and Watergate, Americans were willing to believe almost anything dastardly about their government. But it was precisely this unshockability that indicated how demoralized American democracy had become. John Kennedy, at his inauguration, had urged Americans to ask not what their country could do for them but what they could do for their country; and Americans had thrilled at the high-mindedness of the summons. Lyndon Johnson had conjured an image of a Great Society in the minds of Americans, who proceeded to support its enactment in legislation. Ten years later this sort of idealism seemed woefully naïve. Kennedy and Johnson had been conniving behind their idealism, and Richard Nixon, who lacked even the facade of idealism, had made matters worse. If Americans grew cynical regarding their leaders—and regarding the entire political enterprise—they did so with reason.

## 2. RUNNING ON EMPTY

A page of world history unrelated to American politics began to turn amid the extended Watergate crisis, but distracted Americans could have been forgiven for not noticing. In any event, it was the kind of thing that was hard to summarize in a headline or a television-news teaser. Yet before the turning ended, Americans would have difficulty noticing anything else.

The postwar order of international economics had been based on American industrial supremacy, American financial leadership, and American energy independence. American factories produced as much, at the war's end, as the factories of the rest of the world combined. The American dollar underpinned the Bretton Woods bargain by which other countries fixed their currencies to the dollar and Washington fixed the dollar to gold. America's oil fields provided Americans all the gasoline, diesel, and heating fuel they required and enough extra to send fleets of brimming tankers abroad.

But the system began to erode almost at once. American factories continued to churn out automobiles and washing machines, but the factories of other countries started doing so too. America's industrial lead was, in substantial portion, a war-induced anomaly. Once Britain, France, and Germany recovered from the war, with the help of the American Marshall Plan, their share of world production ate into America's. Japan was slower to challenge the United States in the world markets, mostly because the Japanese economy had been less developed before the war. But American policy encouraged Japan's revival, as it encouraged the revival of Europe, and for the same reasons: prosperous partners made good customers for American products, and happy allies were resistant to communist propaganda. A principal reason the Truman and Eisenhower administrations worried about Southeast Asia—to the point of committing the United States to the defense of Vietnam—was that access to Southeast Asia was considered essential to the economic revival of Japan.

The result of the European and Japanese recovery was that by the late 1960s the United States no longer dictated the course of the world economy.

The United States still enjoyed a trade surplus with the rest of the world—meaning that it sold more goods and services to other countries than they sold to the United States—but the surplus was declining, and with certain countries the trade balance had slipped into deficit. Germany, for example, sold more to the United States than it purchased. The result was that Germany and other countries held larger quantities of dollars than they had been accustomed to holding, and more than they wanted. Their distaste for the dollar was exacerbated by inflation in the United States, which eroded the greenback's purchasing power. The inflation was, in turn, the consequence of record spending by the American government on the war in Vietnam and Johnson's Great Society, and the loose-money policies that, in the absence of counterbalancing increases in taxes, were required to sustain the spending.

Under the Bretton Woods system, dollars held by other countries could be exchanged for gold. Other countries did exchange their dollars during the late 1960s, until the American gold began to run out. The Bretton Woods system began to tremble, and it might have crashed to earth—perhaps bringing destruction comparable to that of the last great global crash, in the early 1930s—had Nixon not suspended gold payments in August 1971. Nixon's move bought enough time for the finance ministers of the major powers to meet at Washington in December 1971 and hammer out a blueprint for Bretton Woods' successor.

The new order was less an order than a managed disorder. No longer would the dollar be fixed in value against other currencies, and no longer would the dollar be convertible to gold. The new regime allowed currencies to rise or fall in value against one another and against gold, which became merely another commodity. The variable exchange rates would reflect global demand for the different currencies: if individuals and (primarily) institutions wanted German marks or Japanese yen, the value of those currencies would rise relative to other currencies.

Most economists liked the new model, which applied the classical laws of supply and demand to financial markets. But by empowering the financial markets, the system of floating currencies disempowered policymakers—especially American policymakers. No longer could they dictate the course of the world economy. Bankers and speculators now had as much clout in international finance as presidents and treasury secretaries. The American economy remained the largest and most powerful in the world, but the dollar was now merely one currency among several, and it was subject to the same insults and vicissitudes as the rest.

With America's industrial supremacy eroded and its financial hegemony compromised, the third pillar of the postwar order—America's energy independence—came under increasing strain. The century after the 1859 discovery of oil in western Pennsylvania had witnessed ever-growing American production, with major discoveries occurring every few decades. In 1945 the United States produced substantially more oil than all other countries together. American consumption of oil and its derivatives increased as well, but until the centennial of Edwin Drake's discovery the production line on energy graphs remained well above the consumption line.

This changed during the 1960s and early 1970s. American consumption continued to climb: the number of cars Americans drove more than doubled between 1950 and 1970. American production meanwhile peaked—and then began to tail off. In 1970 American wells produced eleven million barrels a day, the most they would ever produce. The Texas Railroad Commission, which for decades had served as a de facto regulator of the American oil industry (by virtue of the dominant role of Texas oil fields), in 1971 authorized production at 100 percent of capacity for the first time since World War II. "We feel this to be an historic occasion," the chairman of the commission declared. "Damned historic. And a sad one. Texas oil fields have been like a reliable old warrior that could rise to the task when needed. That old warrior can't rise anymore."

New warriors—foreign ones—took Texas's place. The loss of the spare capacity in the United States increased American exposure to the influence of foreign producers, the most important of whom linked arms in the early 1960s to form the Organization of the Petroleum Exporting Countries. OPEC members, including Saudi Arabia, Iran, Iraq, Venezuela, Kuwait, and eventually several other producing states, compared notes about technology, markets, and how to deal with Western oil companies, but mostly they pondered how to raise prices for the crude they pumped. The narrowing gap between production and consumption gave them an opportunity.

So did an event that had little directly to do with oil but much indirectly. The existence of Israel continued to irk the Arabs of the Middle East; Egypt's president Nasser regularly threatened Israel with war, until the Israelis decided to teach Nasser a lesson. In June 1967 they struck Egypt by surprise and delivered a devastating blow to Egypt's army, its air force, its territory, and its pride. The Six Day War, as the conflict was called (alternatively the June War), ended with Israel occupying large swaths of Egyptian territory, including the Sinai Peninsula and the Gaza Strip. More portentously, Israel occupied the eastern part of Jerusalem and the West Bank of the Jordan River, both of which had been governed by Jordan. The United States had no formal part in the war, but as Israel's unofficial ally, America endured angry criticism from the Arabs as the principal abettor of Israeli policies.

For six years the Egyptians licked their wounds. In October 1973 they returned Israel's gesture of a surprise attack, and on the Jewish holy day of Yom Kippur they launched the fourth war of the Arab-Israeli conflict. The Yom Kippur, or October, War stunned the Israelis, who had assessed the balance of forces between themselves and the Egyptians, determined that they held a decisive advantage, and concluded that Cairo would never be crazy enough to start a war it knew it must lose. The surprise enabled the Egyptians to deliver stinging blows against Israel, which turned in alarm to the United States for material reinforcements. The Nixon administration responded positively, helping rescue Israel but terminating all semblance of evenhandedness between the Arabs and the Israelis.

The outbreak of a war typically drives commodity prices higher, by threatening or disrupting supply and distribution networks. A war's effect on oil prices is magnified by the strategic importance of oil, which fuels the instruments of modern war. A Middle Eastern war, situated amid or adjacent to the most important single oil region on earth, magnifies the effect still further.

The Arab members of OPEC added a final magnifying element. As a political statement, they announced an embargo of oil shipments to the United States. The announcement flabbergasted industry experts. "The possibility of an embargo didn't even enter my mind," one oil company executive remarked. The timing couldn't have been worse from the perspective of the American government. The day the Arabs commenced the embargo was the same day Nixon decimated the leadership of the Justice Department in the Saturday Night Massacre. "All hell has broken loose," Al Haig muttered grimly from the White House.

Combined with the embargo was a series of cutbacks in OPEC production. These, amid the war, had the effect of jolting prices upward. From the low three-dollar range, where the price had hovered for more than a decade, the price leaped to five dollars per barrel, then ten dollars. Panic hit the spot market, where buyers bid against one another for quick delivery. Fifteen dollars was offered and accepted, then seventeen.

The rise in crude prices fueled spikes in the pump price of American gasoline. Motorists watched as prices rose before their eyes—literally. Long lines developed at gas stations, where drivers sat for hours; station owners received regular updates from their suppliers on wholesale price increases, and upon putting down their phones they marched out to change the prices on their signs and pumps. From 30 cents a gallon the price quadrupled to $1.20. Suppliers rationed deliveries to the stations, which often sold their daily allotments long before regular closing time. Signs declaring "Sorry, No Gas Today" popped up at stations all over the country. Lest they lose out, motorists started getting in line hours before the stations opened in the morning; many drivers slept in their vehicles. The crisis became self-reinforcing: as drivers feared being caught short, they insisted on topping off their tanks as soon as their gauges dipped below the three-quarter mark. This practice increased the demand and strained supplies still further.

Fights broke out in gas lines. Cab operators, delivery personnel, sales representatives, and others who drove for a living pleaded for special consideration, generally to little avail, although some dealers did give preference to their regular customers over newcomers. In Oregon, where supplies were particularly tight for reasons no one could adequately explain, stations adopted a routine whereby cars whose license numbers ended in even digits could buy gas on even-numbered dates, and cars with odd numbers on odd dates. The federal government lowered the speed limit on interstate highways from 70 miles per hour to 55 to conserve fuel.

If anything epitomized the waning of America's economic supremacy, it was the gas lines and the lower speed limit. Gas shortages were un-American, something people in other countries endured but not citizens of the United States. And Americans were used to being in a hurry and driving fast. The shortages didn't persist; the Arab producers lifted their embargo in March 1974, and the lines and rationing disappeared. But the new structure of supply and demand remained, and so did the high prices and lower speed limits.

E. F. Schumacher, who for years had preached the virtues of a more modest lifestyle, had the perspicacity or good luck to publish a manifesto on his subject just before the oil shock hit. His book was titled *Small Is Beautiful*, and it suggested that Americans would be happier and more secure consuming fewer natural resources. The oil crunch made him seem a prophet. "The party is over," Schumacher declared, and millions of Americans nodded in sad agreement.

## 3. A FORD, NOT A LINCOLN; A CARTER, NOT A FORD

"At the end of three months, the Ford administration will either have the smell of life or the smell of death," Donald Rumsfeld, Ford's chief of staff, predicted upon his boss's accession. "If it's the smell of death, this White House is going to be torn to pieces by the press, by the Democrats, even by other Republicans."

The Nixon pardon damaged Ford, but perhaps not as much as the economy. The soaring price of oil, atop the lingering costs of the Vietnam War and the Great Society, created a witches' brew of economic ills. Inflation rose to unprecedented levels, sticking in double digits for the first time in living memory. Inflation historically had signaled excessive demand: an economy experiencing too much of a good thing. In this case the inflation was accompanied by high and rising unemployment, which presented both a puzzle for the economists and a dilemma for the policymakers. A basic tool of the economists was the Phillips curve, which posited a tradeoff between inflation and unemployment: as inflation rose, unemployment fell, and vice versa. But the American economy seemed to have careened right off the curve into uncharted territory. The dilemma for the policymakers was that the standard approach to inflation was to chill the economy, chiefly by raising taxes or interest rates; this strategy wasn't especially painful when unemployment was low, as it generally had been during previous inflationary periods, but with unemployment already high, chilling the economy would be very painful, as even more people would be thrown out of work.

Ford first tried to tackle inflation. The White House concocted a campaign to "Whip Inflation Now," and the president, proudly wearing a WIN button, called on Americans to spend less and save more. To facilitate—or force—compliance, he proposed a $5 billion tax hike.

His timing couldn't have been worse. No sooner had he unveiled the new plan than unemployment shot even higher, to an alarming 6.5 percent. Some pundit coined a term to describe the simultaneous inflation and stagnation—"stagflation"—and the label caught on. Ford, a football standout in college, quickly reversed field and proposed tax cuts in place of the tax hike he had just recommended. Had the reversal succeeded, he would have been cheered, but it didn't. Inflation stubbornly stayed in double digits, and unemployment kept rising to nearly 9 percent. Ford simply looked inept.

It didn't help matters that he fell while skiing and bumped his head exiting Air Force One. Late-night comics created a caricature of a bumbler, and as often happens in American politics, the caricature became the reality. It was Ford's misfortune that NBC debuted a new comedy show during just this period. *Saturday Night Live* included strong doses of political satire, and Ford was a target too tempting for Chevy Chase, the show's first star, to resist.

Yet Ford got one back. At an annual dinner of radio and television correspondents, when presidents were expected to poke fun at themselves, Ford consented to share the rostrum with Chase. The comedian reprised his Ford stumbles before giving way to the president, who congratulated him with a straight face: "Mr. Chevy Chase, you are a very, very funny suburb." The reporters, some of whom lived in that tony Maryland enclave, roared with laughter.

Ford's plight was Jimmy Carter's opportunity. The former Georgia governor had been running for president since 1974, yet he was sufficiently unknown that contestants on the television quiz show *What's My Line?* required seven questions (out of a possible ten) to identify him. His competence was rarely questioned—he often seemed a walking compendium of detailed information on matters important to public officials—but his charisma was less obvious, for despite a toothy grin and a twinkle in his eye, he could come across as coldly calculating. His principal qualification for the presidency was that he hadn't been anywhere near Washington during the years of Vietnam, Watergate, and the other blunders of still-painful memory. He didn't exactly trumpet his Christian morality, but neither did he hide it. Only a few years earlier he would have seemed excessively pious, but the code of Sunday school, which Carter still regularly taught, appeared to many Americans to be just what the country needed.

Carter was canny too. He appreciated how the presidency of Lyndon Johnson had broken the prohibition against Southern presidents. He knew that the South was sliding toward the Republican party, but he guessed that sufficient loyalty to the Democrats persisted that a moderate Southern Democrat might hold enough states to be viable in the country at large. He captured the Democratic nomination by stealth, organizing early and campaigning with quiet efficiency in every state that had a caucus or a primary. He knocked off his Democratic rivals one by one, and before he had won a national reputation he bagged the delegates he needed to carry the convention.

He faced Ford in the general election. Ford's nomination was no sure thing, as the president had to beat back a stiff challenge from Ronald Reagan. The former California governor, the darling of conservatives who judged Ford too centrist, defeated Ford in some key primaries. But the president played the incumbent card, wooing and winning uncommitted delegates and ultimately capturing the Republican nomination.

Carter commenced the fall season with a large lead that Ford gradually narrowed. By November the race was a toss-up. Carter won but not by much. His popular margin was less than a million votes of eighty million cast. He carried every Southern state but Virginia and split the Midwest with Ford; the two regions provided the bulk of Carter's 297 electoral votes, against Ford's 240.

## 4. BEYOND CONTAINMENT

"The American dream endures," Carter asserted in his inaugural address. But it had changed. "We have learned that more is not necessarily better, that even our great nation has its recognized limits, and that we can neither answer all questions nor solve all problems." Carter promised to remember America's fundamental values at home and to promote them abroad. "We will not behave in foreign places so as to violate our rules and standards here at home, for we know that the trust which our nation earns is essential to our strength." In a first for a president, Carter promised to make foreign governments' treatment of their own citizens a basis for American diplomacy. "Our moral sense dictates a clear-cut preference for those societies which share with us an abiding respect for individual human rights."

This last point became a touchstone of Carter's foreign policy. He elaborated on the new approach in a widely noted address at Notre Dame. "I believe we can have a foreign policy that is democratic, that is based on fundamental values, and that uses power and influence, which we have, for humane purposes," the president said. "Because we know that democracy works, we can reject the arguments of those rulers who deny human rights to their people." Without uttering the word "containment," Carter distanced himself from the policy that had guided American diplomacy during the Cold War.

> Being confident of our own future, we are now free of that inordinate fear of communism which once led us to embrace any dictator who joined us in that fear. I'm glad that that's being changed. For too many years, we've been willing to adopt the flawed and erroneous principles and tactics of our adversaries, sometimes abandoning our own values for theirs. We've fought fire with fire, never thinking that fire is better quenched with water. This approach failed, with Vietnam the best example of its intellectual and moral poverty. But through failure we have now found our way back to our own principles and values, and we have regained our lost confidence.

So Carter hoped. And so he acted. He established a special office in the State Department for monitoring human rights, and he named as its director Patricia Derian, a veteran of the civil rights struggle in the South. He commenced a correspondence with Andrei Sakharov, the most famous human rights activist in the Soviet Union. "You may rest assured that the American people and our government will continue our firm commitment to promote respect for human rights," he promised Sakharov. He successfully urged Congress to make human rights an important criterion in the distribution of American aid. On his own authority he cut back or canceled aid to repressive regimes in Argentina, Chile, and Nicaragua. He imposed trade sanctions against the white supremacist government of Rhodesia (later Zimbabwe) and against the brutal dictatorship of Idi Amin in Uganda. He halted sales of weapons and police equipment to the apartheid government of South Africa. He warned the authoritarian governments of American allies Iran,

South Korea, and the Philippines to lighten up lest they incur similar penalties.

As part of his rejection of the Cold War model of American diplomacy, he appointed Andrew Young to be American ambassador to the United Nations. Young, a former assistant to Martin Luther King, contended that the East-West framework of the Cold War had been superseded by the North-South structure so evident in the UN General Assembly, where nations of the Third World had long criticized American leaders for ignoring the poverty, disease, and underdevelopment that mattered far more to most Asians, Africans, and Latin Americans than the squabble between the superpowers. Like Carter, Young asserted that the status quo thinking of the Cold War had lost America crucial support abroad. "We need not fear change if we build into it more equity and more participation," he said. "Indeed, fear of social change is the thing we need to fear the most. If we are afraid of it and try to preserve that which is eroding beneath our feet, we will fail."

Carter simultaneously emphasized arms control. The SALT I accords of the Nixon administration had been succeeded by an interim agreement signed at Vladivostok in 1974 by Ford and Leonid Brezhnev. Carter extended the disarmament process, aiming for substantial reductions in the superpower arsenals. The Russians reacted with suspicion, assuming that the American calls for reductions must conceal a trick. But eventually they concluded that the new man in the White House was sincere, and in 1979 Carter and Brezhnev met in Vienna and put their names to the SALT II treaty.

The president's greatest diplomatic triumph involved the most vexatious dispute on earth. Carter approached the Arab-Israeli conflict with the deep interest of a lifelong student of the Bible and the determination of an ambitious public figure who had never yet failed to achieve something he set his heart on. His timing was fortunate. Egypt, the most populous of the Arab states and till now the foremost antagonist of Israel, had regained its self-respect in the 1973 war, which ended in an Israeli victory but only, the Egyptians told themselves, because the United States came to Israel's rescue. Anwar Sadat, the Egyptian president, concluded after the war that eternal enmity against Israel would hinder Egypt's progress, and he was ready to talk peace.

Menachem Begin, the Israeli prime minister, was initially skeptical. Begin, a native Pole who had lost much of his family in Hitler's Holocaust, had been a leader of the most militant anti-British, anti-Palestinian wing of the Zionist movement in the years before Israel's birth; since then he had urged a harsh policy against the Arabs and anyone who challenged Israel's security.

Carter knew that Begin wouldn't come easily to the peace table, but the president guessed that if Begin could be won over, his hard-line reputation would make selling a peace pact to the Israeli people much easier. Even after the downfall of Richard Nixon, it was conventional wisdom among observers of American foreign policy that only a person with the anticommunist track record of Nixon could have pulled off the opening to China; Carter hoped that Begin would be to Egypt what Nixon had been to China.

In September 1978 Carter brought Sadat and Begin to Camp David, the presidential retreat in the Maryland mountains, for a three-day conference that stretched to nearly two weeks. On several occasions the talks ground to a halt; at one point Begin packed his bags and prepared to leave. But each time, Carter coaxed the principals to resume discussions—albeit, by the end, through him, after Begin and Sadat refused to speak to each other. His determination was rewarded. Sadat finally agreed to sign a peace treaty with Israel, making Egypt the first Arab state to recognize that country's legitimacy; and Begin consented to return the Sinai to Egypt. Carter sealed the deal with promises of large amounts of American aid to both Egypt and Israel.

The Camp David accord by no means terminated the Arab-Israeli dispute. The future of the occupied West Bank and Gaza Strip, and the larger question of an independent state for the Palestinian residents of those territories, remained unresolved. But by fostering normal relations between Israel and Egypt, Carter did more for Middle Eastern peace than any president before him—and, it turned out, more than any president after.

## 5. NEITHER CONFIDENCE . . .

Carter could have been forgiven for savoring his foreign policy triumph, for things were not going well domestically. Unemployment eased, but inflation drove interest rates higher than ever, with the prime rate topping 21 percent.

For persons whose incomes increased commensurately with prices, conditions were uncertain but not necessarily bad. But retirees and others on fixed incomes watched their purchasing power dwindle by the week.

Carter couldn't do much about inflation in the short term, yet he did take one step that ultimately tamed the beast. In 1979 he appointed Paul Volcker to head the Federal Reserve. Volcker was an economist by training and experience, and a believer in the importance of curbing the money supply as a way of curtailing inflation. Putting his beliefs into action required time—more time than Carter was allowed, as matters proved—but when the Fed's new policy took hold, inflation finally fell to acceptable levels.

Carter meanwhile tried to tackle another contributor to inflation. The exploding cost of energy contributed powerfully to price rises elsewhere in the economy, for the reason that nearly everything sold in America contained elements of energy in its production or distribution. The energy problem, besides making Americans poorer, also made them less secure. By the late 1970s OPEC's stranglehold on world oil markets had grown stronger than ever; the United States, now a major importer of oil, found itself at the mercy of the foreign producers. Carter addressed the energy issue institutionally by persuading Congress to create a new Department of Energy, charged with overseeing Americans' energy use and encouraging conservation. He set the mood and offered an example, lowering the thermostats in the White House during the winter to 65 degrees and raising them to 78 during the summer. He had solar panels installed on the roof of the building and a wood-burning stove inside. He conspicuously wore a cardigan sweater as a reminder that conservation could be comfortable (if not necessarily fashionable).

In July 1979 the White House scheduled a presidential address on energy. Carter had spoken on the subject several times before; he hoped to summarize what he had said and push a bit further. "But as I was preparing to speak, I began to ask myself the same question that I now know has been troubling many of you," Carter told his television audience. "Why have we not been able to get together as a nation to resolve our serious energy problem?" He explained that he had solicited comments from ordinary Americans. He quoted several, including one that he said summarized the others: "Mr. President, we are confronted with a moral and a spiritual crisis." Accordingly Carter addressed the moral and spiritual crisis.

> It is a crisis of confidence. It is a crisis that strikes at the very heart and soul and spirit of our national will. We can see this crisis in the growing doubt about the meaning of our own lives and in the loss of a unity of purpose for our nation. The erosion of our confidence in the future is threatening to destroy the social and the political fabric of America.

The president proceeded to lay out a six-point program to enhance America's energy security. The measures were realistic and reasonable. But what everyone remembered was the "crisis of confidence." Critics alleged that Carter was blaming the American people for the failures of government. Some pundit, or perhaps a space-strapped headline writer, applied the term "malaise" to the speech, which became known by that label even though the president hadn't uttered the word.

## 6. . . . NOR DECISIVENESS

The malaise speech marked a low point in Carter's presidency—but, unfortunately for him, not the lowest. As trying as domestic affairs could be for a president during the late 1970s, foreign affairs were worse. Some of the trouble Carter brought on himself; some came with the commitments he inherited from his predecessors.

Among those commitments was American support for an ugly regime in Nicaragua. The United States government had been backing the Somoza family in Nicaragua for decades. The Somozas were never democrats, but neither were they so egregiously despotic that their sins against civil liberties reflected unacceptably upon the United States. Such, at any rate, was the verdict of the pre-Carter presidents. Carter's higher standard put the current incumbent in Managua, Anastasio Somoza (nicknamed Tachito, to distinguish him from his father, also Anastasio, nicknamed Tacho), in a difficult position. Pleasing the Americans required relaxing his rule, but relaxing his rule encouraged those who wanted to oust him. The most important of Somoza's challengers were the Sandinistas, who took their name from a nationalist hero martyred by forces under the leadership of the current Somoza's father. The Sandinistas had waged a guerrilla war against Somoza's regime since the 1960s, but their campaign caught fire following a massive 1972 earthquake that leveled large parts of Managua and killed many thousands. As international relief poured in, Somoza and his cronies siphoned much of it into their own accounts, outraging Nicaraguans who till then had refused to take sides between the Sandinistas and the government. Somoza responded to the growing popularity of the insurgency by ordering harsher measures against anyone caught collaborating with the Sandinistas or even suspected of doing so.

These measures drew the attention of international human rights monitors, as well as the human rights office of Carter's State Department. Washington chided Somoza and delayed aid payments. Somoza, not wishing to alienate the Americans, pledged reforms. Carter ordered the aid released.

But this solved neither Somoza's problems nor Carter's. The Sandinistas lay low for a time, but in early 1978 the regime committed another outrage, more egregious in its way than anything before. Pedro Chamorro was the editor of *La Prensa*, the leading opposition newspaper; his columns had annoyed Somoza for years, but his social and political connections preserved him from physical harm. In January 1978 his connections failed, and he was assassinated. The people of Managua responded by staging a general strike, weakening the Somoza regime further. The Sandinistas followed up with a spectacular raid against the national palace in the capital. The rebels seized the building and took hundreds of hostages, including many members of Nicaragua's parliament. With his regime on the verge of collapse, Somoza appealed to Washington.

What he received were mixed signals. Carter had lacked experience in foreign policy before arriving in Washington; he studied the subject diligently, but like all presidents of similar inexperience, he depended heavily on his advisers. Two mattered more than the rest. Cyrus Vance, Carter's secretary of state, shared the president's belief in accommodating change and emphasizing human rights. Zbigniew Brzezinski, Carter's national security adviser, took the opposite view, being skeptical of change and more confident than Vance of the status quo. Carter allowed the two men and their respective staffs to argue about the appropriate American response to events abroad—including the developments in Nicaragua. Vance contended that Somoza was finished and that the United States should make overtures to the Sandinistas.

Brzezinski said not so fast: the Sandinistas were radical leftists with ties to Cuba and the Soviet Union; their accession could only damage American interests.

Had Carter decided between Vance and Brzezinski and ended the debate, American policy might not have been perfect, but it would have been less disjointed than it proved to be. Instead Carter vacillated between Vance and Brzezinski. One month he insisted that Somoza stop torturing his opponents; the next month he looked the other way. Carter's carrot-and-stick approach simply confused Somoza. The Nicaraguan autocrat agreed to ransom the government officials kidnapped by the Sandinistas and to release some Sandinistas previously jailed. This bought him time, but it invited further insurgent actions, which duly occurred.

Carter belatedly sought a middle ground between the rightist dictator and the leftist rebels. He appealed to the Organization of American States and encouraged middle-class Nicaraguans to establish a coalition government. But nothing worked, and in the spring of 1979 the Sandinistas launched their final anti-Somoza offensive. The dictator fought desperately, bombing his own capital after rebel troops entered Managua. The rebels wouldn't be dislodged, and in midsummer Somoza gave up. He and his closest associates abandoned the country and flew off to exile in Florida.

Somoza's fall coincided with Carter's "crisis of confidence" speech and the crisis of confidence in Carter's leadership that followed. His opponents seized on his vacillations regarding Nicaragua as additional evidence of an inability to lead. The president fended off the criticism as best he could. A reporter at a press conference asked if America faced the prospect of another Cuba in Nicaragua. Carter dismissed the question. "It's a mistake for Americans to assume or to claim that every time an evolutionary change takes place, or even an abrupt change takes place in this hemisphere, that somehow it's the result of secret, massive Cuban intervention," he said. "The incumbent government, the Somoza regime, lost the confidence of the Nicaraguan people." American policy was simply to let the Nicaraguan people have the government they wanted. "We have a good relationship with the new government. We hope to improve it."

Hope was a weak reed for policy. Carter sought accommodation with the Sandinistas, but they, for the most part, weren't interested. Their revolution, like many revolutions, grew more radical with time, and the non-Marxist members of the government were gradually marginalized. The Sandinista leaders were willing to accept American money; Carter rescheduled repayment of old loans and pushed Congress to send new money south. But the Sandinistas refused to retreat from their revolution or to forgo closer ties to Cuba.

## 7. TRAPPED IN TEHRAN

No less vexing to Carter and even more alarming to most Americans was a simultaneous revolution in Iran. Since his American- and British-sponsored restoration in 1953, the shah of Iran had ruled the former Persia with a bewildering combination of repression and modernization. It was bewildering, at any rate, to many Iranians, including both the Westernizing middle class, who wanted more influence in the governing of the country, and Iran's Islamic fundamentalists, who wanted less Westernization and more traditional religion. The shah straddled the divide between the two groups with the assistance of American aid and Iran's oil revenues. The former supplied his army and police with weapons, the latter with the means to assuage the demands of Iran's poor, who outnumbered both the Westernizers and the Islamists.

Washington wasn't unaware of the shah's repression or of the challenges to his rule. But as part of the pullback from Vietnam, Richard Nixon unveiled something called the Nixon Doctrine, which handed responsibility for regional security to regional powers, with the United States providing the arms. Iran was nominated to protect the crucial oil region of the Persian Gulf. The shah accepted the responsibility, assuming it would tie Washington even more closely to his regime. The policy meanwhile appealed to American weapons manufacturers, whose representatives filled the flights to Tehran. "It was a salesman's dream," the chief of the American military advisory group in Iran recalled.

The policy encouraged the shah to ignore signs that pressure for change in Iran was reaching explosive levels. His secret police arrested and tortured dissidents, which measures simply stoked the boiler further. Amnesty International and other human rights groups put the shah's regime at the top of the world list of repressors.

Jimmy Carter was caught in the same dilemma regarding Iran as he faced with Nicaragua. To push the shah too hard toward reform might destabilize a government that, for all its faults, had supported the United States for a quarter-century. To push him too gently would contradict Carter's asserted belief in the importance of human rights and might result in an even greater disaster down the road.

Complicating the picture was the fact that American intelligence regarding Iran was abysmal. Few American officers could speak Farsi, the predominant language, and the shah discouraged contacts with Iranian dissidents. American officials tended to rely on what the shah's agents told them, which naturally favored the shah's point of view.

Carter's policy toward Iran wavered in much the same way as his policy toward Nicaragua. The president sent Cyrus Vance to Tehran in 1977 to lecture the shah on the importance of human rights, but when the shah ignored the warning he suffered no sanctions. On the contrary, Carter brought the shah to Washington, where the president affirmed the "unbreakable ties of friendship" that joined the United States to Iran. "We look upon Iran as a very stabilizing force in the world at large," Carter said. "We don't fear the future when we have friends like this great country."

The stabilizing force was becoming less stable by the month. Religious dissidents gathered at the holy city of Qom; the shah's police fired on the crowd, killing dozens. The violation of the shrine and the identity of the victims—mostly young theology students—angered even Iranians who didn't endorse the fundamentalists' views. Riots spread across the country; the violent response of the police produced hundreds of additional martyrs to the cause. In September 1978 a huge crowd filled the main square of Tehran; police fire killed or wounded more than a thousand.

Had Carter not been closeted with Egypt's Sadat and Israel's Begin at Camp David during just this period, he might have responded more quickly to events in Iran. But there was little he or anyone else could do. The unrest continued to escalate until December 1978, when the shah, who knew he was dying of cancer, relinquished power and fled the country.

Briefly it appeared that Iran might enjoy a moderate post-shah government. But the Islamists were better organized and more self-confident than the moderates, and within weeks they seized control. In February 1979 the ayatollah—or religious leader—Ruhollah Khomeini returned from exile, to massive displays of devotion by millions of Iranians. Khomeini had long denounced the United States for supporting the shah; he continued to do so, more sulfurously than ever. America, Khomeini said, was the "Great Satan," the source of evil in the world and the mortal enemy of Islam.

For several months Khomeini confined himself and the Islamic revolution to verbal assaults on the United States. But in the autumn of 1979 Carter, from an excess of generosity, allowed the dying shah to enter America for medical treatment. Khomeini and the Islamists asserted that this was a trick: the shah was consulting with the CIA for a return to Iran. Khomeini's followers staged giant demonstrations outside the American embassy in Tehran; in early November the demonstrators scaled the walls, overpowered the embassy guards, and seized seventy hostages.

Carter responded cautiously, hoping that quiet diplomacy would effect the hostages' release. But Khomeini was in no mood for quiet diplomacy; he liked the thrill the hostage taking injected into Iranian politics. He ordered the release of the African Americans and women among the hostages, evidently considering them less culpable in the sins of the Great Satan, and subsequently let a sick hostage go. But the remaining fifty-two Americans remained in captivity.

## 8. THE BAD NEWS GETS WORSE

From its start in the early 1970s détente had been surprisingly unpopular. Certain groups—farmers, who could now sell wheat to the Soviet Union; disarmament activists, who praised the slowing of the arms race—liked the loosening toward Moscow, but others distrusted it, and some bitterly opposed it. The opponents included a small faction with loud voices and easy access to print, many of whom had been leftists during the 1930s but had leaped to the other end of the ideological spectrum by the 1950s. Calling themselves neoconservatives, these intellectuals and polemicists decried détente as a unilateral American ceasefire in the never-ending struggle between freedom and tyranny.

Norman Podhoretz, a leader of the neoconservatives and the editor of *Commentary* magazine, the house organ of the American Jewish Committee, slammed détente as a strategy for "making the world safe for communism," as he put it in a piece with that title in 1976. Podhoretz attacked Henry Kissinger for modern-day appeasement (he would have gone after Richard Nixon, but the latter hadn't emerged from his post-resignation hiding in San Clemente). Kissinger talked tough but acted weak, Podhoretz asserted. The result would be nothing but disaster for America and the cause of freedom.

As much as the neoconservatives disliked the Republican version of détente, they absolutely loathed the Democratic version. Neocon Jeane Kirkpatrick, writing in Podhoretz's *Commentary*, in 1979 accused Carter of adopting a double standard for dictators. Carter had lost Iran and Nicaragua, Kirkpatrick said, because he treated friendly dictators more harshly than he did the unfriendly ones. Carter insisted that Nicaragua's Somoza and Iran's shah meet the human rights standards of Amnesty International while he ignored the far more egregious violations of the Soviet and Chinese governments. Besides being immoral, the Carter policy was perverse. "In each country," Kirkpatrick asserted, "the Carter administration not only failed to prevent the undesired outcome, it actively collaborated in the replacement of moderate autocrats friendly to American interests with less friendly autocrats of extremist persuasion."

By the end of 1979 Carter had little with which to counter the criticism. And what little he did have exploded in his face when Soviet troops invaded Afghanistan. The Kremlin had observed the progress of the Islamic revolution in Iran with growing concern for the security of the largely Muslim republics of Soviet Central Asia. The peoples of Kazakhstan, Tajikistan, and the other "-stans" had never warmed to communism, and the success of Khomeini in Iran might be all the encouragement they needed to rise in revolt against Marx, Lenin, and Brezhnev. Already the Islamic revolution was sweeping into Afghanistan, where a government quietly backed by the Kremlin had failed to slow the fundamentalist tide. Taking Carter's diffidence toward Iran as an example of how *not* to deal with religious fanatics, the Kremlin in the last week of 1979 airlifted thousands of Red Army troops over the mountains that separate Afghanistan from the Soviet Union. Tanks and infantry followed.

The Soviet action stunned Carter, who made no secret of his shock. (Carter had never been good at keeping secrets. Earlier he gave an interview to *Playboy* magazine in which, while professing love and fidelity toward his wife, Rosalyn, he confessed to having "lusted" after other women. Rosalyn may have understood what he meant, but millions of Americans scratched their heads at his candor.) Upon learning of the Soviet invasion of Afghanistan, Carter declared, "My opinion of the Russians has changed more drastically in the last week than in the two-and-a-half years before that."

Carter's admission signaled a surrender to the neoconservatives, whose opinion of the Russians was simply confirmed by the new aggression. Carter completed his capitulation by withdrawing the SALT II treaty from the Senate, where it was awaiting ratification. The neoconservatives had lambasted the treaty as more of the modern Munich syndrome, and although the invasion of Afghanistan had nothing to do with strategic weapons, the Soviet action lent credence to neoconservative warnings.

Carter took additional anti-Soviet steps. He embargoed grain shipments to Russia, banned the sale of high-technology equipment, suspended Russian fishing rights in American waters, canceled cultural and academic exchanges, and in the most symbolically important measure, ordered American athletes to stay home from the 1980 Summer Olympics, to be held in Moscow.

Beyond all this, Carter articulated a new doctrine of American foreign policy. His State of the Union address of January 1980 was unusually explicit, for that typically vague genre, in condemning Soviet adventurism. Carter remarked that the assault on Afghanistan had carried the Red Army to within three hundred miles of the Indian Ocean and alarmingly close to the Strait of Hormuz, the choke point for oil exiting the Persian Gulf. He warned the Kremlin against any further move south. "Let our position be absolutely clear," the president intoned. "An attempt by any outside force to gain control of the Persian Gulf region will be regarded as an assault on the vital interests of the United States of America, and such an assault will be repelled by any means necessary, including military force."

No president had spoken so bluntly to the Russians since John Kennedy told Khrushchev to get his missiles out of Cuba in 1962. In this instance the American president wasn't making a positive demand, but instead was warning the Kremlin against something it probably had no intention of doing. (Afghanistan soon gave the Soviets more than they could handle, leaving neither the resources nor the inclination for a push to the Persian Gulf.) All the same, Carter's warning got the attention of the world, as well as of Congress, which approved the large increase in the American defense budget

Carter requested as part of his sudden conversion from human rights liberal to born-again Cold Warrior.

Détente might have collapsed under its own weight even without the invasion of Afghanistan. A generation of Americans had grown accustomed to treating the Soviet Union as an enemy, and the idea that Moscow might be a friend could be disconcerting. Some of the reluctance to relinquish the enemy was a matter of material and political self-interest. Weapons makers and their suppliers and employees had a vested interest in continued tension between East and West. Red-baiting politicians had long found the Kremlin to be an easy target. But much of the détente-era nostalgia for the Cold War represented a desire for landmarks in a confusing international landscape. The Soviet Union served as a negative navigational guide; by steering away from Moscow, Americans could find safe harbor. Without Moscow as an enemy, the task grew harder. Nostalgia alone wouldn't have brought back the Cold War. But when the Soviets began acting like enemies once again, more than a few Americans took odd comfort in the familiar hostility.

# 9 | South by Southwest

## 1979–1983

### 1. FROM HOLLYWOOD TO WASHINGTON

After Lyndon Johnson demolished Barry Goldwater in the 1964 election, it was tempting to think that Americans had seen the last of conservatism for a long time to come. The trajectory of American politics since the 1930s had been in a decidedly liberal direction, and Johnson's Great Society promised to extend and elaborate the New Deal reforms of Franklin Roosevelt. Americans might differ on social issues, but on the underlying political question that had always formed the crux of the contest between liberals and conservatives—the question of whether the important problems of American life were better addressed by the private sector (the conservatives' answer) or the public sector (the liberals' choice)—Americans sided with the liberals and government. Americans who came of age during the 1960s—the Baby Boomers, for instance—unsurprisingly thought that liberalism was the wave of America's future and always had been.

But America's future was more complicated than that and always had been. Americans were not congenital liberals; if anything, they were natural skeptics of big government—which is to say, they were conservatives. Americans had typically looked first to themselves and their families for support and assistance and only second to government. The principal exceptions to this rule of individualism and self-help were wars and national emergencies. When the nation was attacked, the national government was the obvious instrument of defense. And when a national calamity struck—the Great Depression, for example—Americans were willing to look to Washington for help, which was generally expected to be temporary. After the wars ended and the emergencies passed, Americans turned back to their private affairs and once again preferred the private sector.

Such a turning away from government might well have occurred after World War II, as it had after each previous war. But the world war segued almost seamlessly into the Cold War, which fostered a similar wartime mind-set. Americans spoke not of the "war effort," as they had during the world war, but of "national security," a term better suited to the open-ended character of the Cold War. Over time the concept of national security grew, and with it the size and intrusiveness of government. National security demanded the reorganization of the War and Navy departments and the creation of the CIA and the NSC. National security required curbs on free speech, as the numerous objects of the McCarthy and House Un-American Activities Committee probes discovered. National security suggested the construction of an interstate highway system and, after Sputnik, the expenditure of federal dollars on science education. National security insisted that Americans beat the Russians to the moon. National security made imperative the solving of America's race question: the world was watching to see whether democracy or communism was the more honestly egalitarian.

For as long as the national government delivered on its promises of national security—as long as the Cold War went well for the United States—the American people were content to place their confidence in Washington. But when the Cold War went wrong—in the wake of the Tet offensive, as victory in Vietnam slipped from America's grasp—Americans began to withdraw their confidence. To be sure, other factors contributed to the loss of trust in government. Watergate was the most obvious. But Watergate grew out of the failing war in Vietnam; the leak of the Pentagon Papers, which prompted the creation of Nixon's Plumbers, resulted from the refusal of the government to level with Americans regarding conditions in Vietnam. In any case, when Americans decided that the government didn't know what it was doing in Vietnam, and when Nixon declared, via détente, that the Cold War, as Americans had known it, was over, they did what Americans had done after every previous war. They turned away from government and looked to the private sector once more. They reverted to their historically conservative habits and expectations.

No one benefited more from the reversion than Ronald Reagan. An Illinoisan by birth, with a sunny disposition, bright hopes, and a photogenic face, Reagan moved west to Southern California in the 1930s to try his hand at the movies. His coming-out role was the doomed footballer George Gipp in *Knute Rockne, All American*; subsequent credits included *King's Row* and *Bedtime for Bonzo*. Reagan made training films for the army during World War II and realized, by the war's end, that though he might continue to receive supporting roles, he'd never crack the A-list of big stars. He turned his energies to the politics of his craft, winning election as president of the Screen Actors Guild. He negotiated the narrow road between his union constituency and the communist-hunting committees of Congress, defending freedom of speech while acknowledging the legitimacy of government concern regarding the infiltration of subversive ideologies into America's movies. As his film career waned, he shifted to television. He signed on as host of the *General Electric Theater*, which allowed him to reach a new audience and to demonstrate his remarkable skills on the small screen.

He jumped to public politics—and to a new party—in the early 1960s. Reagan had been a New Deal Democrat during the 1930s, but as his income increased he felt the pain of taxes more acutely and began to lean to the right. He backed Dwight Eisenhower over fellow Illinoisan Adlai Stevenson in 1952 and 1956, and fellow Californian Richard Nixon over John Kennedy in 1960. In 1962 he forsook the Democrats formally and was rebaptized as a Republican. His television presence won him a spot on the platform at the 1964 Republican convention at San Francisco, which nominated Goldwater but cheered loudest for Reagan. The speech Reagan delivered at the convention went over so well that Republicans insisted he repeat it during the campaign and purchased television time to air it just before the election. "I have spent most of my life as a Democrat," Reagan said. "I have recently seen fit to follow another course." Government had grown too large. "No nation in history has ever survived a tax burden that reached a third of its national income. Today, thirty-seven cents out of every dollar earned in this country is the tax collector's share." The question facing ordinary Americans, Reagan said, was whether they would recapture the power big government had usurped. "This is the issue of this election: whether we believe in our capacity for self-government or whether we abandon the American Revolution and confess that a little intellectual elite in a far-distant capital can plan our lives for us better than we can plan them ourselves."

Lyndon Johnson won the election a week later, but Reagan ran a close second in terms of career boost from the campaign. Reagan was handed the 1966 Republican nomination for California governor and swept to victory on a wave of voter shock at the Watts riots and the countercultural excesses of the hippies. He continued to rail against big government, although as head of the largest state government in America he aimed most of his charges at what he called "the Goliath that is the federal government." In two terms as governor he continued to migrate rightward. He approved a large tax increase during his first term, to bring the state budget into balance, but subsequently became a devoted tax cutter. He signed a bill easing restrictions on abortion but afterward adopted a hard line against the practice. He supported the death penalty, sent national guard troops against protesters at the University of California at Berkeley, and regularly railed against "welfare bums."

He probably would have run for president in 1972 had Nixon not claimed the prerogative of Republican incumbency; he did run for president in 1976, even though Gerald Ford made the same assertion. Reagan won enough primaries to challenge Ford at the convention, held in Kansas City. He lost narrowly but was granted an unheard-of opportunity to address the convention after Ford had secured the nomination. Ford and most of the others at the convention assumed that Reagan—"at 65 years of age, too old to consider seriously another run at the Presidency," the *New York Times* explained—would retire from public life. But Reagan fooled them. "Nancy and I aren't going back, sitting on a rocking chair and say that's all there is for us," he told the convention, prompting many delegates—"eyes glistening with tears," the *Times* observed—to conclude that the convention had chosen the wrong candidate.

When Ford lost to Carter that fall, Reagan became the favorite for the Republican nomination in 1980. He fended off a challenge from adoptive Texan George H. W. Bush, whom he added to the ticket in the vice-presidential slot. Beating Carter in the general election wasn't difficult, as events and Carter himself conspired against the Democratic president. The American economy continued to sputter, and the Republicans popularized the term "misery index"—defined as the sum of the inflation and unemployment rates—to measure the economy's underperformance. In the last year of Carter's term the index hit a postwar high of 22 percent. Little of this was Carter's doing, but it guaranteed his *un*doing. No incumbent had ever survived such an abysmal economy, and Carter wasn't the one to break the streak.

The international situation was no more promising—although as had been the case for some time, the distinction between domestic and foreign affairs grew increasingly blurry. Much of the inflation in America resulted from the second oil shock of the 1970s, this one coinciding with the Iranian revolution, which frightened the other oil producers of the Persian Gulf and spooked the spot market. Petroleum prices doubled from their previous highs, and the oil increases surged through the rest of the economy.

The Iranian revolution also hurt Carter more directly. The hostage crisis of 1979 became the hostage crisis of 1980 as the Iranian revolutionaries realized what leverage the hostages afforded them with the Great Satan of the West. Carter proclaimed that he would put other issues aside until the hostages were freed, and when they weren't freed he became a prisoner in the White House. Television news programs and the print media counted the days of the hostage crisis, which stretched into the hundreds. Against his better judgment—and the judgment of some of his top advisers—Carter ordered a rescue operation in April 1980. The operation was exceedingly risky, and it failed spectacularly, with eight American soldiers killed when a helicopter and a transport plane crashed and burned in the desert. The failure epitomized American frustration with the state of the world and seemed to underscore Carter's ineptitude in managing foreign affairs.

What Carter had been in 1976—the outsider untainted by the failures of the Washington in-crowd—Reagan became in 1980. "Are you better off than you were four years ago?" Reagan asked voters. "Is America as respected throughout the world as it was four years ago?" In that almost no one could answer these questions affirmatively, it wasn't surprising that Reagan won handily, with 51 percent of the popular vote to 41 percent for Carter. (Independent John Anderson got most of the rest.)

## 2. STANDING TALL

Reagan was inaugurated two weeks before his seventieth birthday, making him the oldest incoming president in American history. His age worried some supporters; the date of his election others, especially the superstitious. Since 1840, every president elected in a year divisible by twenty had died in office, four of them by assassination (Lincoln, Garfield, McKinley, Kennedy), and three by natural causes (William Henry Harrison, Harding, Franklin Roosevelt). The latter possibility seemed the more likely for Reagan, if the curse were to continue. But it was a would-be assassin's bullet that almost did him in. In March 1981, after a mere two months in office, Reagan was shot in Washington by an unbalanced young man named John Hinckley, who apparently thought the fame he would achieve by killing the president would win him the love of actress Jodie Foster, with whom he was obsessed. Reagan was badly wounded (as were three members of his entourage). A bullet punctured his lung and lodged a mere inch from his heart. He underwent emergency surgery to remove the bullet, reportedly remarking to the surgeon, before going under, "I hope you're a Republican." The surgeon responded, "Mr. President, we're all Republicans today."

The surgery went well and the president recovered quickly. The foremost public memory of the event involved an agitated Al Haig, Reagan's secretary of state, taking charge of the White House and telling reporters, "I am in control here." In fact the line of succession ran through three others before it reached Haig, who didn't last much longer in office, being too jumpy and combative for Reagan's taste.

Aside from this large detour, the Reagan presidency got off to a promising start. The new president earned the name "the great communicator," not least from a brilliant inaugural address. He spoke at the west side of the Capitol, from which he and his audience could see the Washington Monument, the Lincoln Memorial, and Arlington National Cemetery across the Potomac. At the distance of the Capitol it was just possible to make out the many rows of grave markers climbing the cemetery's hillsides. "Under one such marker lies a young man, Martin Treptow, who left his job in a small town barbershop in 1917 to go to France with the famed Rainbow Division," Reagan said.

> There, on the western front, he was killed trying to carry a message between battalions under heavy artillery fire. We're told that on his body was found a diary. On the flyleaf under the heading, "My Pledge," he had written these words: "America must win this war. Therefore I

will work, I will save, I will sacrifice, I will endure, I will fight cheerfully and do my utmost, as if the issue of the whole struggle depended on me alone."

Reagan acknowledged that the crisis facing America in 1981 did not require the same kind of sacrifice Martin Treptow had made. "It does require, however, our best effort and our willingness to believe in ourselves and to believe in our capacity to perform great deeds, to believe that together with God's help we can and will resolve the problems which now confront us. And after all, why shouldn't we believe that? We are Americans."

Reagan received an inaugural gift from an unlikely source. Even as he spoke, the American hostages were being released in Iran. The government of the Islamic republic, as Iran now styled itself, had decided it had squeezed as much political use from the hostages as it could, and it let them go. "Just what was needed to make the day perfect," Reagan remarked to reporters on hearing the news.

The hostages' release fit neatly into the theme of Reagan's first year in office: the restoration of American self-confidence. Reagan himself didn't claim credit for Tehran's decision, but his supporters intimated—and some stated flatly—that fear of the wrath of Reagan inspired the release. His critics later alleged that members of Reagan's campaign team had secretly sabotaged Carter's pre-election efforts to arrange a release, that their man win the credit—after winning the presidency. Whatever the cause of the timing, the end of the standoff with Iran freed the new president to deal with other matters.

The first was the Cold War. The Soviet invasion of Afghanistan had killed détente, and the Carter Doctrine had buried it, but Carter never convincingly reembraced the Cold War, certainly not the way Reagan did. Despite being religiously tepid, Reagan had no compunction about speaking of international affairs in terms of good and evil. The Soviet Union, he said, was an "evil empire" and the "focus of evil in the modern world." This being the case, American morality as much as American interest required all the resistance to communism America could summon.

Reagan urged Congress to expand the arms buildup commenced in Carter's last year, and Congress complied. The Pentagon's budget swelled by a third during Reagan's first term, with each service battening after several lean post-Vietnam years. The navy laid keels for a six-hundred-ship navy. The air force ordered stealth fighters and bombers, and cruise missiles of unprecedented range and accuracy. The army bought more-powerful tanks, more-accurate artillery, and dozens of other weapons systems.

The centerpiece of the Reagan buildup was the Strategic Defense Initiative, a projected space-based antimissile system. Reagan had long rejected the premise of American nuclear strategy: that survival in the modern age depended on the good sense of America's adversaries in not starting a war, lest they be annihilated in response. But what, Reagan asked, if the adversaries *lacked* good sense? What if they were suicidal? Reagan's SDI, quickly dubbed "Stars Wars" by skeptics and some irreverent supporters, envisioned complementing the psychological defenses of mutual assured destruction with physical defenses that could obliterate incoming missiles.

The skepticism arose from the lack of the technological means to put Reagan's vision into practice. No one had ever figured out how to shoot down ballistic missiles, and no one currently had a convincing plan for doing so. Reagan's approach appeared to be to throw money at the problem in the hope that something would turn up.

But SDI had supporters, especially among individuals and groups with a stake in the defense industry. The Reagan defense expansion was the best thing to befall American arms makers since the big buildup of the 1950s (the one that prompted Eisenhower's warning against the military-industrial complex). They greeted the new orders with delight. Defense industry employment increased; profits soared; share prices hit new highs. The Star Wars gambit, precisely because its required technology didn't exist, promised to extend the bonanza far into the future. "For defense contractors across America, President Reagan's Star Wars program is more than a new strategy for defense," the *Wall Street Journal* observed. "It is the business opportunity of a generation, a chance to cash in on billions of dollars in federal contracts." The *Journal* quoted a defense industry insider who called the clamor for SDI contracts "a fish-feeding frenzy." The official in charge of coordinating efforts among private contractors told a reporter, with obvious pleasure: "There will be many, many Manhattan Projects in this."

Whatever the new program did for the arms industry, it threatened to touch off a fresh arms race with the Soviets. Disarmament advocates were uniformly dismayed. The arms treaties of détente hadn't stuffed the nuclear genie back into the bottle, but they had kept the genie from growing to even more daunting size and power. Reagan's SDI, coming after the demise of the SALT II treaty, would let the genie run amok. Not even the most ardent advocates of SDI projected total effectiveness in shooting down Russian rockets; if even a few out of a hundred got through, they could devastate American society—especially if the Kremlin enlarged its nuclear force, as it seemed certain to do in response to SDI. Because offensive missiles were cheaper than defensive ones, the financial arithmetic would favor Moscow.

Reagan defied the critics and pressed ahead. He wasn't always the most effective advocate of his program, in that his knowledge of nuclear technology was alarmingly incomplete. Brent Scowcroft, who chaired a commission Reagan appointed to examine nuclear issues, was astonished to learn that the president didn't realize that the most formidable part of the Soviet arsenal was its large land-based intercontinental missiles—something even casual readers of the newspapers of the period couldn't have missed. But Reagan apparently didn't read newspapers. When reporters inquired about this lack in his knowledge, he said, "I never heard anyone of our negotiators or any of our military people or anyone else bring up that particular point." A few months later he told several members of Congress that submarines and bombers did not carry nuclear missiles—a statement the legislators knew to be so wrong as to cast serious doubt on the president's capacity to direct American defense policy.

But the arms buildup served enough constituencies that no one effectively called the president on his ignorance. Most voters, who themselves knew no more than Reagan about this seemingly esoteric subject, ignored his miscues.

## 3. THE ONLY GOOD TAX . . .

Simultaneously he implemented the other half of his confidence-restoring campaign. The Reagan of the early 1980s differed from the Reagan of the 1960s in considering tax cuts the indispensable element of economic revival. Reagan subscribed to a theory of federal finance called "supply-side economics," which contended that tax cuts need not diminish federal revenues but could actually increase them. High tax rates, the supply-siders argued, discouraged economic activity and thereby reduced the tax base. Low tax rates had the opposite effect, encouraging productive activity, expanding the tax base, and potentially increasing overall revenues. As an illustrative example, the supply-siders posited a punitive tax rate of 90 percent. Who, they asked, would want to work knowing that the government would take 90 cents of every dollar earned? But if the tax rate were lowered to 30 percent, plenty of people would work, since they now would keep 70 cents of every dollar they earned, rather than a meager 10 cents. All those energetic people would toil away, and their larger incomes would increase government revenues, even taxed at a third the former rate. Yet the real benefit would be the revival of the American economy. Lift the heavy tax burden, Reagan and the supply-siders said, and the economy would spring back to life.

Congress gave Reagan most of the tax cuts he wanted. Conservative Southern Democrats called "boll weevils" joined Reagan's fellow Republicans in supporting the cuts, which reduced tax rates by a quarter, in three steps over two years. Whether the tax cuts produced economic growth was something Republicans and Democrats would argue about for the next three decades; ascribing causation is as difficult in economics as in most realms of human behavior. But there was no denying that economic growth did not occur at once. On the contrary, the economy slipped into a serious recession in 1982, with unemployment reaching double digits for the first time since the Great Depression of the 1930s.

This was hardly what Reagan had promised, and for months he denied it was happening. "A recession is when your neighbor loses his job," he often joked. "A depression is when you lose yours." After the bad news became incontrovertible, Reagan and his supporters blamed Carter and the mess he had left behind. Or they blamed Paul Volcker and the Federal Reserve, which was ratcheting up interest rates to wring the inflation out of the system.

Reagan did not entirely understand Volcker's strategy. The president made no claims to being a financial expert; only days after his inauguration he walked from the White House to the Treasury Department for a lunch meeting with Volcker. "I was wondering if you could help with a question that's often put to me," he told the Fed chairman. "I've had several letters from people who raise the question of why we need any Federal Reserve at all. They seem to feel that it is the Fed that causes much of our monetary problems and that we would be better off if we abolished it. Why do we need the Federal Reserve?"

Martin Anderson, a Reagan loyalist, later remembered Volcker's reaction. "His face muscles went slack and his lower jaw literally sagged a half-inch or so as his mouth fell open," Anderson said. "For several seconds he just looked at Reagan, stunned and speechless. It is a good thing Volcker had not had time to light one of his long cigars because he might have swallowed it." But Volcker recovered, and he provided the new president a primer on the nature and operation of the American money supply and the Fed's role in supervising it. Reagan accepted the explanation, realized he was in over his head on monetary matters, and left Volcker alone.

One result was the recession; another was the defeat of inflation, which fell by half during Reagan's first year in office and continued to decline. And as employers, workers, consumers, and investors became convinced that prices and wages would not inevitably increase, or at least would not rise as fast as they had been rising, the economy corrected itself. By 1983 unemployment was down and most positive measures of economic health were up.

## 4. WITH GOD ON OUR SIDE

Reagan was possibly the least pious of America's postwar presidents, which made it ironic—his opponents called it hypocritical—that he leaned so heavily on supporters for whom religion was the most important thing in life. Americans had always been religious, but rarely did religion enter directly into politics. The generation of America's founding were children of the Enlightenment, tending to look to human reason rather than divine revelation as their source for political principles and philosophy. During the nineteenth century religion became more obvious in the public arena, largely on account of the efforts of abolitionists, temperance advocates, and others who hoped to inject the body politic with a stronger dose of personal morality. The arrival of millions of Catholic Irish immigrants starting at mid-century caused the native-born Protestant majority some angst, which was compounded by the advent of Jews from Eastern Europe at the end of the century. But though the Irish entered politics at the local level, especially in Boston and New York, national politics remained a Protestant preserve, and candidates rarely raised the religious issue. The emergence of an avowedly atheistic regime in Russia made Americans cling more tightly to Christianity, or to Judeo-Christianity, as the ecumenical were willing to put it. During the Cold War this clinging grew more explicit and fervent; Congress and Dwight Eisenhower in 1954 added "under God" to the Pledge of Allegiance.

Religion entered national partisan politics explicitly in 1960, when John Kennedy became the first Catholic to have a serious chance at winning the presidency. (Al Smith in 1928 led a divided Democratic party to a smashing defeat at the hands of Herbert Hoover and the Republicans.) Kennedy felt obliged to assert that he would not be taking orders from the pope and that his Catholic faith, while important to him personally, would not intrude upon his performance as president. Some voters nonetheless held his beliefs against him, although perhaps no more than others held his Catholicism *for* him. In any event he won, breaking an old if unspoken taboo against Catholics in the White House.

Whether this had anything to do with the emergence of evangelical Christianity as a political force in the decade that followed is unclear. Evangelicals, who believe in the inerrancy and often the literal truth of the Bible and who emphasize a personal conversion experience—typically referred to as being "born again"—traced their American roots at least to the Great Awakening of the eighteenth century. Then and later they held outdoor revivals; in the twentieth century they added modern communications media, first radio and then television, to their conversion campaigns.

The most influential of the modern revivalists was Billy Graham, a North Carolina native who preached to millions in stadiums, parks, parking lots, and amphitheaters all over America and around the world starting in the late 1940s, and to hundreds of millions via his weekly radio show, *The Hour of Decision*. Graham was a riveting speaker and a canny operator; every president and nearly every public figure during the second half of the twentieth century courted Graham and wished to be considered his friend. Graham counseled Eisenhower and Johnson regarding civil rights; he prayed with Nixon over Watergate. Graham's appeal was partly personal and partly political. Despite his careful avoidance of explicit endorsements, every politician knew that his blessing carried weight with tens of millions of Christian voters.

Jerry Falwell wasn't so fastidious in avoiding partisanship. Falwell lacked the almost Mosaic stature of Graham, but he possessed even more media savvy. At the tender age of twenty-two in Lynchburg, Virginia, he founded the Thomas Road Baptist Church, which became one of the first of America's "mega-churches"—congregations unaffiliated with mainstream denominations but boasting thousands of members who were typically attracted by a charismatic minister. Falwell exuded charisma, as well as empire-building tendencies. His church spun off a Bible college that evolved into Liberty University and eventually enrolled twenty thousand students. Falwell meanwhile established himself as one of the most successful of the new breed of "televangelists" who broadcast their sermons and services to national television audiences.

Like many conservative Christians, Falwell grew distressed during the 1960s at what he took to be the hedonistic excesses of that turbulent decade. Rampant drug use, the sexual revolution, and the increasing openness of homosexuals suggested that the moral fabric of America was shredding badly. Falwell preached against these and other modern evils—especially abortion, after the 1973 *Roe v. Wade* decision—and in 1979 gave organizational form to his complaints with the creation of the Moral Majority. From the outset the Moral Majority was plainly political; it lobbied elected officials and campaigned for candidates in order to write its code of morals into law. It opposed Carter's reelection in 1980 and sided with Reagan, despite the fact that Carter was a devout churchgoer and faithful family man while Reagan rarely attended services and was divorced. Falwell took credit for delivering the conservative Christian vote to Reagan and thereby helping to put him in the White House. Reagan returned the favor by appointing Falwell-friendly persons to numerous administration posts.

Yet Reagan never gave the Christian conservatives all they wanted. He ignored their opposition to his nomination of Sandra Day O'Connor to the Supreme Court. Some of the opposition reflected the simple fact that O'Connor was a woman—the first woman nominated to the high court. Many Christian conservatives believed that women should be subordinate to men and certainly should not be judging men. O'Connor also drew opposition for her comparatively liberal views on contraception and abortion. But Reagan liked her. "She was forthright and convincing," he said, reflecting on the one pre-nomination meeting he had with her. "I had no doubt she was the right woman for the job."

All the same, the Christian right wielded more political influence during the 1980s than organized religion ever had in American history till then. Other televangelists—Pat Robertson, Oral Roberts, Jim Bakker, Jimmy Swaggart—also held large audiences in thrall every Sunday morning, and they encouraged their listeners and viewers to vote for the candidates who promised to put God's will, conservatively interpreted, into action. They campaigned to restore prayer to public schools (it had been banned since the early 1960s) and allow federal support to religious schools. They opposed equal rights for women and gays, the teaching of evolution and contraception in the schools, and arms control. "Our government has the right to use its armaments to bring wrath upon those who would do evil by hurting other people," Falwell explained.

The Christian right contended that American values, including the Christian religion, were under assault from something called "secular humanism," which looked to reason rather than revelation for guidance. According to a group called the Pro-Family Forum, secular humanism:

> Denies the existence of God, the inspiration of the Bible and the divinity of Jesus Christ.
>
> Denies the existence of the soul, life after death, salvation and heaven, damnation and hell.
>
> Believes that there are no absolutes, no right, no wrong—that moral values are self-determined and situational. Do your own thing, "as long as it does not harm anyone else."
>
> Believes in the removal of distinctive roles of male and female.
>
> Believes in sexual freedom between consenting individuals, regardless of age, including premarital sex, homosexuality, lesbianism and incest.
>
> Believes in the right to abortion, euthanasia (mercy killing) and suicide.
>
> Believes in equal distribution of America's wealth to reduce poverty and bring about equality.
>
> Believes in control of the environment, control of energy and its limitation.
>
> Believes in removal of American patriotism and the free enter-

prise system, disarmament, and the creation of a one-world socialistic government.

This indictment reflected the shrewdness of the Christian right. From the denial of the inerrancy of the Bible to an endorsement of incest and world socialism was one steep slippery slope, the antihumanists contended; to deny the existence of hell was to trample the American flag.

Richard Viguerie wasn't a televangelist, but he had friends who were. Jerry Falwell wrote the introduction to Viguerie's *The New Right: We're Ready to Lead* and lauded Viguerie's "courage to speak out regarding liberals"—a label synonymous with "secular humanists" for most Christian conservatives—"and their actions that have significantly occasioned America's perilous condition." Viguerie argued that the liberals had long refused to recognize the threat facing the United States from the Soviet Union and communism, with dire consequences for American security. "Clearly, we have fallen from being the Number One military power in the world to the Number Two power, behind a country whose leaders are totally committed to defeating America and conquering the world." The contest for the world continued, Viguerie said, except that the liberals didn't realize it. Other Americans must seize control of policy and re-gird the country at once. "The alternative to such an all-out American effort is simple. The Soviets will either force us into a war we will lose, or we will be forced to surrender."

Some elements of the Christian right thought a war with the Soviets wouldn't be a bad thing. The movement included a powerful millenarian strain, which contended that the second coming of Jesus was at hand. One indication was the "gathering of Zion," interpreted as the creation of modern Israel, for which the Christian conservatives expressed special solicitude. (Their support evoked ambivalence in many Jews, who appreciated the backing for the Jewish homeland but had painful memories of anti-Semitism among some of the same groups that now applauded Zionism.)

Another sign of the approaching final days was the Cold War. The most widely read account of the end times was Hal Lindsey's *The Late Great Planet Earth*, a book that sold eighteen million copies and claimed to discover a description of the current state of the world in the ancient books of the Bible. Ezekiel had identified the evil empire of Gog as the ruler of Rosh, Meshech, and Tubal. Rosh, Lindsey explained, was none other than Russia, and Meshech was Moscow. (He was still working on Tubal.) Like certain radicals at times past, Lindsey and the Christian millenarians believed that the worse things got, the better for their cause. The Book of Revelation forecast the climactic war of good against evil. "The apostle John predicts that so many people will be slaughtered in the conflict that blood will stand to the horses' bridles for a total distance of 200 miles northward and southward of Jerusalem," Lindsey wrote. Had John known about tanks and nuclear weapons, he would have used another yardstick, but the message was plain. Confrontation, even to the point of war, was not to be shunned but embraced.

The Christian conservatives won some battles and lost others. Sandra O'Connor was confirmed as an associate justice ("She turned out to be everything I hoped for," Reagan remarked later). The Christian conservatives buried the equal rights amendment and SALT II, but they didn't get prayer back in the schools and they didn't force gays back into the closet. In several states, however, they got a moment of silence, during which children could pray if they chose. At times and in particular school districts they ejected Darwin from the classroom and required sex-education teachers to preach abstinence as the only effective form of birth control.

More broadly they contributed to the conservative turn in American politics. The Christian right was at least as right as it was Christian. "If you would like to know where I am politically," Falwell explained, "I am to the right of wherever you are. I thought Goldwater was too liberal." Falwell didn't speak for all Christian conservatives, but he spoke for many. And Congress listened, as Congress does to large and insistent constituencies.

## 5. DAWN FOR THE SUNBELT

It was no accident that Falwell's church and university were located in Virginia. One of the most striking developments of the 1970s and 1980s was the transformation of the old South into something new and decidedly different. There had been previous incarnations of the "New South," most notably in the wake of the Civil War and Reconstruction, as the plantation economy gave way to industrial enterprise in Atlanta, Birmingham, and other Southern cities. But the reinvention of the South was never fully persuasive as long as the region clung to its antebellum attitudes regarding race. The civil rights revolution of the 1960s did more for the South—despite the opposition of most of the white majority—than anything that had happened during the previous eight decades. The South reentered the political mainstream; being Southern no longer disqualified one for national office, as Jimmy Carter first convincingly demonstrated.

Other factors contributed to the evolution of the new New South. One was a lowly bit of technology that nonetheless made all the difference. In the early twentieth century a Brooklyn publishing company hired Willis Carrier, a recent graduate of Cornell University's engineering school, to devise a method for keeping its printing presses working efficiently in the summer. The pages stuck together and the ink bled when the heat and humidity got too high. Carrier came up with a system of condensers and blowers that cooled and dried the air, to the publisher's profit—and the delight of the printers, who basked in the "conditioned" air of the press rooms. Carrier saw no reason that the benefits of his invention should be the monopoly of printers, and so, after patenting his device and forming the Carrier Air Conditioning Company, he set out to make America more comfortable.

The first installations were cumbersome and expensive and were confined to commercial buildings, including movie theaters, hotel lobbies, and banks. The technology gained broader acceptance during the 1920s but was still deemed a frill when the Great Depression made frills unaffordable and then World War II made them unpatriotic. But after the war air conditioning became a standard feature of new commercial buildings and many private homes. It was especially favored in the South, where the long, humid summers had made the locals sweat and nonresidents stay away. For the first time Northerners would consider relocating to the South, and not simply for the winter. Corporations could transfer executives to cities like Atlanta or Houston without compunction; executives could accept the transfers without feeling they were consigning their families to tropical hardship posts.

During the 1960s air conditioning became a common option on new automobiles. This development fueled additional growth in what was just beginning to be called the Sunbelt—the South plus the Southwest. Air-conditioned cars connected the air-conditioned homes of Sunbelt workers to their air-conditioned jobs, and their children to air-conditioned schools. For decades the North had been the climatically favored region of the country, its cold winters kept at bay by the relatively more advanced technology of heating. Now the South was where people wanted to go—to the land of sunshine to soak up and no snow to shovel or get stuck in.

The South appealed to employers for other reasons as well. Labor unions had never caught on in the South, partly because white workers refused to make effective common cause with black workers and partly because employers persuaded Southern legislatures, under the provisions of the 1947 Taft-Hartley Act, to pass "right to work" laws barring union membership as a condition of employment—a condition that was standard in the industrial states of the North. The right-to-work laws rendered unions' organizing efforts difficult and generally unsuccessful. Employers applauded their failure and pocketed the resulting profit.

A lower cost of living made the South appealing as well. Workers could live on less than in the North, and in part as a result received less. Poor whites were eager for whatever jobs came their way. Poor blacks were, too. In the Southwest, poor Hispanics, including undocumented immigrants from Mexico, were the most eager of all.

The lower cost of living applied to the middle classes as well. At a time when housing prices were increasing sharply in much of the rest of the country, homes remained comparatively affordable in the South and sections of the Southwest. The lower home prices reflected lower costs of both land and construction; the modest total made the American dream of home ownership more attainable in the Sunbelt than elsewhere.

The blossoming of the Sunbelt also reflected positive decisions by the federal government. Lyndon Johnson remembered when the Texas Hill Country had lacked electricity; he determined to make his home state and its region the equal of the rest of the country with respect to infrastructure and whatever else federal money could buy. Much of the Great Society's war on poverty was aimed directly at the undeveloped portions of the South and the Southwest. Defense contracts were awarded to Sunbelt manufacturers, and Houston received NASA's Manned Spacecraft Center because Johnson insisted that America's race to the moon should be directed from Texas.

From such causes the Sunbelt grew rapidly during the second half of the twentieth century. The South's share of the total American population increased by a quarter after 1950, till nearly one out of three Americans lived in the states of the old Confederacy. The Southwest grew even faster, with

California passing New York during the 1960s to become the most populous state in the Union. Texas was catching New York and would overtake it in the 1990s. Florida, Georgia, and Arizona added several million each. Of the eight states that grew by more than a million residents each during the 1990s, six were Sunbelt states. Nevada grew by an eye-popping two-thirds during that decade. Las Vegas leaped from almost nothing to more than a million and kept growing at a faster rate than any other large city in the country. By 2000 thirteen Sunbelt cities were among America's twenty most populous cities.

The growing numbers translated into increased political influence. In the House of Representatives the burgeoning states of the Sunbelt stole seats from the shrinking states of the Northern "Rustbelt." The shift was even more striking, if less automatic, at the presidential level. Following the long drought from the 1840s to the 1960s, the South or Southwest produced every elected president from 1963 to 2008. (The Sunbelt would have made a clean sweep of the White House during this period if not for the appointed presidency of Michigan's Gerald Ford.)

The increased influence of the Sunbelt strengthened the conservative trend in American politics. The South had always been conservative, but during the century after the Civil War, Southern conservatives, nearly all Democrats, had been divided from their ideological kin in the Republican party. Now those Southern conservatives migrated to the Republicans, some informally, by changing their votes, others explicitly, by changing their stated affiliation. The migration mortally fractured the Democratic coalition devised by Franklin Roosevelt, of Northern cities and Southern whites, which had never been more than a shotgun marriage anyway. The Southern whites found true love among the Republicans, who became stronger as a party than they had been since the 1920s.

And as the South grew more Republican, the Republicans grew more Southern. From the 1940s to the 1960s the GOP had included a moderate Northeastern wing, conservative on economic issues but comparatively liberal on social issues like abortion and prayer in the schools. The rise of the South—combined with the emergence of the Christian right—compelled the moderates to leave the party or shut up.

The result was a two-party system that more clearly distinguished liberals from conservatives. Nearly all conservatives were Republicans, and nearly all liberals were Democrats. This made for easier voter identification—and, as matters would demonstrate, nastier politics.

## 6. RED INK AND RED TAPE

Ronald Reagan for decades had castigated the evils of big government, but many observers assumed this to be political posturing, at least in part. After all, if he was so opposed to the federal government, why did he want to head the monster? In certain respects the doubters were right. Reagan never met a weapons program he didn't like. "Defense is not a budget item," he explained to his staff. "You spend what you need." Nor was it the growth of the Pentagon alone that belied the Reagan message. The federal government as a whole expanded, with government outlays climbing steadily during the Reagan years and nearly doubling by the time he left office.

One thing that did diminish under Reagan was the solvency of the federal government. The 1980s marked a new era in American government finance, in which Washington ran large and chronic budget deficits. Reagan's supply-side theories didn't pan out in practice; far from reducing the deficits the country experienced under Carter, Reagan's tax cuts—combined with the record defense spending and the growth of other programs—produced deficits that dwarfed Carter's. The annual excess of expenditures over revenues initially hit twelve figures—$100 billion—during Reagan's first term, and it topped $200 billion in his second term. As a result of the actual and prospective deficit, interest payments on the national debt—which itself tripled, to nearly $3 trillion—became the fastest-growing item in the federal budget.

Another troublesome deficit involved international trade. The shift in America's trade balance, which had contributed to the demise of the Bretton Woods system, continued during the 1970s and 1980s. America's last trade surplus occurred in 1975; from there till the end of the century and beyond, it was red ink as far as the eye could see. By the conclusion of the Reagan presidency, the annual shortfall amounted to $150 billion. From 1920 until 1970 the United States had been the world's largest creditor; by the 1980s it was the world's largest debtor.

What this meant was that foreigners gained increasing influence over the American economy and American life. Some of the excess dollars returned to America as loans to the federal government—which was to say that foreign governments, banks, and individuals purchased U.S. government bonds (the bonds necessary to sustain the massive federal deficits). Foreigners held as much as a fifth of the American national debt by the late 1980s. As long as those foreigners were content to keep buying the bonds, the investment kept American interest rates lower than they otherwise would have been. But should the Bank of Japan and German money managers develop doubts about America's future and dump their bonds, Americans would feel the impact in interest rates on home mortgages, automobiles, and credit card balances.

Another chunk of the foreign dollars returned to America in the form of direct investment—that is, foreign-purchased American companies and other assets. Again, if the foreign owners were content with the status quo, the American employees of those companies need hardly notice the difference. But often they weren't content, and the decisions the absentee owners made resulted in corporate restructurings that affected many thousands of jobs. Losing one's job had never been easy; for the ax to be wielded by a foreigner made it that much more painful.

The Reagan revolution wasn't all rhetoric and red ink, however. Reagan really believed that government employed too many people, and given the right opportunity he trimmed the payrolls. In August 1981 the thirteen thousand members of the Professional Air Traffic Controllers Organization walked off their jobs directing American airliners to and from their destinations. The PATCO strikers demanded shorter hours and higher pay, contending that their jobs were stressful and that inflation had eroded their income. They assumed that the Federal Aviation Administration would have to meet their demands, as they exercised a near monopoly on commercial air traffic control. Besides, PATCO, a rarity among labor unions, had contributed to Reagan's 1980 campaign. Surely he would remember the support and respond accordingly.

Reagan shocked the controllers, surprised the country, and impressed even his close associates by rejecting the PATCO demands and refusing to negotiate with the union. Reagan harbored less animosity toward unions than many other Republicans did, and he boasted of being the only president with a lifetime membership in the AFL-CIO, from his days with the Screen Actors Guild; but the PATCO strike violated federal law, which forbade strikes against the "public safety" by unions of federal employees. Consequently Reagan announced, regarding the strikers: "If they do not report for work within forty-eight hours, they have forfeited their jobs and will be terminated." When the PATCO members did not report to work, the president fired the whole union. Supervisors kept most of the planes in the air until replacement controllers were trained and hired.

The action revealed a decisiveness in Reagan many people hadn't expected. "It struck me as singular," remarked Donald Rumsfeld, who had been Gerald Ford's chief of staff and would go on to become secretary of defense. "You had a president who was new to the office and not taken seriously by a lot of people. It showed a decisiveness and an ease with his instincts."

It also showed that the era of labor's ascendancy was truly over. From the nineteenth century till the 1930s, government had usually sided with management against labor. Franklin Roosevelt and the New Deal Congress tipped the balance in the other direction, giving labor the benefit of most doubts. Reagan tipped the balance back against labor. Business leaders, especially those with a comparative perspective, understood at once the significance of his move. "I've asked many leading European financiers when and why they started pumping money into this country, and they all said the same thing," one consultant observed: "When Reagan broke the controllers' strike."

Reagan's assault on the environment was somewhat more subtle. Like many Western landowners—upon leaving the governorship in Sacramento, Reagan purchased the seven-hundred-acre Rancho del Cielo, above the Pacific Ocean north of Los Angeles—Reagan resented efforts by the government to tell private individuals what they could do with their property. He also joined some other Westerners in resenting efforts by the government to tell them what they could do with *government* property. Reagan subscribed to the historic Western creed of development, which started with the premise that public lands and other resources should be transferred to the private sector as soon as possible. Private enterprise, according to this view, always knew better than government bureaucrats.

Reagan meanwhile lacked the aesthetic sensibility that made environmentalists out of many Westerners. At a time when Californians were trying to protect the last of the giant redwoods, Reagan dismissively remarked, "A tree is a tree. How many more do you need to look at?" Reagan relied on the good sense of private owners to protect the forest patriarchs. "People seem to think that all the redwoods that are not protected through a national park will disappear." They wouldn't, he said. And even if they did, the loss wouldn't be so great as the tree huggers contended. "Has anybody ever asked the Sierra Club if they think these trees will grow forever?" On one occasion Reagan asserted that trees caused most air pollution.

Reagan's cabinet appointments reflected his environmental insensitivity. Interior secretary James Watt was every Western developer's dream. He notoriously divided Americans into two categories, "liberals and Americans," and he lumped environmentalists among the un-Americans. He took a raft trip down the Grand Canyon and proclaimed it boring. "We were praying for helicopters," he said. Watt, who hailed from Wyoming, where the federal government owned half the land, pledged to promote development of property previously withheld from the market. "We will mine more, drill more, cut more timber," he promised.

Watt tried to honor his promise, but he proved too controversial for his own policies. He attacked groups that could hardly defend themselves, calling Indian reservations "exercises in failed socialism." He suggested that conserving resources for future generations was a waste of time, in that Jesus would probably return—Watt was a Christian millenarian—before most of those generations were born. He became a poster boy for everything the environmental movement loathed, and thereby served as the movement's most bankable bogie. "If there hadn't been a James Watt," a spokesperson for the Sierra Club explained, "we would have had to invent one." The Sierra Club and other environmental groups grew rapidly during the Reagan years, largely in reaction to the efforts of Watt and his co-ideologists.

Yet below the radar Reagan's appointees weakened many of the environmental regulations introduced during the 1970s. Corporations lobbied the Environmental Protection Agency to delay or roll back restrictions on what they could emit into the air and water, and received a sympathetic hearing. Coal-fired power plants in the Midwest spewed tons of oxides of sulfur and nitrogen into the atmosphere; these combined with water vapor to produce "acid rain," a corrosive kind of precipitation that killed millions of acres of forests downwind in the American Northeast and Canada. Jimmy Carter had negotiated an agreement with Canadian premier Pierre Trudeau to scrub the Midwestern emissions, but Reagan scrubbed the agreement instead, angering the Canadians and consigning the forests to a slow, ugly death.

Deregulation had more benign consequences as well. Until the late 1970s air travel was one of the most tightly regulated industries in America. The regulation had originated in a desire by the federal government to guarantee the safety of passengers; it survived as an effort by the airlines to ensure their profits. Travelers rarely had much choice in airlines, which monopolized or oligopolized routes. The federal government began dismantling the regulatory framework during the 1970s, and the process accelerated during the 1980s and early 1990s. The resulting competition drove fares down drastically. Average ticket prices fell in real—inflation-adjusted—terms by 40 percent between 1977 and 1993. As prices fell, the number of passengers rose, until airports became as crowded as train stations had once been.

Deregulation benefited other industries too. Cargo haulers became freer to operate where and when they wanted; among the most visible results were the ubiquitous brown trucks of the United Parcel Service, which elbowed the federal postal service out of much of parcel delivery, and the orange and blue logo of Federal Express, which stole a large chunk of first-class mail. The bracing wind of competition blew through the telecommunications industry, cracking monopolies, reducing prices, and preparing the way for the proliferation of cellular phones and the creation of the Internet in the 1990s.

# 10 | Fire or Iceland

## 1983–1986

### 1. Tough Talk, Soft Walk?

The election of Ronald Reagan delighted the neoconservatives, who hoped the new president would pursue a more aggressive foreign policy. The neoconservatives differed among themselves as to which had been more dangerous: the conservative realism of Nixon and Kissinger, which had given rise to détente's live-and-let-live attitude toward the communists, or the liberal idealism of Carter, which tried to fashion a foreign policy around human rights. But both forms of error were now in the past, the neoconservatives told themselves. Reagan would lead America into a new era, marked by a self-confident assertion of American power and American values.

Things didn't work out quite as the neocons expected. Reagan did indeed excoriate the Russians rhetorically, and he did order the biggest defense buildup in American history. But he shied away from actual confrontation with the Kremlin, and he exhibited real reluctance to put all those new weapons to work. On two occasions in particular, Reagan responded quite moderately to what many people saw as Soviet provocation. In late 1981, after months of demonstrations by dissident Polish workers, led by the Solidarity movement, the Polish military cracked down, imposing martial law and imprisoning the Solidarity leaders. The move had the clear approval of the Kremlin and recalled similar actions against dissidents in Hungary in 1956 and Czechoslovakia in 1968. The neoconservatives had long pointed to those cases of Soviet brutality as the kind of thing American policy ought to prevent, and many anticipated a forceful response from the Reagan administration against the repression in Poland.

Reagan spoke forcefully enough. "We view the current situation in Poland in the gravest of terms," he said. "Our nation was born in resistance to arbitrary power and has been repeatedly enriched by immigrants from Poland and other great nations of Europe. So we feel a special kinship with the Polish people in their struggle against Soviet opposition to their reforms."

But Reagan's asserted kinship to the Poles produced no measures that gave the Soviets serious pause. The administration suspended the landing rights of the Soviet airline Aeroflot, and it curtailed scientific exchanges and the Soviet purchase of grain and high-technology products. Moreover, it took several actions that punished *Poland*, which seemed odd to many observers, in that Poland was the country the administration said it wanted to help. (The administration's rationale was that it was punishing the *government* of Poland rather than the Polish people.) But Washington did *not* suspend talks on the reduction of intermediate-range nuclear weapons in Europe, it did *not* withdraw American negotiators from discussions of human rights, it did *not* cancel a scheduled meeting between the American secretary of state and the Soviet foreign minister, and it did *not* stop shipments of grain already paid for by the Russians. Before long, in fact, the administration arranged a new grain deal and lifted the restrictions on some high-technology items.

A second illustration of Reagan's caution occurred two years later. In the summer of 1983 a Soviet fighter plane shot down a Korean passenger airliner that had strayed into Soviet airspace. Again the president voiced outrage, condemning "this murder of innocent civilians." But again his bark exceeded his bite. He suspended Aeroflot landings (which had been reinstated since the suppression of Solidarity) but otherwise let the misdeed pass.

There was good reason for the careful treading. No matter how quickly the administration strengthened America's military forces, the Soviet Union remained a dangerous rival. The Russians possessed thousands of nuclear weapons targeted at the United States. As a consequence Washington's ability to manhandle Moscow was decidedly limited. The neoconservatives didn't like to admit this fact, and Reagan hadn't liked it while merely a candidate. But as president he had to take it into account.

All the same, there were ways of weakening communism without risking nuclear war. Such, at any rate, was the premise of what came to be called the

Reagan Doctrine. No single speech—nothing like the March 1947 address announcing the Truman Doctrine—codified the new approach. But Reagan's actions toward various countries added up to a policy that pushed beyond the containment doctrine that had formed the basis of America's Cold War strategy for thirty-five years. In Cambodia, the administration provided aid to a coalition of insurgents challenging the communist regime installed by the army of communist Vietnam following a 1978 invasion. In Afghanistan, American agents worked with fighters called *mujahideen* who battled the Soviet invaders and the pro-Soviet government. In Angola, Washington assisted a pro-Western faction in a long-running civil war. In Nicaragua, the United States supported right-wing rebels attacking the revolutionary Sandinistas.

What connected these policies, and formed the essence of the Reagan Doctrine, was a belief that the United States must replace the fundamental defensiveness of containment, which focused on preventing Soviet expansion, with an offensive strategy of rolling back communist power. The Truman Doctrine had sustained the status quo, bolstering rightist regimes confronting leftist insurgencies. The Reagan Doctrine challenged the status quo, assisting rightist insurgencies against leftist regimes. Such assistance would benefit the insurgents, the Reaganites said; it would also serve the United States. "Support for freedom fighters is self-defense," the president declared, employing his favorite synonym for right-wing insurgents.

The Reagan Doctrine received its fullest application in Nicaragua. Reagan ordered the CIA to raise a rebel army—called the *contras*—from among soldiers of the former regime and disaffected elements of the revolutionary front. At first the CIA relied on proxies: military officers from Argentina who were even more anticommunist than the Reagan administration. But Argentina and Britain got into a war over the Falkland Islands in the South Atlantic, and the Reagan administration sided with the British, angering the Argentines and terminating the Buenos Aires connection to the contras. The rebels became utterly dependent on their covert aid from America, as even their supporters acknowledged. American money fed and clothed the contras; American weapons armed them; American operatives trained them; American officials devised their strategies and identified targets. The contras blew up bridges and bombed oil depots; they planted mines in the harbor of Corinto, on Nicaragua's Pacific Coast. When the mines exploded beneath foreign ships, the contra war created international controversy.

It also attracted the attention of Congress. The contra war had already put the United States perilously close to violations of international law, in that Washington was underwriting rebels who regularly violated the human rights of ordinary Nicaraguans; but the Corinto mining seemed to carry the administration over the edge. Congress objected and passed a series of amendments named for Edward Boland, a Democratic representative from Massachusetts, which forbade the administration from spending federal money on the contras for the purpose of overthrowing the Nicaraguan government. Boland and most of the Democrats would have preferred a complete cutoff of the contras, but they lacked the votes and had to settle for the language targeting the overthrow of the government.

Reagan rejected even this version. The Boland amendments illegitimately constrained his capacity to defend the United States, he contended, besides jeopardizing the future of Central American freedom. In public he said he would obey the law, but in private he let his subordinates know that the contra war must continue, by one means or another.

## 2. WHOSE SIDE ARE WE ON?

"Mr. President, have you approved of covert activity to destabilize the present government of Nicaragua?" a reporter asked in a 1982 news conference.

"Well, no, we're supporting them," the president replied. "Oh, wait a minute, wait a minute. I'm sorry. I was thinking El Salvador."

Reagan wasn't the only one confused. American policy toward Central America consisted of supporting one rightist insurgency against a leftist government, and one rightist government against a leftist insurgency; keeping the former (Nicaragua) distinct from the latter (El Salvador) often required a conscious effort.

El Salvador in the 1980s should have been easy for Americans to understand, in that it resembled the typical American client state from just about any decade of the twentieth century. A rightist coalition headed by President José Napoleon Duarte was challenged by the leftist Farabundo Martí National Liberation Front (FMLN), which conducted a political and military insurgency. Had the government and the FMLN been content to slug it out among themselves, the American role might have been small. But the Duarte government, branding the rebels as Castro-sympathizing communists, unleashed death squads not only against the rebels but against their civilian sympathizers. In 1980 the archbishop of San Salvador, Oscar Romero, was assassinated while celebrating mass. Romero had criticized the government for abusing the citizens of El Salvador and violating their human rights; his final words were a sermon calling on Salvadoran soldiers to disobey the murderous orders of their superiors. The bishop's blood spilled across the altar; widely credited reports held that some splashed into the communion wine, where it mingled with what would have been consecrated as blood of Christ.

The Romero assassination indirectly implicated the United States. The bishop had criticized Washington for its aid to the Salvadoran government, asserting that the American money and weapons fueled the atrocities perpetrated by the government. Romero's murder lent credence to his critique, and it mobilized American liberals to demand that Reagan sever the aid connection.

Reagan refused. The president didn't condone the tactics of the Salvadoran death squads, but he agreed with the Salvadoran government's assertions that the FMLN rebels were communists and that their victory would result in a significant gain for the Soviet Union in Central America. "The Soviets are, you might say, trying to do the same thing in El Salvador that they did in Afghanistan, but by using proxy troops through Cuba and the guerrillas," Reagan told reporter Walter Cronkite.

Far from reducing the American commitment to the Salvadoran government, Reagan escalated it. He increased American funding of the government, and he dispatched American military advisers to El Salvador. In response to complaints that these actions simply magnified the American complicity in the death-squad atrocities, the president split what the critics considered to be fine hairs. "You could say they are advisers in that they're training," Reagan said. "But when it's used as 'adviser,' that means military men who go in and accompany the forces into combat, advise on strategy and tactics. We have no one of that kind."

Neither the money nor the advisers enabled the Duarte government to suppress the rebellion, which intensified until the FMLN controlled large sections of certain provinces. The government responded by stepping up its antirebel activities. At El Mozote in late 1981 government forces killed several hundred persons alleged to be rebels or sympathizers. The killing was covered up for a time but surfaced in 1982. The Reagan administration dismissed the story as overblown and said that the controversy simply underscored the stakes of the struggle in Central America.

The administration's arguments raised new questions about the present and future American role in El Salvador. "Could you tell us, Mr. President, why American soldiers are carrying M-16s in El Salvador?" a reporter asked.

Reagan backhanded the query. "The only thing I can assume is that they were for personal protection, and I think that's understandable."

Another reporter followed up: "Can you envision any circumstances under which we would be sending U.S. combat troops to El Salvador?"

Reagan made a joke: "Well, maybe if they dropped a bomb on the White House, I might get mad."

But the president and his administration were deadly serious about preventing the rebels from toppling the Salvadoran government. Reagan invited Duarte to Washington and lavished praise and money on him. He called the Salvadoran rebels "terrorists" and joined arms with Duarte in a hemispheric struggle against terrorism. "Terrorism is the antithesis of democracy," Reagan declared in a published letter to the Salvadoran president. "By brutal acts against innocent persons, terrorists seek to exaggerate their strength and undermine confidence in responsible government, publicize their cause, intimidate the populace, and pressure national leaders to accede to demands conceived in violence."

Throughout his tenure Reagan linked Nicaragua and El Salvador as two sides of the one struggle against Central American communism. In Nicaragua the communists had already gained a foothold in the government, which was why the administration supported the insurgents. In El Salvador the communists were on the outside trying to get in, which was why the administration backed the government. "In El Salvador we've worked with Congress and stood firmly behind President Duarte and the democratic forces," Reagan explained in a 1985 radio address. "We seek the same goals in Nicaragua."

## 3. BOMBED IN BEIRUT

Central America was hardly the sum of Reagan's foreign policy challenges. His presidency had begun with a Middle Eastern triumph—the release of the

American hostages from Iran—but things went downhill from there. In the summer of 1982 the Israeli army rolled into Lebanon to clear out elements of the Palestine Liberation Organization that had been targeting northern Israel with guerrilla attacks. The PLO, led by Yasser Arafat, refused to accept the existence of Israel, contending that the Jewish state had stolen the homeland of the Palestinian people; to manifest its displeasure the PLO conducted a low-grade war against Israeli soldiers and civilians. Israel had retaliated singly against the PLO attacks, conducting air strikes and cross-border raids in response to each new assault. But these hadn't succeeded in stopping the attacks, and the Israeli government decided a larger response—the invasion of Lebanon—was in order. The Israelis announced that "Operation Peace for Galilee" would establish a PLO-free zone in the southern part of Lebanon.

In fact the Israeli aim was more ambitious than that, as became apparent when Israeli forces continued north to the Lebanese capital of Beirut, where they engaged in house-to-house fighting against the PLO. Meanwhile the Israelis attacked Syrian troops that had occupied parts of Lebanon, and blasted the Syrian air force.

Arabs had long viewed Israel as a stalking horse for the United States, and the fact that most of the damage now done by the Israeli forces was inflicted by American weapons appeared to confirm the impression. Reagan indeed favored Israel in that country's conflict with its Arab neighbors, but he judged that his administration had better quell the conflict in Lebanon before American credibility in the region was totally destroyed. The president sent a negotiator, Philip Habib, to arrange a ceasefire, which Habib did. To supervise the separation of combatants, Habib promised, and Reagan approved, an American peacekeeping force.

The decision seemed innocuous at the moment it was made. And the commitment of American troops went well at first. The PLO left Beirut, and the Syrians withdrew to their home country. The Americans themselves departed shortly thereafter, mission apparently accomplished.

But the sudden exit of all the organized fighters left Lebanon prey to irregular militias who took the opportunity to settle scores among themselves and with noncombatants. Assassins murdered the Christian president of Lebanon, provoking Christian militias to enter two Palestinian refugee camps and massacre several hundred civilians. Israeli troops stood by and let the massacre proceed.

Reagan felt obliged to send American troops back into Lebanon. This time, however, their mission was unclear. They were supposed to help the Lebanese government restore order, but just what that meant was anyone's guess. Lebanon, long considered a haven of tolerant calm and prosperity in the Middle East, spiraled downward into civil war, and the Americans found themselves at the vortex.

As friends of the government, the American troops became the enemies of the government's enemies. Shiite Muslim militiamen fired at the American soldiers and rocketed the American positions. In April 1983 a suicide bomber drove a van packed with two thousand pounds of explosives to the American embassy and set it off. The explosion killed several dozen people, including seventeen Americans, and wounded more than a hundred. Among the dead were the CIA station chief in Beirut and the agency's top Middle East analyst.

Despite concerns that the United States was being dragged into another Vietnam, Reagan authorized the American forces to return the fire of their attackers. The American Sixth Fleet steamed to the coast of Lebanon, launching carrier-based planes against the insurgent positions and bombarding the mountains behind Beirut with sixteen-inch shells from the World War II–vintage battleship *New Jersey*.

The escalation predictably identified the Americans more closely with the government. In October 1983 a Shiite bomber detonated a truck filled with explosives near a marine barracks in the American sector of the Beirut airport. The explosion killed 241 American marines, among numerous other victims.

If the Lebanon war had been less confusing, Americans might have responded with a redoubled commitment to see the peacekeeping through. But the multiple factions and convoluted agendas made the conflict incomprehensible to most nonexperts. Even the Reagan administration found itself at a loss to explain the American mission. The president in early 1984 ordered the withdrawal of the American soldiers from Lebanon to ships offshore. He tried to explain that this wasn't a retreat but rather a redeployment. "We're not bugging out," he said. "We're just going to a little more defensible position."

## 4. NAILS IN THE LIBERAL COFFIN

The 1984 election took nearly everyone by surprise. In the 1982 midterms Reagan hadn't done well: the Republicans had lost ground, surrendering twenty-six seats in the House to the Democrats, who remained entrenched in the leadership of the lower chamber. The parties broke even in the Senate, with the Republicans maintaining their modest lead there. The most salient issue was the recession; voters liked Reagan but had to blame their frustrations and fears on someone and so smacked the president's party.

By 1984 the recession had ended and the economy was recovering strongly, which boded well for Reagan. Moreover, election contests involving White House incumbents are always clearer referendums on presidents than congressional elections, and Reagan's personal popularity was expected to serve him well. Age was an issue: the president turned seventy-three in February 1984, and so if reelected would be almost seventy-eight by the time he left office. The Democrats nominated Walter Mondale, the vice president under Carter and a man who was a generation younger than Reagan. Mondale added fizz to his candidacy by tapping Geraldine Ferraro to be his running mate. Ferraro, a U.S. representative from New York, was the first woman on the ticket of a major party in American history.

An initial debate between Reagan and Mondale suggested that the president's age might indeed be a concern. Mondale appeared physically stronger, mentally sharper, and more fully in command of himself and his facts. Reagan privately admitted he'd been bested. "Reagan always knows when he's done well on stage and when he hasn't," one of his aides remarked. "He told me right away that he was terrible." Even the president's supporters began to wonder about him. "Is the Oldest U.S. President Now Showing His Age?" headlined the *Wall Street Journal*.

The president prepared more carefully for the next debate, and generally acquitted himself more effectively. But what turned the tide was a one-liner he held in reserve till halfway into the session. Henry Trewhitt of the *Baltimore Sun*, a member of the panel of questioners, had the turn. "You already are the oldest president in history, and some of your staff say you were tired after your most recent encounter with Mr. Mondale," Trewhitt said. "I recall that President Kennedy had to go for days on end with very little sleep during the Cuba missile crisis. Is there any doubt in your mind that you would be able to function in such circumstances?"

Reagan's response didn't quite fit the question, but it came close enough for his purposes. "Not at all, Mr. Trewhitt," the president said. "And I want you to know that I will not make age an issue in this campaign. I am not going to exploit for political purposes my opponent's youth and inexperience."

Henry Trewhitt laughed. The audience in the Kansas City auditorium laughed. Television viewers laughed. Even Mondale laughed. But as he did, the Democratic nominee realized that Reagan, with a single sentence, had swept away the single biggest obstacle to his reelection. The theme of the election was the same as in 1980, and when Reagan asked whether voters were better off than they had been four years ago, a majority answered yes.

The fact of Reagan's victory was no surprise. An improving economy almost always returns incumbents to office. But the magnitude of Reagan's triumph *was* a surprise. The president buried his challenger in one of the deepest landslides in American history. Reagan carried 49 of the 50 states, and lost Mondale's home state of Minnesota by less than four thousand votes. He garnered 59 percent of the popular vote to Mondale's 41 percent.

Twenty years earlier the liberal Democrat Lyndon Johnson had defeated the conservative Barry Goldwater by almost the same popular margin. The difference between the two elections marked the distance the conservatives had climbed, and the liberals fallen, since then. The liberals naturally hoped they could revive their cause in the future; the conservatives worked to ensure they didn't.

## 5. TO TEHRAN WITH CHOCOLATE

A small issue in the election was a minor achievement of American arms. Forty-eight hours after the 1983 suicide bombing at the Beirut airport, Reagan ordered the invasion of the Caribbean island of Grenada. The invasion took the world aback; most Americans had no idea where Grenada was and no conception of why American soldiers should be landing there. The government of Grenada was only slightly less surprised, although it had received some warning from Washington. Grenada's prime minister, Maurice Bishop, had cultivated warm relations with Cuba and accepted aid from the Soviet Union. The Reagan administration feared that this portended a Soviet military presence in the southern Caribbean—which, Americans belatedly discovered, was where Grenada was located. The president pointed out that Bishop's government, with Cuban and Soviet assistance, had built an unusually long runway, one suitable for heavy Soviet transports (or tourist-filled airliners, as Bishop rejoined). "Who is it intended for?" Reagan demanded. The president provided the answer: "The rapid buildup of Grenada's military potential is unrelated to any conceivable threat. . . . The Soviet-Cuban militarization of Grenada, in short, can only be seen as power projection into the region."

To forestall this development, the Reagan administration sought a pretext for moving against Grenada. It found one when a faction even more radical than Bishop overthrew the prime minister. The uncertainty and confusion following the coup plausibly threatened several hundred Americans attending medical school in the capital, St. George's. The students seemed unconcerned, but the Reagan administration determined to take no chances. Besides, in the immediate aftermath of the bombing in Beirut, when the efficacy of American military power was being questioned, the president doubtless wished to show the world that the United States was not a helpless giant.

The American marines landed and quickly seized control of the small island. Had the students' safety been the only concern, the marines might have airlifted them out and left. Instead the soldiers stuck around to topple the Grenadan radicals and disperse their followers. The Pentagon claimed a victory for American arms and awarded ribbons by the basketful. The White House claimed a victory for freedom and helped a conservative successor government clean up the mess the invasion caused.

The victory in Grenada, such as it was, distracted Americans from the troubles in Lebanon, as intended, and contributed, if only a little, to Reagan's reelection. But it did nothing to calm the situation in the Middle East. And though the withdrawal of the American soldiers from Lebanon lessened the danger to them, it increased the exposure of American civilians in that country. Shiite insurgents backed by the revolutionary government of Iran began killing and kidnapping Americans. The president of the American University of Beirut was murdered, and the new CIA station chief in Beirut was kidnapped and apparently tortured to death. Several other Americans, including relief workers and the head of one of Beirut's main hospitals, were snatched from the streets.

The Reagan administration adopted the stance that it did not negotiate with kidnappers. "The United States gives terrorists no rewards," the president declared. "We make no concessions. We make no deals."

In truth, however, the administration did make deals. For several months American officials had been quietly exploring the possibility of better relations with Iran. Leaders of the Islamic republic still excoriated the American Satan, but both Tehran and Washington detected some common ground between them. Iran's neighbor and historic rival Iraq—from the era when Iran was Persia and Iraq Mesopotamia—had opportunistically attacked Iran shortly after the toppling of the shah. Iraq's leader, military strongman Saddam Hussein, sought to capitalize on the confusion in Iran to settle age-old grievances and claim ascendancy in the Persian Gulf. Iran absorbed the initial invasion and fought back—with the American weapons that constituted most of the country's arsenal, delivered when the shah was one of the American defense industry's best clients. The weapons required ammunition and spare parts, and Iran was desperate to acquire them.

From the American side, a rapprochement made sense as well. Iran, for all its recent belligerence, remained the most powerful country in the Persian Gulf, and the Gulf, on account of its oil, remained one of the most economically and strategically crucial regions on earth. Washington saw no reason at this point to take sides in the Iran-Iraq war, except to prevent a collapse of either side. Neither country was likely to become an open American ally; the next best outcome would be a balance of power between the two. If this required supplying Iran with weapons, a method ought to be found to do so.

Beyond such strategic considerations were the hostages. Iran had leverage with the Lebanese factions responsible for the kidnappings, as it funded and trained their fighters. If Iran applied that leverage, presumably the hostages could be freed.

Various obstacles, though, stood between the Reagan White House and a deal with Iran. One was the administration's own publicly stated policy, which opposed the transfer of weapons to either side in the Iran-Iraq war. Another was the opposition of influential individuals within the Reagan administration. Secretary of State George Shultz and Secretary of Defense

Caspar Weinberger both objected, with Shultz calling a White House proposal for arms transfers "contrary to our interests both in containing Khomeinism and in ending the excesses of this regime," and Weinberger dismissing it as "almost too absurd to comment on."

The plan went forward anyway. It did so because it served another purpose of the White House, one that had nothing to do with the hostages, Lebanon, or the Middle East. The congressional cutoff of funding for the Nicaraguan contras had left the administration two choices in Central America: to abandon the contra war or to find alternative funding. Reagan honestly believed that the contras were fighting America's battle against hemispheric revolution, and he was loath to let them go. He communicated this sentiment to members of his National Security Council staff, who were simultaneously wrestling with the Iran issue. They concocted a scheme that would solve both problems at once. The United States would secretly sell weapons to Iran, and it would use the proceeds from the secret sales to fund the contras.

Such was the origin of the Iran-contra affair. The details of the White House plan put spy novelists to shame. The point man for the project was Oliver North, a deputy to Reagan's national security adviser. A career officer in the Marine Corps, North was a gung-ho type who refused to let the law or other trivialities stand in the way of what his superiors, in this case including the president, wanted done. North arranged the shipment of antitank and anti-aircraft missiles to Iran. He devised a coded formula for part of the delivery schedule:

H-hour: 1 707 w/300 TOWs = 1 AMCIT
H + 10 hrs: 1 707 (same A/C) w/300 TOWs = 1 AMCIT
H + 16 hrs: 1 747 w/50 HAWKs & 400 TOWs = 2 AMCITs
H + 20 hrs: 1 707 w/300 TOWs = 1 AMCIT
H + 24 hrs: 1 747 w/2000 TOWs = 1 French hostage

(Translation: The operation would begin when a Boeing 707 delivered 300 TOW antitank missiles, in exchange for one American hostage. The same plane would return ten hours later with another 300 missiles, in exchange for another hostage. This would be followed by a 747 with 50 Hawk anti-aircraft missiles and 400 TOWs, for which 2 Americans would be released. Another 707-load would yield another hostage, and a final 747 flight with

2,000 antitank missiles would spring a French hostage, as an American gesture of goodwill to an ally.)

The project ran into difficulties. The Iranian government was deeply divided regarding a rapprochement with America, and those in favor tried to conceal their actions from those opposed. Initial sales of arms yielded modest profits—which were in fact funneled to the Nicaraguan contras—but fewer hostage releases than expected. To lubricate matters North and Robert McFarlane, a recent national security adviser who was still involved in the operation, flew to Tehran in May 1986. They traveled in disguise, carrying false Irish passports, a chocolate cake for their Iranian counterparts, six fancy .357 Magnum pistols in display boxes as presents, and some spare parts for Hawk missiles.

But the yield proved as disappointing this time as before. The hardliners in Tehran remained opposed to bargaining with the American infidels, and the hardliners were the ones with the greatest influence over the hostage holders. The scheme sputtered forward for a few additional months until November 1986, when a Lebanese magazine broke the story of the secret American dealings with Iran.

The Reagan administration couldn't well deny the fact of the dealings; too many people knew too much about them. But the president tried to minimize the damage, in a special address from the Oval Office:

> The charge has been made that the United States has shipped weapons to Iran as ransom payment for the release of American hostages in Lebanon, that the United States undercut its allies and secretly violated American policy against trafficking with terrorists.
>
> Those charges are utterly false. The United States has not made concessions to those who hold our people captive in Lebanon. And we will not. The United States has not swapped boatloads or planeloads of American weapons for the return of American hostages. And we will not.

Reagan apparently believed what he said. In fact, he went to his grave contending that the arms shipments to Iran were not ransom for hostages. Interested parties made the shipments *look* like ransom, he wrote in his memoirs. "Then our press took it up and printed the same false story—to this day, they still are—that we were doing business with the ayatollah, trading arms for hostages. We weren't. We had never had any contacts with the kidnappers, had seen to it that the defensive weapons that went to Iran never got into the hands of the people who held our hostages."

Reagan was right that the missiles never went to the hostage takers. But no one said they had, and the rest of his tortured argument fell apart as congressional investigators probed the Iran-contra story. North, McFarlane, and other administration officials were subpoenaed and compelled to testify. The obvious question hanging over the inquiry was how much Reagan knew of what had been done in his name. Yet it was a question the investigators danced around. Almost no one wanted to repeat the experience of Watergate, and, anyway, Reagan was much better liked than Nixon had been. Reagan's famously detached leadership style made it perfectly plausible that North and the others acted to some extent without the president's knowledge. And when Reagan professed an inability to recall the details of certain meetings, many Americans were willing to ascribe the lapse to age. (Later, after leaving the White House, Reagan was diagnosed with Alzheimer's disease, which made the memory lapses even more believable.)

The most thorough investigation of the Iran-contra affair, conducted over several years by independent counsel Lawrence Walsh, gave Reagan a partial pass. "No direct evidence was developed that the President authorized or was informed of the profiteering on the Iran arms sales or of the diversion of proceeds to aid the contras," the Walsh report explained. "Yet, it was doubtful that President Reagan would tolerate the successive Iranian affronts during 1986 unless he knew that the arms sales continued to supply funds to the contras. . . . The wide destruction of records by North eliminated any possible documentary proof."

## 6. BEYOND THE CLOSET

"I feel like number one, like a teen-ager again," Rock Hudson told the reporter for the *Los Angeles Times*. "I have the energy of a teen-ager. I feel better than I ever felt before in my life. I have stamina and energy, and if I tell you my eyesight is better, you won't believe me. My doctors don't."

The reporter wasn't sure she believed him, either. The face of the fifty-eight-year-old actor was gaunt and deeply lined. He laughingly blamed it on having spent ten days on location in Israel, where the sun was brutal and the food worse. He mentioned a heart operation of three years earlier—"a quintuple bypass," he said, holding up five fingers of his right hand. But he was fully recovered from that, and he spent hours each day exercising outdoors: walking, swimming, and gardening. He also made batches of peach ice cream, his favorite. He said he had almost given up cigarettes—but only almost, as became apparent an hour into the interview when he succumbed to the urge and lit up, and then lit up again. He asked the reporter, through the cigarette smoke, not to write about the smoking, as it would upset his doctor.

He reemphasized how good he felt. "My concentration is better," he said. "For years my mind would just drift. I'd go off to Tahiti, I don't know where I'd go." This would happen in the middle of conversations. "Maybe I'd get back in time, maybe I wouldn't. But now I stay right with them. Concentration." He explained that before the bypass surgery five of his six coronary arteries were blocked. "My mind was barely operating. No blood was getting to my brain." The bypasses changed everything.

He paused, with a twinkle in his eye. "I don't think I have any brain damage." He laughed, and the reporter did too. "I'm not sure. It remains to be seen."

The reporter had a long list of questions, for Hudson had been in the news recently. He fended her off, with grinning good humor for the most part. But the grin disappeared when the questions got personal. "People write a lot of stuff about me," he said. "I'm not going to get into *that*. . . . I laugh it off, and then spit in their face, if I get a chance." But he did offer that he valued each day more than he had before. "Underlying everything, I have to say, in all truth, I appreciate things more. . . . Like the last two or three nights, how warm they were. I sat on the patio, had the music going." Meanwhile he had lost patience with the banalities of celebrity life. "I hear stupid, pointless discussion. And I want to say, Why are you both so dumb? Why are you wasting time like this?"

The interview didn't quiet the rumors Rock Hudson refused to discuss. His appearance grew more haggard until the summer of 1985, when he admitted what the Hollywood gossips had been saying for many months: that he was dying of acquired immunodeficiency syndrome, or AIDS. His condition continued to decline, and at the beginning of October his ravaged body gave out.

The Rock Hudson story occasioned comment from all corners of the political and cultural world, for the actor's death brought into the open two aspects of American life that hitherto had been largely hidden. Neither was peculiar to America, although Americans handled both in distinctively American fashion.

The first involved sexual orientation and identity. For most of American history, homosexuality had been denied or outlawed or both. Artists of a particular bohemian type could survive rumors of a preference for members of the same sex; Walt Whitman and Gertrude Stein, after they achieved a certain stature, hardly bothered to deny their homosexuality. Yet neither was embraced by the keepers of convention until long after their deaths, and often not even then. But for nearly everyone else, to reveal one's homosexuality would be to commit occupational and social suicide. Voters would abandon elected officials shown to be gay; school superintendents would fire teachers; bishops would defrock ministers; audiences would boycott actors.

Things started to change during the 1960s. For all the repression—both external and internal—of homosexuality, most American cities contained neighborhoods where gay men and women gathered in bars, restaurants, and coffeehouses. The Stonewall Inn, in New York's Greenwich Village, had an ambiguous relationship with the city's authorities. Usually they let the bar and its patrons alone, but when morals became an issue in New York politics, as they periodically did, the mayor and the police would make a show of cracking down on the gay life there. In June 1969 police raided the Stonewall, but only after telling the management in advance, so that the patrons might clear out ahead of the cops. The management and the patrons understood the drill; they all expected the bar to be back in business before the night was over.

Something went wrong, though. Perhaps a new customer didn't get the message; perhaps the police moved too swiftly for one of the regulars, or the regular too slowly for the police. Doubtless many of the neighborhood's gay residents considered the charade of the announced sweeps stupid and, at the end of a decade in which other long-standing taboos had been challenged, anachronistic. Whatever the cause, the Stonewall raid this night provoked a riot. Thousands of gay men and women and their supporters filled the streets; hundreds of police responded to the call for backup.

The Stonewall riot assumed nothing like the scale of the race riots in Los Angeles, Newark, and Detroit, but it did create headlines, and it forced the issue of gay rights into the public arena. "Gay Power" joined "Black Power" on marchers' signs; members of the Gay Liberation Front likened their cultural insurgency to the insurgency of the National Liberation Front in Vietnam. One by one, then in larger numbers, gay men and lesbian women came out of the closet. The bolder ones went first; the more diffident—or, often, those who thought they had more at stake—waited longer. Across the country people who hadn't realized they knew anyone who was gay discovered they did. The discoveries went far to demystify the whole issue of homosexuality; gradually, over the 1970s and 1980s, the conventional thinking began to change.

Yet as it did it intersected the other current of American culture on the subject, the one of more recent provenance. During the early 1980s physicians in San Francisco, Los Angeles, and New York began reporting an unusual incidence of a rare disease called Kaposi's sarcoma. The disease, a form of cancer, was quite aggressive and almost always killed its victims in comparatively short order. Doctors and public health officials, inquiring into the origins of what they feared might become an urban epidemic, noted that the victims, who were nearly all men, had engaged in regular or intermittent sex with other men.

By the time the disease had a new name—AIDS—it had been labeled the "gay disease." Christian conservatives pointed the finger of blame at the regnant liberalism. "AIDS is God's judgment on a society that does not live by His rules," Jerry Falwell intoned. Patrick Buchanan, who had written speeches for Richard Nixon and now books for conservative readers, asserted, "The poor homosexuals—they have declared war upon nature, and now nature is exacting an awful retribution." The disease cast a long shadow over the gay community. In the first several years of what soon was called the "AIDS epidemic," a positive diagnosis was tantamount to a death sentence, and the death came at the end of months of wasting and pain. Each diagnosis touched off a round of whispers as those who knew the victim wondered about those he might have had sex with; gay men with multiple partners in their pasts shuddered to think what other partners those partners might have had.

Rock Hudson seems to have been diagnosed during the summer of 1984. Rumors of his sexual orientation had floated around Hollywood for years. But the diagnosis of AIDS lent credence to the rumors, and even if the disease hadn't made him too sick to work, it would have ended his career. Hudson had been one of the movie industry's leading men; he appeared on screen opposite Elizabeth Taylor, Doris Day, and other female beauties. The thought that he might have been faking the cinematic chemistry—that he might have been *acting* in all those love scenes—was more than many moviegoers were ready to accept.

Yet the final months of his life did more to soften attitudes toward AIDS victims—and to some extent, toward gay people generally—than just about anything else in the mid-1980s. Rock Hudson had exuded wholesome manliness; if *he* could contract AIDS, if *he* was gay, maybe the disease wasn't so exotic or the lifestyle so perverted. "I am not happy that I have AIDS," Hudson explained not long before his death. "But if that is helping others, I can, at least, know that my own misfortune has had some positive worth." Ronald Reagan went back decades with Hudson, and though the gesture risked offending party conservatives, the president offered public condolences. "Nancy and I are saddened by the news of Rock Hudson's death," he said from the White House. "May God rest his soul."

Reagan's statement was something of a breakthrough for the president. Reagan's administration had tried to ignore the disease; until just weeks before Hudson died, Reagan himself refused to utter the word "AIDS" in speeches or press conferences. But as the gravity of the disease became undeniable, Reagan changed his position. He increased the federal budget for AIDS research, to a half-billion dollars over five years. "This is a top priority with us," the president said. "There's no question about the seriousness of this and the need to find an answer."

Answers came slowly. The causative agent was identified as a human immunodeficiency virus (HIV), but an effective treatment, let alone a cure, was elusive. The death toll mounted, to 12,000 per year in 1986 and 20,000 in 1988. In October 1987, as part of a march on Washington for gay rights, friends and families of the deceased spread a giant quilt upon the Mall, with panels representing thousands of the victims. The quilt returned to the Mall the next year and the year after that; each time the number of panels grew dramatically.

The collective mind of America was torn. Sympathy for the victims battled fear for the safety of one's self and family. As it became apparent that AIDS wasn't simply a gay disease—that HIV would be transmitted through heterosexual contact, through blood transfusions, and through exposure to infected hypodermic needles—many Americans shunned proximity to the infected. A thirteen-year-old boy named Ryan White, a hemophiliac who contracted the infection through a transfusion, was expelled from school in Indiana for fear he would pass the virus to his classmates. When Earvin "Magic" Johnson, a pro basketball superstar, became infected, other players in the league expressed reluctance to take the court against him.

The fear diminished, albeit slowly, as science and medicine made progress against the disease. Researchers discovered that a drug called AZT inhibited the proliferation of HIV within the body and delayed the onset of AIDS; in 1987 the federal Food and Drug Administration approved AZT for clinical use with patients. The drug was expensive but broadly effective. Two years later Louis Sullivan, the secretary of health and human services, was able to announce, "Today we are witnessing a turning point in the battle to change AIDS from a fatal disease to a treatable one."

## 7. APOCALYPSE OVER MANHATTAN

"Burst some eighty-five hundred feet above the Empire State Building, a one-megaton bomb would gut or flatten almost every building between Battery Park and 125th Street," Jonathan Schell wrote.

> The physical collapse of the city would certainly kill millions of people. The streets of New York are narrow ravines running between the high walls of the city's buildings. In a nuclear attack the walls would fall and the ravines would fill up. The people in the buildings would fall to the street with the debris of the buildings, and the people in the street would be crushed by this avalanche of people and buildings. . . . A dazzling white light from the fireball would illuminate the scene, continuing for

> perhaps thirty seconds. Simultaneously, searing heat would ignite everything flammable and start to melt windows, cars, buses, lampposts, and everything else made of metal or glass. People in the street would immediately catch fire, and would shortly be reduced to heavily charred corpses. . . . Soon huge, thick clouds of dust and smoke would envelop the scene, and as the mushroom cloud rushed overhead (it would have a diameter of about twelve miles) the light from the sun would be blotted out, and day would turn into night. . . . Before long, the individual fires would coalesce into a mass fire, which, depending on the winds, would become either a conflagration or a firestorm. In a conflagration, prevailing winds spread a wall of fire as far as there is any combustible material to sustain it; in a firestorm, a vertical updraft caused by the fire itself sucks the surrounding air in toward a central point, and the fires therefore converge in a fire of extreme heat. . . . In this vast theater of physical effects, all the scenes of agony and death that took place at Hiroshima would again take place, but now involving millions of people rather than hundreds of thousands.

If the world didn't end in fire, it would end in ice. Schell's description of a nuclear attack originated as a *New Yorker* article, but after it evoked a tremendous reader response, it was expanded into what became one of the bestselling books of the 1980s, *The Fate of the Earth.* Reagan's arms buildup and bellicose rhetoric—including a tasteless joke delivered when he thought he was off-microphone, about how the bombing of Moscow was to begin shortly—had set millions of Americans on edge. Whatever détente had or hadn't accomplished to alter relations between the superpowers, it had altered perceptions of those relations within the United States. Millions of Americans, having felt themselves on the brink of the nuclear abyss during and after the Cuban missile crisis of 1962, breathed great sighs of relief that Washington and Moscow were scaling back their nuclear ambitions and pulling away from confrontation. The "doomsday clock," a metaphor regarding humanity's nearness to the apocalypse, had been maintained and recalibrated, as events suggested, by the board of directors of the *Bulletin of the Atomic Scientists* since just after World War II. Originally set at seven minutes to midnight, it was moved forward to three minutes in 1949, when the Soviet Union acquired its atomic bomb, and to two minutes in 1953, when both the

Americans and the Russians unveiled their thermonuclear weapons. It gradually fell back as doomsday didn't arrive; in the détente era it stood at twelve minutes to midnight. The policies of the Reagan administration pushed it forward again, to three minutes.

Schell's book gave rise to a new genre of end-times literature and art—a genre distinct from but not unrelated to the end-times predictions of the Christian fundamentalists. The ABC television network produced a program called *The Day After*, depicting a nuclear war and its aftermath. The story was centered in the American Midwest, where survivors staggered through the rubble, sorting the dead and dying from the living, wondering how many of those spared by the blast would succumb to the radiation then or later. The show took no side in the nuclear debate, fudging even the issue of which country fired first. The special effects were amateurish (the Reagan administration denied the producers access to Department of Defense footage of real mushroom clouds), but the psychological effects were profound. Tens of millions of viewers turned off their sets wondering how long the human species had left.

The species question constituted the heart of the debate over "nuclear winter." Carl Sagan was an astronomer and Cornell professor who attracted national attention with a 1980 series called *Cosmos* on the Public Broadcasting System. Sagan subsequently became the face and voice of science to millions of Americans. And so when he predicted, with other scientists, that a nuclear war would not merely incinerate and poison the human race but also cast a pall of dust over the planet that would block out the sun and lower temperatures dramatically, killing plant and animal species and eventually most of those humans who had survived the initial onslaught, his warning had a predictably chilling effect.

One result was the not-coincidentally-named "nuclear freeze" movement, which demanded that the Reagan administration halt its arms buildup. Another was calls for a pledge by the administration that it would not resort to nuclear weapons until some other country—presumably the Soviet Union—did so. The pedigree of the no-first-users was more distinguished, in a foreign policy sense, than that of Sagan or Schell or the ABC producers: their number included such eminent figures as George Kennan, the coiner of containment; McGeorge Bundy, the national security adviser to Kennedy and Johnson; Robert McNamara, defense secretary to same; and Gerard Smith, a veteran of several administrations. "It is time to recognize that no one has ever succeeded in advancing any persuasive reason to believe that any use of nuclear weapons, even on the smallest scale, could reliably be expected to remain limited," the four experts jointly asserted in an article in *Foreign Affairs*. "Any use of nuclear weapons in Europe, by the Alliance"—NATO—"or against it, carries with it a high and inescapable risk of escalation into general nuclear war, which would bring ruin to all and victory to none."

The Reagan administration rejected the demands for a no-first-use pledge, contending that it would yield an advantage to the Soviets and their larger conventional forces. The president similarly rebuffed the nuclear freezers. "A freeze now would make us less, not more, secure and would raise, not reduce, the risks of war," he told a national television audience. "It would reward the Soviets for their massive military buildup while preventing us from modernizing our aging and increasingly vulnerable forces."

## 8. SO CLOSE

Yet Reagan was too canny a politician to ignore the popular fears entirely, and when he found a suitable partner in the Kremlin, he began changing his bellicose tune and policies.

The Soviet Union had never figured out how to manage its regime transitions, which was why Soviet leaders tended to die with their boots on. Leonid Brezhnev, only the fourth Soviet head man in the sixty-five years since the 1917 revolution, died in 1982. History suggested another long reign by his successor. But Yuri Andropov died after less than two years in charge, and *his* successor, Konstantin Chernenko, lasted only a year. In early 1985 the Politburo tried another approach, selecting a much younger and more vigorous figure. Mikhail Gorbachev was a son of peasants from southwestern Russia; he grew up under Stalin and learned what was not to like about that brutal dictator's brand of communism. He nonetheless joined the Young Communist League as a teenager and steadily climbed the ranks of the party. By 1984 he was commonly accounted the heir apparent to Chernenko, whose sudden death catapulted him to power as general secretary of the Communist party.

Gorbachev had added an aversion to Brezhnevism—interpreted as the bureaucratic rule that stifled the Soviet economy—to his existing distaste for Stalinism, and in his new position he determined to eliminate both. He launched a two-pronged campaign of *glasnost*, or openness, which allowed greater freedom of speech and the press, and *perestroika*, or restructuring, which provided Russians their first taste of democracy and capitalism. The purpose of the twin initiatives was to modernize the Soviet system and improve the lot of Soviet citizens.

As part of his reform package, Gorbachev sought ways to trim government spending. Defense formed an even larger part of the Soviet budget than of the American budget; to lessen his defense burden, Gorbachev revamped the Soviet approach to the arms race. Hitherto Moscow had tried to match the Americans at each step of the technological way, building a fission bomb after the Americans built theirs, a fusion bomb almost simultaneously with the Americans, then big bombers and missiles. By the early 1980s the Soviet Union was fully the equal of the United States in nuclear weaponry, but it was also nearly bankrupt. Consequently, when the Reagan administration proposed to take the arms race into outer space with the Strategic Defense Initiative, Gorbachev decided the time had come to halt the competition.

The death of détente hadn't entirely derailed arms control, but it had slowed the process to a crawl. American and Soviet negotiators haggled endlessly over matters substantial and trivial, with the haggling in the mid-1980s centering on intermediate-range missiles in Europe. Gorbachev jolted the talks forward by giving the Americans all they asked for. This was indeed a jolt, in that certain elements of the Reagan administration, and most of the administration's neoconservative supporters, distrusted the whole idea of disarmament. They had never expected the Kremlin to accept what Reagan's negotiators had put on the table regarding the intermediate missiles; when Gorbachev did accept it, they immediately began to think they should have asked for more.

The administration responded to Gorbachev's agreement to ban intermediate missiles from Europe by proposing to eliminate *all* nuclear missiles, not just the intermediate ones. As the Soviet arsenal depended more heavily on missiles than the American arsenal did, Reagan's team was sure Gorbachev would reject the proposal.

Like a riverboat gambler, Gorbachev matched the American bet and raised it. Why not eliminate all nuclear *weapons*, he said, not just the weapons mounted on missiles? Gorbachev's offer was a public relations coup. The world had watched the back-and-forth between Washington and Moscow, and for the most part it hailed the Kremlin's new man as a great peacemaker. (He would win the Nobel Peace Prize in 1990.) American leaders, having grown accustomed to a glacial tempo in Soviet decision making under Brezhnev, found themselves panting to keep up with Gorbachev's sprint.

The critical moment came in October 1986, when Reagan and Gorbachev met in Iceland. Some of Reagan's advisers were worried; the president had become better educated in the nuances of nuclear arms than he had been at the outset of his administration, but he was still no expert. The details of disarmament bored him, but in matters of weapons technology the details could mean everything. His advisers feared that in a one-on-one session with Gorbachev, he might inadvertently yield crucial points to the Soviets. Richard Nixon, just emerging from his post-Watergate isolation, was appalled at what Reagan might do. "There is no way he can ever be allowed to participate in a private meeting with Gorbachev," the pioneer arms controller declared.

Reagan and Gorbachev talked for two days at Reykjavík. The world media covered the conference, which many observers considered the most important Soviet-American meeting since Truman's conference with Stalin at Potsdam in 1945. The president and the general secretary and their respective advisers thrashed out one aspect after another of a potential bargain on missiles and warheads. On the third day Gorbachev returned to his grand proposal for the elimination of all nuclear weapons. Why not do it? he asked Reagan. Why not simply get rid of them all?

Reagan nodded agreement. "It would be fine with me if we eliminated all nuclear weapons," he said. The president's advisers almost choked. The United States had long justified its nuclear arsenal as necessary to counter the Soviet advantage in conventional weapons. Without nuclear weapons, how would the United States prevent the Red Army from overrunning Western Europe? At the very least, how would the administration explain to America's European allies that the president had just negotiated away the nuclear umbrella that had shielded them since the creation of NATO?

Things didn't quite come to that. Gorbachev had a condition for agreeing to eliminate nuclear weapons: the United States must confine research on

SDI to the laboratory. Retiring and destroying all the nuclear weapons would take years; in the meantime the United States must not deploy a space-based defensive system.

Reagan reacted sharply. "I've said again and again that SDI wasn't a bargaining chip," he declared angrily. At least he seemed angry: Reagan retained enough of the actor's skills that one could never be sure when he was being sincere and when he was acting. Yet he truly believed that SDI would be a force for peace. At Reykjavík he likened SDI to a gas mask, which protected the wearer while threatening no one. Gorbachev rejected the analogy, arguing that an effective nuclear defense would remove the psychological deterrent that had kept both sides in check for decades. Besides, even if he trusted Reagan not to exploit an American advantage in defensive systems, how could he be sure about Reagan's successors? It would be years before any Reykjavík deal became fully operational.

On this point the talks stalled. Reagan gathered his papers and stood up. "The meeting is over," he said. He turned to Secretary of State Shultz. "Let's go, George."

The failure of the Reykjavík summit was widely mourned. For a moment the fondest dream of billions of people since 1945—that the leaders of the superpowers would summon the sense and courage to banish the specter of nuclear annihilation—had seemed possible. Perhaps the dreamers deluded themselves; perhaps the nuclear genie could never be returned to the bottle. Perhaps the fine plans of Gorbachev and Reagan would have been frustrated in the implementation. But for that moment in Reykjavík, humanity had allowed itself to dream.

And in the time it took the American president to walk out of his meeting with the Soviet general secretary, the dream dissolved in the frosty Iceland air.

# III

# Silicon Schemes and Global Connections

1987–2010

# 11 | History Without End

## 1987–1991

### 1. St. Alan and the Dragon

The autumn of 1987 was a turbulent period on Wall Street. The twin deficits—the federal budget deficit and the trade deficit—had pushed interest rates up, not to the historic levels of the late 1970s but to an altitude from which those daunting heights were visible. Stock prices skidded, then recovered, then skidded some more. On Friday, October 16, the Dow Jones average suffered its first hundred-point loss on a single day in history, plummeting 108 points, or 5 percent of its value. *Time* magazine went to press that weekend with a story headlined "Wall Street's October Massacre."

Then the really bad news hit. Alan Greenspan had only just taken his seat as chairman of the Federal Reserve Board. On Monday he was scheduled to fly from Washington to Dallas, where he would address the American Bankers Association and reassure them that the Fed was monitoring the stock market carefully. He checked the Dow as he was boarding the plane for the three-hour flight; it was already down another two hundred points. En route he considered how to strengthen his remarks. He was greeted at the airport in Dallas by an employee of the Federal Reserve branch of that city. Greenspan asked how the market had fared. "Down five-oh-eight," he was told. "Great!" Greenspan replied, assuming the employee meant 5.08 points. "What a terrific rally!"

The sickened look on the face of the Dallas man told him that there hadn't been a rally—"five-oh-eight" meant 508 points, nearly a quarter of the Dow's value, a portion larger than any single-day loss during the Great Crash of 1929, the previous benchmark of investor doom. The volume was immense: six hundred million shares, almost double the previous record. In the space of hours, trillions of dollars of market value had vanished; it was, the chairman of the New York Stock Exchange said, "the nearest thing to a meltdown that I ever want to see."

The titans of American business were mystified. "I have never experienced anything like this, so it is difficult to have clear vision," Robert E. Allen, the president of AT&T, said. "I don't understand it in terms of the fundamentals of the economy." Thomas Labrecque of Chase Manhattan Bank declared: "The fundamentals don't call for it. The activity far exceeds the facts." John Rolls of United Technologies asserted: "We believe it is an overreaction. We don't know how to interpret it, and we don't think anyone else does either."

As bad as the news was for the investment pros, the greater fear was that the Wall Street collapse would devastate the larger economy. "When people see a selloff like this they tend to panic, even if they don't own stock," Paul Getman, a financial consultant, explained. "My 55-year-old mother called me twice today to ask if we're going into a depression, and she doesn't own a share."

Black Monday, as the day came to be known, put the skills of Alan Greenspan and the powers of the Federal Reserve to the test. Greenspan's predecessors and the earlier Fed had flunked a similar test in 1929, with the result that the Great Crash had segued into the Great Depression. Greenspan knew that story, and he understood the danger. "I went straight to the hotel, where I stayed on the phone into the night," he recollected.

> The Fed's job during a stock-market panic is to ward off financial paralysis—a chaotic state in which businesses and banks stop making the payments they owe each other and the economy grinds to a halt. To the senior people on the phone with me that night, the urgency and gravity of the situation was apparent—even if the markets got no worse, the system would be reeling for weeks. We started exploring ways we might have to supply liquidity if major institutions ran short of cash.

Some of Greenspan's associates, especially the younger ones, who couldn't remember the Great Crash and the depression, suggested taking things slowly. "Why not wait a few days and see what happens?" one asked.

"We don't need to wait to see what happens," Greenspan retorted. "We know what's going to happen. You know what people say about getting shot? You feel like you've been punched, but the trauma is such that you don't feel the pain right away? In twenty-four or forty-eight hours, we're going to be feeling a lot of pain."

Greenspan flew by military jet—placed at his disposal by the White House—back to Washington for an emergency meeting of the Fed board. Lately the Fed had been tightening credit by contracting the money supply; Greenspan and the board now declared a reversal of course. "The Federal Reserve, consistent with its responsibilities as the nation's central bank, affirmed today its readiness to serve as a source of liquidity to support the economic and financial system," the board announced. The Fed began buying billions of dollars of Treasury securities, thereby injecting those billions into the money supply.

The strategy worked miraculously well. Interest rates declined, and the financial system began operating normally again. Far from plunging into depression, the economy resumed its growth, expanding robustly during 1988. The Dow recovered the ground it had yielded; investors recouped their losses; and Wall Street promoted Alan Greenspan for early canonization.

## 2. JUST SAY . . . MAYBE?

The role of the president in these dramatic events was modest. Ronald Reagan was no master of finance, and he didn't pretend to be one. He uttered the expected reassurances but did little more. Yet even if he had been an expert, he would have had difficulty concentrating on Wall Street's troubles. "I confess this was a period of time in which I was more concerned about the possibility of an even greater tragedy in my own life than I was about the stock market," he wrote.

Nancy Reagan was Ronald Reagan's second wife. He had divorced Jane Wyman in 1948, long before he developed political aspirations. Some social and religious conservatives held the divorce against him, but most forgave him as the depth and sincerity of his devotion to Nancy became apparent. As president he reserved an honored place for her at the State of the Union and other speeches; when her work as first lady took her away from Washington, he counted the days and hours till her return. He accorded her more influence over policy than was generally known. Donald Regan, the White House chief of staff, later recounted that Mrs. Reagan consulted an astrologer to determine auspicious dates for presidential announcements and meetings. Other administration insiders confirmed the story and added that Reagan knowingly went along with his wife's superstition. "He is definitely aware of it," one said. "He approved of it."

In October 1987, weeks before Black Monday, a routine exam revealed a lump in Nancy Reagan's left breast. "The next ten days may have been the longest ten days of our lives," Reagan recalled. A biopsy revealed that the tumor was malignant. The doctors gave the president the bad news. "I couldn't reply to them. I just dropped my head and cried. After they left, I remained at the table, motionless and unable to speak." The surgery went as well as a mastectomy could go. "She was devastated by the loss of her breast—not because she was worried about herself, but because she was worried about me and how I would feel about her as a woman." Reagan reassured her, "It doesn't matter: I love *you*." He kissed her and smiled. "But seeing that sadness in her eyes, it was all I could do to avoid breaking up again."

Forty-eight hours later Wall Street walked off its cliff. Reagan hardly noticed. "Stock market or no stock market, it was mainly Nancy, not Wall Street, I worried about." Nancy recovered, albeit more slowly than the stock market, and returned to her various duties as first lady.

The most important of these was one she had chosen herself. She afterward said that her travels on her husband's behalf during the months before the 1980 election alerted her to the ravages drug abuse was having on American society. "Not only can it tear down an entire nation," she explained, "it also brings danger into the lives of our most precious resource: our children. It is up to our generation to protect them and provide for them a drug-free world in which to live. We must act now, not tomorrow, or the next day." Nancy Reagan crisscrossed the country preaching abstinence from drugs; she spearheaded a movement summarized in the slogan "Just Say No."

In part because of her influence, the war against drugs escalated beyond America's borders. The Reagan administration pressured foreign governments to act against producers and traffickers of opiates, cocaine, marijuana, and other illicit drugs. In 1988 a cabinet-level office was created to coordinate the war; its head, universally called the "drug czar," reported directly to the president.

The war on drugs became an enduring feature of American domestic politics and foreign policy; over the course of the ensuing decades the federal government would spend hundreds of billions of dollars on the project. Several states and the federal government rewrote criminal codes to punish violators of drug laws more harshly; prison populations swelled with convicted offenders. Candidates for elective office vied to present themselves as the ones most willing and able to bring the drug pushers and traffickers to justice.

Victories in the war on drugs were elusive. Because it was illegal, drug use was difficult to document, but evidence indicated that after an initial decrease, unlawful use actually spread. A 1995 survey of fifty thousand teenagers across the country revealed that 20 percent of eighth graders, 30 percent of tenth graders, and 40 percent of twelfth graders had used illegal drugs during the previous year. Half of those reporting use during the year said they had used drugs during the previous month. These numbers were up sharply from a similar study four years earlier. A separate study released in 1996, documenting the rise in adolescent marijuana use in particular, declared, "A profound reversal in adolescent drug trends is continuing. . . . Today's teens are less likely to consider drug use harmful and risky, more likely to believe that drug use is widespread and tolerated, and feel more pressure to try illegal drugs than teens did just two years ago."

New and newly popular drugs complemented the old standbys. Ecstasy, a stimulant favored by the hard-partying crowd, flooded the cities. "In 1997 we seized 400,000 pills," an official of the U.S. customs service told a reporter in early 2001. "We seized 9 million pills in 2000, and in the last four months we have seized 3 million. We are on pace to set a record year of 12 million tablets of Ecstasy this year. It's just coming at us fast and furious."

The heightened efforts to intercept imports of illegal drugs had the perverse but predictable effect of encouraging production within the United States. Government statistics for 2005 estimated that illicit producers in basements, back lots, and rural hideaways harvested twenty-two million pounds of marijuana. This was ten times the amount produced when Nancy Reagan's antidrug campaign began, and it had a market value of more than $35 billion, making it the most lucrative cash crop in America.

## 3. THEIR WAY

The failure of the Reykjavík summit dealt a blow to arms control and the budding rapprochement between the United States and the Soviet Union, but it didn't derail the process entirely. As Gorbachev's reforms took hold in Russia, the Soviet leader gained confidence in his ability to cut deals with Reagan, who for his part didn't want to leave office under the cloud of the Iran-contra scandal. Six weeks after the stock swoon in the autumn of 1987, Reagan hosted Gorbachev for a Washington visit, during which the two leaders signed an agreement calling for the elimination of their countries' intermediate nuclear forces. "This treaty represents a landmark in postwar history, because it is not just an arms control but an arms reduction agreement," Reagan explained in a television address to the country. "Unlike treaties of the past, this agreement does not simply establish ceilings for new weapons; it actually reduces the number of such weapons. In fact, it altogether abolishes an entire class of U.S. and Soviet nuclear missiles."

This was a remarkable statement, and the INF treaty, as it was called, was a remarkable pact. Reagan had entered office contending that the United States must build weapons; now he was destroying them. He claimed a logic beneath the apparent inconsistency: the buildup had been necessary to bring the Russians to the bargaining table. And certain aspects of the buildup continued. The Strategic Defense Initiative remained a centerpiece of American planning. "We will research it, we will test it, and when it is ready we will deploy it," Reagan vowed. "We will move forward with SDI; it is our moral duty." All the same, the shift from the old Reagan to the new, from Cold Warrior to arms controller, was striking. Even as Reagan told Americans they could relegate "INF" to the storage files of the alphabet-soup vernacular of international affairs, he introduced a new combination. "Other letters you'll hear more about are START, Strategic Arms Reduction Talks, because we've made progress toward fifty-percent reductions in strategic nuclear arsenals," he declared at the end of Gorbachev's visit. "This could be another historic achievement."

And so it would be, albeit under another president. Reagan's time in office was waning, but he retained sufficient loyalty among the Republican faithful to ensure the 1988 nomination of his vice president, George H. W. Bush, to be his successor. Bush originally hailed from the moderate Northeastern wing of the Republican party, and though he had moved to Texas as a young man and had prospered in politics with the Sunbelt shift of the GOP, many of the traits of his youth survived. "I want a kinder, gentler nation," he told the Republican convention, in implicit rebuke to those members of the party who demanded a no-holds-barred campaign against the Democrats. Yet Bush had imbibed enough of the Reagan philosophy to embrace tax cuts at all costs. "I'm the one who will not raise taxes," he said. "My opponent"—Massachusetts governor Michael Dukakis—"now says he'll raise them as a last resort or a third resort. When a politician talks like that, you know that's one resort he'll be checking into. My opponent won't rule out raising taxes, but I will, and the Congress will push me to raise taxes, and I'll say no, and they'll push, and I'll say no, and they'll push again, and I'll say to them, 'Read my lips: no new taxes.'"

This last line, which referenced a tough-guy movie role of Clint Eastwood's, got a laugh, and it got the attention of the country. The Bush campaign made its candidate the heir to Reagan and branded Dukakis a Massachusetts liberal; voters bought the characterization sufficiently to award Bush the presidency, by a popular margin of 53 percent to 47 percent and an electoral advantage of 426 to 112. The election suggested even better things for the Republicans in the years to come. Reagan's 1980 and 1984 victories had resulted in no small part from his personal appeal; when the less charismatic Bush carried the entire South and most of the Midwest in 1988, it signaled that the Republicans now owned Dixie and had a strong claim on the American heartland.

Bush was happy to identify himself with Reagan during the campaign, but he proved to be a different sort of president. His speaking skills fell short of those of the Great Communicator; Dana Carvey of *Saturday Night Live* launched a career lampooning Bush's telegraphic style. Bush distanced himself from grand schemes for remaking the world; he said he lacked the "vision thing."

Yet he demonstrated a quiet competence born of years in vital, if often unnoticed, appointed positions. He had been ambassador to the United Nations, where he got to know many of those who would go on to become leaders of their countries. He had headed the Republican national committee in the wake of Watergate, earning the gratitude of party regulars. He was the first American envoy to China and took lessons in diplomacy from Zhou Enlai, one of the modern masters of the diplomatic arts. He headed the CIA as the Church committee was airing the agency's dirty linen; for decades afterward American intelligence professionals avowed their esteem for him at every opportunity.

Yet for all his experience in foreign affairs, Bush as president proceeded cautiously at first. He studied Gorbachev and the Soviet Union for three months before calling on his Russian counterpart to live up to the peaceful promises he had made. "A new relationship cannot simply be declared by Moscow," Bush said. "It must be earned." He proposed to move "beyond containment," saying the Cold War should end. But reaching the end would require care and resolve. "Many dangers and uncertainties are ahead. We must not forget that the Soviet Union has acquired awesome military capabilities. That was a fact of life for my predecessors. . . . That is a fact of life for me today."

Gorbachev responded to Bush's challenge by maintaining the reform course he had sketched out and extending it to Moscow's allies. Since 1945 the Red Army had rarely retreated from territory taken during the war; the Kremlin's policy was summarized in the Brezhnev Doctrine—a Soviet counterpart to the Truman Doctrine—that asserted that a country that once fell under Soviet sway would remain under Soviet sway. The Brezhnev Doctrine had received its definitive application in 1968 when Red Army tanks rolled into Prague and crushed efforts by Czech dissidents to loosen Moscow's grip on their homeland.

Gorbachev rescinded the doctrine, at first obliquely by withdrawing Soviet troops from Afghanistan, and then directly by announcing a new policy toward the satellite states of Eastern Europe. Gorbachev urged the members of the Warsaw Pact to seek their own paths toward *perestroika*, and he declared that the Soviet Union had "no moral or political right to interfere in events" in those countries. His foreign policy spokesman went on American television to give the new approach a name. Gennady Gerasimov was a fan of American music, and he explained that the Kremlin was replacing the Brezhnev Doctrine with the "Sinatra Doctrine." Hungary and Poland were reforming rapidly, with Moscow's blessing, Gerasimov said. "You know the Frank Sinatra song 'I Did It My Way'? Hungary and Poland are doing it their way."

Their way caught on in a rush. Reformers in one country of Eastern Europe after another barged through the door Gorbachev had opened. The critical moment occurred in November 1989 when large crowds gathered in East Berlin. For four decades Berlin had symbolized and embodied the Cold War division of Europe; for nearly three decades the hated Berlin Wall had split the old German capital in two. John Kennedy had stood at the wall and flung democracy's defiance at the authoritarians beyond; more recently Ronald Reagan had approached the Brandenburg Gate and demanded: "Mr. Gorbachev, open this gate! Mr. Gorbachev, tear down this wall!"

Now the people of East Berlin and East Germany made the same demand—from their own side of the wall. For several excruciating hours no one knew what would happen. East German troops had been trained to guard the wall with their lives and to kill anyone who tried to breach or scale it. The citizens of East Berlin had painful memories of those spots along the wall where their comrades had indeed been gunned down trying to flee. But the government of East Germany had lapsed into chaos, and on this November evening the guards didn't know whether the old orders stood, and the demonstrators didn't know whether the guards would obey the orders, if the orders did stand.

Finally word came from headquarters that the gates should be opened. An immediate thrill coursed through the crowd, and then the crowd pushed through the gates into a city they hadn't seen for twenty-eight years. The neighborhoods near the wall celebrated throughout the night and far into the next day. "We've Done It! The Wall Is Open!" the West German tabloid *Bild* exulted in a banner headline. The mayor of West Berlin declared, "The whole city and all its citizens will never forget November 9, 1989. For twenty-eight years since the wall was built we have yearned for this day. We Germans are now the happiest people on earth."

## 4. SOFT LANDING

Americans were happy, too, but also perplexed. "I was at my desk about mid-afternoon when an excited Brent"—Scowcroft, the national security adviser—"came in and told me there were reports that the Wall had been opened," George Bush remembered. "We went into the study off the Oval Office and turned on the television to live coverage of the jubilant crowds in Berlin." Bush's press secretary arrived with wire-service reports confirming what the television pictures showed. He recommended that the president make a statement. Bush demurred. "Although I was elated over what appeared to have happened, I was wary about offering hasty comments. . . . I did not want to jump in before we really knew the details. More important, I knew we had to be careful how we portrayed our response to the good news. I had to anticipate Gorbachev's reaction—and that of his opposition. As Brent pointed out, this was not the time to gloat."

But he had to say something. Bush went before reporters with a brief statement: "I welcome the decision by the East German leadership to open the borders to those wishing to emigrate or travel. I am very pleased with this development."

The reporters wanted more. "Is this the end of the Iron Curtain?" one asked.

"Well, I don't think any single event is the end of what you might call the Iron Curtain," Bush replied. "But clearly this is a long way from the harshest Iron Curtain days—a long way from that."

"Did you ever imagine anything like this happening?"

"We've imagined it, but I can't say that I foresaw this development at this stage."

"You don't seem elated."

"I'm not an emotional kind of guy."

"How elated are you?"

"I'm very pleased. . . . The fact that I'm not bubbling over—maybe it's getting along towards evening. . . . I feel very good about it."

Bush continued to feel good about it, largely because things continued to go America's way. One by one the communist regimes in Eastern Europe disintegrated. Most went peacefully; others put up a struggle. In Poland the Solidarity movement supplanted the communist government following elections. In Hungary reformers proclaimed the third Hungarian republic and moved quickly to restore ties to Western Europe. In Romania the odious Nicolae Ceausescu met a violent end before a firing squad, which also dispatched his wife.

Germany drew the greatest attention. The opening of the Berlin Wall suggested a larger opening of East Germany to West Germany, yet many people within Germany and especially outside the country registered doubts. For all the costs the Cold War had inflicted on Europe, they were far less than the costs of the two world wars, and though no one could prove it, the division of Germany plausibly had something to do with the comparative calm since 1945. An irreverent cliché about NATO, not articulated in polite company but neither denied, asserted that the purpose of the alliance for the British and French was to keep the Americans in, the Russians out, and the Germans down. American leaders had long endorsed the reunification of Germany, but that was during a time when reunification seemed impossible. Now that it appeared possible, they might reconsider.

Bush and his advisers did reconsider, and in doing so they developed a set of conditions reunification ought to meet. It should reflect the will of the German people, it should preserve Germany's membership in NATO and the European Community, and it should be accomplished gradually and without alarming Germany's neighbors. The first two conditions were readily met; the third was harder. Once the Germans discovered that the Cold War no longer barred their path to reunification, they demanded a rapid rejoining of the two parts of their severed country. Meanwhile the prospect of a reconstructed German juggernaut indeed alarmed the neighbors. In Britain, France, and the Soviet Union, millions of people had personal recollections of Hitler's Germany and the horrendous harm it had visited upon them and their countries. The tramp of German jackboots, the rumble of German tank treads, and the scream of German rocket-bombs still echoed in the minds of the survivors of Nazi aggression.

But Bush decided that European stability required a German anchor, and he joined forces with West German chancellor Helmut Kohl to make reunification a reality. The president reiterated America's commitment to European security and he spent long hours in meetings and on the telephone reassuring the British, French, and Soviets that the Germany of 1990 wasn't the Germany of 1940. Bush's efforts paid off, and when the Germans formally retied the knot in October 1990, he was the first to offer congratulations. "Today begins a new chapter in the history of your nation," he told the Germans. "Forty-five years of conflict and confrontation between East and West are now behind us. At long last the day has come: Germany is united; Germany is fully free."

The reunification of Germany might have marked the definitive end of the Cold War—which, after all, had started with the division of Germany—had another event, still more definitive in concluding the contest between the United States and the Soviet Union, not followed within several months. Gorbachev's reforms had not been universally popular within the Soviet Union. The old guard of the Communist party objected to the derogation of its authority the reforms entailed. Soviet military leaders, having spent two generations preparing to fight the Americans and their allies, found it difficult to relinquish their weapons. Government elites, accustomed to the perquisites of office and authority, felt threatened by their loss of prestige. Members of the security forces feared what *glasnost* might reveal about their complicity in the activities of the Soviet police apparatus. Soviet citizens from all stations complained that Gorbachev was unilaterally surrendering the superpower status their country had won at such cost during World War II.

During the summer of 1991 a cabal of the Communist hardliners attempted a coup against Gorbachev. He was arrested while on vacation near the Black Sea, and the hardliners declared a state of emergency. But the effort was poorly organized, and it began falling apart at once. Large crowds gathered in Moscow, where they confronted troops sent by the leaders of the anti-Gorbachev plot. A long, tense moment ensued, with the troops unsure whether to shoot the protesters or join them. In the end the soldiers simply stood down, and the coup collapsed.

But so did Gorbachev's government. The man of the hour was Boris Yeltsin, the elected president of the Russian republic (the largest of the subdivisions of the Soviet Union). At the crucial moment Yeltsin mounted one of the tanks sent against the demonstrators and dared the soldiers to fire. When they didn't, his popularity soared. Already power had been drifting away from the Soviet central government to the governments of the several republics; Yeltsin's heroics accelerated the trend. During the next few months Gorbachev tried to paper over the breakup, but at the end of 1991 the Soviet Union quietly slipped out of existence.

With it disappeared, finally and forever, the Cold War. As long as the Soviet Union survived, Gorbachev's reforms could have been reversed, just as détente had been reversed. But after the Soviet Union sank beneath the waves of *glasnost, perestroika*, and the preexisting strains of communist politics and socialist economics, no such reversal was possible. Russia persisted, as did the other republics of the erstwhile union. Yet they were as dysfunctional in their own ways as the larger union had been. And in any event, without the confidence the communist ideology had inspired, they lacked the assertiveness that for nearly half a century had made Moscow always a worry to Americans and often a fright.

## 5. WHO'S NEXT?

"It was over," Brent Scowcroft recalled. "An event I had never imagined I would see in my lifetime had actually taken place. It left me feeling numb, disbelieving." Many Americans felt similarly. The end of the Cold War deprived Americans of much of the sense of purpose and direction that had guided their country's actions since 1945. As trying as the struggle against the Soviet Union had been, it had the singular advantage of focusing the attention of the American political system.

American lawmakers and American voters prior to 1941 had paid little heed to the world beyond American borders; their intermittent endorsements of foreign ventures were typically followed by retreats to isolationism. The 1898 imperialist burst that made the Philippines an American colony fizzled out in an anti-imperial discouragement that precluded the taking of any more colonies. The rally to arms behind Wilson's 1917 call to make the world safe for democracy gave way, within little more than two years, to a rejection of Wilson, his vision, and the world in general. Many Americans had expected, and more than a few hoped for, a similar retreat from the world after 1945. Robert Taft and Henry Wallace, from different ends of the political spectrum, had encouraged such thinking. But the Truman administration interpreted Soviet actions as threatening and responded in a confrontational manner, the Kremlin acted analogously, and the Cold War resulted.

Now, forty-five years later, the Cold War was over. What would follow was anyone's guess. Francis Fukuyama offered one prediction. Fukuyama worked for the State Department's policy planning staff, the idea shop George Kennan had headed at the time he outlined the containment policy. Fukuyama contended that the end of the Cold War marked not simply the end of a phase of history but of history itself. This argument wasn't quite as nonsensical as it sounded; a philosopher by training, Fukuyama considered history to be the struggle of ideas. Modern Western history, which had become modern world history, was the struggle between liberalism, in the sense of democracy and capitalism, and authoritarianism, as embodied originally by monarchism but more recently by fascism and communism. Liberalism had bested monarchism in the eighteenth and nineteenth centuries, and it had defeated fascism and communism in the twentieth. With no other competitors, liberalism had won—and history had ended.

This was a mixed blessing, Fukuyama asserted. He appreciated the virtues of liberalism, but he also valued the effort its victory had required. "The end of history will be a very sad time," he predicted. "The struggle for recognition, the willingness to risk one's life for a purely abstract goal, the worldwide ideological struggle that called forth daring, courage, imagination, and idealism, will be replaced by economic calculation, the endless solving of technical problems, environmental concerns, and the satisfaction of sophisticated consumer demands. In the post-historical period there will be neither art nor philosophy, just the perpetual caretaking of the museum of human history."

Fukuyama needn't have worried. Almost no one outside the American policy elite read *National Interest*, the journal that published his musings; the other 99.99 percent of the world carried on as though history had neither ended nor even slowed down. The war between Iraq and Iran had continued amid the crumbling of the Soviet empire. The Reagan administration, initially neutral in public, tilted toward Iraq after Iran began winning—and after the Reagan White House got caught illegally shipping arms to Iran. Iranian gunboats targeted oil tankers loading at Kuwait, the oil emirate at the head of the gulf; Kuwait appealed for international assistance, cannily calling on both the United States and the Soviet Union to uphold the maritime rights of neutrals during wartime. Washington might well have acceded to an exclusive Kuwaiti appeal; the unfettered flow of oil was essential to the American and world economies. But the Soviet angle decided the matter. "I was quite sure," Caspar Weinberger, Reagan's secretary of defense, explained afterward, "that if we did not respond positively the USSR would quickly fill the vacuum, and that the Gulf states, already concerned for a number of reasons"—especially the fall of the shah—"about American reliability, would not be able to deny basing and port facilities to their new protectors."

The Reagan administration approved the reflagging of Kuwaiti ships under American registry. It presented the decision as balanced between Iran and Iraq, but no one was fooled. The American tilt against Iran became clearer as American warships escorting the reflagged tankers started trading fire with Iranian gunboats. Iranian vessels laid mines in the shipping lanes; after an American destroyer hit one of the mines, the Pentagon ordered reprisals against Iranian oil rigs in the gulf. Tensions escalated until July 1988, when an American guided-missile cruiser, the *Vincennes*, spotted an Iranian aircraft approaching along what seemed a threatening trajectory. The officers and crew of the *Vincennes* were on hair-trigger alert against Iranian gunboats and mines; they required little imagination to perceive the approaching plane as dangerous. The ship's commander ordered his rocket crews to fire. The missiles streaked toward the target, which exploded in a ball of flame and plunged into the sea. To his horror, the captain later discovered that the plane was no attacker but a civilian airliner, and that his rockets had killed nearly three hundred noncombatants.

The Iranian government and people rejected Washington's claim of mistaken identity; the shoot-down evinced the depths to which the Great Satan would sink in its efforts to roll back the Islamic revolution, they claimed. The incident doubtless would have provoked a further escalation of hostility between the United States and Iran had the Iranian government not concluded, at just this time, that the war with Iraq had to end. A July 1988 ceasefire terminated the fighting between Iran and Iraq, and with it the skirmishing between Iran and the United States.

Perhaps paradoxically—but perhaps not, such being the complexities of Middle Eastern politics—the ceasefire freed Iraq to cross swords with the United States. The war ended with Iraq's economy in tatters and the country deeply in debt; Saddam Hussein sought all means of increasing Iraq's oil revenues. Neither he nor most other Iraqis had ever acknowledged the legitimacy of Kuwait as an independent country; they deemed the 1961 transfer of authority from Britain to the al-Sabah family of Kuwait a cynical attempt by London to weaken Iraq. Saddam plotted a takeover of Kuwait and its oil fields and commenced a campaign of saber rattling.

The United States government watched with concern but something less than alarm. President Bush ordered the American ambassador to Iraq to speak with Saddam on the subject of Kuwait. Exactly what April Glaspie told the Iraqi leader at a crucial meeting in July 1990 occasioned subsequent dispute. She claimed that she warned Saddam that the United States would not tolerate any aggression toward Kuwait. He asserted that she said that the United States would take no sides in inter-Arab quarrels. About the only thing certain was that Washington did not go public with whatever warning it gave Saddam. American intelligence agencies thought Saddam was bluffing. He would settle, they said, for a rescheduling of the debt Iraq owed Kuwait from the war against Iran, for Kuwait's support in raising oil prices, or for a larger share of an oil field that underlay the Iraq-Kuwait border. The saber rattling was a tactic in the negotiation.

Bush considered the analysis sound, and so was stunned to be told on August 1 that Iraqi troops were poised to attack Kuwait. It was a Wednesday evening, and Bush was in the medical office in the White House basement. "I was sitting on the edge of the exam table in a T-shirt getting a deep heat treatment to relieve my sore shoulders, the result of hitting a bucket's worth of golf balls earlier in the day," he remembered. Brent Scowcroft appeared in the door. "Mr. President," the national security adviser said, "it looks very bad. Iraq may be about to invade Kuwait."

The invasion indeed occurred, and before Bush could do anything about it Saddam controlled Kuwait. This was alarming enough, in that it afforded Saddam control of Kuwait's oil in addition to Iraq's own and thereby increased his leverage in world oil markets. But Washington's larger worry was that Kuwait was merely a warm-up: that Saddam's army would shortly roll into Saudi Arabia, the whale of world oil in comparison to Kuwait's tuna. If Saddam gained control of Saudi oil, there was no end to the mischief he might cause.

Bush had another concern as well. With the Cold War ending, the structure of world order required remodeling. For four decades much of the planet had been divided into Soviet and American spheres, with each superpower enforcing at least a modicum of good behavior on those countries within its sphere. America's allies couldn't freelance excessively without risking a cut-off of their aid from Washington; Soviet clients encountered similar kinds of discipline. But as the Soviet Union withdrew from world affairs—on the way to withdrawing from existence—the discipline of the superpower duopoly diminished.

Bush proposed to replace this with something he would call a "new world order," a regime of responsibility enforced by the United States in league with like-minded countries. The United Nations would be the venue for discussions and decisions, but the muscle would be provided by American arms and those of the other big powers.

Iraq's invasion of Kuwait provided an early test of the concept. Bush quickly contacted the leaders of America's principal allies. Margaret Thatcher supplied the greatest encouragement. "If Iraq wins, no small state is safe," the British prime minister told the president. "It's got to be stopped. We must do everything possible. . . . We cannot give in to dictators."

Bush agreed, and seventy-two hours after the Iraqi invasion the president vowed to reverse it. "This will not stand," he told reporters. "This will not stand, this aggression against Kuwait."

## 6. BUSH VS. SADDAM (I)

Accomplishing the reversal took time. Bush sent envoys to the Middle East seeking the cooperation of Saudi Arabia, Egypt, and other governments in a diplomatic and quite possibly military initiative against Saddam. The Saudis were especially nervous. They had watched American forces land in Lebanon seven years before, only to withdraw after a single suicide bombing. Bush's emissaries wanted the Saudis to open their country to American troops, perhaps hundreds of thousands of them. The presence of so many infidels—and not just infidels but allies of the Zionists of Israel—in Muhammad's homeland would outrage Muslim sentiment across the region and the world, potentially endangering the Saudi monarchy. The Saudis demanded a promise from Washington that if they let the Americans attack Saddam from Saudi soil, Saddam would not survive. Apparently they got the promise, or something close to it, for they gave the requested permission.

As American troops poured into Saudi Arabia, complemented by a buildup of ground, sea, and air forces in the surrounding region, the Bush administration worked the corridors of the United Nations. The president's prior experience as American ambassador to the UN made him respectful of the international body's prerogatives, but he would have sought UN approval anyway for action against Saddam. To a greater degree than any president before or after him, Bush appreciated the value of international opinion. His new world order would require the cooperation of many other countries, for as powerful as the United States might be, it couldn't police the world alone.

Bush's diplomatic offensive paid off. One by one the most important governments signaled their support for efforts to eject Iraq from Kuwait. Nearly all preferred economic sanctions to military force; Bush consented to give economic sanctions a try, even as he insisted that force be prepared in case the sanctions failed. Indispensable assistance came from Moscow. Time and again during the Cold War, substantive measures on just about any weighty subject had failed to survive scrutiny by the Security Council, where the United States and the Soviet Union traded vetoes. But Gorbachev's reforms had converted the Soviet Union into a de facto ally of the United States, at least for the moment and on the subject of Iraq. When Moscow joined Washington in condemning Saddam, the Iraqi leader's diplomatic fate was sealed.

Bush meanwhile cultivated American domestic opinion. For many Americans the mere thought of war in the Middle East came as a shock. The end of the Cold War was supposed to inaugurate an era of peace; after forty years defending freedom against the communists, Americans expected a respite. They were already spending, in their imaginations at any rate, the "peace dividend" that would accrue when the Cold War swords were beaten into post–Cold War plowshares. But now, in the very weeks when German reunification was being finalized, the president was saying they might have to strap on the armor again.

Bush administration officials made some of the same arguments their predecessors had made early in the Cold War. If the United States didn't halt aggression as soon as it started, the bad guys would gain momentum and spawn imitators. The more pragmatic among the Bush spokesmen distilled the argument to its material essence. James Baker, the secretary of state, told reporters that America's economic well-being was at stake. "To bring it down to the level of the average American citizen," Baker told reporters, "let me say that means jobs. If you want to sum it up in one word, it's jobs."

Congress hadn't voted a war declaration in half a century, since just after Pearl Harbor. Not once during the Cold War did a president ask for war. Harry Truman fought the Korean War on his own authority; Kennedy, Johnson, and Nixon did the same regarding Vietnam. Congress acquiesced in this undermining of its constitutional prerogative, informally in the case of Korea, formally—via the Gulf of Tonkin Resolution—on Vietnam. Bush adopted the Johnson approach, asking Congress for a resolution authorizing his employment of force against Iraq.

The answer wasn't foreordained. Sam Nunn, the Georgia Democrat who headed the Senate Armed Services Committee, conducted hearings on the constitutionality and political prudence of the resolution the president sought. Nunn and most of the witnesses—who included military officers, diplomats, constitutional scholars, and foreign policy experts—counseled against war, contending that the Middle East would become a quagmire for American troops and that an American-led operation would alienate Arabs across the region and Muslims around the world. At the very least, most said, the administration should give economic sanctions time to bite. "I'm willing to use force after all other avenues are explored," Nunn conceded. "Over half the Iraqi GNP has been taken away. I believe that every month that goes by Saddam gets weaker."

But the mood shifted after Bush vowed to go to war even without congressional approval. A majority of the lawmakers decided they didn't want to undercut the president on a crucial issue of foreign policy. The margin in the House was comfortable: 250 to 183. The vote in the Senate was far closer: 52 to 47. "I felt the heavy weight that I might be faced with impeachment"—for ignoring Congress and going to war without approval—"lifted from my shoulders as I heard the results," Bush recalled.

The only question that remained was whether Saddam would yield without a fight. A Security Council deadline of January 15, 1991, neared, and the Iraqi leader engaged in some final diplomatic feints. But nothing came of them, and on January 16 Bush ordered American forces into action.

America's first Middle Eastern war began with five weeks of bombing. American planners were reluctant to commit ground forces to battle until Saddam's army had been thoroughly softened up. The initial blows were delivered by Tomahawk cruise missiles launched from American ships in the Persian Gulf; these hugged the desert terrain en route to Baghdad. American bombers followed close behind, escorted by electronic-warfare planes that neutralized Iraqi air defenses and allowed the bombers almost unchallenged access to high-value targets. Some of the bombers employed "stealth" technology that rendered them essentially invisible to radar, and they dropped laser-guided bombs that found their targets with unprecedented precision. At the outset of the aerial campaign, Iraq scrambled its fighter-jet force to contest the attack, but the overmatched planes and pilots were shot down in large numbers until the surviving pilots flew the surviving planes off to Iran, where they sat out the rest of the war.

Iraq did succeed in launching a number of medium-range Scud missiles against Saudi Arabia and Israel. Those aimed at Saudi Arabia had the purpose of hitting American troops and installations and their Saudi hosts; those targeting Israel were intended to provoke an Israeli response. The Bush administration had made sure the United States did not go to war alone; with the approval of the United Nations, several other countries, starting with Margaret Thatcher's Britain, joined the anti-Iraq coalition. But Bush kept Israel out of the fight lest the contest over Kuwait become conflated with the Arab-Israeli struggle. And when Iraqi Scud missiles began raining down on Israel's cities and countryside, all of Bush's persuasiveness was required to keep Israel from striking back. The Pentagon rushed Patriot antimissile missiles to Israel; these failed to intercept many of the Scuds (or perhaps any of them: the Patriots' functionality was hotly debated during and after the war), but they did provide a certain psychological protection.

During the five weeks of the air war American leaders hoped, without really expecting, that Saddam might give way and pull his troops out of Kuwait. When he didn't, Bush ordered the ground operations to begin. American troops, joined by units from other coalition members, poured across the border from Saudi Arabia into Kuwait and Iraq. The Iraqis were driven quickly from Kuwait back into Iraq, where they raced toward what they guessed would be the relative safety of Baghdad.

Their guess proved accurate, but only because Bush called off the ground war on the fifth day, with American troops well short of the Iraqi capital. American units had been killing Iraqis in large numbers on what was being called the "highway of death" from Kuwait City to Basra in Iraq, and Bush feared losing the moral high ground if the slaughter continued.

There were other reasons for not pressing on to Baghdad and ousting Saddam. The war's objective had been to liberate Kuwait; this was now accomplished. To expand the mission would bring new elements into play. "We would have been forced to occupy Baghdad and, in effect, rule Iraq," Bush and Scowcroft recalled in their joint memoir. "The coalition would instantly have collapsed, the Arabs deserting it in anger and other allies pulling out as well. Under those circumstances, there was no viable 'exit strategy' we could see." Moreover, the war against Iraq had been designed, from the start, as a model for countering aggression in the post–Cold War world. "Going in and occupying Iraq, thus unilaterally exceeding the United Nations' mandate, would have destroyed the precedent of international response to aggression that we hoped to establish." Bush and Scowcroft were writing in 1998, but their words would have resonance during the following decade: "Had we gone the invasion route, the United States could conceivably still be an occupying power in a bitterly hostile land. It would have been a dramatically different—and perhaps barren—outcome."

And so the war ended. American casualties were lighter than expected, and far lighter than the predictions of some opponents of the war. Approximately three hundred Americans died and about five hundred were wounded. Iraqi combat deaths could only be estimated, but were probably between ten thousand and forty thousand. A few thousand to several thousand Iraqi civilians were also killed.

The central objective, the liberation of Kuwait, was accomplished. "No one country can claim this victory as its own," Bush told America and the world. "It was not only a victory for Kuwait but a victory for all the coalition partners. This is a victory for the United Nations, for all mankind, for the rule of law, and for what is right."

And yet Saddam survived, to the annoyance of the Saudis, who thought they had an American promise that he wouldn't, and to the frustration of many in the Middle East and beyond, who thought him a source of continued trouble.

## 7. THE WORLD IN REAL TIME

"I was sitting in my office with Richard Haass and Bob Gates"—the administration's top Middle East expert and its intelligence chief, respectively—"watching CNN when the air campaign began," Brent Scowcroft recalled.

> It was an eerie experience. There I was, with the time lines of the attack in my lap, simultaneously looking at the targets on television as they were struck. It was as if I were reading a script of a movie as it played out before my eyes. I was actually watching a war begin. At about 6:40 p.m., Bernard Shaw of CNN, stationed in a hotel in downtown Baghdad, said there were reports of firing near the southern border. That would be the attack on the Iraqi warning radars, I thought. Right on time. Then I watched as the night sky over the city on the TV screen began to light up with anti-aircraft tracers—gunners firing at nothing out of nervousness. At precisely 7:00, the screen filled with bomb bursts.

Scowcroft wasn't the only one amazed to watch a war in real time. Just as military technology had historically developed from war to war, so had the technology to communicate what the military was up to. The Civil War was the first American conflict to be reported by telegraph and photograph, World War I the first conflict covered by radio. Film—newsreels, mostly—brought World War II back to the home front. The Vietnam War was widely regarded as the first war of the television era.

In each case the new technology disconcerted government authorities, who often tried to curtail what the novel devices could record and relay. And what the officials didn't disallow, the users of the technology sometimes censored on their own. Mathew Brady was appalled by the carnage of the great battles of the Civil War; he turned his cameras away from the corpses (although his assistants sometimes turned them back). During World War I the Navy Department seized control of radio facilities of the American Marconi Company for the government's own use and to prevent the company from transmitting messages that might aid Germany. American reporters and film crews rode and sailed into battle with American forces during World War II, but in exchange for their front-line perspective they submitted to military discipline and control. The relationship between the media and the military grew more fractious in Vietnam, not because the media were inherently antagonistic to the military or the war but because military and civilian officials failed to level with the reporters, who then determined to dig out the story on their own.

The tension increased still further with the war against Iraq. The two decades between Vietnam and the Persian Gulf War witnessed a revolution in television news. During the 1960s the major television networks—CBS, NBC, ABC—typically broadcast a total of ninety minutes of news per day. Walter Cronkite on CBS, Frank Reynolds on ABC, and the duo of Chet Huntley and David Brinkley on NBC each had their evening half hour to convey and explain the major developments in the nation and the world that day. The limit was enforced by a combination of cost and government edict. Television was a broadcast medium and hence subject to the supervision of the Federal Communications Commission, which effectively guaranteed the three networks their triopoly of the airwaves. And television news was expensive to gather and produce. Cameras and sound equipment were heavy and bulky; transmitting what the cameras recorded was difficult and time-consuming, especially from distant locations like the jungles of Vietnam. For such reasons the evening news often consisted of the anchormen simply reading reports from the field, with still photos or very brief clips punctuating rather than carrying the story.

Technology and practice changed during the 1970s and 1980s. Cable television began to challenge the hegemony of the broadcast networks. Precisely because cable television was delivered via cable, rather than over the airwaves, it circumvented the broadcast restrictions of the FCC. There was effectively no limit on the number of channels a cable operator could deliver to households; as a result, a much freer market in television emerged. The trend was abetted by, and in turn abetted, the deregulating mood that characterized Congress and the executive branch during this period.

Equally important, advances in electronics made possible smaller, lighter, less expensive cameras and sound equipment. What had required a truck to transport in the 1960s could now be fitted into a backpack. And communications satellites allowed the images to be transmitted to headquarters and thence out over the cables even as they were recorded. For the first time it became possible for viewers at home to watch the news as it unfolded halfway around the world.

The first person to appreciate the possibilities of real-time news was Ted Turner, a mercurial Atlantan known to friends as "Captain Outrageous" and "the Mouth of the South" (his rivals and enemies had less printable names for him). Turner was a visionary whose visions varied in quality. "Ted Turner is without doubt one of the very smartest people I had ever met," an associate later observed. "But it took me just two seconds to figure out that he was also completely wacko. He is a brilliant idea man, but he's been a plunger from the beginning. A plunger with extraordinary business judgment."

Turner plunged into radio in the late 1960s and television in the early 1970s. He transformed a local Atlanta television station, WJRJ, into WTBS, "the superstation that serves the nation," by bouncing its signal off an early communications satellite. The station showed old movies and lots of baseball, in particular every game of the hometown Atlanta Braves.

Turner's bigger breakthrough was the Cable News Network, a twenty-four-hour news network that went on the air in June 1980. "I think the people of America need this in-depth news service," Turner said. "And I've been willing all along to risk everything I have to provide it." At a time when television stations typically signed off after midnight, Turner vowed, "Barring satellite problems, we won't be signing off until the world ends. We'll be on and we will cover the end of the world, live, and that will be our last event."

Industry observers and potential viewers initially wondered how Turner would fill the twenty-four hours of programming each day. Was there really that much news to report? A partial answer appeared on CNN's very first day, when Turner broke into the regular programming to carry an extemporaneous address by President Carter from the hospital where civil rights leader Vernon Jordan was being treated for a gunshot wound. It was a minor story, but it foreshadowed much to come. Certain earlier events had been carried live, of course: presidential addresses, political conventions, sports contests. But these had all been predictable and indeed were typically scheduled well in advance, allowing the television networks to pre-position crews and reporters. The CNN breakthrough was its ability to respond to unexpected events as they occurred.

Almost overnight CNN changed the media landscape. Households and offices left television sets on and tuned to CNN, expecting to see the news as it occurred. The evening news programs found themselves scooped by CNN; the news they showed was often stale by the time they aired. As additional all-news cable stations popped up in CNN's wake, the other media were affected as well. Newspapers lost readers, who had already seen and heard much of what the papers were reporting. All-news radio stations gave way to all-talk radio, as listeners discovered they could get the same breaking news, but now with pictures, that only radio had previously delivered.

The "CNN effect," as it came to be called, extended beyond the media. Elected officials saw the same news, at the same time, as their constituents, and when the news provoked an emotional response—as in the wake of natural or man-made disasters—they had to take action. A drought in Africa or an earthquake in Afghanistan became real when the cameras beamed the suffering into American homes, and Congress and the president often felt compelled to send American aid.

At times CNN complemented or even replaced traditional means of diplomatic communication. In the weeks before the Persian Gulf War, as the Security Council's deadline for an Iraqi withdrawal from Kuwait approached, Saddam Hussein conducted his diplomacy via interviews and speeches he knew CNN would carry to American households, including the White House. In the summer of 1991 the Bush administration followed the attempted coup against Mikhail Gorbachev not by means of the CIA but through CNN. "The live CNN pictures are stark," Bush wrote in his diary. "Bumper to bumper APCs"—armored personnel carriers—"parked in Moscow. Tanks moving down the streets."

The CNN effect sometimes put American officials in awkward positions. After the Chinese government had brutally suppressed pro-democracy demonstrations in Beijing's Tiananmen Square in the spring of 1989, the Bush administration came under political pressure to register America's outrage. Bush didn't think the pressure would do any good, and he didn't want to jeopardize the progress he thought he was making in other areas of U.S.-China relations. He dispatched Brent Scowcroft to Beijing to conduct some quiet diplomacy—only to have Scowcroft run into a CNN crew at a dinner held in his honor. "I could go through with the ceremony and be seen as toasting those the press was labeling 'the butchers of Tiananmen Square,' or refuse to toast and put in jeopardy the whole trip," Scowcroft recalled. "I chose the former and became, to my deep chagrin, an instant celebrity—in the most negative sense of the term."

The CNN effect could be eerie, as Scowcroft noted during the Gulf War.

In former wars military planners would select targets, launch bombers or missiles, and assess the accuracy of the strikes afterward. Now Bush and Scowcroft could watch the attacks as they took place. The reporters and cameras of CNN became, in effect, the forward spotters of the American military.

As in other wars, the new services of the news services weren't always appreciated. Peter Arnett, CNN's Baghdad correspondent, became notorious in some American circles for what seemed his softball coverage of Saddam Hussein before and during the war. "The Iraqis went to great lengths to take the CNN people to orchestrated events, where the journalists duly recorded whatever they were told," Scowcroft complained. Even his fellow journalists wondered where Arnett's sympathies lay. "Is Mr. Arnett, the only American correspondent left in the Iraqi capital, sending out enemy propaganda, or is he doing the journalist's job under difficult conditions, or both?" the *New York Times*'s Walter Goodman asked.

Arnett's boss, Ted Turner, rejected the criticism. By 1991 CNN had outgrown its American roots, and it reported the world accordingly. Iraq was currently an enemy of the United States, Turner acknowledged. "But CNN has had, as an international global network, to step a little beyond that. . . . We try to present facts not from a U.S. perspective but from a human perspective."

# 12 | The Good Old Bad Old Days

## 1992–1996

### 1. READ THEIR LIPS: NO SECOND TERM

George Bush should have won reelection easily. At the moment of victory over Saddam Hussein, various polls put his public approval rating at 90 percent, the highest in history till then. His larger victory was something long thought impossible: a final resolution of the conflict with Soviet communism. Those few who had foreseen the demise of the Soviet empire had generally expected the breakup to occur violently, with civil wars inside and among the Soviet republics possibly spreading into other countries of Europe or Central Asia. But the dismantling of the empire forged by Peter the Great and his czarist and communist successors had occurred peacefully, for the most part. That it did so owed a great deal to the diplomacy of George Bush. Any number of things could have gone wrong: American officials might have pushed too hard too fast, the successor regimes in the Eastern European countries might have indulged in score-settling that would have required a response from Russia, rogue generals might have seized Soviet nuclear weapons and used them for who knew what. The absence of such dire developments was the result of many factors, but not the least of these was the ability of Bush to steer a steady course between timidity and triumphalism.

The avoidance of disaster rarely registers for long, though. Politics takes place in the present tense; voters want to know what their elected officials have done for them lately. And positive results are far more impressive than the absence of negative outcomes. Moreover, American politics skews toward domestic affairs: foreign triumphs are fine, but if they come at the expense of domestic achievements they can open a president to charges that he has neglected the home front.

Such charges were precisely what the campaign of Bill Clinton leveled at Bush in 1992. Clinton became the Democratic nominee primarily because of the daunting approval ratings Bush boasted during the year before the election. The big names of the Democratic party, including New York governor Mario Cuomo and Georgia senator Sam Nunn, considered Bush unbeatable and sat out the contest. But Clinton, a six-term Arkansas governor, decided he had done about all he could do in his home state, and he guessed that Bush might be more vulnerable than the polls indicated.

The economy proved him right when it slipped into recession. Alan Greenspan's valiant efforts in the wake of 1987's Black Monday proved beneficial for a couple of years, but the federal and trade deficits persisted and eventually dragged the economy down. Corporations dismissed large numbers of workers; many of those who kept their jobs nonetheless wondered if they would be next. Under the circumstances it was easy for Clinton to argue that Bush had spent too much time saving the world and not enough time securing American jobs and promoting American prosperity.

Bush didn't help his case politically by reneging on his promise not to raise taxes. The growing federal deficit was spooking the stock market and deterring investment; nearly all economists concurred that it had to be reduced. But the Democrats who controlled Congress refused to countenance deficit reduction that focused solely on spending cuts in such popular programs as Social Security and Medicare. A bargain was struck in the autumn of 1990: Bush accepted some modest tax increases, and the Democrats swallowed some spending cuts.

It was a perfectly reasonable, perhaps even necessary, compromise from the standpoint of economics. And it would contribute to the exuberant prosperity of the following decade. But from the political standpoint of the approaching presidential election it opened Bush to criticism for having violated his categorical promise not to raise taxes. Republican conservatives revolted; editorialists and headline writers lampooned and tut-tutted the president. "Read my lips: I lied," joked David Letterman, the host of *Late Night* on NBC.

Another Bush measure, likewise praised by economists, did him further political harm. Since the Bretton Woods conference of 1944, American trade policy had been consistently aimed at reducing barriers to trade, including tariffs and import quotas. Progress had been slow but cumulative, and by the early 1990s world trade was probably freer than it had been at any time in history. In certain regions the reduction of barriers was almost complete. The European Common Market, which had grown out of the cooperation the Truman administration required as a condition of Marshall Plan aid, had evolved into the European Community, which established a single market for most of Europe, one in which goods crossed borders without quotas or tariffs. The European Community (which would become the European Union in 1993, following further economic and political integration) promised to give the Europeans an advantage in trade, as the larger market it created allowed European manufacturers to build larger factories that operated more efficiently than small ones.

Not to be outdone, the Bush administration in 1992 negotiated the North American Free Trade Agreement, a pact among the United States, Canada, and Mexico eliminating nearly all barriers to trade. NAFTA, as the agreement was called, was a logical extension of the trade policies eight presidents before Bush had pursued, and it received almost universal acclaim from economists, who generally favored whatever reduced artificial—that is, noneconomic—barriers to trade.

But it sparked political protests among individuals and groups who feared the competition from low-wage Mexico. H. Ross Perot, a Texas billionaire of nonetheless populist political views, mounted a challenge to Bush and NAFTA. Perot figuratively but flamboyantly cocked an ear and professed to hear a "giant sucking sound" as American jobs were swept south to Mexico.

Perot's complaint caught on, especially in the context of the layoffs afflicting the American economy, and his self-financed independent challenge to Bush gave dissident Republicans an alternative to the president. The three-way race among Bush, Clinton, and Perot focused on economic affairs, with the Clinton team adopting the informal slogan "It's the economy, stupid." As it happened, the economy pulled out of its recession before the election, but because job growth typically lags behind recovery in production, the upturn didn't register with voters.

Bush tried to balance the bad news on the economic front with his few positive accomplishments in domestic affairs, particularly the Americans with Disabilities Act, which mandated efforts to accommodate persons with various disabilities and bring them into the mainstream of American life. To many of those affected, the ADA was hardly less than an emancipation proclamation, opening doors to work, education, and other activities that had been closed before. But it was in the nature of the subject that the affected persons constituted a small part of the American population, and as important as the ADA was to them, it didn't change many votes among the electorate at large.

The dissatisfaction with the economy proved Bush's undoing. On election day Clinton received 43 percent of the popular vote, against Bush's 37 percent and Perot's 19 percent. Bush would have benefited without Perot on the ballot, but perhaps not enough to beat Clinton, who carried the electoral college with 370 electors to Bush's 168 and Perot's none.

## 2. DON'T ASK OR TELL

Bill Clinton was the first president born after World War II, and the first since Franklin Roosevelt not to have served in the military. During the campaign he had revealed a desire to apply the mores of the Baby Boom generation to military culture when he suggested that homosexuals ought to be allowed to serve in the military. He hadn't even been inaugurated when representatives of gay groups insisted that he make good on his pledge.

The issue spoiled Clinton's political honeymoon, such as it was for a president elected with a minority of the popular vote. Social conservatives castigated the idea of gays in the military as public condoning of immoral behavior. Some generals and admirals shared that view; others followed Joint Chiefs chairman Colin Powell in basing their opposition on the belief that letting gays serve would diminish the effectiveness of American military units. "The presence of homosexuals in the force would be detrimental to good order and discipline, for a variety of reasons, principally relating around the issue of privacy," Powell told an audience at the U.S. Naval Academy. He repeated this sentiment in meetings with Clinton and with congressional committees examining the issue.

Clinton thought Powell was wrong. He cited government reports saying that gays had served honorably and could continue to do so. He quoted the Pentagon's own figures, which showed that $500 million had been spent discharging seventeen thousand homosexuals during the previous decade, and he said he thought the money could have been put to far better use. He reminded Powell—who as a black man and a career officer hardly needed reminding—that the arguments being made against gays in the military were strikingly similar to arguments that had been made against the integration of African Americans into the services under Harry Truman.

But Powell had stature on military affairs Clinton couldn't even approach. Powell was the 1990s equivalent of George Marshall, having guided American forces to victory during the Persian Gulf War. And when he hinted that he might resign if the president overruled him on the gay issue, the mere thought gave Clinton pause.

Meanwhile the House and Senate hearings proceeded. Witnesses testified for and mostly against allowing gays to serve openly in the armed forces, and the legislators themselves weighed in. Former marine lieutenant colonel Oliver North, who was mounting a comeback among conservatives following his disgrace in the Iran-contra scandal, considered the president's mere proposal the beginning of the end. "With free access for homosexuals to our military," North said, "we have finally succeeded in doing what Hitler's legions, Japan's forces and the Soviet empire never could—destroy our armed forces." Democratic senator Robert Byrd of West Virginia declared that the Roman empire had fallen at least in part because of rampant homosexuality in the ranks of the legions. Georgia's Nunn, the Democratic chairman of the Senate Armed Services Committee, didn't share such extreme views but contended that deference must be paid to the judgment of the generals.

Yet the opinions, while mostly predictable, weren't uniformly so. Some of Clinton's liberal supporters recommended maintaining the ban, while certain conservatives wanted it lifted. Barry Goldwater told of being a white officer in charge of a black unit during the military's era of racial segregation, when African Americans were said to lack leadership potential. "That seems ridiculous now, as it should," the Arizona senator and former Republican nominee for president wrote in the *Washington Post*. The gay ban was discriminatorily un-American and counterproductive besides. "You don't need to be straight to fight and die for your country," Goldwater said. "You just need to shoot straight."

But the opposition was too strong for Clinton to overcome. The House voted overwhelmingly to reject opening the military to gays. The Senate followed suit by a somewhat less lopsided margin. Clinton could have issued an executive order allowing gays to serve, but Congress would have overturned the order, entrenching the discriminatory policy in law.

So Clinton struck a compromise. The months of testimony and the long days and nights of closed-door talks produced a policy of "don't ask, don't tell." What this meant was that military recruiters and officers would not be allowed to inquire as to the sexual orientation of recruits and soldiers, but neither should homosexuals in the military announce their orientation. "It is not a perfect solution," Clinton conceded in a speech at the National Defense University. "It is not identical with some of my own goals. And it certainly will not please everyone, perhaps not anyone, and clearly not those who hold the most adamant opinions on either side of this issue."

Clinton was right about not pleasing people. The whole affair nearly destroyed his credibility as president before his administration had fairly begun. "I got the worst of both worlds," he reflected later. "I lost the fight, and the gay community was highly critical of me for the compromise, simply refusing to acknowledge the consequences of having so little support in Congress." The Republicans hammered Clinton mercilessly on the issue. "It appeared I was working on little else, which caused a lot of Americans who had elected me to fix the economy to wonder what on earth I was doing and whether they'd made a mistake."

## 3. ONE PLUS ONE EQUALS . . . ?

When Clinton had been campaigning, he liked to say, half-jokingly but half-seriously, that voters would be getting a two-for-one deal if they elected him. As a student at Yale Law School, he had encountered a young woman he couldn't take his eyes off. She returned his gaze, then walked up to him. "If you're going to keep staring at me and I'm going to keep staring back, we ought to at least know each other's names. Mine's Hillary Rodham. What's yours?" Clinton remembered these words many years later; he also remembered his reaction to her forthrightness. "I was impressed and so stunned I couldn't say anything for a few seconds. Finally I blurted my name out. We exchanged a few words, and she left." Some days after this he ran into her as she was heading to register for the next semester's classes. He said he'd do the same. "We stood in line and talked. I thought I was doing pretty well until we got to the front of the line. The registrar looked up at me and said, 'Bill, what are you doing back here? You registered this morning.' I turned beet red, and Hillary laughed that big laugh of hers. My cover was blown."

Hillary Rodham's career started faster than Clinton's. She worked with the Children's Defense Fund upon graduating from law school, and then advised the House Judiciary Committee as it prepared to impeach Richard Nixon. But her career took a sideways turn after she married Clinton in 1975 and he was elected governor of Arkansas in 1978. As Arkansas's first lady she did what first ladies did, and a bit more. She chaired and otherwise assisted various worthy causes, most having to do with education and children's services.

The experience and her general competence inspired Clinton, upon his election as president, to give her an office in the West Wing of the White House, the operational side of the building, rather than the East Wing, where the social business was conducted and first ladies typically had their offices. This signal that he hadn't been kidding about the two-for-one deal struck some observers as a positive blow for women and a good thing for the country, and others as an end run around the Constitution, which makes no allowance for co-presidents.

The complaints grew louder when the president appointed Hillary Clinton head of a task force charged with revising America's national health care policy. "This health care system of ours is badly broken, and it is time to fix it," Clinton told a joint session of Congress in September 1993. "Despite the dedication of literally millions of talented health care professionals, our health care is too uncertain and too expensive, too bureaucratic and too wasteful. It has too much fraud and too much greed." What the Clintons proposed was what Franklin Roosevelt had been tempted to include with the original Social Security bill, what Harry Truman had unsuccessfully urged Congress to enact, and what Lyndon Johnson had partially achieved with Medicare and Medicaid—guaranteed health care for all Americans. "Millions of Americans are just a pink slip away from losing their health insurance and one serious illness away from losing all their savings," Bill Clinton explained. "Millions more are locked into the jobs they have now just because they or someone in their family has once been sick and they have what is called a preexisting condition. And on any given day, over 37 million Americans, most of them working people and their little children, have no health insurance at all." The Clinton plan would provide universal coverage—"a comprehensive package of benefits over the course of an entire lifetime, roughly comparable to the benefit package offered by most Fortune 500 companies." Coverage would be partly public, partly private, with the private portion regulated by the federal government to ensure quality care at moderate prices. Costs would be borne by workers, employers, and taxpayers.

Clinton knew he was asking a lot. But health care was a challenge the country couldn't ignore, he said. "Our history and our heritage tell us that we can meet this challenge. Let us guarantee every American comprehensive health benefits that can never be taken away."

The Clinton health care plan would have run into trouble even if Hillary Clinton had had nothing to do with it. Insurance companies lobbied hard and expensively to keep the government from stealing their business or telling them how to run it. Pharmaceutical manufacturers, hospitals, and doctors feared red tape and cost caps. Conservatives denounced it as another government boondoggle designed by tax-and-spend liberals. Republicans refused on partisan grounds to have anything to do with it. The most telling—or at least the most memorable—blow against the Clinton plan came in an insurance-sponsored television commercial depicting a middle-class couple, Harry and Louise, puzzling over the complexities of the proposed program and fearing that it would force them out of their current plan, which they liked.

The White House pointed out the exaggerations and downright falsehoods, not to mention the self-interested motives, of the campaign against their health care plan. But they couldn't overcome the central truth that the Harry and Louise commercial conveyed (and which polls confirmed): that most Americans who had health insurance were reasonably happy with their coverage. They constituted a majority of voters, and the changes the administration proposed appeared threatening.

That Hillary Clinton was the face of health care reform simply made it easier for the opponents to demonize the entire initiative. In contrast to her husband, who exuded charisma, Hillary came across as cold and businesslike. "A lot of the students we both knew talked about Hillary as if they were a little intimidated by her," Bill Clinton recalled of their law school days; and her demeanor hadn't softened much by 1993. The opponents demanded to know who had elected Hillary Clinton to anything, let alone health care czar. Not for the last time, Clinton's political enemies found his wife to be an easier target than he was, and they went after her to weaken him.

The result was that the Clinton health care plan died an early death. Unloved by the public, it expired in Congress and was little mourned upon its passing. "We are going to keep up this fight and we will prevail," Clinton bravely promised. But he never revived the issue.

## 4. HIS AIRNESS

As vital as health care reform appeared to the Clintons in the autumn of 1993, it paled in the minds of millions of Americans next to another development. Shortly before the beginning of the 1993–94 professional basketball season, Michael Jordan announced his retirement from the game, saying he was switching to baseball. The announcement was stunning; Jordan was widely acknowledged to be the greatest player in the history of the National Basketball Association, and he was still in his prime. He had led the Chicago Bulls to three consecutive NBA championships, and he seemed likely to have several more championships left in him. Chicago fans fell into despair, asking how they had failed their hero and what they would do without him.

The fans weren't the only ones at a loss. Michael Jordan was the preeminent example of the emerging phenomenon of sports-star-as-pitchman. Not long after leaving the University of North Carolina, Jordan signed a contract with the Nike corporation, a manufacturer of athletic shoes. The Oregon-based Nike was the brainchild of Phil Knight, who had run track for the University of Oregon before attending Stanford business school, where a class project became the basis for a company that would provide runners better shoes than had been available before. Knight's timing was exquisite; millions of recreational runners were taking to the streets and paths of America in search of health and longevity. He teamed up with his old coach at Oregon, Bill Bowerman, to try to invent the perfect shoe. Bowerman tinkered with designs; his most successful sported a textured sole first fabricated on his wife's waffle iron. Bowerman tested his designs on the feet of his Oregon team, and Knight marketed the ones that worked. The Nike logo, a "swoosh" designed for thirty-five dollars by an art student Knight met in a hallway at Portland State University, where he was moonlighting teaching an accounting class, became the signature of the growing business. (Knight later supplemented the artist's fee with a swoosh-adorned diamond ring and an undisclosed number of shares of Nike stock.)

Knight and Nike were soon thinking beyond runners to participants in other sports. Basketball wasn't an obvious choice; in the early 1980s the sport ranked well below baseball and football in the affections of fans and the ratings of television viewers. But basketball had an advantage for Nike over the two turf sports in that basketball shoes, unlike the cleated shoes worn by baseball and football players, could be worn on the street. To publicize its new departure, Nike enlisted Michael Jordan, who wasn't yet the best basketball player in America but who did have a magnetic off-court presence and eye-popping on-court abilities, including the capacity to leap higher than anyone else and seemingly hang in the air after his opponents succumbed to the force of gravity. Nike built an entire line of shoes around the "Air Jordan" model, the shoe it paid Jordan $2.5 million to wear for the Chicago Bulls.

The launch of the Air Jordan line at first ran afoul of NBA rules, which required uniformity in teams' uniforms. The league threatened to fine the Bulls for letting Jordan wear his signature shoes. Knight, who had cultivated a kind of outlaw persona for Nike, was delighted at the furor and the publicity it generated. He promised to pay any fines the league levied against Jordan and the Bulls, and he built an advertising campaign based on freedom of feet. "On September 15 Nike created a revolutionary new basketball shoe," one ad asserted. "On October 18, the NBA threw them out of the game. Fortunately the NBA can't stop you from wearing them. Air Jordans from Nike."

David Stern, the NBA commissioner, soon came to realize that Michael Jordan could be the league's ticket to popularity and profit, and after some minor modifications to the shoe, he let Jordan wear the previously forbidden footwear. The endorsement practice caught on, and Nike and other companies signed additional athletes to endorsement deals. Nike prospered the most, in large part because of its good luck—or good judgment—in hitching its star to Jordan, who by the 1990s was a celebrity with stature that transcended basketball and even sports in general. Nike also paid college coaches to put Nike shoes on the feet of their basketball, football, and baseball teams, and as the company broadened its product lines further, the Nike swoosh appeared on jerseys, shorts, and caps.

Nike was clever and resourceful. The company failed to win the contract to outfit the 1992 U.S. Olympic basketball team, the first American team to feature NBA players, who previously had been barred from the formerly amateur Olympic competition. Rival company Reebok got the uniform deal instead. But several of the players, including Jordan, were under contract to Nike, and at a critical moment of the television coverage they contrived to cover the Reebok logo with artfully draped American flags. "It was a disgrace to the Olympics and to America," the head of Reebok spluttered. Knight responded, "That moment was by no means orchestrated from headquarters, but I thought it was great."

Jordan was the most prominent example of the commercialization of sports during the 1990s, expanding beyond Nike and shoes to Wheaties, Coca-Cola, Gatorade, Chevrolet, McDonald's, and Hanes underwear; but the phenomenon of market-driven athletics ranged the entire sports spectrum. Football's Super Bowl had begun its existence as a poor cousin to baseball's World Series and a pale imitation of the Rose Bowl. The first Super Bowl, played in January 1967 in Los Angeles, pitted the Green Bay Packers of the established National Football League against the Kansas City Chiefs of the upstart American Football League. The Packers won without breaking a sweat, and a similar breeze the next year over the Oakland Raiders caused the Super Bowl's sponsors to wonder if the game had a future. But upsets by the AFL in 1969 and 1970 lent interest to the rivalry, and even after the two leagues merged, the Super Bowl remained the climax of the professional football season.

In time the event evolved from game to spectacle. Marching bands from local schools gave way as halftime features to nationally and internationally popular musicians. The growth of the television audience prompted advertisers to prepare special commercials to air during the game, and to pay the hosting network handsomely for the privilege. By the 1990s the commercials drew as much attention as the game; many people who cared little about the contest tuned in for the ads. Super Bowl parties became as common as New Year's Eve parties, drawing fans and nonfans alike.

The game produced a windfall for the city that hosted it, with scores of thousands of fans—and almost as many sportswriters and sportscasters, it sometimes seemed—descending on Los Angeles, New Orleans, Miami, and the other cities that staged the event. The visiting hordes spent millions of dollars in hotels, restaurants, and clubs. The game generated hundreds of millions of dollars for the television networks, which bid aggressively against one another for the broadcast rights. The networks' payments, to the NFL and its teams, made the team owners and many of the players rich. The American gambling industry, including the legal bookies in Nevada and the illegals in the rest of the country, looked forward to each "Super Sunday" as the industry's biggest day of the year. The game even inspired urban legends, such as one asserting that the water pressure in cities around the country plummeted at halftime when millions of viewers went to the bathroom simultaneously. The NFL boasted that a billion people could watch the game worldwide; the actual audience, as opposed to the potential audience, was closer to one hundred million, but this still made the game the most-watched event on American television.

As for Michael Jordan, the basketball superstar found baseball a harder game to master. He spent a lackluster season in the minor leagues before rejoining the Bulls in early 1995. He led Chicago to three more NBA championships, in each case being named the most valuable player of the championship series. His fame and endorsements continued to grow. His 1997 income was estimated at $78 million, making him the best-paid sportsman in the world.

## 5. FIRST GLIMPSES OF A NEW SPECTER

It was snowing in New York City on Friday afternoon, February 26, 1993, and workers in the financial district of lower Manhattan were trying to figure out how to get home for the weekend, when a huge explosion ripped through the base of the Twin Towers of the World Trade Center. Police and firefighters quickly ruled out an accident; the detonation was too large, and the location too suspicious. The World Trade Center was the most prominent symbol of American commerce and finance; one hundred thousand workers and visitors entered its halls and elevators every day, busily extending the reach of American capitalism to the far corners of the world. The towers had opened in the early 1970s, and federal officials feared from the start that the buildings would be a target for terrorists. "When the people responsible for anticipating terrorist attacks began to run scenarios on this kind of thing, this was one of the places," former CIA deputy director Bob Inman explained. To strike a blow against the Twin Towers would be to register displeasure or outrage against America's global power. The trade center, moreover, sat atop a train and subway station, through which hundreds of thousands of people passed daily. Attacking the station could kill many of those commuters outright, and it would tangle the New York underground system for months. Equally important, it would terrify the millions who depended on the system and who would naturally fear future bombings.

The explosion blasted a hole two hundred feet long, one hundred feet wide, and five stories deep. Several floors of the building structure collapsed, and large segments of the concrete ceiling of the train station smashed down upon the tracks and platform. The blast caused the Twin Towers to tremble; many of those inside thought they were feeling an earthquake. The motion shook slabs of marble off the facade of the building; the shock wave propelled windows out of their frames. Electrical wires shorted and steam pipes burst, spewing a scalding fog into the building and the surrounding area.

Miraculously, only six people were killed, although a thousand were injured. The FBI immediately took charge of the case and began searching for evidence pointing to the makers and planters of a car or truck bomb. Terrorists based in the Middle East or perhaps the Balkans seemed the most likely suspects. "The car bomb is very much the signature of these groups," one terrorist expert explained. Bob Inman agreed that foreigners were the most likely culprits. "There hasn't been a domestic development of the kind of skills that are needed for this, as there has been in Northern Ireland or the Middle East," the ex–CIA officer said.

In time the trail would lead to several conspirators funded by a shadowy group called al Qaeda. Six men were convicted, but little definitive was discovered about al Qaeda, which apparently had been founded in the 1980s by Osama bin Laden, a member of a wealthy family based in Saudi Arabia, and other militant Islamic fundamentalists who vowed to rid the Arab homeland and the Muslim holy places of American and Zionist influences.

Even as the investigation and prosecution of the World Trade Center bombing proceeded, another explosion, far more deadly, blew the front off the Alfred P. Murrah Federal Building in Oklahoma City on the morning of

April 19, 1995. One hundred sixty-eight people were killed and eight hundred injured. Officials and the general public again suspected foreign terrorists, perhaps connected to al Qaeda. But in this case the trail ran in a different direction. Timothy McVeigh and Terry Nichols were Americans associated with self-styled militia groups that believed the federal government was conspiring against the liberties of ordinary Americans. They evidently shared the outrage of many in the militia movement regarding the federal government's handling of a 1992 incident at Ruby Ridge in northern Idaho, involving a fatal shootout between federal agents and a militia family, and another at Waco, Texas, in 1993, in which an exchange of shots between a militant cult calling itself the Branch Davidians and federal agents killed several persons and led to a seven-week siege that ended in a fiery blaze claiming seventy-six more people, including two dozen women and children.

McVeigh had rented a Ryder truck, which he and Nichols filled with five thousand pounds of homemade explosive consisting of ammonium nitrate fertilizer and liquid nitromethane. On the second anniversary of the Waco fire, McVeigh parked the truck in a loading zone beside the Murrah building, where a timed fuse subsequently ignited the explosive. The blast ripped the near wall off the building, besides damaging dozens of other structures in the surrounding blocks. The sound of the blast was heard as far as fifty miles away and registered on seismographs as a low-grade earthquake.

McVeigh was captured within two hours of the bombing, albeit by accident. He was stopped for driving a car without a license plate, and was arrested for carrying a concealed weapon without a permit. Only later was he linked to the bombing. His arrest implicated Nichols, who turned himself in. McVeigh was tried, convicted, and ultimately, in 2001, executed. Nichols was tried, convicted, and sentenced to life in prison.

Meanwhile the American people, not long after consigning the Cold War specter of nuclear annihilation to the distant rear of their collective memory, learned to live with a new threat—terrorism—looming above their future.

## 6. BOTH SIDES BLINKED

The timing of the Clinton administration's defeat on health care couldn't have been better for the Republicans. The 1994 midterm elections were less than two months away, and the Republicans could portray themselves as the defenders of the honest folks of the heartland against the know-it-all liberals of Washington.

Two Republicans jockeyed for leadership of the party: Bob Dole of Kansas, the Senate minority leader, and Newt Gingrich of Georgia, the House minority whip. Dole had the more impressive résumé, having served in the Senate for a quarter-century after four terms in the House, and that after distinguished and decorated service in the military during World War II. But Gingrich had the better ideas, among them the comparatively novel concept of waging the congressional elections on a national platform.

Conventional wisdom had long held that congressional midterm elections were best fought district by district, with candidates appealing to voters on issues of local concern. Gingrich nationalized the 1994 election by writing a playbook for Republicans across the country to use. The positive part of the playbook was something he called the "Contract with America," which stated in constructive and forthright fashion what the House Republicans would do if voters gave them a majority. They pledged to bring to the House floor within the first hundred days of the new Congress ten bills that would, if enacted, amend the Constitution to require a balanced budget and to grant the president a line-item veto, with the goal of curtailing spending; strengthen law enforcement and stiffen prison sentences, to reduce crime; deny payments to minor unmarried mothers and trim welfare payments generally, to promote personal responsibility; limit damage awards in product liability lawsuits, to discourage excessive litigation; impose term limits on legislators, to prevent the congealing of a permanent political class; and effect various other reforms.

On the negative side, Gingrich had had his political action committee, GOPAC, circulate to Republicans a memo entitled "Language: A Key Mechanism of Control," which listed pejorative words to employ when describing Democrats and their policies. The demonizing list included "greed," "corruption," "radical," "bizarre," "permissive," "sick." The executive director of GOPAC explained: "So often legislative candidates are not used to speaking and not used to putting together phrases with sound-bite words." The memo was intended to assist them.

It worked. The Republicans lashed the Democrats unmercifully, and to great effect at the polls. "We got the living daylights beat out of us," Clinton acknowledged afterward. "Gingrich had proved to be a better politician than I was." The Democrats lost eight seats in the Senate and fifty-four in the House, making it the worst day for Democrats since the post-Roosevelt reaction of 1946. The Republicans seized control of both chambers, making Dole the Senate majority leader and Gingrich the speaker of the House. The GOP did well in state races too. George Pataki ousted Mario Cuomo in the New York governor's race, while George W. Bush, the son of the former president, beat Democratic incumbent Ann Richards in Texas.

Clinton absorbed the meaning of the election. "If we agree on nothing else tonight," he said in his State of the Union address in January 1995, "we must agree that the American people certainly voted for change." The president proposed to get in front of that change. He proposed a "new covenant" with the American people. "I think we all agree that we have to change the way the government works. Let's make it smaller, less costly, and smarter. . . . Our job here is to expand opportunity, not bureaucracy, to empower people to make the most of their own lives, and to enhance our security here at home and abroad. We must not ask government to do what we should do for ourselves." Clinton asserted that the trimming had already begun in the executive branch. He boasted of having cut a quarter-trillion dollars from the budget and one hundred thousand positions from the federal payroll. Yet more needed to be done. "We have to cut yesterday's government to help solve tomorrow's problems."

Having spoken his piece, Clinton prudently stepped aside to let the Republicans savor their moment. Gingrich was as good as his campaign word, and he brought the several clauses of the Contract with America to the House floor. In short order the House approved the balanced budget amendment, the line-item veto, welfare retrenchment, tort (that is, lawsuit) reform, limits on federal paperwork and unfunded mandates (orders by the federal government to the states to spend their own money for federally specified purposes), and other aspects of their national platform.

The Republican contract had never bound the Senate, in part because the senators considered themselves above such pandering, and in part because Bob Dole didn't want to be seen as marching to the Gingrich tune. The House measures fared less well at the north end of the Capitol. The Senate accepted the line-item veto and the limits on paperwork and unfunded mandates, but the rest of the House package bogged down. Some sections fell victim to the long-winded debate for which the Senate is famous; others got lost in committee. The balanced budget amendment claimed a majority but not the two-thirds required to alter the Constitution.

The excitement in Washington thereupon shifted to the shaping of the federal budget. Gingrich and the House Republicans wanted to balance the budget by making deep cuts in social, educational, and environmental programs, including Medicare and other favorites of the Democrats. Senate Republicans adopted a less draconian attitude, while Clinton threatened to veto the kind of budget Gingrich was proposing. A standoff ensued, and the end of the fiscal year—September 30—came and went with no budget in place. Gingrich matched Clinton's veto threats with a threat of his own: to refuse to pass legislation raising the federal debt limit. Such legislation had been pro forma previously, and it remained a largely technical matter. But without an increase in the debt limit, Clinton's Treasury couldn't borrow the money needed to fund the federal government, which would go into default. This had never happened, and no one knew what it would mean. Clinton didn't want to find out, and he thought Gingrich didn't really want to either.

The government muddled through by means of continuing resolutions until November, when Gingrich partially relented and allowed the debt limit to go up, but only for thirty days. Unless a new budget was approved by then, the government might have to shut down.

Clinton convened a summit meeting with the Republican leadership at the White House. Gingrich and Dole brought their lieutenants; Clinton mustered Vice President Al Gore and the administration's top money men. Gingrich was his usual confrontational self; Dole was more statesmanlike and said he didn't want to see a government shutdown. Richard Armey of Texas, the House majority leader, interrupted to say that Dole didn't speak for all Republicans. "Armey was a big man who always wore cowboy boots and seemed to be in a constant state of agitation," Clinton remembered. "He launched into a tirade about how the House Republicans were determined to be true to their principles, and how angry he was that my TV ads on the Medicare cuts had frightened his elderly mother-in-law. I replied that I didn't know about his mother-in-law, but if the Republican budget cuts were to become law, large numbers of elderly people would be forced out of nursing homes or lose their home health care."

The meeting ended with the impasse unbroken, and in mid-November the government began to close down. Eight hundred thousand federal workers were furloughed; federal offices operated with skeleton staffs; many federal services were suspended. The Grand Canyon and other national parks shut their gates, turning away visitors. The museums of the Smithsonian Institution in Washington buttoned up. Environmental inspections ceased. College students needing loans heard recordings telling them to call back when the government reopened. Vendors to the government went unpaid. Applicants for Social Security benefits encountered locked doors. Travelers awaiting passports had to cancel trips.

After public opinion polls showed that voters tended to blame the Republicans for the shutdown—partly because the Republicans had been ranting about big government for years, partly because Clinton simply seemed more likable than Gingrich—the Republicans flinched. They sent Clinton a new continuing resolution, which allowed the government to reopen.

But only temporarily. The Republicans still differed with the president over the substance of the budget, and by mid-December Gingrich, Dole, and the others were willing to have another test of strength. The second shutdown wasn't as severe as the first—only a quarter-million workers were sent home—but it lasted longer. The furloughs cast a pall over Christmas for the workers and their families, and for holiday retailers in communities with large numbers of federal employees, who unsurprisingly didn't do much shopping. The effects rippled outward: Philadelphia, which normally greeted crowds of tourists to Independence Hall and the other sites associated with the nation's founding, fell quiet as the tourists knew not to come. Restaurants and hotels suffered from their absence, as did the suppliers to those establishments, and their employees. Even businesses unrelated to tourism suffered. "Just dead—dead" was how the owner of a shoe repair shop not far from Independence Hall described business and the neighborhood in general.

By the third week of the second shutdown, Dole was willing to compromise. The Kansas senator was running for president, and he appreciated the incongruity of asking voters to elect him to run a government he was in the process of closing down. "Enough is enough," he said in early January. "I think we've made our point."

But Gingrich and the House Republicans disagreed. "If he wants to cave to the wishes of the White House, he can do it," Tom DeLay of Texas, one of the House hardliners, said of Dole. "But we are going to get a balanced budget."

The uncompromising stand of Gingrich and the House Republicans made them look even more the heavies in the shutdown story, and the rift between Dole and Gingrich weakened the Republican party as a whole. As election-year alarm spread through the GOP, even Gingrich finally had to come around. The House joined the Senate in approving another continuing resolution, which brought back the federal workers.

Clinton might have exploited his victory by lambasting the Republicans; instead he offered an olive branch. The president too had taken a lesson from the shutdown, and from the Republicans' success in getting as far as they did. In his 1996 State of the Union address he introduced Americans to Richard Dean. The cameras panned to Dean, sitting in the gallery, as Clinton told Dean's story:

> He's a forty-nine-year-old Vietnam veteran who's worked for the Social Security Administration for twenty-two years now. Last year he was hard at work in the federal building in Oklahoma City when the blast killed 168 people and brought the rubble down all around him. He reentered that building four times. He saved the lives of three women. He's here with us this evening, and I want to recognize Richard and applaud both his public service and his extraordinary personal heroism.
>
> But Richard Dean's story doesn't end there. This last November, he was forced out of his office when the government shut down. And the second time the government shut down he continued helping Social Security recipients, but he was working without pay.
>
> On behalf of Richard Dean and his family, and all the other people who are out there working every day doing a good job for the American people, I challenge all of you in this chamber: Let's never, ever shut the federal government down again.

The applause for Dean had hardly died when Clinton said something the Republicans had thought they would go to their graves without hearing from a Democratic president: "The era of big government is over." Clinton explained that he had already reduced the number of federal employees by two hundred thousand and that the number would continue to decline. "Our federal government today is the smallest it has been in thirty years," he said, with pride unthinkable in a Democrat not long before. "And it's getting smaller every day."

## 7. MISSING THE COLD WAR

Clinton entered office having campaigned almost exclusively on domestic issues. In this he was no different from most successful presidential candidates, who had long recognized that foreign affairs rarely engage voters sufficiently to decide elections. But like many other successful candidates, Clinton discovered that the world couldn't be ignored for long.

Clinton was the first post–Cold War president, and it fell to him to devise an American foreign policy for the post–Cold War world. George Bush's "new world order" could have furnished a starting point, if Clinton chose to go down that path. But having criticized Bush for spending too much time trying to save the world, Clinton was in no position to turn around and start saving it himself.

The world, moreover, resisted saving. The end of the Cold War, far from inaugurating an era of peace, ushered in an age of chaos. The Persian Gulf War was one manifestation of the confusion; the breakup of Yugoslavia another. For forty years Yugoslavia had been held together by the charisma and iron will of Josip Broz Tito, and for ten years after Tito's 1980 death by the continuing pressure of the Cold War. But the disintegration of the Soviet Union released the pressure from the East, even as it encouraged the constituent elements of Yugoslavia to strike out on their own. In 1991 two provinces, Croatia and Slovenia, declared independence. Macedonia followed suit later that year, and Bosnia did the same in 1992.

Serbia was the dominant province in Yugoslavia, and the Serbs had long considered themselves the heart of the nation. Serbia opposed the serial secessions, partly because they weakened the country as a whole and partly because some of the seceding provinces contained large numbers of Serbs, who feared being separated from their cousins in Serbia. In Croatia, local Serbs encouraged by Serbia mounted an armed campaign against the new Croat government. The fighting produced heavy casualties and large numbers of refugees, with Serbs fleeing the areas controlled by Croats, and Croats fleeing the Serb-dominated regions.

Fighting in Bosnia was even more intense. Three groups vied for influence: the Bosnian Muslims, who were the most numerous, at nearly half the population; the Serbs, at a third; and the Croats, about a sixth. The Bosnian Serbs, as in Croatia assisted by Serbia, had resisted Bosnian independence, and once it came they fought to detach their sector of the new country and reattach it to Serbia. The Bosnian Muslims might have been tempted to let them go, had the populations in Bosnia been neatly segregated. But the populations had been intermingling for centuries, making separation a logistical nightmare. The Serbs attempted to undo the intermingling by a brutal campaign of what came to be called "ethnic cleansing": driving the Muslims out of the Serb regions.

Clinton inherited the Bosnian conflict and the halfhearted attempts of the outside world to resolve it. The European Community, the United Nations, and NATO had all weighed in, with the EC leading efforts to negotiate a settlement, the UN imposing economic sanctions against Serbia and an arms embargo against all parties in Bosnia, and NATO blockading the Adriatic coast and threatening air strikes against the Serbs.

But none of the measures brought the fighting to anything like an end. In early 1994 NATO, with Clinton's encouragement, decided to go ahead with the air strikes, and that spring American and other NATO warplanes began bombing Serb forces in Bosnia. The Serbs held out against the NATO bombardment, later supplemented by missile strikes, for more than a year.

Finally, though, in the autumn of 1995, the leader of Serbia, Slobodan Milosevic, consented to travel to the United States and engage in peace talks with Alija Izetbegovic of Bosnia and Franjo Tudjman of Croatia. The Balkan head men spent three weeks at Wright-Patterson Air Force Base near Dayton, Ohio, where they argued, obstructed, and postured under the dour gaze of Clinton's secretary of state, Warren Christopher. The foursome finally concluded what came to be called the Dayton accords, confirming Bosnian independence and territorial integrity while securing a degree of autonomy for the Serbs within the Bosnian republic. A complicated system of power sharing in the Bosnian government was part of the deal; a determination of the fate of the Bosnian Serbs responsible for the worst of the atrocities was not.

A pledge of American troops to help enforce the agreement nudged the three Balkan leaders the final steps to the signing.

Clinton hadn't wanted to involve the United States directly, but he saw no alternative. "America cannot and must not be the world's policeman," he told the American people in explaining his—and their—role in the Bosnia accord. "We cannot stop all war for all time. But we can stop some wars. We cannot save all women and all children, but we can save many of them. We can't do everything, but we must do what we can."

Clinton took pains to assure the American people that the commitment to Bosnia would be closely constrained and carefully monitored. Twenty thousand American troops would constitute but a third of the international peacekeeping force, drawn from more than two dozen countries. The American troops would take orders from an American commander. "They will be heavily armed and thoroughly trained," Clinton said. "By making an overwhelming show of force, they will lessen the need to use force." The troops were going not to fight but to keep the fighting from breaking out again. "Our mission is clear and limited, and our troops are strong and very well-prepared."

The reason Clinton made such a point of the clarity of the American mission in Bosnia and the strength of the American force was that in another conflict during this same period America's mission was not clear and the American force was not strong. The dissolution of Somalia had little to do with the end of the Cold War, but the American decision to intervene in the Somali civil war had much to do with it. The Somali war was a case study in the CNN effect: after television cameras brought the plight of starving Somali refugees into American living rooms, the American government felt great pressure to aid the sufferers. The United Nations was providing food and medicine, but the rival factions fighting the war prevented the supplies from reaching those who needed them. During his last month in office George Bush sent troops to Somalia to safeguard the relief effort. Clinton as president-elect concurred in the effort, and as president he inherited responsibility for it. The mission went well throughout the spring of 1993; the aid reached its recipients, and life in Somalia returned to a semblance of normality. UN peacekeepers entered the country, and as they did so, Clinton withdrew most of the American troops. By June only four thousand remained.

But then militiamen loyal to one of the Somali clan leaders, Muhammad

Farrah Aidid, killed twenty-four of the UN peacekeepers. Continued conflict apparently suited Aidid better than peace; by attacking the peacekeepers he hoped to keep the pot boiling. The secretary general of the UN, Boutros Boutros-Ghali, requested American help in bringing Aidid to justice. Clinton weighed the request carefully, consulting with Colin Powell and his other military advisers. Powell concluded that the mission would be difficult but was worth doing, lest the credibility of the UN—and implicitly of the United States—suffer grievous harm.

Clinton approved, and in early October a task force of U.S. Army Rangers helicoptered into Mogadishu, the Somali capital. The force encountered unexpectedly strong resistance from Aidid's militiamen; two of the Black Hawk helicopters were shot down by rocket-propelled grenades. Some of those injured in the downings were rescued and evacuated, but the pilot of one of the Black Hawks was trapped in the wreckage. The Rangers' code forbade leaving a comrade in the field, and so some of the Rangers stayed with him while calling for reinforcements. A bitter urban battle resulted, in which eighteen American soldiers died and scores were wounded. Somali dead numbered in the hundreds, with many more wounded. The American pilot, Mike Durant, was captured by the Somali militiamen.

The American losses were painful and embarrassing to the army and to the administration, both of which wondered how a ragtag militia could have inflicted such damage on the best-trained and best-armed soldiers in the world. The losses were puzzling to the American people, who weren't sure what the troops were still doing in Somalia. The pain, embarrassment, and puzzlement turned to outrage when the Somali fighters dragged the bodies of some of the slain Americans through the streets of Mogadishu, and television cameras recorded and relayed the images.

Members of Congress from both parties received constituent calls demanding that the American troops be withdrawn at once. Many callers complained that the American soldiers in Somalia were doing the dirty work of the United Nations, rather than defending the national interests of the United States. Senators and representatives echoed this sentiment. "Americans by the dozens are paying with their lives and limbs for a misplaced policy on the altar of some fuzzy multilateralism," Democratic senator Robert Byrd of West Virginia asserted. Senate Republican leader Dole declared, "As the body bags pile up in Mogadishu, the confusion over U.S. objectives increases."

Dole insisted that Clinton present Congress a "blueprint for how and when the U.S. leaves Somalia for good."

Clinton initially defended his policy. "We started this mission for the right reasons, and we're going to finish it in the right way," he said. "In a sense, we came to Somalia to rescue innocent people in a burning house. We've nearly put the fire out, but some smoldering embers remain. If we leave them now, those embers will reignite into flames, and people will die again."

But as the criticism mounted, and as the complexity of the conflict in Somalia grew ever more apparent, Clinton sought an exit strategy. "I was sick about the loss of our troops and I wanted Aidid to pay," he recalled later. "If getting him was worth eighteen dead and eighty-four wounded Americans, wasn't it worth finishing the job?" But going after Aidid again, even successfully, would carry a cost. "If we went back in and nabbed Aidid, dead or alive, then we, not the UN, would own Somalia, and there was no guarantee that we could put it together politically any better than the UN had."

Clinton decided on a phased withdrawal, to take place over six months. Meanwhile he dispatched an envoy to arrange the release of Mike Durant, the captured pilot. The American offer was that the United States would not attack Aidid if he released Durant at once; the accompanying threat was that the American forces would hit Aidid harder than ever if he didn't release Durant. Aidid accepted the offer.

During the subsequent weeks Clinton visited the wounded soldiers at Walter Reed Army Hospital, and he met with the families of the soldiers who had been killed. Two of the fathers pressed him hard, asking why their sons had died if the job wasn't important enough to finish. Another father told the president to his face that he was not fit to be commander-in-chief. "I couldn't tell if he felt the way he did because I had not served in Vietnam, because I had approved the policy that led to the raid, or because I had declined to go back after Aidid," Clinton reflected.

As for himself, the president shared a sentiment articulated by Tony Lake, his national security adviser, who remarked amid the troubles in the Balkans and East Africa: "Sometimes I really miss the Cold War."

# 13 | Culture Clash

## 1996–2000

### 1. NOT SINCE FDR

Rarely does the American presidency seek out individuals; almost always the seeking works the other way around. The principal exceptions have been victorious generals—the likes of Washington, Jackson, Grant, Eisenhower. Even rarer are the instances when a general sought has declined the honor. William Sherman rebuffed repeated efforts by the Republicans to nominate him; his categorical rejection—"If nominated I will not accept; if elected I will not serve"—became the gold standard for political denial and added an adjective, "Shermanesque," to the American lexicon.

Colin Powell's denial of interest in the Republican nomination wasn't exactly Shermanesque. By 1996 Americans were starving for heroic leadership. Three wars had been fought since Eisenhower won his laurels, and of Korea, Vietnam, and the Persian Gulf War, only the last had been successful enough to propel a general into the political arena. Powell had other things working for him, too. As a black man he appealed to minorities even as he made many white liberals feel good about themselves for admiring him. As a successful soldier he had earned the respect of conservatives and others for whom the military remained a noble calling. He was clearly competent, having climbed the ladder from the Harlem and South Bronx of his childhood through officer training at the City College of New York and thirty-five years with the army, including service in Vietnam and culminating in the rank of four-star general. He chaired the Joint Chiefs of Staff under George Bush and briefly Bill Clinton, and he commanded American forces during the Gulf War.

He might have had the Republican nomination in 1996 for the asking. His approval rating far surpassed that of other likely candidates, and he tested favorably against Clinton. His memoir, *My American Journey*, published in late 1995, was a runaway bestseller.

But Powell said he wasn't a candidate. Others had said the same thing, hoping to be asked again. Powell was asked again—and again and again. His reiterated denials of interest were artful enough to elicit admiration from his potential opponents, who noted that he never quite slammed the door. In fact, though, he really didn't want the job—or at least he didn't want to run for the job. He kept voters hopeful long enough to promote his book, which while interesting as a tale of poor-boy-makes-good was absolutely riveting as long as the last, unwritten chapter might land the author in the White House. Perhaps Powell, having seen the presidency up close, didn't think it warranted the sacrifices one had to make, for oneself and one's family, to achieve it. Almost certainly, observing what Clinton was going through, he judged politics a sorry substitute for the more straightforward world of the military.

When he finally convinced the Republicans that he would not run, the field of potential challengers to Clinton narrowed quickly. Senator Phil Gramm of Texas filled a war chest with campaign contributions but discovered that money couldn't buy love, or even a single delegate. Bob Dole, the majority leader, survived an early scare from Pat Buchanan, the former Nixon speechwriter who turned phrases and a few heads, and won the GOP nomination with ultimate ease.

Political observers who knew Dole hoped to see some of his wicked humor on display. At a gathering of former presidents, Dole observed Gerald Ford, Jimmy Carter, and Richard Nixon in a row. Dole looked down the line and quipped: "See no evil . . . Hear no evil . . . Evil." But his humor didn't translate well to television, and after some awkward moments that left viewers puzzling, his handlers reined him in.

Clinton meanwhile hit his stride. When he declared that "the era of big government is over," he wasn't kidding. He wrung all the political benefit he could out of his confrontation with Gingrich and the House Republicans over the budget, then accepted their timetable for reducing the federal deficit. He advocated welfare reform, adopting language of individual responsibility no Republican could have imagined improving upon. "People on welfare who can work should go to work," Clinton said. "Parents who owe child support should pay it. Governments don't raise children; people do." He sponsored what became the 1996 Welfare Reform Act—formally, the Personal Responsibility and Work Opportunity Reconciliation Act—and he praised the bipartisan legislation for "ending welfare as we know it." He endorsed the same year's Freedom to Farm Act, which set government subsidies on the road to retirement. "Farmers will be free to plant for the market, not for government programs," Clinton said, on signing the measure.

Clinton's repositioning certainly enhanced his reelection prospects, but not as much as the improving economy did. After the recession of the Bush years, the economy surged back, in part because investors took heart from the shrinking federal deficits. Clinton was able to boast in his acceptance speech to the Democratic convention in August 1996 that America currently enjoyed the lowest combined rates of unemployment, inflation, and home mortgage interest in nearly three decades. Ten million new jobs had been created, more than half in technology and other high-wage sectors. Four million Americans owned homes for the first time. Record numbers of small businesses, many operated by women and minorities, had been established. American exports were at an all-time high. Clinton proposed to extend the recovery by continuing to close the budget gap. "Tonight let us proclaim to the American people that we will balance the budget," Clinton urged the convention. "And let us also proclaim we will do it in a way that preserves Medicare, Medicaid, education, the environment, the integrity of our pensions, the strength of our people."

That a Democrat was running on a pledge to balance the budget was historically surprising; the last one to do so had been Franklin Roosevelt, and he hadn't come anywhere near achieving the goal. But Clinton was serious and, on current trends, perfectly credible. Voters liked his prospects and returned him to office easily, making him the first Democrat since Roosevelt to be elected a second time. Clinton won 49 percent of the popular vote to Dole's 41 percent; Ross Perot, trying again, received 8 percent. The electoral tally magnified the popular margin, as usual; Clinton got 379 electoral votes to Dole's 159.

## 2. SLICK WILLY IN THE STARR CHAMBER

His victory didn't appease his critics—far from it. From the start of his presidency, Clinton had inspired expressions of loathing seldom witnessed in American politics. Partisan calculation explained some of the animosity. "I think one of the great problems we have in the Republican Party is that we don't encourage you to be nasty," Gingrich told a faction of the GOP faithful. The House speaker instructed by example, calling the Democratic party the "enemy of normal Americans," and other Republicans adopted the practice and applied it to Clinton.

Commercial opportunity accounted for some of the anti-Clinton vitriol. In talk radio, Rush Limbaugh built a conservative empire that operated on the premise that Clinton was evil incarnate and liberals were his ungodly acolytes. Limbaugh's success owed much to the Reagan-era deregulation, in particular the FCC's rescission of the fairness doctrine, which had required radio stations to balance liberal and conservative opinions in their programming. Stations discovered, post-deregulation, that conservative talk shows sold more ads than liberal ones. No one knew quite why; some conjectured that the liberals were listening to FM stations rather than the AM stations favored by the talk show listeners. Whatever the reason for the imbalance, Limbaugh capitalized on it. His daily talk show, which was syndicated coast to coast and beyond, starting in the late 1980s, enjoyed huge ratings. Limbaugh's listeners, the self-styled "Dittoheads," called their hero on air to cheer him on. Limbaugh grew rich and powerful condemning "Clintonistas," "feminazis," and other elements of the "liberal elite."

Much of the hatred of Clinton was deeply personal. Clinton could talk circles around nearly all his opponents, which made him seem too facile. Anyone so glib couldn't be sincere, they reasoned. They dubbed him "Slick Willy," as though he were an oily used-car salesman. There were stories of shady dealings in Arkansas real estate from Clinton's pre-presidential days; the Whitewater affair—named for the firm involved—became the object of formal investigation after the Republicans took control of Congress following the 1994 elections.

There were also stories of illicit liaisons. During the 1992 campaign a woman named Gennifer Flowers claimed to have had a long relationship with Clinton while he was governor of Arkansas. He neither quite confirmed nor explicitly denied the allegation. He and Hillary went on the CBS news show *60 Minutes,* where he obliquely addressed the issue, saying he regretted having caused pain to Hillary in their marriage. He added that he had already revealed more personal information than any other politician had, and he concluded by declaring that he would say no more on the subject. He thought he had put the allegation to rest. "The public understood that I hadn't been perfect and wasn't pretending to be," he recalled. "But people also knew that there were many more important issues confronting the country."

Yet the issue wouldn't rest, not least because Gennifer Flowers wasn't the only woman who had stories about him. In 1994 Paula Jones sued Clinton for sexual harassment, claiming he had propositioned her in a hotel in Little Rock in 1991. Clinton denied the harassment charge, and he rebuffed attempts to reach an out-of-court settlement. The lawsuit gained traction after Kenneth Starr was appointed independent counsel to investigate the Whitewater affair. Starr interpreted his charge broadly and branched out from Whitewater to probe Clinton's misbehavior generally. The investigation went slowly until the beginning of 1997, when the *Drudge Report,* a Web-based news site best known for spreading gossip, broke a story about a White House intern named Monica Lewinsky who alleged having a sexual relationship with Clinton. Matt Drudge went on to assert that the mainstream media, which he regularly derided, knew the story but had refused to publish it.

This latter allegation gave the Lewinsky story legs. Even in the 1990s the major papers, newsmagazines, and networks hesitated to dig too deeply into the private lives of public figures; but Drudge's claim of a cover-up put the underlying assertion on a new level. The plot thickened as the media heavyweights went to work; four days after the original Drudge allegation, the *Washington Post* reported that Starr and his investigators were pursuing reports that Clinton and his close friend Vernon Jordan had tried to persuade Lewinsky to lie about her relationship with Clinton to lawyers for Paula Jones, who were trying to establish the credibility of their client by corroborating the infidelity of the president. Within ninety-six hours a dismissible Internet report about a personal lapse had become a front-page account of possible witness tampering and obstruction of justice at the highest level.

Clinton loyalists exhibited a combination of disbelief and outrage. "This story seems ridiculous," Robert Bennett, the president's lawyer, declared.

"Frankly, I smell a rat." Sidney Blumenthal, a senior aide, recalled, "My initial instinct was more than extreme skepticism that the President and Vernon Jordan were locked in a criminal conspiracy. I could not imagine that such careful political men would be reckless lawbreakers. An affair? I had no idea. But obstructing justice? Suborning perjury? This seemed impossible."

The timing of the story appeared no accident. Just days earlier Clinton had given a deposition in the Paula Jones case. Clinton's lawyers had contended that the president should not be made to testify while he remained in office; his forced involvement in the case would distract him from his executive duties, they said. Moreover, to require a president to testify would encourage other lawsuits in the future by plaintiffs simply trying to make political trouble. The Supreme Court disagreed and ordered Clinton to answer the questions of the lawyers for Jones. Robert Bennett subsequently urged Clinton to settle. "I didn't want to," Clinton explained afterward, "because it would take about half of everything Hillary and I had saved over twenty years, and because I knew, on the basis of the investigative work my legal team had done, that we would win the case if it ever went to trial." But neither did he want to waste presidential time on the case, and he told Bennett to work out a deal. The bargaining stuck, however, on Jones's insistence that Clinton apologize for sexually harassing her. "I couldn't do that because it wasn't true," Clinton said. The case continued.

The president's deposition lasted several hours, of which only a small portion related to Paula Jones or what Clinton had done with or to her. Most of the questioning had to do with other people Clinton had known, including Monica Lewinsky. This surprised Bennett, who knew little about Lewinsky beyond the fact that she had been a White House intern. After a long series of introductory questions, Jones's lawyer at the deposition put the matter to Clinton directly: "Did you have an extramarital sexual affair with Monica Lewinsky?"

"No," the president responded.

"If she told someone that she had a sexual affair with you beginning in November of 1995, would that be a lie?"

"It's certainly not the truth. It would not be the truth."

"I think I used the term 'sexual affair.' And so the record is completely clear, have you ever had sexual relations with Monica Lewinsky?"

"I have never had sexual relations with Monica Lewinsky. I've never had an affair with her."

Clinton later asserted that he had answered truthfully in the deposition. "During the government shutdown in late 1995," he explained in his memoir, "when very few people were allowed to come to work in the White House and those who were there were working late, I'd had an inappropriate encounter with Monica Lewinsky and would do so again on other occasions between November and April." Lewinsky subsequently took a new assignment at the Pentagon, and for ten months he didn't see her, although they spoke by phone. She returned to the White House in February 1997. "She was among the guests at an evening taping of my weekly radio address, after which I met with her alone again for about fifteen minutes. I was disgusted with myself for doing it, and in the spring, when I saw her again, I told her that it was wrong for me, wrong for my family, and wrong for her, and I couldn't do it anymore."

This ended things until the Jones case required Clinton to explain. "What I had done with Monica Lewinsky was immoral and foolish," he said later. "I was deeply ashamed of it and I didn't want it to come out. In the deposition, I was trying to protect my family and myself from my selfish stupidity. I believed that the contorted definition of 'sexual relations'"—the legal framework established in the course of the investigation—"enabled me to do so."

He soon discovered that he had outfoxed himself. In fact, he concluded he had been deliberately drawn into a trap. The Drudge story broke the next day. "The deposition had been a setup," Clinton wrote.

If so, it worked, for now the issue wasn't infidelity but perjury. The president proceeded to dig his hole deeper. "Is there any truth to the allegation of an affair between you and the young woman?" a reporter from National Public Radio asked him just hours after the *Washington Post* follow-up to the Drudge story appeared.

"No, that's not true," the president replied. "The charges are not true."

"Did you have any kind of relationship with her that could have been misconstrued?"

"There wasn't improper relations."

That night he went on the PBS *NewsHour* and told host Jim Lehrer that there was "no improper relationship" with Monica Lewinsky.

"Define what you mean by that," Lehrer pressed.

"I think you know what it means. It means that there is not a sexual relationship, an improper sexual relationship, or any other kind of improper relationship."

A few days later he issued his most emphatic denial. "I want to say one thing to the American people," he declared on television from the White House. "I want you to listen to me. I'm going to say this again. I did not have sexual relations with that woman, Miss Lewinsky. . . . These allegations are false."

But they weren't false, which became apparent as more details of the Lewinsky story leaked to the press. Lewinsky's former colleague and ostensible friend Linda Tripp tape-recorded some conversations with Lewinsky, in which Lewinsky detailed her relationship with Clinton and made clear that it involved oral sex, if not sexual intercourse. Tripp's motives weren't transparent; she may have been out to get Clinton, as Clinton's supporters alleged, or she may have been protecting herself in the event *she* was drawn into the investigation. But whatever her motives, when her story surfaced, it added to the perception that Clinton was lying about his relationship with Lewinsky.

It also lent credence to suspicions that he might have been lying about other matters, including whether he had tried to get Lewinsky to commit perjury in the Jones case. This would have been not simply bad faith or bad judgment but a crime, and a grand jury was empaneled. The jurors convened in the White House Map Room in August 1998, and Clinton was questioned not only about his relationship with Lewinsky but about his testimony in the Jones deposition. "Mr. President, were you physically intimate with Monica Lewinsky?" Robert Bittman of Starr's office asked.

"Mr. Bittman, I think maybe I can save you and the grand jurors a lot of time if I read a statement, which I think will make it clear what the nature of my relationship with Monica Lewinsky was and how it related to the testimony I gave, what I was trying to do in that testimony. And I think it will perhaps make it possible for you to ask even more relevant questions from your point of view. And, with your permission, I'd like to read that statement."

"Absolutely. Please, Mr. President."

"When I was alone with Monica Lewinsky on certain occasions in early 1996 and once in early 1997, I engaged in conduct that was wrong. These encounters did not consist of sexual intercourse. They did not constitute sexual relations as I understood that term to be defined at my January 17th,

1998, deposition. But they did involve inappropriate intimate contact." Clinton then stated that he would say no more about the specifics of the relationship, out of a desire to protect his family from embarrassment and preserve the dignity of the office of the president.

He didn't get off so easily. One of Bittman's associates read a statement by Robert Bennett, in which Bennett characterized certain testimony by Lewinsky as claiming that "there is absolutely no sex of any kind in any manner, shape or form" between herself and the president. Clinton was now asked whether his own testimony hadn't shown this statement to be false.

"It depends on what the meaning of the word 'is' is," Clinton replied. "If the—if 'is' means is and never has been, that is not—that is one thing. If it means there is none, that was a completely true statement."

The president guessed, correctly, that his grand jury testimony would surface soon; to regain what control he could of the story, he went on television that night. "This afternoon in this room, from this chair, I testified before the Office of Independent Counsel and the grand jury," he declared from the White House.

> I answered their questions truthfully, including questions about my private life, questions no American citizen would ever want to answer. Still I must take complete responsibility for all my actions, both public and private. And that is why I am speaking to you tonight.
>
> As you know, in a deposition in January I was asked questions about my relationship with Monica Lewinsky. While my answers were legally accurate, I did not volunteer information. Indeed, I did have a relationship with Ms. Lewinsky that was not appropriate. In fact, it was wrong. It constituted a critical lapse in judgment and a personal failure on my part for which I am solely and completely responsible.
>
> But I told the grand jury today, and I say to you now, that at no time did I ask anyone to lie, to hide or destroy evidence, or to take any other unlawful action. I know that my public comments and my silence about this matter gave a false impression. I misled people, including even my wife. I deeply regret that.

Clinton tried to take the offensive. He blamed the Starr investigation for exceeding its charge and scrutinizing people who had nothing to do with the original issue. "This has gone on too long, cost too much, and hurt too many innocent people," Clinton said. It was time for the inquisition to end.

> Now this matter is between me, the two people I love most, my wife and our daughter, and our God. I must put it right, and I am prepared to do whatever it takes to do so. Nothing is more important to me personally. But it is private. And I intend to reclaim my family life for my family. It's nobody's business but ours. Even presidents have private lives.

## 3. SEX, LIES, AND POLITICS

But not this president, and not after all that had happened. The Republicans in Congress weren't going to let Clinton go, and they began talking seriously of impeachment. The House voted, on party lines, to commence an inquiry leading toward articles of impeachment. The matter became, not surprisingly, an issue in the 1998 congressional elections, as the Republicans expected to exploit Clinton's weakness for their own gains. To their surprise, voters handed the victory to the Democrats, who picked up five seats in the House and held their ground in the Senate. The Republicans still controlled both chambers but with considerably less confidence than before.

All the same, the House Republicans went forward with the impeachment proceedings. In December the House approved two articles, one asserting perjury and the other obstruction of justice.

The trial—the first impeachment trial since Andrew Johnson's in 1868—took place before the Senate in January and February 1999. William Rehnquist, the chief justice of the United States, presided, and the entire Senate sat as jury. Thirteen Republicans from the House Judiciary Committee served as "managers" of the impeachment—that is, as prosecutors. Over three days they reiterated the evidence against Clinton, contending that the president should be held to the same standards as the humblest citizen. Charles Canady of Florida declared that Clinton must be convicted and removed from office because he had made himself "a notorious example of lawlessness." Steve Buyer of Indiana observed that federal prisons currently held more than a hundred persons convicted of perjury. "Where is the fairness to these Americans," Buyer demanded, "if they stay in jail and the president stays in the Oval Office?" Lindsay Graham of South Carolina responded to assertions that the punishment of removal from office was excessive, compared to the offense, by saying, "Impeachment is not punishment. Impeachment is about cleansing the office."

Henry Hyde of Illinois, the chairman of the Judiciary Committee and the leader of the prosecution, summarized the case against Clinton in an emotional speech that drew passion and pathos from the Ten Commandments, the Magna Carta, the Bill of Rights, the Gettysburg Address, and the battles of Bunker Hill, Omaha Beach, and Kuwait City. Hyde declared that the Clinton case was not about sex, as the president's defenders complained, but about "the rule of law." Americans—and the world—must be able to trust the country's chief executive. Having a "presidential perjurer" in the White House would undermine faith in government and America's international credibility. Hyde read a letter he said came from a Chicago third grader who asked, "If you cannot believe the President, who can you believe? If you have no one to believe in, then how do you run your life?" Hyde closed with an appeal to the conscience of the senators: "My solitary, solitary hope is that a hundred years from today, people will look back at what we have done and say, 'They kept the faith.'"

Clinton turned to Dale Bumpers to make the case for acquittal. Bumpers had just left the Senate after four terms, and he reminded the senators of the personal element in the matter at hand. "The President has said for all to hear that he misled, he deceived, he did not want to be helpful to the prosecution," Bumpers acknowledged.

> Why would he do that? Well, he knew this whole affair was about to bring unspeakable embarrassment and humiliation on himself, his wife whom he adored, and a child that he worshipped with every fiber in his body, and for whom he would happily have died to spare her this or to ameliorate her shame and her grief.
>
> The House managers have said shame and embarrassment is no excuse for lying. Well, the question about lying, that's your decision. But I can tell you, you put yourself in his position, and you've already had this big moral lapse, as to what you would do. We are none of us perfect. Sure, you say, he should have thought of all that beforehand. And indeed he should. Just as Adam and Eve should have. Just as you and you

> and you and you, and millions of other people who have been caught in similar circumstances, should have thought of it before. And I say none of us are perfect.

Bumpers contended that there were degrees of perjury. He said that in his career as a lawyer he had tried hundreds of divorce cases, and in most of them someone lied about something intimate. He had also tried many murder cases. "There's a very big difference in perjury about a marital infidelity in a divorce case and perjury about whether I bought the murder weapon or whether I concealed the murder weapon or not. And to charge somebody with the first and punish them as though it were the second stands justice, our sense of justice, on its head."

Bumpers noted that Henry Hyde had said the present case wasn't about sex. But it was about sex, Bumpers rejoined. "We're here today because the president suffered a terrible moral lapse, a marital infidelity; not a breach of the public trust, not a crime against society. . . . It is a sex scandal. H. L. Mencken said one time, 'When you hear somebody say, "This is not about money"—it's about money.' And when you hear somebody say, 'This is not about sex'—it's about sex." The senators should keep this in mind.

> An unfaithful relationship does not even come close to being an impeachable offense. Nobody has suggested that Bill Clinton committed a political crime against the state. So, colleagues, if you honor the Constitution, you must look at the history of the Constitution and how we got to the impeachment clause. And if you do that, and you do that honestly according to the oath you took, you cannot—you can censure Bill Clinton; you can hand him over to the prosecutor for him to be prosecuted, but you cannot convict him.

Some of the senators doubtless were moved by Bumpers's appeal to history and conscience. Some surely took heed of the results of the recent elections. Many must have read a Gallup poll taken just after the House voted to impeach that registered a ten-point jump in Clinton's approval rating, to an all-time high of 73 percent (which was higher than Ronald Reagan's best). The same poll revealed that fewer than three respondents in ten wanted the Senate to convict, and fewer than a third approved of the Republican party.

Whatever the senators' reasoning, they refused to convict the president. Both articles fell far short of the required two-thirds approval. The vote on the perjury charge was 45 in favor and 55 against. The vote on obstruction was 50 to 50.

## 4. BUBBLE AND BOIL

Clinton's trial in the Senate was one of America's most celebrated legal confrontations in the 1990s, but it wasn't the most important. And while Clinton's squirming under oath made him look foolish and deceitful, his performance didn't make him look as stupid as Bill Gates looked when it was Gates's turn to squirm.

Gates was the cofounder of Microsoft Corporation, and by the 1990s he was the wealthiest man in America. The roots of both Gates and Microsoft lay in Seattle, where as a six-year-old he attended the 1962 World's Fair. One of the exhibits was an IBM showcase, forecasting an information revolution driven by computers. Gates took note. In eighth grade he logged onto a General Electric mainframe computer via teletype terminal and shortly thereafter began programming. Gates and Paul Allen, a schoolmate, hacked their way past security systems to get free time on the GE computer; when their break-in was discovered, the company that owned the computer was more intrigued than miffed and wanted to know how they had done it. Gates and Allen were programming for pay by the time they finished high school.

Gates went east to Harvard for college but didn't last. "He was a hell of a good programmer," the head of Harvard's computer lab recalled. Gates's personal skills were another matter. "In terms of being a pain in the ass, he was second in my whole career here. He's an obnoxious human being. . . . He'd put people down when it wasn't necessary, and just generally not be a pleasant fellow to have around the place."

Gates dropped out of Harvard to form a partnership with Allen that evolved into Microsoft. The coup on which the company's initial success depended was a contract with IBM to write the operating system for IBM's breakthrough personal computer, the PC. What made the contract special—and specially advantageous to Microsoft—was that Microsoft retained the rights to the operating system. Gates intuited—against the conventional wisdom of the day—that software would be more important than hardware in the dawning computer age, and that by controlling the software Microsoft would go far toward controlling the revolution.

Events proved Gates right. The engineers who designed the microprocessors that powered the computers learned to cram more and more transistors onto each sliver of silicon; the number of transistors, and with them the computing horsepower, doubled every eighteen months or so (establishing a pattern called "Moore's Law," after engineer Gordon Moore); and the number of computers in use expanded dramatically. And as the computers proliferated, so did the Microsoft operating system, which became the industry standard. By the 1990s some nineteen out of twenty computers required the Microsoft system, brand-named Windows. Microsoft also developed application software—word processing, spreadsheet, financial, and presentation programs—to complement Windows; these didn't dominate the market quite so thoroughly as Windows but still far outstripped the competition.

By this time Gates and Allen were billionaires. Allen left the company to pursue other interests (although he held on to the Microsoft shares that made him so wealthy); Gates drove the company relentlessly forward. It was his relentlessness—and a rare slip by Gates—that prompted the Justice Department to charge Microsoft with antitrust violations.

Gates's foresight was as good as anyone's in the business, but he initially overlooked the Internet. Following the Soviet launch of Sputnik in 1957, the American government established the Advanced Research Projects Agency to facilitate American scientific research. ARPA funded research at various laboratories across the country; to allow the researchers to communicate more effectively, the agency constructed a network, called Arpanet, that linked computers in the different labs. Arpanet was expanded during the 1970s and early 1980s, but not until the late 1980s was it opened to outside users. Meanwhile the network grew beyond the borders of the United States, and in the early 1990s the European research consortium CERN launched the World Wide Web project, to link documents, databases, and additional sources of information over what now was known as the Internet. Between the Web and such other Internet applications as e-mail, Internet usage exploded during the late 1990s, with the number of users doubling each year.

The explosion of the Internet prompted entrepreneurs to establish businesses based on the increasingly ubiquitous network. Jeff Bezos founded

Amazon.com as an online—Internet-based—bookstore in 1995. Buyers cruised the bookshelves, so to speak, of Amazon from their home computers; they placed their orders over the Internet, paid with credit cards, and received their books by mail or delivery service.

The Bezos model didn't make money during its first several years, but the idea caught on—in a huge way. Dozens, then hundreds, then thousands of companies staked their claim to the Internet. Pets.com sold supplies for dogs, cats, and goldfish; eBay auctioned everything under the sun; Yahoo provided news, e-mail, and search services; Expedia reserved airplane tickets and hotel rooms. The new companies attracted investors who judged Silicon Valley, the region just north of San Jose, California, that epitomized the computer industry and its Internet spin-offs, to be the site of a modern gold rush. One venture capitalist—the name given to the financiers who funded the Internet start-ups—described the "vein of gold" that ran through Silicon Valley. "Anybody can reach down into it and strike it rich," he said. Another Silicon Valley veteran called the Internet boom "the largest legal creation of wealth in the history of the planet."

So it seemed through the end of the 1990s. The NASDAQ Composite index, the most commonly cited measure of technology share prices, quintupled between 1995 and early 2000. Tens of thousands of employees of tech companies who took part of their pay in stock shares became millionaires on paper—or millionaires in cash if they sold their shares. "Microsoft millionaires" were thick on the ground near Redmond, Washington, the Seattle suburb Gates had made the headquarters of Microsoft. "Dellionaires" were the Central Texas equivalent, enriched by their shares of Dell computer. The money sloshing around Silicon Valley and the other hotbeds of technology drove real estate to unheard-of levels, spreading the wealth to the lucky people who bought their homes before the boom began, but spreading distress among those who found themselves priced out of once affordable neighborhoods.

The dot-com bubble, as the phenomenon was called, reached its maximum volume in March 2000 when the NASDAQ topped 5100, or twice its level of just a year before. And then the bubble burst. Within weeks the NASDAQ lost a third of its value; by the end of 2002 it had fallen nearly four-fifths.

The collapse was attributed to various causes. Some blamed a lack of business savvy on the part of the tech types who were dazzled by the capabilities of the Internet but couldn't read an annual report, let alone write one. Others faulted investor overconfidence, arguing that only in the fevered imaginations of the most self-deluded could all or even many of the start-ups yield profits to warrant the astronomical share prices they boasted.

Still others blamed the federal court that brought Bill Gates and Microsoft to trial. The Justice Department sued Microsoft for monopoly violations, under laws dating back to the Gilded Age, when such corporate titans as John D. Rockefeller, Andrew Carnegie, and J. P. Morgan had built industrial and financial empires that threatened to dwarf democracy and crush the ordinary people of America. No one seriously accused Microsoft of attempting to overawe the federal government; if anything, Gates and Microsoft had shown themselves to be ineptly innocent at the political arts. But many feared that Microsoft so dominated computer software that the kind of innovation that had characterized the industry—and had made Microsoft itself possible—no longer stood a chance.

The government's case against Gates and company centered on allegations that Microsoft had leveraged its Windows monopoly to try to control the market for Web browsers, the software that allowed users to navigate the Internet. Though Gates had been slow to appreciate the significance of the Internet, once he caught on his company launched a remorseless campaign against the makers of the existing browsers. Microsoft bundled Internet Explorer, its browser, with Windows, essentially making it free to everyone who bought Windows—which was to say, nearly everyone who used a personal computer. The makers of the other browsers complained that this constituted unfair and illegal practice, and the Justice Department concurred.

The federal prosecution of Microsoft required Gates to testify. The Justice Department's David Boies strove to show that Gates and Microsoft had tried to destroy the opposition by any and all means. Gates had long taken pride in being the smartest person in almost any room in which he found himself, but in his duel with Boies he played dumb. Boies handed him an e-mail he had written in 1996 that said: "Winning Internet browser share is a very, very important goal for us."

Gates replied he didn't remember writing it.

Boies pressed him.

Gates responded, "I'm very confused about what you're asking."

Boies showed Gates a message sent to him by Brad Chase, one of the vice presidents at Microsoft. "We need to continue our jihad next year," Chase's message asserted. "Browser share needs to remain a key priority for our field and marketing efforts."

"It doesn't say Microsoft," Gates parried.

"When it says 'we' there, do you understand that means something other than Microsoft?"

"It could mean Brad Chase's group."

Boies demanded to know what Chase meant by "jihad."

"I think he is referring to our vigorous efforts to make a superior product and to market that product."

Boies showed Gates an e-mail he himself had written in January 1996, in which he expressed concern about the success of "non-Microsoft browsers." What browsers were those?

Gates feigned confusion. "I'm sure . . . what's the question? Is it . . . are you asking me about when I wrote this e-mail? . . . What are you asking me about?"

"I'm asking you about January of 1996."

"That month?"

"Yes, sir."

"And what about it?"

Boies shifted course slightly to probe Gates on what he meant when he had written that he was "concerned" about the rival browsers.

Gates acted puzzled regarding the word.

Boies had been calm and polite till now, but Gates's continued evasions drove him to sarcasm. "Is the term 'concerned' a term that you're familiar with in the English language?" he demanded.

Judge Thomas Penfield Jackson grew even more impatient with Gates than Boies did, and he ruled that Microsoft had abused its power, as the Justice Department alleged. Jackson found Microsoft guilty of monopoly practice and in early 2000 ordered a drastic remedy: that the company be broken in two, with one part to handle Windows, the other Internet Explorer and the rest of the applications.

It was this decision, some industry observers said, that burst the dot-com bubble. At the very least, the judgment suggested that the gold rush days of the Internet had ended. The computer industry and especially the Internet had grown up with little government oversight; this freedom from supervision contributed to the feeling that in Silicon Valley and on the Internet all things were possible. Judge Jackson, by imposing the harshest kind of oversight, eliminated at least the wildest possibilities.

Ironically, the mandated breakup never occurred. Gates's lawyers appealed Jackson's decision, and the appellate court set aside Jackson's remedy, without reversing his finding of violation. The appeals court instructed the Justice Department to seek a less draconian remedy.

But by this time the Justice Department was under new management. The 2000 election of George W. Bush installed business-friendly Republicans in the seats of executive power in Washington, and Bush's attorney general, John Ashcroft, opted to settle the Microsoft case out of court. The company made some cosmetic concessions but remained in one piece, almost as powerful as ever.

And Bill Gates remained the wealthiest man in America.

## 5. The Battle of Seattle

Few single events in American history—and certainly none in the history of the Pacific Northwest—ever received more global coverage than a meeting of the World Trade Organization in Seattle in November 1999. The accounts were full of drama. The Montreal *Gazette* called the affair a "Three-Ring Circus." The London *Guardian* declared, "Robocops Face Down Protesters." The *Japan Times* reported, "New Luddites at the Gates." The *South China Morning Post* asserted, "Ugly from Start to Finish." Malaysia's *New Straits Times* said, "Violent Protesters Disrupt WTO Meeting." The Melbourne *Age* remarked, "Seattle Feels World's Anger."

The WTO had convened before, but never in such a hostile atmosphere. Some of the ruckus seemed a throwback to the days when Seattle had been a hotbed of labor radicalism. A general strike in 1919 closed the city for a week and helped trigger the "red scare" of the post–World War I era. Although Seattle had evolved considerably since then, becoming more a haven for hippies and tree huggers than a nest of anarcho-syndicalists, the anti-WTO protesters of 1999 hoped to rekindle the old radical spirit and shut the city down again, or at least alert the country and the world to the dangers of globalization.

The revolt against globalization was paradoxical on its face. As the 1990s drew to a close it was apparent that the decade had been the most prosperous for Americans in the aggregate since the 1920s. Nearly all measures of economic well-being were up: employment, gross domestic product, home ownership, personal wealth. The stock market was surging, fattening the retirement accounts of the Baby Boomers. Alan Greenspan and the Federal Reserve were keeping inflation under control. Clinton and Congress, for all their reciprocal finger-pointing, had struck a bargain that, in combination with the booming economy, did not simply balance the federal budget but in 1998 delivered a surplus (for the first time in thirty years). The 1998 surplus of $69 billion nearly doubled to $125 billion in 1999 and would nearly double again to $236 billion in 2000. Three decades of dismal expectations about an ever-increasing national debt were reversed; for the first time in living memory, it became unlaughable to talk about paying off the debt. Given that the Baby Boomers would begin retiring in another decade and would make unprecedented demands on Social Security and Medicare, this was welcome news indeed.

But the general prosperity of the 1990s masked underlying concerns. Americans have never worried about inequalities of wealth as much as people in many other countries have; the American dream always allowed that some people might get richer than others. But the dream also insisted that the most talented and energetic of the less-rich be able to join the more-rich in time. During the 1990s this second aspect of the dream came under serious question. The distribution of wealth and income grew ever more skewed. The income of the households in the bottom two-fifths of the income scale rose very slightly (in real, inflation-adjusted terms) between 1990 and 2000, while the income of households in the top tenth rose substantially, and that of the top twentieth rose even more. In other words, most of the prosperity of the decade was accruing to the economic upper half of American society, while the lower half was just holding its own.

Many individuals and families within the lower half weren't even holding their own. The American economy had continued to evolve since the 1950s. The manufacturing jobs that had constituted the core of America's industrial economy at mid-century increasingly gave way to service jobs. Some of this transformation was natural, inevitable, and cause for congratulation. When countries modernize they tend to focus on physical fundamentals first—on those material objects necessary to everyday life and livelihoods. America built highways, bridges, office buildings, houses, apartments, automobiles, appliances, and myriad other goods. As the material needs of Americans were fulfilled, they increasingly turned to services—nonessentials, in many cases, but attractive nonetheless. Americans ate more often in restaurants. They had pizza delivered. They hired people to cut their lawns, paint their houses, and wash their cars. They traveled more frequently. Typically the people employed as waiters, pizza deliverers, gardeners, house painters, car washers, and hotel custodians received lower wages than industrial workers. At the same time, other service workers were highly paid: doctors, lawyers, business executives, scientists, movie actors, television producers. The result was a bifurcation of income, with people clustered at the top and bottom and fewer in the middle.

The erosion of the middle class reflected something else: the integration of the world economy. America's official embrace of free trade meant that American workers competed with workers from other countries for world markets. In 1945 American workers and American industry were more efficient than most of their counterparts elsewhere, and Americans tended to win the competition. But as Europe and Japan recovered from the war, and as previously nonindustrial countries began to modernize, the terms of the competition changed. The modernizing countries in particular benefited from low wage rates that allowed manufacturers based there to undercut American producers. And with little to impede the flow of goods across borders—transportation costs were falling, along with the tariffs and quotas—the foreign goods increasingly displaced American products.

Industry after industry felt the pressure. Textile manufacturers had been priced out of New England, the birthplace of the American textile industry, decades earlier, as employers moved their factories to the low-wage South. But even the South proved too expensive after free trade opened American markets to fabric and clothing produced in Mexico, China, and Southeast Asia. The mill towns of the Carolinas joined the mill towns of Massachusetts as outdoor museums.

The steel industry experienced similar strains. Born around Pittsburgh in the mid-nineteenth century, American steel had subsequently opened a Southern front near Birmingham, Alabama, where wages were lower. But during the 1970s the American steel industry found itself under attack from even-lower-wage Brazil and Korea. Pennsylvanians and Alabamians breathed cleaner air than before, but they paid for the improvement with fewer jobs.

American auto manufacturers had laughed at the German Volkswagens and Japanese Datsuns and Toyotas that tested the American market during the 1950s and 1960s. But Detroit's Big Three weren't laughing after General Motors, Ford, and Chrysler found the foreigners claiming an ever larger share of the American market.

The effects of de-industrialization, as the loss of manufacturing and the shift to services was called, transcended the loss of jobs. Organized labor was grievously weakened. The unions had emerged under one set of conditions, in which America led the world in manufacturing and blue-collar jobs lasted a lifetime. As those conditions changed, the unions suffered. They defended their members against pay cuts and workforce reductions where they could, but they couldn't defend entire industries against international competition. In some cases they made the competition worse, when their refusal to accept pay cuts accelerated the flight of jobs to foreign countries. Labor recouped some of its losses by organizing the service sector, but the low wages of service workers and their comparative interchangeability diminished the financial resources available to the unions and reduced the unions' leverage with employers. Unfriendly state legislation, including the right-to-work laws, didn't help matters; the unfriendliness of the legislation simply confirmed the declining influence of the unions.

By the 1990s the fashionable term for the integration of world markets was "globalization." Economists lauded the concept and its effects. They pointed to companies like Wal-Mart, which scoured the earth for the most efficient producers and passed the savings along to customers. They noted that globalization allowed coffee drinkers to choose from a whole range of flavors and aromas, where their parents had made do with a few. Globalization brought apples to American tables from New Zealand and grapes from Chile, not to mention lettuce and strawberries from Mexico, and in the bargain stretched the season for fresh produce to a full year. Globalization reduced the price of computers and televisions, allowing consumers to purchase for a pittance what a king's ransom couldn't command a generation earlier.

Many politicians praised globalization. Every president from Truman to Clinton strove to extend the principle to new products and areas. Clinton ensured that Congress approved the NAFTA treaty negotiated by Bush, and he embraced the global economy with conviction. He was tactful enough to acknowledge that nothing came without cost, but he consistently favored moving forward toward more globalization rather than pulling back. "The challenge before us is to adapt our international institutions, to deepen the cooperation between nations so that we can confront a new generation of problems that know no national borders," he told the World Economic Forum in January 1995. "Indeed, the job of constructing a new international economic architecture through our trade agreements and the revitalization of our institutions is, for our generation, as pressing and important as building the postwar system was to the generation of the Marshall plan and Bretton Woods."

Clinton continued to defend globalization in November 1999, as the WTO gathered in Seattle. "We live in a global economy that on balance has been quite good for the United States, but also good for developing countries," he told a reporter as he flew to Seattle. To the delegates themselves he declared, "No one in this room can seriously argue that the world would have been a better place today if our forebears over the last fifty years had not done their work to bring us closer together. . . . Whatever the legitimacy of any of the criticism against us, this is a stronger, more prosperous world because we have worked to expand the frontiers of cooperation and reduce the barriers to trade among people."

The Seattle protesters disagreed. Labor advocates blamed globalization for driving American jobs overseas while forcing foreign workers to slave at low wages and in dangerous and unhealthy conditions. Environmental activists condemned globalization for allowing multinational corporations to ravage region after region while leaving the local populations to suffer the ecological consequences of their rapacity. Proponents of localism held globalization responsible for the extinction of difference—for compelling the peoples of the world to eat Big Macs and drink Coca-Cola whether they liked it or not.

A rapt world watched as the Seattle protests erupted into violence. Looting and vandalism caused the police to employ tear gas and rubber bullets to disperse the crowds. Most of the protesters and the authorities concurred that the violence was the work of a small fraction of the antiglobalization contingent; some singled out international anarchists whose logistical coordination was made possible by the very phenomena they decried. Seattle mayor Paul Schell professed shock at what he had been compelled to do. "This administration has people who marched in the 1960s," he said. "The last thing I wanted was to be mayor of a city that called in the national guard." Many Seattle residents shared his astonishment. "I mean, here we are in what is supposed to be the happiest, mellowest city on the planet, and look what's happening," remarked one man who came downtown to watch the protests but got caught in the blast of rubber bullets. "I'm a lifelong native of this city, and I simply can't believe what I'm seeing."

The protesters didn't prevent the trade talks from proceeding. The WTO delegates met behind barricades and police cordons. But the demonstrations did reveal the dissatisfaction many people felt at a process that often seemed beyond the ability of individuals or even countries to control. And they raised the potential cost to American leaders of a continued embrace of a philosophy that had guided American economic diplomacy since 1945.

## 6. NOT QUITE WAR, NOT QUITE PEACE

The Dayton accords of 1995 didn't end the Balkan wars, although they and the peacekeepers who entered Bosnia in their wake did stem the bloodletting in that country, pending a hoped-for resolution of the ethnic and political conflicts there. Bosnia's success in breaking free of Serbia inspired imitators, including the ethnic Albanians of Kosovo, one of the Yugoslav provinces that remained attached to Serbia. Under Tito the Kosovars, as they were called, had enjoyed substantial autonomy, which the post-Tito government rescinded. The Kosovars agitated, some peacefully and some violently, for a restoration of autonomy, which Belgrade interpreted as a precursor to secession. Serbian forces entered Kosovo to suppress the insurgency, and did so with the brutality that characterized their leader, Slobodan Milosevic.

In the spring of 1998 the United Nations embargoed weapons to Serbia in an effort to restrain Milosevic. The United States and NATO complemented the arms ban with economic sanctions and warnings of military strikes against Serbian targets. Clinton's negotiator, Richard Holbrooke, traveled to the region to try to broker a deal. The talking lasted till early 1999, culminating in a conference at Rambouillet, France. The conference produced a plan for Kosovo to regain its autonomy within what was left of Yugoslavia, and for NATO to guarantee that autonomy. Milosevic and Serbia rejected the plan and received support for the rejection from the government of Russia, which had long considered itself the sponsor of the Serbs, ethnic cousins to the Russians.

NATO thereupon repeated its warnings of military action against Serbia, and despite some eleventh-hour wriggling by Milosevic, the alliance commenced a bombing campaign in late March 1999. "We act to protect thousands of innocent people in Kosovo from a mounting military offensive," Clinton explained in a televised address. "We act to prevent a wider war, to defuse a powder keg at the heart of Europe that has exploded twice before in this century with catastrophic results." Clinton cast the Kosovo campaign in the tradition of American concern for Europe, the focus of American foreign policy since 1945. "If we've learned anything from the century drawing to a close, it is that if America is going to be prosperous and secure, we need a Europe that is prosperous, secure, undivided, and free. We need a Europe that is coming together, not falling apart."

The NATO bombing lasted eleven weeks. American planes flew from NATO bases in Italy, from American aircraft carriers in the Adriatic, and, in a display of technological prowess, from U.S. mainland air force bases, which sent B-2 stealth bombers on nonstop, undetectable flights to Serbia and back.

The bombardment confirmed the belief of Milosevic and the Serbs that America and Western Europe hated and despised them; it also persuaded Milosevic and the Serbs to accept the American and NATO terms for ending the fighting in Kosovo. A tense moment occurred when NATO peacekeepers encountered Serb-friendly Russian troops at the airport at Pristina, the Kosovo capital, but the moment passed without violence.

Clinton accounted the campaign a victory. "I felt an enormous sense of relief and satisfaction," he recalled. "Slobodan Milosevic's bloody ten-year campaign to exploit ethnic and religious differences to impose his will on the former Yugoslavia was on its last legs. The burning of villages and killing of innocents was history." And so it was, for the most part, although working out the consequences of that history would take time and considerable effort.

Clinton had less cause for satisfaction at the outcome of another international initiative. For a decade after the evacuation of American forces from Lebanon following the 1983 Beirut airport bombing, the United States had kept its distance from the Arab-Israeli conflict. Clinton and especially his first secretary of state, Warren Christopher, helped nudge negotiators from Israel and the Palestine Liberation Organization toward agreement in secret talks at Oslo in 1993, and after the Oslo meeting produced a pact in which the PLO for the first time conceded Israel's right to exist, in exchange for Israeli agreement to grant Palestinians a measure of self-rule in the West Bank and Gaza Strip, Clinton hosted a signing ceremony at the White House. It was a memorable occasion but personally awkward. Israeli prime minister Yitzhak Rabin didn't want to shake hands with PLO chief Yasser Arafat, whom he considered a terrorist. Clinton argued that Rabin must. "The whole world will be watching, and the handshake is what they will be looking for," he told the Israeli leader.

Rabin grudgingly agreed. "I suppose one does not make peace with one's friends," he said.

"Then you'll do it?" Clinton asked.

"All right. All right. But no kissing." Rabin knew the Arabs, and he knew a kiss on the cheek was part of a heartfelt greeting. He drew the line short of a kiss.

Clinton realized this might be a problem. Arafat might well try to plant a kiss on Rabin's cheek, and if Rabin backed away the whole effect of the ceremony would be spoiled. National security adviser Tony Lake devised a plan. "He described the procedure and we practiced it," Clinton recalled. "I played Arafat and he played me, showing me what to do. When I shook his hand and moved in for the kiss, he put his left hand on my right arm where it was bent at the elbow, and squeezed it; it stopped me cold. We practiced it a couple of more times until I felt sure Rabin's cheek would remain untouched. We all laughed about it, but I knew avoiding the kiss was deadly serious for Rabin."

Rabin dodged the kiss, and the White House ceremony went well. But even Arafat's handshake proved deadly. Radicals in Israel who wanted no peace with the Palestinians excoriated the prime minister, and in 1995 one of them assassinated Rabin in Tel Aviv.

The murder dismayed advocates of peace and retarded additional steps in that direction, but in July 2000 Clinton brought Arafat and Ehud Barak, the new Israeli prime minister, to Camp David in a last-ditch—for Clinton, at any rate—effort to resolve the long-standing dispute. The central issues were control of the West Bank and Gaza, the fate of Palestinian refugees, and the future of Jerusalem. Many Israelis had grown to believe that the occupation of the Palestinian territories was an insupportable burden; reflecting this belief, Barak was willing to transfer control of the largest portion of the territories to Arafat and the Palestinian Authority, the shadow government of the proto-Palestine. Jewish settlements established in the territories since 1967 complicated a handover; some of these would be retained by Israel, others would be dismantled. How many would fall into each category was a principal point of dispute. On the question of the Palestinian refugees, the controversy hinged on whether the Palestinians displaced by the creation of Israel would be allowed to return to their homes. The refugees and their descendants insisted that the answer be yes; the Israelis that it be no. As to the future of Jerusalem, this was the hardest problem of all. The Temple Mount was sacred to both Jews and Muslims, not to mention Christians; deciding who would govern and safeguard the holy ground would test the wisdom and patience of even the best-intentioned peacemakers.

Clinton held Arafat and Barak at Camp David for two weeks. He jawboned hard with the two leaders and shuttled back and forth between their cabins at the presidential retreat when they refused to speak directly. He came close to a deal. Barak consented to hand over more than nine-tenths of the territories. Arafat might have accepted this, and he and Barak might have finessed the Palestinian right of return by retaining it in principle while hedging it in practice. But on Jerusalem the two men couldn't agree, and on that rock the summit broke down.

Clinton blamed Arafat. He recalled former Israeli foreign minister Abba Eban's remark that the Palestinians never missed an opportunity to miss an opportunity, and he characterized Arafat's refusal to accept Israel's offer as a "colossal mistake." Just before leaving office, Clinton spoke to Arafat again. The Palestinian leader thanked the president for his efforts and told him he was a great man. "Mr. Chairman," Clinton answered, "I am not a great man. I am a failure. And you have made me one."

# 14 | Blowback

## 2000–2004

### 1. BUSH 5, GORE 4

Al Gore would have waltzed into the White House, if not for the albatross around his neck. Few vice presidents ever received the presidential nomination of their parties under more favorable economic circumstances. The expansion of the 1990s continued, making it America's longest stretch of unbroken growth since the nineteenth century. To be sure, the bursting of the dot-com bubble during the spring of 2000 suggested that future growth wouldn't be as headlong as in the most recent past, but the NASDAQ's slide hadn't much affected the broader economy. And an argument could be made that the pricking of the bubble would actually strengthen the economy by restoring balance between the tech and other sectors. If the first rule of American politics is that voters reward incumbents for prosperity (and it is), then Al Gore could anticipate collecting his reward—the presidency—in the 2000 election.

But there was that albatross: the Clinton scandals. Clinton had survived the impeachment trial, and he proclaimed his survival a victory over his persecutors. But the triumphant mood didn't last. Many Americans were glad he hadn't been convicted, if only because the Republicans had made themselves even more unlikable than Clinton, but no one defended his conduct, and few found much in him to admire.

Gore had to decide whether to embrace Clinton in the 2000 campaign or avoid him. The argument for embracing Clinton was the peace and prosperity of the Clinton years, with which Gore naturally wanted to be associated. Gore in addition desired to assert that his eight years as vice president had seasoned him for the top job; to do so he had to point out that he and Clinton had been close, at least professionally. The argument for avoiding Clinton was the moral taint of illicit affairs conducted in the Oval Office and elsewhere and dissected, condemned, and lampooned in the press, on talk shows, and by the late-night comics, and of the lying that followed the affairs and likewise became the stuff of disapproval and derision. Every vice president running for president has tried to show he was his own man; in Gore's case, he had to show he was a different kind of man.

Gore's Republican opponent had issues of his own. George W. Bush was the governor of Texas and the son of Clinton's predecessor. Only once before had a son followed in his father's presidential footsteps, but in that case twenty-four years had separated the service of the son, John Quincy Adams, from the tenure of the father, John Adams. (The only other direct-descent presidency was Benjamin Harrison's, which began in 1889, forty-eight years after the death in office of his grandfather, William Henry Harrison.) For a son to try to follow the father after a mere eight years seemed rather pushy.

In the case of George W. Bush, it had also seemed quite unlikely for most of the younger Bush's life. Bush had a brother, Jeb, who appeared to have inherited the political genes in the family; George worked in the family oil business and directed the operations of the Texas Rangers baseball team.

But as the state of Texas began tipping decisively to the Republican party, George W. Bush detected the merit in politics, and he ran for governor in 1994. He won and was reelected in 1998, by which time he had his eye on the White House, and he surprised no one when he mounted an early campaign for the Republican nomination. The Republicans were desperate for a winner, anyone who could rescue the country from Clintonism. Bush had name recognition, access to his father's friends and their checkbooks, and credibility with the Christian right. This last advantage was crucial in the primary campaign, in which party activists played their typically decisive role. Bush was "born again" and could speak to the religious conservatives in their own language. That he was a Southerner, at a time when the South had become the geographic core of the Republican party, certainly helped.

Bush dispatched his Republican rivals with ease and captured the nomination. He thereupon appointed former defense secretary Dick Cheney to head a committee to consider running mates; Cheney's committee concluded that none of those suggested supplied what the ticket needed, prompting Bush to choose Cheney himself.

Bush presented himself to the nation as the candidate of "compassionate conservatism." Newt Gingrich and the House Republican class of 1994 had hardened and sharpened American conservatism; Bush proposed to soften and humanize it. "We will give low-income Americans tax credits to buy the private health insurance they need and deserve," he told the Republican convention. "We will transform today's housing rental program to help hundreds of thousands of low-income families find stability and dignity in a home of their own. And, in the next bold step of welfare reform, we will support the heroic work of homeless shelters and hospices, food pantries and crisis pregnancy centers. . . . Government cannot do this work. It can feed the body, but it cannot reach the soul. Yet government can take the side of these groups, helping the helper, encouraging the inspired."

Americans liked what they heard. They also liked what Clinton and the Democrats had done. The result was a dead heat in the November election. Gore won the popular vote by five hundred thousand, but the electoral tally was too close to call. National attention focused on Florida, where Bush led the preliminary popular count by less than a thousand votes, a margin that triggered a recount—and prompted the Bush and Gore camps to send teams of lawyers to Florida to supervise, and if possible influence, the recount. Americans were treated to abstruse discussions of the "butterfly ballot," an allegedly confusing arrangement of the candidates' names on the pages presented to voters in the voting booths, and "hanging chads," tiny bits of paper imperfectly punched out of contested ballots. Competing lawsuits compelled the Florida supreme court to consider whether to prohibit, allow, or order the recount to proceed in some or all of the state's counties. The issue was finally decided, more than a month after the election, when the federal Supreme Court stepped in and by a five-to-four vote halted the recounting and thereby awarded Florida's electors to Bush. The one-vote margin in the Supreme Court translated into a five-vote margin for Bush in the electoral college. Al Gore conceded gracefully, but many Democrats deemed the election stolen, citing the Republican antecedents of the five majority justices (and subsequently dismissing evidence that a full recount would have awarded Florida's electors to Bush anyway).

## 2. THAT OLD-TIME RELIGION

Bush's victory wasn't much of a mandate, but he made the most of it. In the first inaugural address by a president in the twenty-first century, he reiterated the central theme of his campaign. "Today we affirm a new commitment to live out our nation's promise through civility, courage, compassion and character," he said. "America, at its best, is compassionate. In the quiet of American conscience, we know that deep, persistent poverty is unworthy of our nation's promise. . . . Where there is suffering, there is duty. Americans in need are not strangers, they are citizens, not problems, but priorities. And all of us are diminished when any are hopeless." Yet compassion was not the responsibility of government alone. "Compassion is the work of a nation. . . . Some needs and hurts are so deep they will only respond to a mentor's touch or a pastor's prayer. Church and charity, synagogue and mosque lend our communities their humanity, and they will have an honored place in our plans and in our laws." But whoever did the work, it had to be done. And it would be done. "I can pledge our nation to a goal: When we see that wounded traveler on the road to Jericho, we will not pass to the other side."

Bush may or may not have been thinking about that wounded traveler when he launched his first initiative in Congress: tax cuts. In the Reagan years, tax cuts had been Republican gospel, and they remained gospel with party conservatives. But the tax increases approved by the first President Bush had helped bring down the federal deficit and make possible the surpluses the nation enjoyed under Clinton. The rosy projections of debt reduction—and even elimination—from Clinton's second term had dimmed a bit with the slide in the stock market and the less exuberant economic growth that followed, but many Democrats and some Republicans still hoped that the surplus could be used to continue to pay down the debt and perhaps shore up Social Security in time for the Baby Boomers' retirement.

For Republican conservatives and for Bush, however, the surplus wasn't part of the solution to America's problems; it was part of the problem. Taxes were bad, and the surplus was evidence that they were worse than they needed to be. Besides, the surplus tempted the profligates in Congress to find new programs to spend the money on. Without the surplus they wouldn't be tempted. Moreover, despite the evidence from the Reagan years, some Republicans still subscribed to supply-side economics: the belief that reducing tax rates could actually increase tax revenues, by stimulating productive activity. There was something of a contradiction in this reasoning, for if taxes were bad, why should Republicans endorse action that would *increase* tax revenues? Those Republicans who noticed this contradiction sometimes answered that they would simply reduce rates further when the time came.

Economic reasoning aside, Bush recognized that when a president pushes tax cuts, Congress has great difficulty pushing back. Tax cuts may have negative consequences in the long term, but they almost always feel good in the short term. Taxpayers—that is, voters—have more money in their pockets, which makes them happy. They spend some or all of that money, making merchants and producers happy. The merchants and producers hire workers, making the workers happy.

The Bush tax bill encountered little meaningful resistance in Congress and soon became law. The measure projected tax cuts of $1.35 trillion over the next decade, and would have projected more but for a quirk in the law that mandated repeal of the cuts on December 31, 2010, to accommodate congressional constraints on forecasting too far into the future. The immediate impact of the new law was a rebate of $300 to most taxpayers, paid in the form of checks sent out by the Treasury. More important for the long term were the reduction of the tax rates on personal income, from 15 percent to 10 percent in the lowest bracket and 39.6 percent to 35 percent in the highest, and the gradual elimination of the estate tax (the tax on inheritances, insistently called the "death tax" by Republicans).

"Across the board tax relief does not happen often in Washington, D.C.," Bush observed upon signing the law. "In fact, since World War II it has happened only twice: President Kennedy's tax cut in the 1960s and President Reagan's tax cuts in the 1980s. And now it's happening for the third time, and it's about time." Tax cuts were about more than money, Bush said. "Tax relief expands individual freedom. The money we return, or don't take in the first place, can be saved for a child's education, spent on family needs, invested in a home or in a business or a mutual fund or used to reduce personal debt." Bush didn't deny that the tax cuts would reduce the federal surplus; that, he said, was the point. "The surplus is not the government's money. The surplus is the people's money."

## 3. SEPTEMBER 11

At six o'clock on the morning of September 11, 2001, Mohamed Atta and Abdul Aziz al Omari boarded a plane in Portland, Maine, for the short flight to Boston. They arrived at Boston's Logan Airport at quarter to seven. They rendezvoused with three other men, also of Arab descent, at Logan, and all five passed through a security checkpoint, where their carry-on bags were X-rayed and they themselves were screened for metal objects. Nothing unusual was detected. The five boarded American Airlines flight 11, scheduled to depart at quarter to eight for Los Angeles.

Meanwhile five other men, also Arabs, gathered in a separate terminal at Logan before boarding United Airlines 175, likewise bound for Los Angeles, scheduled for an eight o'clock departure. At about the same time, at Dulles Airport outside Washington, another quintet boarded American 77, bound for Los Angeles. The American Airlines counter agent at Dulles thought two of the men appeared suspicious; the agent, instructed to look out for potential bombers who might check luggage onto a flight but then not board the flight themselves, ordered that their checked bags be held until the gate agent confirmed that the two had boarded the plane. They did board, and the bags were loaded. Two others of the five at Dulles tripped the metal detector at the security checkpoint. One was directed through a second metal detector, which indicated nothing amiss. The other was inspected by a security agent with a metal-sensing wand that similarly found nothing. Finally, at Newark Airport, across the Hudson River from New York's Manhattan Island, four men boarded United Airlines flight 93, bound for San Francisco.

Had anyone realized that these nineteen Arab men were traveling to California on the same morning at the same time, such a person might have concluded that something was happening on the West Coast of particular interest to young Arab men. That person would have been mistaken. The reason the nineteen had chosen planes scheduled to fly to California was that these four planes would be taking off with full tanks of fuel.

American Airlines flight 11 from Boston departed a little behind schedule, at 7:59. The Boeing 767 climbed toward its initial cruising altitude of 29,000 feet as it headed west. At 8:14 the pilots acknowledged a message from the

Boston air traffic control center, and several seconds later the control center instructed the plane to climb to 35,000 feet.

This message was not acknowledged, apparently because Mohamed Atta and his companions had stabbed two of the flight attendants with weapons they had managed to conceal from the security scanners, and had forced open the cockpit door and seized control of the plane. Hijackings weren't unheard of in American aviation history; past hijackings had prompted the security precautions in effect that morning. Some hijackings had ended violently but most had not, and when Atta and the others announced that they had a bomb and were hijacking the plane, the passengers and surviving crew had little reason to think the plane wouldn't eventually land in one piece. Atta had taken flying lessons and learned to fly an airliner; he settled into the pilot's seat and put his training to work.

About ten minutes after the seizure, the plane turned south, according to one of the flight attendants, Betty Ong, who used a phone on the plane to communicate with an American Airlines office in North Carolina. Air traffic radar observed the plane descending in the direction of New York City. Air controllers thought the hijackers were taking the plane to Kennedy Airport and cleared other planes out of the way. Betty Ong's call lost contact with the ground, but another attendant, Amy Sweeney, got through. "We are flying low," she said. "We are flying very, very low. We are flying way too low. . . . Oh my God, we are way too low."

The phone call ended as American Airlines 11 slammed into the North Tower of the World Trade Center in lower Manhattan at 490 miles per hour. The time was 8:46. The New York financial district, where the trade center was located, was just beginning its business day.

At almost the same moment, the hijacking of United 175, the other plane from Boston, commenced. The modus operandi was similar to that aboard American 11; in this case the pilot and copilot were murdered in the assault on the cockpit. The hijacker who began flying the plane initially did a poor job of it; the plane pitched, swerved, and rose and fell rapidly. One of the passengers, Peter Hanson, called his father in Connecticut:

> It's getting bad, Dad. A stewardess was stabbed. They seem to have knives and Mace. They said they have a bomb. It's getting very bad on

> the plane. Passengers are throwing up and getting sick. The plane is making jerky movements. I don't think the pilot is flying the plane. I think we are going down. I think they intend to go to Chicago or someplace and fly into a building. Don't worry, Dad. If it happens, it'll be very fast. My God, my God.

Lee Hanson, Peter's father, had turned on his television after the first plane hit the North Tower of the World Trade Center. Lee lost the connection with Peter as Peter's plane crashed into the South Tower of the trade center at 545 miles per hour, with Lee watching on television. The time was 9:03.

By then the hijacking of American 77, the flight from Dulles, had been under way for ten minutes. One of the passengers was Barbara Olson, the wife of Ted Olson, the solicitor general of the United States. Barbara Olson called her husband and said that the hijackers had knives and box cutters. The call failed after about a minute, and Ted Olson attempted to contact the Justice Department. He couldn't get through, but then his wife called again. He asked her where the plane was. She said they were flying over houses, but otherwise she couldn't discern the location. The connection was cut off again. A few minutes later the control tower at Reagan National Airport in Washington notified the Secret Service of an unidentified plane flying in the direction of the White House. The plane then made a sharp turn as the hijacker pilot advanced the throttle to full power. The plane descended rapidly and hit the Pentagon at a speed of 530 miles per hour. The time was 9:37.

The fourth plane, United 93, left Newark half an hour behind schedule, and just minutes before the first plane hit the World Trade Center. The Boeing 757 flew west over New Jersey and Pennsylvania for forty-five minutes. Just before 9:30 the hijackers stormed the cockpit. The plane dove abruptly, losing a thousand feet of altitude in mere seconds. But then the pilot among the hijackers gained control and the plane leveled off. Passengers began making phone calls; some learned of the other hijackings and the fact that these had ended with the planes being used as guided missiles against targets on the ground. The passengers pooled their information and determined to retake the plane from the hijackers. As they prepared to do so, one of the passengers signed off her telephone call: "Everyone's running up to first class. I've got to go. Bye." The passenger attack prompted the hijacker pilot to cause the plane to lurch violently left and right, in an effort to throw the passengers off balance. He pitched the nose up and down. The hijackers held off the passengers for a few minutes, until the pilot shouted, *"Allahu Akbar! Allahu Akbar!"* (God is the greatest). The cockpit recorder captured this statement and the pilot's question that followed: "Shall we put it down?" One of the conspirators answered, "Yes, put it in it, and pull it down." The plane nosed forward, then rolled to its right and onto its back. "Allah is the greatest! Allah is the greatest!" another hijacker shouted. Seconds later United 93 slammed into the ground near Shanksville, Pennsylvania, at 580 miles per hour. The time was 10:03.

From the perspective of the hijackers, the mission that ended in Pennsylvania failed, for it killed only the hijackers and the 44 passengers and crew. The other missions succeeded. The plane that hit the Pentagon literally rocked the symbol of American military power, blasting a huge hole in the side of the building and killing some 125 military personnel and civilians, in addition to the 64 persons on board the plane. The final descent and deliberate crash were witnessed by thousands of people in and around the nation's capital, and the smoke from the fires the plane and its fuel ignited was clearly visible from the White House and the Capitol.

The suicide missions that ended at the Twin Towers of the World Trade Center in New York succeeded beyond the terrorists' wildest dreams. The first plane hit the North Tower between the 94th and 98th floors. The momentum of the aircraft drove it through the comparatively flimsy walls of the building into the building's structural core, which supported the weight of the 110 stories. The impact spewed fuel from the plane's nearly full tanks throughout the building; this immediately caught fire and ignited flammable material in the building. Within a short while the top tenth of the building was an inferno.

By now the cameras of CNN and other networks were capturing pictures of the developing disaster and broadcasting them around the world. Viewers watched the fire spread; they could imagine with horror the feelings of those trapped amid the flames. They supposed that persons on the floors below the burning portion would evacuate the building, terrified no doubt but physically unharmed. At this point, none of the news organizations could say whether the crash was accidental or deliberate.

Evidence for the latter—a deliberate attack—mounted exponentially just minutes later when viewers saw the most appalling footage any but a few had ever observed. On live television the second Boston plane slammed into the South Tower of the trade center. This plane struck its target lower, at about the 80th floor. The 65 persons aboard, including the five hijackers, were killed instantly; hundreds in the building were killed by the impact. The unknown number of persons on the floors above the impact zone were trapped as the plane's ten thousand gallons of fuel touched off another inferno.

The horror mounted as the fires grew larger and more intense. Some of those trapped in the buildings escaped slow death by fire only by leaping to instant death from the shattered windows. New York City firefighters and other emergency personnel rushed to the scene and into the buildings. As terrible as the situation was, it still appeared that the danger to life was concentrated in the upper portions of the two towers. An orderly evacuation would save those below.

Then, at 9:59, not quite an hour after United 175 slammed into the South Tower, the upper part of that building collapsed upon the lower part with a force that smashed the entire structure to the ground below. The implosion took eleven seconds, and it killed nearly everyone still alive in the building. The tens of millions of viewers who watched the disaster on television were rendered speechless.

They had hardly regained their voices when the North Tower collapsed twenty-nine minutes later. The billowing plumes of smoke from the fires were subsumed in monstrous clouds of dust and debris that rolled across lower Manhattan, choking Wall Street and bringing the epicenter of American capitalism to a dazed standstill.

## 4. A NEW KIND OF WAR

The shock of "9/11"—the shorthand soon applied to the events of September 11, 2001—was unlike anything in American history. The successful attacks on the World Trade Center and the Pentagon, and the foiled attack—on what? The White House? The Capitol?—that ended in Pennsylvania, were compared by some to Pearl Harbor. But months of tension, and years of war in Asia and Europe, had preceded the Japanese attack on Hawaii, giving Americans a frame of reference for interpreting the 1941 attack. More to the point, no one outside Hawaii saw the attack occur; Americans read about it after it was over. The utterly unexpected events of 9/11 unfolded in real time on television in the homes and offices of the entire country.

The shock of the day evolved into mourning for the thousands killed in the attacks. For weeks no one could say how many had died; estimates of ten thousand were reduced to six thousand and then four thousand. The statistical uncertainty as to the overall number reflected the individual uncertainty among families and friends of the missing. Popular media gravitate to emotional stories; in the months that followed 9/11, newspapers and television shows were filled with heart-wrenching tales of loss, of last moments shared via cell phone, of persons whom happenstance took to the World Trade Center that morning and doomed—or took somewhere else and delivered.

For weeks Americans couldn't laugh. At first nothing seemed funny; the pain was too great. Then, as the pain diminished, laughter still often seemed inappropriate. *The Onion*, a satirical newspaper that almost never pulled its punches, wrestled with how to handle 9/11. "When you make a joke about a huge tragedy, you don't make a joke about the tragedy itself," John Krewson, a writer for the paper, explained. "You make a joke about all the confusion and terrible stuff surrounding it. Your laughter is coming from 'Oh yeah, this is hell.'" *The Onion*'s early efforts were more angry than humorous. "U.S. Vows to Defeat Whoever It Is We're at War With," one headline asserted. "American Life Turns into Bad Jerry Bruckheimer Movie"; "God Angrily Clarifies 'Don't Kill' Rule."

In their pain and disorientation, Americans rallied around their elected officials. New York mayor Rudy Giuliani became an overnight hero for the calm reassurance he projected amid the chaos. Many Americans had long distrusted New York City as a place whose residents looked down on them; the perception was often warranted. But the distrust disappeared in the sense of solidarity Americans felt for one another after the attack, and Giuliani, whose popularity even in his own city had been declining for years, suddenly became "America's mayor." Americans all over the country silently—or loudly—agreed as Giuliani promised: "We're going to rebuild. We're going to come out of this stronger than we were before: emotionally stronger, politically stronger, economically stronger."

The terrorist attacks transformed the presidency of George W. Bush. Unlike Giuliani, who made his presence felt from the moment of first impact, Bush spent the hours after the attacks largely incommunicado. He was in

Florida that morning; he got the news of the crash into the North Tower while visiting an elementary school in Sarasota. Bush had planned to return to Washington directly after the visit, but at the urging of Vice President Cheney and the Secret Service, who feared that the Pentagon attack foretold further assaults on the capital, Air Force One was routed to Barksdale Air Force Base in Louisiana. The president taped a statement for later broadcast, rather than airing it live, lest would-be assassins learn his location. He re-boarded his plane and flew to Offutt Air Force Base in Nebraska, where he consulted remotely with his national security team in Washington. Not till late that afternoon did he return to Washington.

At 8:30 p.m. he spoke to the American people. "Today our fellow citizens, our way of life, our very freedom came under attack in a series of deliberate and deadly terrorist acts," the president declared. "The victims were in airplanes or in their offices: secretaries, business men and women, military and federal workers, moms and dads, friends and neighbors. Thousands of lives were suddenly ended by evil, despicable acts of terror." The terrorists had intended to intimidate America and its people. But they had failed, Bush said. "Our country is strong."

Three days later—a long three days, Bush's critics asserted; a respectful three days, his supporters rejoined—the president visited the pile of rubble that had been the Twin Towers. His appearance prompted the firefighters, the police, and the rescue workers to applaud and chant spontaneously: "U.S.A.! U.S.A.! U.S.A.!" Bush replied through a bullhorn: "I can hear you. I can hear you. The rest of the world hears you. And the people who knocked these buildings down will hear all of us soon." The applause and chanting grew louder: "U.S.A.! U.S.A.! U.S.A.!"

Bush's popularity soared in the wake of 9/11, to the highest level recorded for any president since polling began. More than 90 percent of Americans approved of his handling of his job. Even eight of ten Democrats endorsed his actions.

Bush understood that the effect was fleeting. "It won't last," White House spokesman Ari Fleischer predicted, citing the natural tendency of Americans to rally around their leaders in times of crisis. "The president is appreciative, but it won't last."

Yet the administration made every effort to prolong the effect. Bush proclaimed a national emergency, in light of what he described as "the continuing and immediate threat of further attacks on the United States." He went before Congress to declare a "war on terror," a construction he proceed to justify:

> On September 11th, enemies of freedom committed an act of war against our country. Americans have known wars, but for the past 136 years, they have been wars on foreign soil, except for one Sunday in 1941. Americans have known the casualties of war, but not at the center of a great city on a peaceful morning. Americans have known surprise attacks but never before on thousands of civilians. All of this was brought upon us in a single day, and night fell on a different world, a world where freedom itself is under attack.

Bush shared some of what he knew about the perpetrators of the attacks. The evidence pointed to al Qaeda and Osama bin Laden. "Al Qaeda is to terror what the Mafia is to crime," Bush said. "But its goal is not making money. Its goal is remaking the world and imposing its radical beliefs on people everywhere."

The war on terror would place demands on American resources and American resolve, Bush said.

> This war will not be like the war against Iraq a decade ago, with a decisive liberation of territory and a swift conclusion. It will not look like the air war above Kosovo two years ago, where no ground troops were used and not a single American was lost in combat. Our response involves far more than instant retaliation and isolated strikes. Americans should not expect one battle but a lengthy campaign, unlike any other we have ever seen. It may include dramatic strikes, visible on TV, and covert operations, secret even in success. We will starve terrorists of funding, turn them one against another, drive them from place to place, until there is no refuge or no rest. And we will pursue nations that provide aid or safe haven to terrorism.
>
> Every nation, in every region, now has a decision to make. Either you are with us, or you are with the terrorists. From this day forward, any nation that continues to harbor or support terrorism will be regarded by the United States as a hostile regime.

Americans would persevere, the president said. And they would prevail. "The course of this conflict is not known, yet its outcome is certain. Freedom and fear, justice and cruelty have always been at war, and we know that God is not neutral between them."

## 5. STRIKE ONE, STRIKE TWO

The war on terror commenced with a war on the Taliban, the Islamic fundamentalist regime that governed Afghanistan and harbored al Qaeda. Bush proclaimed that the Taliban had a simple choice: "They will hand over the terrorists, or they will share in their fate." When the Taliban rejected the president's ultimatum, he ordered American forces into action. On October 7, 2001, American warplanes began bombing Taliban targets and al Qaeda camps. British planes joined the attack, as did a group of anti-Taliban Afghans called the Northern Alliance. Troops of the Northern Alliance captured Kabul, the Afghan capital, in early November while the al Qaeda fighters, possibly including Osama bin Laden, and some Taliban forces retreated to the mountains of the border region between Afghanistan and Pakistan. They holed up in a warren of caves called Tora Bora, while American bombs, directed to their targets by U.S. Special Forces on the ground, exploded all around them. The caves were taken in December, and hundreds of the defenders were captured or killed. But bin Laden was not among them. Somehow he had slipped away, perhaps with the assistance of locals who admired him for taking on the Americans.

While the fighting in Afghanistan continued and the search for bin Laden resumed, the president and his associates prepared to widen the war on terror. Since the end of the Cold War a decade earlier, a new generation of neoconservatives—spiritual and in some cases actual descendants of the anti-détente activists of the 1970s—had been agitating for a more assertive role for the United States in the world. Like their forebears, the 1990s neocons contended that America served itself best when it took the offensive internationally. Many of them worried that in the wake of the Cold War, Americans would retreat to a modern isolationism, leaving the world to the thugs and miscreants with which the world has always abounded. Some spoke openly of leveraging America's military advantage as the sole remaining superpower to create a Pax Americana, a global system in which American values, undergirded by American arms, reigned supreme. Others were more modest, at least in public, calling for specific sanctions against particular villains.

Iraq's Saddam Hussein headed the list of neocon targets. In 1998 eighteen neoconservatives and allies wrote an open letter to Bill Clinton decrying the current policy toward Iraq—chiefly economic sanctions and occasional air strikes, inflicted for violation of international mandates—as "dangerously inadequate." Saddam, they said, either possessed or was attempting to acquire or develop "weapons of mass destruction," a category that included chemical, biological, and nuclear weapons. If the United States did nothing, Saddam would surely obtain such weapons and thereby threaten the Persian Gulf, the broader Middle East, and possibly the world at large. The administration must adopt a new strategy, one aiming at "the removal of Saddam Hussein's regime from power."

Clinton rejected the advice, and so did Bush before 9/11. But in the wake of the terrorist attacks, the neoconservatives escalated their political offensive against Saddam. It helped their case that some of the signers of the anti-Saddam letter had been appointed to positions within the Republican administration. Donald Rumsfeld was secretary of defense; Paul Wolfowitz was his deputy; Elliott Abrams was a special assistant to the president; Zalmay Khalilzad spearheaded Middle Eastern policy for the National Security Council. The anti-Saddam faction contended that the Iraqi strongman was more dangerous than ever and that the time was ripe for moving against him. "It may be that the Iraqi government provided assistance in some form to the recent attack on the United States," another open letter, this time to Bush, declared. "But even if evidence does not link Iraq directly to the attack, any strategy aimed at the eradication of terrorism and its sponsors must include a determined effort to remove Saddam. . . . Failure to undertake such an effort will constitute an early and perhaps decisive surrender in the war on international terrorism."

The argument against Saddam took hold in the Bush administration in the context of the evolving war on terror. In September 2002 the White House produced a document called *The National Security Strategy of the United States of America* that codified administration thinking on the importance of preventive action. "Given the goals of rogue states and terrorists, the United States can no longer solely rely on a reactive posture as we have in the past," the policy paper asserted. "The inability to deter a potential attacker, the immediacy of today's threats, and the magnitude of potential harm that could be caused by our adversaries' choice of weapons, do not permit that option. We cannot let our enemies strike first." An explicit policy of prevention was new, but it comported with historic American principles. "The United States has long maintained the option of preemptive actions to counter a sufficient threat to our national security. The greater the threat, the greater is the risk of inaction—and the more compelling the case for taking anticipatory action to defend ourselves, even if uncertainty remains as to the time and place of the enemy's attack."

The document didn't single out Saddam by name, but administration officials soon began doing so. The president and his advisers took every opportunity to alert America and the world to the growing menace of Saddam and the weapons of mass destruction he was said to possess. "He has broken every pledge he made to the United Nations and the world since his invasion of Kuwait was rolled back in 1991," Bush declared in the autumn of 2002. "Sixteen times the United Nations Security Council has passed resolutions designed to ensure that Iraq does not pose a threat to international peace and security. Saddam Hussein has violated every one of these sixteen resolutions—not once, but many times." Saddam supported terrorist groups and brutalized the Iraqi people.

> And although the regime agreed in 1991 to destroy and stop developing all weapons of mass destruction and long-range missiles, it has broken every aspect of this fundamental pledge. Today this regime likely maintains stockpiles of chemical and biological agents, and is improving and expanding facilities capable of producing chemical and biological weapons. Today Saddam Hussein has the scientists and infrastructure for a nuclear weapons program, and has illicitly sought to purchase the equipment needed to enrich uranium for a nuclear weapon. Should his regime acquire fissile material, it would be able to build a nuclear weapon within a year.

Hardly a day passed during the final months of 2002 and the first months of 2003 that the president didn't condemn Saddam and bolster the case for war. "Some ask why Iraq is different from other countries or regimes that also have terrible weapons," Bush reflected in October 2002. The answer lay in the character and performance of Saddam. "Iraq's weapons of mass destruction are controlled by a murderous tyrant who has already used chemical weapons to kill thousands of people. This same tyrant has tried to dominate the Middle East, has invaded and brutally occupied a small neighbor, has struck other nations without warning, and holds an unrelenting hostility toward the United States." Bush quoted a former UN weapons inspector: "'The fundamental problem with Iraq remains the nature of the regime itself. Saddam Hussein is a homicidal dictator who is addicted to weapons of mass destruction.'" And time was on his side. "The danger is already significant, and it only grows worse," Bush said. "If we know Saddam Hussein has dangerous weapons today—and we do—does it make any sense for the world to wait to confront him as he grows even stronger and develops even more dangerous weapons?"

Bush and his advisers took pains to link Saddam to the perpetrators of the 9/11 attacks. Most neutral observers found this argument implausible, in that Saddam was rigidly secular while Osama bin Laden and al Qaeda were fanatically religious. The evidence of a connection, moreover, was circumstantial and imperfectly corroborated. But Bush emphasized it anyway. "We know that Iraq and the al Qaeda terrorist network share a common enemy—the United States of America," he told a national television audience.

> We know that Iraq and al Qaeda have had high-level contacts that go back a decade. Some al Qaeda leaders who fled Afghanistan went to Iraq. These include one very senior al Qaeda leader who received medical treatment in Baghdad this year, and who has been associated with planning for chemical and biological attacks. We've learned that Iraq has trained al Qaeda members in bomb-making and poisons and deadly gases. And we know that after September the 11th, Saddam Hussein's regime gleefully celebrated the terrorist attacks on America.

If Iraq should develop nuclear weapons, Saddam would have no compunctions about passing them to al Qaeda. This was what made the present situation so dire.

> We've experienced the horror of September the 11th. We have seen that those who hate America are willing to crash airplanes into buildings full of innocent people. Our enemies would be no less willing—in fact, they would be eager—to use biological or chemical or a nuclear weapon.
>
> Knowing these realities, America must not ignore the threat gathering against us. Facing clear evidence of peril, we cannot wait for the final proof, the smoking gun, that could come in the form of a mushroom cloud.

The administration's arguments persuaded Congress. Some members voiced doubts about the Saddam-Osama connection and the imminence of the danger Saddam posed, but most senators and representatives chose to trust the president. In October 2002 the legislature adopted a resolution authorizing the use of force against Saddam. The votes weren't close: the Senate approved the force resolution by 77 to 23, the House by 296 to 133. Nor were the votes particularly partisan: 29 Democratic senators and 81 Democratic representatives backed the president.

Bush took his case against Saddam to the United Nations. "We have been more than patient," he asserted. "We've tried sanctions. We've tried the carrot of oil for food and the stick of coalition military strikes. But Saddam Hussein has defied all these efforts and continues to develop weapons of mass destruction. The first time we may be completely certain he has nuclear weapons is when, God forbid, he uses one. We owe it to all our citizens to do everything in our power to prevent that day from coming."

When the Security Council balked, Bush sent his secretary of state. Colin Powell displayed photographs and much other evidence that conclusively demonstrated, he said, Iraq's relentless quest for weapons of mass destruction. "There can be no doubt that Saddam Hussein has biological weapons and the capability to rapidly produce more, many more," Powell declared. "He has the ability to dispense these lethal poisons and diseases in ways that can cause massive death and destruction." The intelligence on chemical weapons was equally alarming. "Our conservative estimate is that Iraq today has a stockpile of between 100 and 500 tons of chemical weapons agent. That is enough agent to fill 16,000 battlefield rockets. Even the low end of 100 tons of agent would enable Saddam Hussein to cause mass casualties across more than 100 square miles of territory, an area nearly five times the size of

Manhattan." As for Saddam and nuclear weapons: "We have more than a decade of proof that he remains determined to acquire nuclear weapons." Powell delineated the ingredients and techniques needed to build nuclear weapons, and said that Saddam possessed or would imminently acquire all but one of these. He added that Saddam's agents were scouring the earth for the final ingredient, uranium.

The Security Council was not convinced. Some members of the UN body simply didn't believe the Bush administration; others wanted to give inspections and sanctions more time to work. The council refused to authorize the use of force against Iraq.

Bush was disappointed but not deterred. "The United Nations Security Council has not lived up to its responsibilities, so we will rise to ours," he asserted in March 2003. The time for action had come. "In one year, or five years, the power of Iraq to inflict harm on all free nations would be multiplied many times over. With these capabilities, Saddam Hussein and his terrorist allies could choose the moment of deadly conflict when they are strongest. We choose to meet that threat now, where it arises, before it can appear suddenly in our skies and cities."

## 6. THE ROAD TO BAGHDAD

America's second war against Iraq began in the hours of darkness between sunset on March 19 and sunrise on March 20. The war plan, months in the making, called for the fighting to commence with the destruction of Iraqi observation posts along the country's perimeter, to blind the Iraqi command. Attacks against the interior of the country would follow. But at the last minute American intelligence received word that Saddam and his two sons were meeting at a compound in a southern neighborhood of Baghdad. The opportunity appeared too promising to pass up. This wasn't a war against Iraq per se but against Saddam's regime. A single air strike might "decapitate" the regime, taking out Saddam and his heirs apparent. Two F-117 stealth fighter-bombers were dispatched. The planes looped over Baghdad just before sunrise and dropped four 2,000-pound GPS-guided bombs—the first time such munitions had ever been used in combat. Tomahawk cruise missiles completed the strike.

Saddam and his sons escaped, perhaps because their plans had changed. "But it had been worth the effort," General Tommy Franks, the American commander of the war, said later. "Never again would they feel secure among their most-trusted advisers. Who had betrayed their presence at that location? . . . Had we zeroed in on their encrypted cell phones? Were our satellites tracking their vehicles' unique heat signatures from space?"

As in the Gulf War of 1991, American troops went into battle with allies. The 120,000 American troops were joined by 45,000 British soldiers and much smaller contingents from several other countries. In contrast to the earlier war, however, which was conducted from the air for five weeks before the ground units engaged the enemy, the 2003 war saw action on the ground from the start. This was a battle to the death against Saddam's regime, and none of the American military or civilian officials thought he could be ousted short of the seizure of his capital. Besides, in the Gulf War Iraqi units had set the oil fields of Kuwait on fire as they left the country; this time the American commanders didn't want to give Saddam a chance to destroy Iraq's oil fields. Oil played a central role in American planning for Iraq after Saddam; the country's oil revenues would support Iraqi development for decades to come. To lose the oil would jeopardize Iraq's future, besides wreaking havoc on world oil markets.

The original American plan called for simultaneous invasions of Iraq from the north and the south. But when Turkey refused to allow its territory to be used as a staging ground, only the southern invasion took place. Yet it was swift and effective. The attackers seized the oil fields before the Iraqis could ignite more than a few dozen wells. The invaders moved north along the valley of the Tigris and Euphrates rivers.

As they advanced, they expected to encounter the weapons of mass destruction that had been the principal argument for the invasion. "The Iraqis had prepared themselves to fight in a WMD environment," Tommy Franks wrote. "The regime had used chemical weapons before. Indications were that they had WMDs. And we were advancing on their capital." Franks didn't profess to know when Saddam's soldiers would employ the WMDs. "But I was certain it would be soon."

American forces reached Baghdad in early April. Some of Saddam's Republican Guards put up last-ditch resistance, but much of the Iraqi army and many other officials associated with the regime simply melted away. The world watched on television on April 9 as an American armored vehicle helped a crowd of anti-Saddam Iraqis topple an oversize statue of the dictator.

Bush explained what was supposed to happen next. "The goals of our coalition are clear and limited," the American president announced to the Iraqi people. "We will end a brutal regime, whose aggression and weapons of mass destruction make it a unique threat to the world. Coalition forces will help maintain law and order so that Iraqis can live in security. . . . We will help you build a peaceful and representative government that protects the rights of all citizens. And then our military forces will leave."

Some details remained. Saddam had fled and was on the loose; he would have to be run to ground. And the weapons of mass destruction—which, to the surprise of Franks and other Americans, had not yet been used by Saddam's soldiers—would have to be located.

But by the beginning of May the president was confident enough of the outcome to make a dramatic visit to one of America's warships. Bush arrived aboard the *Abraham Lincoln* via fighter plane; he emerged from the cockpit in a flight suit to the thunderous applause of the aircraft carrier's crew of thousands. A huge banner proclaimed: "Mission Accomplished." The president, smiling proudly, congratulated the crew and all the military personnel who had made the victory possible. "Major combat operations in Iraq have ended," Bush declared. "The tyrant has fallen, and Iraq is free."

## 7. THE MORNING AFTER

For a few weeks the president's positive assessment appeared in order. To be sure, the disappearance of the police and the Iraqi security apparatus allowed looting and other violations of civic order. And the collapse of Saddam's government took with it much of the expertise and simple manpower that had kept the electrical grid working, the water flowing, and the garbage picked up. Yet these deficiencies seemed to many Iraqis merely the loose ends of freedom, and they were broadly accepted as the price of ridding Iraq of Saddam.

During the summer of 2003, though, conditions grew more ominous. The first director of the American occupation, Jay Garner, decided to disband the Iraqi army rather than attempt to reorient or reconstruct it. Garner's decision threw many thousands of Iraqis, a large portion of whom resented the American presence in their country, out of work. Their training in the use of weapons made some of them likely subjects of persuasion by those of their colleagues determined to act on their resentment and challenge the American occupation. These insurgents targeted American troops and positions; they also targeted persons and offices seen as assisting the Americans. In August 2003 a suicide bomber drove a cement truck packed with explosives up to a converted hotel in Baghdad where the special representative of the UN secretary general had his headquarters. The detonation of the explosives demolished the building and killed seventeen people, including the special representative, Sergio Vieira de Mello. Although the secretary general initially declared the UN's determination to remain in Iraq to assist in the rebuilding of the country, within little more than a month he changed his mind. Nearly all the organization's personnel were withdrawn.

Better news for the United States came in December with the capture of Saddam. The ex-dictator had been hiding in and sometimes under a farmhouse near his ancestral city of Tikrit; American troops, acting on a tip, discovered him in a hole in the ground, dirty, disheveled, unshaven, but still defiant. He was imprisoned while the occupation authority decided what to do with him.

The positive turn didn't last. During the spring of 2004 the insurgency escalated. Iraq had long been divided culturally and religiously among three groups: the Shiites, who formed a majority in the southern and western parts of the roughly triangular country; the Sunnis, who constituted a minority; and the Kurds, who lived in the north. The Kurds had never much liked being part of Iraq; many longed to join with fellow Kurds in Turkey, Iran, and Syria to form an independent Kurdistan. For several years under Saddam, the Kurds had exercised a de facto autonomy guaranteed by American and UN sanctions against Saddam. The Kurds were delighted at the arrival of the Americans; Kurd militiamen fought alongside the Americans against Saddam's army. The Kurds continued to exercise autonomy within the occupation, and many believed that Kurdistan was closer than ever.

Most of the Sunnis and some of the Shiites, by contrast to the Kurds, were the ones who objected to the American presence. The split between the two groups had originated in a quarrel over the succession to Muhammad, and this doctrinal dispute still resonated centuries later. But in Iraq the division had serious political and cultural overtones as well. The Sunnis, despite being a majority among the Arabs across the Middle East, were a minority in Iraq, and yet they had contrived to dominate the country's politics and public life. They were Saddam's people; his regime had favored them, and they returned the favor. The regime's downfall was their downfall; they confronted an ominous future in which the Shiites would do to them what they had long done to the Shiites.

The bad omens became more prominent as a result of a shift in American thinking regarding Iraq. To the surprise of Tommy Franks and other American commanders, their troops never encountered the use of chemical or biological weapons. Nor did the troops or the investigating teams the American government sent to scour every inch of Iraq discover those kinds of weapons or anything looking at all like nuclear weapons. The specter of weapons of mass destruction, which had provided the principal justification for the American invasion, proved to be nothing more than a specter, the result of faulty intelligence and, no doubt, excessive eagerness to find a reason to take down Saddam.

Without the weapons, the Bush administration fell back on another reason. Democracy for Iraq had always been part of the agenda; now it jumped to the top of the priority list. "The United States and its coalition partners will remain in Iraq as long as necessary to help put Iraq on the path toward democracy," Bush declared two months after the invasion. Another two months later the president asserted: "The creation of a strong and stable Iraqi democracy is not easy, but it's an essential part of the war against terror." At the eight-month mark of the conflict, he promised: "Iraqi democracy will succeed, and that success will send forth the news, from Damascus to Tehran, that freedom can be the future of every nation."

Democracy sounded good to Americans, and it sounded good to many Shiites, who expected, by virtue of their majority, to dominate a democratic Iraq. But for precisely that reason it frightened the Sunnis. Many of them joined the insurgency, battling both the Americans, who were seen as imposing democracy on Iraq, and the Shiites, who would benefit from this foreign form of government. When the American occupation authorities in June 2004 handed limited control of the country to a provisional government headed by Shiites, and tasked that government with preparing Iraq for democratic elections, the Sunnis felt more threatened still.

Part of democracy's promise was that it would bring dignity to ordinary Iraqis, who had long suffered under the tyrannical misrule of Saddam. This part of the promise suffered a grave loss of credibility in the spring of 2004 when American news outlets broke the story of the abuse of detainees at the Abu Ghraib prison near Baghdad. The prison had acquired an unsavory reputation under Saddam, a circumstance that heightened the outrage when the news reports made clear that despicable acts were still being perpetrated there—but now by Americans. Graphic photos and videotapes revealed prisoners being paraded naked through the corridors and being forced to engage in sex acts with one another. Additional evidence pointed to beatings and other forms of physical and psychological abuse.

The Bush administration immediately sought to contain the damage. Defense secretary Donald Rumsfeld blamed the events at Abu Ghraib on "a few who have betrayed our values and sullied the reputation of our country." Richard Myers, the chairman of the Joint Chiefs of Staff, promised, "Those who committed crimes will be dealt with and the American people will be proud of it and the Iraqi people will be proud." Bush went on Arab television. "I want to tell the people of the Middle East that the practices that took place in that prison are abhorrent, and they don't represent America," he said in an interview with al Arabiya, a television news channel based in Dubai. The perpetrators would be brought to justice. "We're a great country because we're a free country, and we do not tolerate these kind of abuses."

The Abu Ghraib story broke at a bad time for Bush. The failure to find the weapons the president had seemed so certain Saddam possessed had put his judgment, if not his honesty, into question. The growing insurgency undercut the administration's prewar claims that Iraqis would greet American troops as liberators. The rising death toll among those American troops tarnished the luster of the initial easy victory over Saddam. Reports of shortages of body armor and other equipment cast doubt upon the competence of the Pentagon. The Abu Ghraib revelations caused Americans to wonder whether the occupation was making monsters of their own young men and women. The revelations diminished respect for America in the world at large, discouraging even many of America's allies from cooperating with Washington.

The doubts regarding Iraq compounded complaints about the war on terror in general. Civil libertarians and others had worried that the administration's post-9/11 policies eroded basic freedoms in the United States. They pointed with particular concern at the Patriot Act, passed in October 2001, which expanded the powers of government to intercept telephone calls and e-mails, to enter homes and places of business, to search medical and financial records, and to detain and deport immigrants. The Patriot Act passed both houses of Congress by wide margins, but as the shock of 9/11 wore off, opposition to the act increased. Administration critics also challenged the indefinite imprisonment of terrorism suspects at the American base at Guantànamo Bay, Cuba, and the practice of American intelligence and military officers of handing detainees over to interrogators in other countries, where American laws against torture did not apply.

The questions and complaints contributed to a dramatic decline in Bush's approval rating, which hit a till-then low for him of 42 percent in June 2004. Conventional wisdom held that an incumbent with an approval rating below 50 percent could expect to lose a contest for reelection. By the summer of 2004 John Kerry had locked up the Democratic nomination for president. The Massachusetts senator made much of his decorated military service in Vietnam, which contrasted with the absence of any comparable service by Bush. "I'm John Kerry and I'm reporting for duty," he told the Democratic convention, gathered in Boston. "I know what kids go through when they are carrying an M-16 in a dangerous place and they can't tell friend from foe. I know what they go through when they're out on patrol at night and they don't know what's coming around the next bend." Kerry hadn't opposed the war in Iraq, and he didn't oppose it now. He simply promised to conduct it more effectively. "As president, I will wage this war with the lessons I learned in war." He would clean up Abu Ghraib, provide American troops with better equipment and sounder strategy, and engage America's allies more fully. Kerry also promised to fight "a smarter, more effective war on terror. We will deploy every tool in our arsenal: our economic as well as our military might; our principles as well as our firepower."

Kerry's criticism of Bush made sense, but it also played into the president's hands. Not once in their history had Americans voted a wartime incumbent out of office, and Bush calculated that they wouldn't do so this time. He and his supporters harked back to 9/11 at every opportunity; they suggested that a vote for Kerry was a vote against the commander-in-chief and a slap at American soldiers. They warned that Osama bin Laden and al Qaeda were watching; if Americans rejected the president, the terrorists would take heart.

Meanwhile Republican low-roaders attacked Kerry personally. They mounted a campaign to discredit his Vietnam War record, asserting that his medals weren't honorably won and that his subsequent criticism of the Vietnam War had disgraced his uniform and defamed those who died in Southeast Asia. They ridiculed his wife and his reliance on her money.

The double whammy succeeded, but barely. Some voters stuck with Bush out of patriotism and confidence in his leadership; others voted for the president out of dislike of Kerry. Their numbers were just sufficient to return Bush to the White House. The president received 50.7 percent of the popular vote to 48.3 percent for Kerry. Alleged irregularities in Ohio—whose electoral votes, if shifted to the Democratic column, would have reversed the outcome—tempted Kerry to challenge the result, but lacking hard evidence, he let the result stand.

# 15 | Still Dreaming

## 2005–2010

### 1. THE CHANGING CLIMATE OF CLIMATE CHANGE

No American politician ever made more of losing the presidency than Kerry's predecessor in defeat, Al Gore. After the Supreme Court ruled against him in December 2000, Gore grew a beard, put on some weight, and found a cause that inspired him more than politics ever had. For many years scientists had suspected that human activities that emitted carbon dioxide into the atmosphere—in particular, the burning of fossil fuels such as coal and oil—might have a warming effect on the earth's climate. Carbon dioxide and other "greenhouse gases" trap heat from the sun (in much the same way as the glass windows and roofs in greenhouses). How strong the greenhouse effect was, though, remained a mystery.

During the 1980s and 1990s the mystery began to diminish. Numerous studies indicated that global warming was measurable and significant, and climate-modeling computer programs suggested that greenhouse gases were at least partly to blame. The evidence wasn't definitive; skeptics continued to challenge both the data and the theory, and pointed out that only a few decades earlier the climatologists had been predicting a new Ice Age. Yet gradually scientific opinion coalesced around the view that humans were indeed warming their planet and that something ought to be done about it.

In December 1997 a large conference on global warming convened in Kyoto, Japan. Fifteen hundred delegates from 150 countries produced a set of guidelines, called the Kyoto Protocol, for reducing greenhouse gas emissions. The guidelines were controversial, in that they proposed to commit the industrial nations to curtailing their emissions while leaving developing nations India and China free to emit as much as they wanted. Reducing emissions, moreover, seemed likely to be very expensive, and it was unclear what effect, if any, the Kyoto guidelines would actually have on global warming. Nonetheless nearly all the countries of the world ratified the Kyoto pact.

The United States was the conspicuous exception. As the largest producer of greenhouse gases, the United States would have to make the largest reductions and would thereby incur the greatest expense. Whether the benefit to Americans would match the expense was doubtful. Bill Clinton was favorably inclined toward the Kyoto accord, but by the time the Senate might have taken it up, that body had other business to attend to, in particular Clinton's impeachment trial. Clinton left the Kyoto pact and the broader issue of global warming to his successor.

Had Al Gore won the 2000 election he might have pressed for Kyoto ratification. His loss left the treaty in the unfriendly hands of George W. Bush and the Republicans. Besides having close ties to the oil industry—Bush had worked in his father's oil firm; Dick Cheney's last job before the vice presidency was head of Halliburton, an oil services firm—the administration was philosophically opposed to the government mandates upon business Kyoto required. Moreover, as the administration's decision to defy the UN in waging war in Iraq demonstrated, the Republicans disliked the whole idea of international bodies telling the United States what to do. For nearly a century—since Woodrow Wilson's fight with the Republican Senate over the League of Nations—Americans had debated the merits and demerits of multilateralism versus unilateralism. Like the Republicans in that earlier fight, the Republicans of Bush's day came down on the side of unilateralism.

"I oppose the Kyoto Protocol," Bush explained in a letter to the Senate, "because it exempts eighty percent of the world, including major population centers such as China and India, from compliance, and would cause serious harm to the U.S. economy." The president didn't ignore the concerns of those who had drafted and ratified the Kyoto guidelines, but he placed other concerns first. "We must be very careful not to take actions that could harm consumers. This is especially true given the incomplete state of scientific knowledge of the causes of, and solutions to, global climate change."

The president's approach angered much of the world. "Bush Puts U.S. Above the Globe," the London *Daily Telegraph* asserted. "Bush Defies World on Gas Emissions," the *Weekend Australian* seconded. "Le coup de poignard américain" ("the American stab"), *Le Temps* observed from Paris. "Rendez-vous mit Klimastörungen" ("Rendezvous with climatic chaos"), the *Süddeutsche Zeitung* of Munich predicted.

But Bush's anti-Kyoto stance played well in the United States. Prior to the Kyoto conference, the Senate had passed a resolution opposing any climate treaty that exempted China and India from greenhouse gas curbs, and after the Kyoto pact did precisely that, the senators reiterated their opposition.

Yet as the evidence of human-caused climate change mounted, so did the desire among Americans at large to do something about greenhouse gases. The summer of 2005 produced an unusually severe series of hurricanes in the Atlantic, Caribbean, and Gulf of Mexico. The most destructive of these, Hurricane Katrina, roared across southern Mississippi and Louisiana in late August en route to New Orleans. Officials and residents of the city had long recognized their vulnerability to a large storm, in that much of the urban area lay below sea level, behind levees of dubious reliability. Katrina's storm surge—the high waters literally sucked skyward by the low pressure at the hurricane's heart—swamped and then broke the levees, sending the waters of Lake Pontchartrain pouring into the city. More than eighteen hundred people died as a result of Katrina's flooding and high winds; a million people fled the storm's fury. New Orleans emptied out as the floodwaters filled four-fifths of the city; the residents relocated to Houston and other cities and towns across the South and beyond. The Bush administration—in particular the Federal Emergency Management Agency—suffered heavy criticism for clumsiness in responding to the crisis. Not for weeks were the levees even temporarily restored and the floodwaters pumped out. The first residents who returned found whole neighborhoods beyond repair; as the word spread, many other evacuees simply stayed away. New Orleans had long been poor, but for its residents it had been home. With their homes now destroyed, many saw no reason to come back.

The role of climate change in causing Katrina and other strong storms was a matter of debate. Not many scientists, even among those convinced of the reality of climate change, were willing to point the finger of global warming at particular, discrete events. But Katrina and the other storms made terrifyingly real what could be at stake if the climatologists' theories proved correct.

And Al Gore made it sexy. Gore had long displayed an interest in science; an essentially unobjectionable statement he uttered during the 2000 campaign about his early support for digital communications had been misconstrued to intimate that he boasted of having invented the Internet. After deciding not to run in 2004 he devoted his attention to global warming: He developed a presentation explaining the phenomenon, assessing its likely human costs, and arguing for policy changes to avert disaster. The presentation proved such a hit that he made it into a movie, *An Inconvenient Truth*, that drew raves at film festivals, packed theaters across the country and around the world, and won an Academy Award in 2006 for best documentary film. A companion book by the same title topped the *New York Times* bestseller list. In 2007 Gore won the Nobel Peace Prize. The Nobel citation lauded Gore for his efforts "to build up and disseminate greater knowledge about man-made climate change, and to lay the foundations for the measures that are needed to counteract such change."

Gore's honors and fame didn't impress the Bush administration, which continued to oppose the Kyoto treaty. Nor did they change American policy. Comparatively calm summers in 2006 and 2007 in America's hurricane zones diminished the felt need for quick action, and the soaring price of oil in 2007 and 2008 caused Congress to shy away from measures that would increase the pain at the pump.

Yet none could deny that the politics of global warming were changing. Denials that the earth was warming grew rarer, as did assertions that humans weren't to blame. The opponents of action still clung to the balance sheet argument: that the costs of slowing the warming would outweigh the benefits. But such mercenary considerations didn't prevent several states and cities from adopting measures designed to reduce their "carbon footprints." Almost no one expected the payoff from these measures to outweigh the costs; they were chiefly symbolic. But symbolism mattered, and increasingly it favored what Al Gore preached.

## 2. THE GOLDEN DOOR—AND A CONCRETE WALL?

For most of American history, immigration was an economic issue rather than a political one. The chronic problem of the American economy during the colonial era and for the first century of American independence was a dearth of labor, and government policies aimed to encourage almost anyone even slightly disposed to come to America to do so. For nearly two hundred years those policies also facilitated the immigration of many thousands who did *not* want to come, namely African slaves, who were legally imported against their will until 1808 (and sometimes illegally after that). The first law restricting voluntary immigration was the Chinese Exclusion Act of 1882, which barred Chinese laborers. The ban on Chinese revealed the growing strength of industrial workers, who objected to the low-wage competition; it also reflected a fear on the part of many Americans that their country and culture couldn't assimilate immigrants who seemed so different from the native-born. Both influences increased in strength during the next forty years, as immigration swelled overall and shifted in origin from northern and western Europe, from which most immigrants to America had traditionally come, to southern and eastern Europe. The newer immigrants were typically unskilled and willing to work for low wages; they were Catholic or Jewish rather than Protestant; they were often darker in skin or otherwise exotic in appearance. The complaints about the new immigration culminated in the 1924 Immigration Act, which sharply reduced legal immigration and set quotas for various countries, with preference given to those countries that had supplied most of the earlier generations of immigrants.

The 1924 act furnished the framework for immigration to the United States until 1965, when a new law abolished the regime of quotas based on national origins and gave preference to those persons with skills needed by the American economy, and to individuals with relatives already in the United States. The latter preference, which had no numerical upper limit, proved far more inclusive than the legislators who approved the law imagined. The measure surprised its supporters in another respect. They had assumed that most immigration would continue to come from Europe, but growing prosperity there limited the comparative appeal of the United States; instead the origins of most immigration shifted to Latin America and Asia. Mexico sent the largest number of immigrants, followed by Vietnam, the Philippines, and Korea, with substantial numbers arriving from China, Cuba, and the Dominican Republic as well. Family connections and economic considerations aside, many of the Vietnamese and Cubans fell into a newly broadened category of American immigration law: persons fleeing political persecution. The Vietnamese were fleeing the consequences of the communist victory in their country; the Cubans were fleeing Fidel Castro.

The legal immigrants were accompanied, contemporaneously, by those who came illegally. Most of these came over the border from Mexico, seeking jobs that paid better than those to the south. Mexican laborers had long been coming to the United States. During World War II the American and Mexican governments had arranged for the admission of temporary workers from Mexico to alleviate wartime shortages. The *bracero* program, as it was called, outlasted the war, providing agricultural workers to commercial farms in the United States until 1964, when complaints about abuses of workers led to its termination. But halting the program didn't diminish the demand for labor, and workers continued to come, some with visas but many without.

By the 1980s the undocumented workers formed a large enough group that Congress felt compelled to address their situation. A 1986 law mandated penalties for employers who knowingly hired illegal immigrants, but it also provided amnesty to persons who had arrived illegally before 1982.

The amnesty worked better than the employer penalties, which were enforced only sporadically. Illegal immigration continued and in fact grew significantly. The booming American economy of the 1990s attracted large numbers of workers, and though the slump after the turn of the century reduced the demand somewhat, the influx persisted. The size of the black market in labor was difficult to gauge, as the sizes of black markets generally are. But by 2005 a common estimate was that ten million undocumented immigrants were living in the United States.

The immigration issue prompted demands for reform. Some would-be reformers insisted that those who had arrived illegally be deported and a wall built along the U.S.-Mexican border; others urged a new amnesty along the lines of the 1986 version. Both sides mobilized. The wall builders put volunteers in the field to monitor the border and assist government agents in apprehending illegal crossers; the amnesty advocates sponsored parades in which marchers waved Mexican flags and decried the discrimination they perceived in anti-immigrant measures. Congress attempted to address the issue during the 2007 session, but the politics grew so bitter that the legislature decided to put the question off until after the 2008 elections.

## 3. WIRED

Saddam Hussein's execution, following his trial and conviction in an Iraqi court, was supposed to be a carefully controlled event, with media coverage closely circumscribed. But within hours an unauthorized video recording of the dictator's last seconds and death were playing on television networks around the world. One of the witnesses had smuggled a mobile phone into the execution chamber and documented the hanging; audio disclosed the angry exchange between Saddam and his guards.

The incident revealed one of the most remarkable developments of the first decade of the twenty-first century: the continued erasure of time and distance in communications and information. Mobile telephones first became available in the United States during the 1980s, mostly in cars on account of their bulkiness and power requirements. Smaller versions emerged by the 1990s, made possible by advances in electronics and batteries but also by the adoption of "cellular" transmission technology, which divided service areas into small "cells," with their own individual antennas and towers. The signal from a cell phone only had to reach a nearby tower, from which it was repeated across the cellular grid to the cell phone at the other end of the call.

The adoption of cellular technology caused usage to explode. By 2005 more than two hundred million cell phones were in use in the United States. Nor were Americans by any means the heaviest users. Japan and several other countries had higher usage rates, in part because of different billing customs. (Americans generally did not pay per local call on land lines, while customers in various other countries did.) In 2005 more than two billion cell phones were in use around the world.

Cell phones changed the way people communicated and the way they acted. Phones became constant companions, allowing individuals to communicate at all times and in nearly all places. Travelers could keep in constant touch with their homes or their offices; parents could know where their children were (at least potentially: just because children carried phones didn't mean they always answered them). Phones added the capacity to transmit text, which fostered a shorthand—understood mostly among young people—of abbreviations and symbols. Cell phones and kindred devices developed e-mail and Internet capabilities, allowing users access to the much wider electronic world. Cameras were initially included in phones as a novelty, but they caught on in ways the inventors never imagined. The cameras captured still pictures and video footage, and transmitted them to other phones, to computers, and eventually to the Internet and television. They recorded proud moments (graduations, weddings), embarrassing moments (gaffes by politicians, misbehavior by celebrities), frightening moments (automobile accidents, hurricanes, tsunamis), and just about every other kind of moment. In the same way that CNN had multiplied the events people could witness from afar, so cell phones multiplied them again; now every person became a potential reporter, able to record and transmit the sights and sounds of life on the planet.

In 2007 the cell phone merged with another technology that was equally revolutionary in its own sphere. The Apple corporation had begun life as a maker of personal computers that were stylish but not especially popular commercially. The company branched out in 2001 with a portable music player called the iPod. The iPod wasn't the first device to play digital music files, but its quality and style immediately made it the state of the art. It dominated its own field and had spillover effects into other areas. Users could purchase music by the song over the Internet, a practice that had devastating effects on the existing recorded-music business, which had been built around suites of songs, recorded originally on vinyl albums and later on compact disks, and sold through retail stores. (Another very large segment of digital music consumers didn't purchase their music at all but bootlegged it from the Internet; this practice undercut the music industry even more.) Apple invaded the cell phone market in 2007 with the iPhone, which combined the features of a music player with those of an advanced cell phone, and threatened to do for consumers—and do *to* rival manufacturers—what the iPod had done.

The iPod added momentum to the emergence of what might have been called an "à la carte culture" of consumerism. At the dawn of the industrial age, the state of technology had dictated long production runs to reduce the price of manufactured objects. Henry Ford had perfected the approach with his Model T, which rolled off Ford's assembly line by the million, and he articulated the theory when he reportedly declared that customers could have their cars in any color they wanted, so long as it was black. William Levitt applied the one-size-suits-all to suburban home building; the result was more families owning homes, and the homes looking more alike.

The development of nimbler techniques and faster communications during the 1980s and 1990s allowed a new approach to manufacturing. Dell computer pioneered a build-to-order method of fitting computers to customers. Customers selected the components they wanted in their computers from menus Dell provided, then phoned in their orders or submitted them over the Internet. Dell built the computers to match the orders. Customers got what they wanted, and Dell saved on inventory—and passed part of the savings on to the customers.

Similar trends in other industries caused consumers to expect customizing. Starbucks, which grew from a single coffee stand at Pike and First in Seattle to a global behemoth operating fifteen thousand stores in more than forty countries, let customers select from a dizzying menu of coffees drawn from around the world and prepared in dozens of different ways. The iPod and other vehicles for digital music invited listeners to create what amounted to their own albums. Consumers caught on at an early age: Build-a-Bear let children design their own Teddy bears. And they demanded new habits from old industries: automobile manufacturers began building cars to customers' orders.

The result was an ironic conflation of the individual and the collective. Dell's custom designs allowed it to crowd other manufacturers out of the market, causing Dell computers, in all their singular uniqueness, to proliferate. Starbucks' customers filled their cups with distinctive brews, but the cups all said "Starbucks" as drinkers carried them to work, to school, and to everywhere else. Apple's trademark was its iconoclasm (its most famous commercial, a 1984 spot announcing the Macintosh computer, displayed an anti–Big Brother theme, with IBM cast as the Orwellian heavy); but that very iconoclasm made it an icon in its own right (the distinctive shade of the iPod became known as "mug-me white," for its street appeal).

Whether Americans were becoming more alike or more different was an intriguing question. They were certainly becoming pickier.

## 4. SHADES OF THE THIRTIES

The conflation of the individual and the collective was systemically innocuous, if symbolically significant, in matters of coffee and music, but it was far from innocuous in matters of finance. The consumer revolution of the Nineties and the Noughties (as the cheeky dubbed the first decade of the twenty-first century) pushed Americans more deeply into debt than they had ever been. Or perhaps they were *pulled* into debt by the endless offers of new credit cards that filled mailboxes and asked for little or nothing in the way of credit history. The national savings rate fell below zero, meaning that rather than saving for a rainy day, Americans were banking on sunshine and borrowing against it. The bursting of the dot-com bubble left investors and speculators (two groups that became increasingly difficult to distinguish) looking for fresh opportunities; millions found it in real estate. Prices of homes rose, then soared, then rocketed in market after market around the country. Existing owners felt wise and wealthy as they watched the appraised value of their residences inflate (although owners on fixed incomes often worried about the rising property taxes that accompanied the rising prices). But those persons not yet on the real estate escalator—renters, young couples, and singles—fretted, even panicked, that if they didn't get on now, they'd never be able to afford the first step.

Fortunately for them—or so they thought—a subindustry developed in what were called subprime mortgages. The traditional mortgage—the instrument that had built Levittown, the other suburbs, and much of the postwar American dream—had required borrowers to prove an ability to repay the loan. Lenders scrutinized tax returns, called employers to confirm wages and salaries, queried banks about borrowers' account balances. Much of this was plain sense; more was self-interest, as the banks didn't want to have to deal with deadbeats or people who simply got in over their heads. But bright young minds on Wall Street developed new ways of packaging and selling mortgages, so that the banks that originated the loans—the ones that traditionally checked the background of borrowers—no longer kept the mortgages on their own books, but sold them to other institutions. The banks, which earned fees from making the loans, no longer had to worry about whether the loans were repaid and consequently grew careless. They lowered the limits on income, on down payments, on the principal repaid each month. They offered teaser rates—rates set unsustainably low but scheduled to readjust to a higher rate in the future. Many borrowers expected to be earning more money in the future and intended to cover the higher costs with those bigger paychecks; others thought they would resell—"flip"—their homes for a profit before the higher rates took hold.

The result of all this was a classic speculative bubble. As long as people believed home prices would go up, they did go up. And in the manner of previous bubbles, the beneficiaries persuaded themselves that this bubble was different. Real estate never depreciated, they said. There could never be an oversupply of real estate, they asserted, because the supply of land is finite.

And just like every previous bubble, this one burst. Some people looked at the cost of ownership and decided to rent. Some got nervous about the bigger payments ahead and bailed. Some simply remembered that every other bubble had burst and concluded that this one must too. The combination of factors caused a flattening, then a decline, in real estate prices, starting in 2007. As in other burstings, once the decline commenced, it fed on itself. Borrowers took fright that unless they sold now, they'd have to sell for less in the future. Many borrowers, discovering that they owed more on their homes than the homes were suddenly worth—such homes and owners were said to be "under water"—simply walked away, leaving the properties in the hands of the mortgage holders. That it was often unclear precisely who the mortgage holders were—the repackaging and reselling of the mortgages typically split the loans into many parts—aggravated the situation by making it difficult for borrowers to restructure payments.

The growing crisis in real estate soon became a crisis in finance. Many large institutions had purchased the repackaged mortgages; as the mortgages lost value, the purchasing institutions found themselves unable to pay their own debts. The same interconnections—domestic and international—that had seemed a strength of the modern economy during the good times suddenly became a weakness. Each bank or financial firm that wobbled threatened to bring down dozens of others—and the threats to these others caused still others to pull back in fear, further eroding the confidence on which financial structures always rest. Lenders that specialized in subprime loans failed first, but then firms that invested in the subprime lenders went down. Two huge lenders, the government-sponsored Federal National Mortgage

Association and the Federal Home Mortgage Corporation, nicknamed Fannie Mae and Freddie Mac, found themselves verging on bankruptcy, which likely would have destabilized most of the American financial system and much of the world system; only the emergency extension of federal loans, followed by a federal takeover of the companies, staved off a collapse.

But it didn't solve the problem, which simply grew worse. One investment bank, Lehman Brothers, closed its doors in September 2008; another, Merrill Lynch, avoided a similar fate only by selling itself to Bank of America. Insurance giant AIG had to be saved from financial death by the federal government.

Up to this point, Treasury secretary Henry Paulson and Federal Reserve chairman Ben Bernanke had been willing to treat each emergency as it arrived, but as the ER line grew crowded, they appealed to Congress for greater resources. They proposed a rescue package of $700 billion, initially to be applied to the "toxic mortgages" at the heart of the financial crisis. A frightened Congress approved, and the plan went into operation. But it didn't stop the bleeding, and the damage began to spread from the financial sector to the broader economy. Stock prices plunged, erasing trillions of dollars in investments and making Americans feel collectively much poorer. Consumers stopped spending, forcing retailers to cancel orders and lay off workers. The tourism industry took a beating as vacationers stuck close to home. The American auto industry suffered its worst slump since 1945; General Motors, for decades the bluest of blue chip companies, hemorrhaged cash. Unemployment reached levels not seen for decades, and it threatened to get much worse. No one uttered the d-word, but the recession that loomed caused more than a few old-timers, and a larger number of students of history, to recall the depression of the 1930s.

## 5. DREAMS OF HIS FATHER

Barack Obama presumably didn't wish the economic troubles on his country, but if they had to occur, they arrived at an opportune moment for him. Until 2004 almost no one outside Illinois had heard of Obama, but that summer he was invited to give the keynote address at the Democratic national convention, and his stirring speech—consisting of equal parts policy, personal history, and partisanship—proved the highlight of an otherwise lackluster week. The personal history was particularly riveting: the son of a black African father and a white American mother, Obama grew up in Hawaii and Indonesia before attending Columbia University and Harvard Law School. En route he worked with community groups in Chicago, where he eventually took up residence, with wife Michelle. He entered elective politics in 1996, winning a seat in the Illinois legislature. He tried for Congress in 2000 but lost in the Democratic primary. In 2004 he announced for the Senate and this time won, on a wave of the acclaim from his convention speech.

Soon he was being touted for president. Democratic victories in the 2006 congressional races made the Democratic nomination for 2008 appear particularly valuable. The front-runner was Hillary Clinton, who had been elected to the Senate from New York, to which she and Bill retired from the White House. Clinton displayed a deftness for politics that belied her previous best-known effort, the failed attempt at health care reform in Bill Clinton's first term. She enjoyed the advantages of name recognition, of the support of Clinton loyalists, and of the fervent backing of feminists and others who thought it was finally time for America to elect a woman president.

The 2008 campaign started early, with a large roster of Democratic hopefuls. All the candidates but Clinton hoped for her to stumble, but throughout the run-up to the Iowa caucuses, the traditional start of the primary season, she maintained her footing and her lead in the polls. Yet once Democratic voters actually began voting, as opposed to simply answering pollsters, they revealed a slight preference for Obama, who gradually outpaced Clinton in delegates to the national convention. In June 2008—very deep into the primary season, by recent standards—he crossed the threshold of sufficient delegates to secure the nomination.

The Republicans meanwhile nominated John McCain, a senator from Arizona with a stirring record of wartime service in Vietnam, including five years as a prisoner of war. McCain had sought the Republican nomination in 2000, positioning himself as a maverick and a moderate. He lost the nomination to George W. Bush and took the lesson that Republicans liked mavericks more in theory than in practice and that they didn't like moderates at all. By 2008 he recast himself as a reliable conservative, and he waltzed through the primaries with comparative ease.

During most of the primary season the principal issue on voters' minds was the war in Iraq, and as long as it dominated the news, McCain—the war hero and a strong supporter of Bush's war policies—appeared likely to defeat either Obama or Clinton. But Iraq grew calmer by the summer of 2008, in part because of the "surge" of American troop strength since the previous summer and in part because of shrewd political bargaining between the American occupation command and Sunni insurgents. And while Iraq claimed less of voters' attention, the economy claimed more. As they almost always do, voters responded to the economic troubles by demanding change at the top. Bush wasn't running, so they took out their frustrations on his fellow Republican, McCain. The Arizona senator tried to shift the dynamic by picking Alaska governor Sarah Palin to join him on the Republican ticket. Palin's conservative credentials pleased party members who doubted the sincerity of McCain's conversion to conservatism, but her lack of knowledge on issues of national and international importance put off voters who hadn't decided between the Republican and Democratic tickets.

Obama was the first African American to win the nomination of a major party, a fact that naturally inspired much commentary. Yet Obama's race apparently played a diminishing role as the campaign wore on. Blacks indicated an overwhelming preference for him, and no one doubted that race had much to do with it. But while some white voters likely rejected Obama because of his race, other white voters might well have voted *for* Obama because of his race.

In the end, race mattered less than the economy, which sank McCain's chances. Obama won the popular vote by 53 percent to 46 percent, and the electoral vote by 365 to 173.

## 6. FRANKLIN DELANO OBAMA?

The historic nature of Obama's victory—the first African American president would be inaugurated just weeks before the two hundredth birthday of Abraham Lincoln, the emancipator of African American slaves—brought joyful tears to the eyes of his supporters and a moment of respectful reflection even to many of those who voted against him. "Senator Obama has achieved a great thing for himself and for his country," McCain said in his concession speech. "That he managed to do so by inspiring the hopes of so many millions of Americans who had once wrongly believed that they had little at stake or little influence in the election of an American president is something I deeply admire and commend him for achieving."

As always, though, the sun arose the morning after the election on a world not markedly different from that of the day before. The American economy was more fraught than ever; by now the financial crisis had spread to Europe and Asia, and the global economy appeared recession-bound. President-elect Obama met with President-still Bush in an effort to reassure investors and consumers, but the meeting couldn't calm the markets or persuade customers to return to the stores. Henry Paulson spent half the $700 billion rescue package without observably ameliorating the crisis; the other half looked unlikely to accomplish more.

Foreign affairs offered no respite for the new president. Iraq remained reasonably stable, but Afghanistan, which had long appeared the more tractable of America's Middle Eastern wars, now witnessed increasing, and increasingly successful, insurgent violence. Iran had been edging toward nuclear weapons, frightening the Israelis, who took Iran's president seriously when he said Israel didn't deserve to exist. If Israel launched an air strike against Iran, to disrupt its nuclear program, the United States would surely incur the wrath of the Muslim world. But if Iran acquired the nukes, there was no telling what its government would do with them. China grew more assertive by the day. So far the Chinese government had broadly backed the international status quo, based economically on the U.S. dollar. But with the American economy weakening, Beijing might demand adjustments that acknowledged China's growing strength. Russia was reasserting itself in the region of the old Soviet Union; President Obama would have to decide whether to confront the Russians or accommodate them.

By some accountings, Obama became president at the worst possible time. The strains on America—on its economy, on its foreign policy, on its dreams of a progressively better life for its people—were as great as they had ever been since 1945, and they were growing by the month. What person would want a job in which failure seemed so likely?

By other reckoning, however, Obama's timing couldn't have been better. The greatest presidents—Washington, Lincoln, Franklin Roosevelt—led

America effectively through its moments of greatest crisis, and earned their place in the pantheon for doing so. Washington guided the country to independence; Lincoln secured the Union and freed the slaves; Roosevelt rescued capitalism and defeated fascism. Each extended the dreams of Americans to a new era of national life. No one yet was comparing Obama to Washington or Lincoln, but some saw parallels between the challenges Obama faced and those that had confronted FDR. Roosevelt became president at a moment when many Americans believed that their country's best days were behind them, and despaired that the American dream would survive the Great Depression. Yet under Roosevelt's leadership, the dream not only survived but flourished, and by the time of his death in 1945 the country was stronger and more prosperous than ever.

Obama's first months on the job provided some support to the FDR analogy, to the pleasure of most of Obama's supporters and the pain of his opponents. Congress approved an $800 billion economic stimulus package in February 2009; the purpose was to increase public—that is, government—demand for goods and services at a time when private demand had slackened. The president's supporters hailed it as a sign of bold leadership; his critics complained that it was larded with pork that undid any positive effects it might have produced. Its effects were hard to measure. The unemployment rate continued to rise—to more than 10 percent by autumn of 2009—but it might have risen further without the stimulus.

The financial system stabilized during the same period, or appeared to. Big banks and financial firms stopped collapsing; credit began to flow again. As with the stimulus package, none could say for sure what role government action played in the stabilization. Obama nominated Bernanke for a second term as Fed chief, conveying his belief that Bernanke's forceful response to the crisis had been instrumental in preventing what was already the worst recession in thirty years from becoming the worst depression in eighty. But Bernanke's—and Obama's—critics worried that all the money that had been thrown at the financial problem merely postponed the day of reckoning, when inflation would insidiously erode America's standard of living.

Supporters and critics similarly split on the signature reform effort of Obama's first year. Obama and the Democrats sought to reform America's health care system, at least by extending medical insurance to all Americans, at most by bringing millions of Americans under the umbrella of a publicly funded "single-payer" system—essentially a broader version of Medicare. Nearly all Republicans opposed the reforms, contending that they would raise taxes, increase the size of government, and diminish the realm of personal choice. As 2010 began, the administration and the Democrats had pushed divergent bills through the House and Senate and were hoping to reconcile them; the Republicans had fallen back but were plotting an ambush.

## 7. STILL DREAMING

In the middle of the argument were the Baby Boomers, who were just approaching retirement age. Health care meant more to them than it had before, as they needed more of it than in their youth; but so did the solvency of the government, which would fund—they hoped—the longest retirement of any generation in American history so far.

If they reflected on their place in history—and more of them did, the older they got—they might have noticed an odd inversion in the nature of American dreams during their lifetimes. The dreams of 1945 had been collectively ambitious but individually modest; those of 2010 were collectively modest but individually ambitious. Collectively, the country in 2010 seemed troubled on several fronts, and its dreams were curtailed commensurately. The nation that had put sixteen million soldiers in the field during World War II now had difficulty finding a few hundred thousand to garrison Iraq and Afghanistan. The economic dynamo that had dictated to the global economy at Bretton Woods now labored under a debt that left the dollar at the mercy of central bankers in China and Japan. Proud industrial cities like Pittsburgh, Detroit, and Buffalo, whose factories had rescued democracy during the war, rebuilt Europe afterward, and made the middle-class dreams of fifty million families possible, had become pale shadows of their former selves. The political system that had designed a Great Society, one to make America the envy of the world, agonized over guaranteeing medical care that much of the rest of the world had long taken for granted. Bretton Woods, the Marshall Plan, the Great Society—those were dreams of another age; the nation in 2010 could aspire to nothing so grand.

And yet Americans individually often dreamed more ambitiously than at any time in the country's past. The personal standard of living of the Baby

Boomers—the houses, the cars, the computers, the cell phones, the travel, the cappuccinos—made the lifestyle of their grandparents seem quaint, and if the current recession had trimmed some of the extravagance, no one expected a general rollback to the standard of 1945. For particular groups of individuals, the dreaming had never been more realistically hopeful. The presence of a black man in the White House, who placed a Latina woman, Sonia Sotomayor, on the Supreme Court, signaled to children of color across the land that their dreams weren't limited by the institutionalized prejudice of previous generations. Young women, many of whom had no idea who Betty Friedan was or why women might once have burned their bras, dreamed of careers their grandmothers couldn't have imagined. Gay people lived more openly than their counterparts of previous generations; that several states now let them marry made those in other states dream that they might marry, too. Immigrants dreamed the same dreams that immigrants always have—of opportunity in America for themselves and their children—but they did so in far greater numbers than in the 1940s and 1950s.

All of which suggested that the heart of America's dreams was the act of dreaming itself. No charter of American history explicitly enshrined the right to dream, but it was encoded in the country's DNA from the beginning. Jefferson's triad implied it: the right to life suggested the right to dream of a *better* life; liberty allowed Americans to choose their own dreams, not those imposed by others; and the pursuit of happiness—what was that besides the right to dream and to chase one's dreams?

Americans' collective dreams had always waxed and waned. The Founders' dream of national independence, articulated audaciously at Philadelphia in 1776, struggled against cold and hunger at Valley Forge just two years later. The Jacksonian dream of national democracy, asserting that ordinary Americans could govern themselves peacefully, hit the rocks of secession and civil war. The Jazz Age dream of permanent national prosperity proved an illusion during the Great Depression. The Cold War dream of global hegemony dissolved in Vietnam. The post–Cold War dream of permanent peace exploded in the Balkans, the Middle East, and lower Manhattan.

But Americans' individual dreams stubbornly survived. They adjusted for the cycles of prosperity and depression, of war and peace, of political liberalism and conservatism. They modified themselves to suit the circumstances of the individuals who did the dreaming—the farmers and the city dwellers, rich and poor, native-born and immigrants, men and women, whites and peoples of color. But through everything the dreams remained surprisingly consistent. Americans dreamed that they could chart their own paths in life, that they could better themselves materially, that their children could thrive and prosper. They had dreamed this for two centuries, because it was their national birthright and because, despite reality's refusal to honor all of their dreams, it had delivered more of them than it granted any other people on earth.

Americans had dreamed since our national birth, and in the twenty-first century we were dreaming still.

# ACKNOWLEDGMENTS

I would like to thank the numerous archivists and librarians who have assisted me during the twenty-five years I have been researching and writing about the subjects included in this book. I would also like to thank my many colleagues at the University of Texas at Austin, Texas A&M University, and Vanderbilt University, who have encouraged me to try out ideas and interpretations on them. And I would especially like to thank the thousands of students who have participated in my classes and challenged me to sharpen my thinking, lest I get conceptually lazy, and to emphasize the story in history, lest they become distracted and bored.

# NOTES

## Chapter 1. Last One Standing

4 "My first impression": R. A. Larkin memo, July 27, 1945, Los Alamos National Laboratory website: http://www.lanl.gov/history/atomicbomb/pdf (October 5, 2009).

5 "like the crack of a five-inch anti-aircraft gun . . . one way or the other": Richard Rhodes, *The Making of the Atomic Bomb* (1986), 674–76.

7 "They were nothing . . . end of it": Harry S. Truman, *Memoirs* (1955), 1:341.

7 "Operated on this morning": Rhodes, *Making*, 685.

8 "I casually mentioned": Truman, *Memoirs*, 1:416.

8 "If he had had": Winston Churchill, *Triumph and Tragedy* (1953), 670.

9 "a sort of Grand Canyon . . . blow their brains out": David M. Kennedy, *Freedom from Fear: The American People in Depression and War, 1929–1945* (1999), 653.

12 "If we do not do that": H. W. Brands, *The Devil We Knew: Americans and the Cold War* (1993), 10–11.

21 "Where we had seen a clear city . . . the whole city": Rhodes, *Making*, 710–11.

21 "the enemy has begun to employ": Thomas W. Zeiler, *Unconditional Defeat: Japan, America, and the End of World War II* (2004), 189.

## Chapter 2. The War That Never Ended

24 "If we see that Germany is winning": Wilson D. Miscamble, *From Roosevelt to Truman: Potsdam, Hiroshima, and the Cold War* (2006), 17.

25 "Boys, if you ever pray": David McCullough, *Truman* (1992), 353; Alfred Steinberg, *The Man from Missouri: The Life and Times of Harry S. Truman* (1962), 239.

25 "Big money has too much power": Robert H. Ferrell, *Harry S. Truman and the Modern American Presidency* (1996), 230.

25 "I have pleaded your case": McCullough, *Truman*, 492.

25 "worse than bullets": Robert J. Donovan, *Conflict and Crisis: The Presidency of Harry S. Truman, 1945–1948* (1996), 212.

26 "I am tired . . . by the President": McCullough, *Truman*, 500–505.

27 "Please Mr. Truman": James T. Patterson, *Grand Expectations: The United States, 1945–1974* (1996), 14.

28 "It's going to be a God-damned beefsteak election": William Smith White, *Home Place: The Story of the U.S. House of Representatives* (1965), 60.

28 "clear threat": Truman veto message, July 20, 1947, Papers of the Presidents, www.presidency.ucsb.edu. (Unless otherwise noted, presidential statements below are from this source.)

29 "We shall fight on the beaches": Martin Gilbert, *The Second World War: A Complete History* (2004), 86.
30 "I have never been talked to . . . one-two to the jaw": Daniel Yergin, *Shattered Peace: The Origins of the Cold War and the National Security State* (1977), 83; Miscamble, *Roosevelt to Truman*, 137.
31 "I know that he will have": Donovan, *Conflict and Crisis*, 191.
32 "From Stettin in the Baltic": Churchill speech, March 5, 1946, Churchill Centre website, http://www.winstonchurchill.org.
33 "They have learned . . . to do so": George Kennan, "Long telegram," February 22, 1946, National Security Archive website: http://www.gwu.edu/~nsarchiv/coldwar/documents/episode-1/kennan.htm.
33 "promote tendencies": George Kennan, "The Sources of Soviet Conduct," *Foreign Affairs*, July 1947.
34 "At the present moment": Truman speech, March 12, 1947.
34 "Like the Lend-Lease program": *New York Times*, March 13, 1947.
35 "The president's hands": Joseph M. Jones, *The Fifteen Weeks (February 21–June 5, 1947)* (1955), 174.
35 "The measures undertaken . . . the present war": H. W. Brands, *The Strange Death of American Liberalism* (2001), 58–59; *The Papers of Robert A. Taft*, ed. Clarence E. Wunderlin Jr. (1997), 2:271.
36 "If we assume": *Papers of Taft*, 2:260.
36 "the president's announcements": *New York Times*, April 11, 1947.
37 "Americans would themselves": H. W. Brands, *What America Owes the World: The Struggle for the Soul of Foreign Policy* (1998), 155–56.
38 "Aside from the awful implications": Brands, *Devil We Knew*, 15–16.
38 "Our policy is directed": Marshall Plan speech, Harry S. Truman Presidential Library website, http://www.trumanlibrary.org.
39 "huge taxes . . . communist or not": *Papers of Taft*, 3:204; Greg Behrman, *The Most Noble Adventure: The Marshall Plan and the Time When America Helped Save Europe* (2007), 135; Robert Edward Summers, ed., *Economic Aid to Europe: The Marshall Plan* (1948), 142; Henry W. Berger, *Senator Robert A. Taft and American Foreign Policy* (1961), 74.
40 "If the Soviets go to war": Yergin, *Shattered Peace*, 384.
40 "We stay in Berlin": McCullough, *Truman*, 630.
43 "I just tell the truth": Ferrell, *Truman*, 278.

## Chapter 3. Agnostics and Believers

46 "By executing a treaty . . . its dangerous implications": *Congressional Record*, July 11, 1949.
48 "This treaty . . . one step": Truman statement, July 25, 1949.
51 "It is of vital importance": Executive order 9835, March 21, 1947.
52 "The government is full . . . ought to be impeached": Patterson, *Grand Expectations*, 197; Roy Cohn, *McCarthy* (1968), 246; David Caute, *The Great Fear: The Anti-Communist Purge under Truman and Eisenhower* (1978), 43; Eric Alterman, *When Presidents Lie: A History of Official Deception and Its Consequences* (2005), 76; U.S. Senate, Committee on Rules and Administration, *Hearings of Senator Joseph R. McCarthy* (1952), 29; Richard H. Rovere, *Senator Joe McCarthy* (1996 ed.), 12.
53 "I look at that fellow . . . none of theirs": Patterson, *Grand Expectations*, 201.
54 "I just won't get": Stephen E. Ambrose, *Eisenhower: Soldier and President* (1990), 308.
54 "Let us not assassinate": Arthur Herman, *Joseph McCarthy: Reexamining the Life and Legacy of America's Most Hated Senator* (1999), 276.
56 "open, clear, direct challenge": Melvyn P. Leffler, *A Preponderance of Power: National Security, the Truman Administration, and the Cold War* (1991), 367.

56 "the attack upon Korea": William W. Stueck, *The Korean War: An International History* (1995), 43.
58 "old soldiers never die": Robert J. Donovan, *Tumultuous Years: The Presidency of Harry S. Truman, 1949–1953* (1982), 362.
59 "Most of the senior officers": H. W. Brands, *Cold Warriors: Eisenhower's Generation and American Foreign Policy* (1988), 187.
62 "American Gestapo": Michael J. Hogan, *A Cross of Iron: Harry S. Truman and the Origins of the National Security State* (1998), 61.
63 "Many times": Richard H. Immerman, *John Foster Dulles: Piety, Pragmatism, and Power in U.S. Foreign Policy* (1998), 109.
64 "It is now clear": John Ranelagh, *The Agency: The Rise and Decline of the CIA* (1986), 277; William M. Leary, ed., *The Central Intelligence Agency: History and Documents* (1984), 144.
65 "no limit to the explosive power": Lawrence Freedman, *The Evolution of Nuclear Strategy* (1983), 62.
65 "I believe that the United States": Donovan, *Tumultuous Years*, 153.
66 "The United States would be": Richard Rhodes, *Dark Sun: The Making of the Hydrogen Bomb* (1996), 406.
66 "the man who lives in a tar paper shack": *Science News-Letter*, February 25, 1950.
66 "Can the Russians do it?": McCullough, *Truman*, 763.

## Chapter 4. The Golden Age of the Middle Class

71 "For years I thought": John Steele Gordon, "The Ordeal of Engine Charlie," *American Heritage*, Feb./Mar. 1995.
74 "It is Mickey Mouse's day": H. W. Brands, *Masters of Enterprise: Giants of American Business from John Jacob Astor and J. P. Morgan to Bill Gates and Oprah Winfrey* (1999), 190.
76 "On 1,200 flat acres . . . going on outside": *Time*, July 3, 1950.
84 "racial and religious minorities": Democratic party platform, 1948.
86 "In the field of public education . . . all deliberate speed": *Brown v. Board of Education*, 347 U.S. 483 (1954); *Brown v. Board of Education* (II), 349 U.S. 294 (1955).
88 "You know, my friends": Joshua Gottheimer, ed., *Ripples of Hope: Great American Civil Rights Speeches* (2004), 212–13.
89 "The original Constitution": "Southern Manifesto," *Congressional Record*, March 12, 1956.
90 "These are not bad people . . . act accordingly": Tom Wicker, *Dwight D. Eisenhower* (2002), 54; Ambrose, *Eisenhower*, 368.
90 "The federal Constitution . . . of the United Nations": Eisenhower address to the nation, September 24, 1957.
95 "The Soviet announcement": *New York Times*, October 6, 1957.
95 "If they can launch one that heavy": Eric F. Goldman, *The Crucial Decade and After: America, 1945–1960* (1961), 309.
96 "Since military rocketry was not involved": *New York Times*, December 8, 1957.
97 "It commands our whole attention . . . and will persist": Eisenhower address, January 17, 1961.

## Chapter 5. Abraham Lincoln Walks at Midnight

102 "His style in the press conferences": Norman Mailer, *The Presidential Papers of Norman Mailer* (1964), 45–47.
102 "If you give me a week": Wicker, *Eisenhower*, 118.
103 "Let the word go forth": Kennedy inaugural address, January 20, 1961.
104 "Look, Mr. Chairman": Robert Dallek, *An Unfinished Life: John F. Kennedy, 1917–1963* (2003), 410–13.
104 "As a free man": Kennedy speech, June 26, 1963.

106 "Within the past week": Kennedy address, October 22, 1962.
109 "It is in the American tradition": Taylor Branch, *Parting the Waters: America in the King Years, 1954–1963* (1988), 314.
110 "This is the way all presidents behave": Dallek, *Unfinished*, 381.
110 "Can't you get your goddamned friends": Raymond Arsenault, *Freedom Riders: 1961 and the Struggle for Racial Justice* (2006), 164.
111 "We must either submit": Jack Bass and Walter De Vries, *The Transformation of Southern Politics* (1995), 200.
111 "I have almost reached the regrettable conclusion": Martin Luther King, Jr., *Why We Can't Wait* (2000 ed.), 72–73.
111 "The people in the South": Richard Reeves, *President Kennedy: Profile of Power* (1993), 501.
111 "We are confronted primarily with a moral issue": Kennedy address, June 11, 1963.
112 "We are on a breakthrough": Taylor Branch, *Pillar of Fire: America in the King Years, 1963–1965* (1998), 102.
113 "I'm glad I lived long enough . . . moral leader of our nation": Branch, *Parting the Waters*, 877–81.
113 "We will not be satisfied": King speech, August 28, 1963, http://www.americanrhetoric.com/speeches/mlkihaveadream.htm.
119 "I can't stand the bastard . . . hadn't agreed to it": H. W. Brands, *The Wages of Globalism: Lyndon Johnson and the Limits of American Power* (1995), 25–26.
120 "Dick, you've got to get out . . . free at last": Robert Dallek, *Flawed Giant: Lyndon Johnson and His Times, 1961–1973* (1998), 112–13.
122 "We believe that all men are created equal": Johnson speech, July 2, 1964.
122 "I think we just delivered": Dallek, *Flawed Giant*, 120.
122 "We entered the pool area": Ibid., 80–81.
123 "For a century we labored": Johnson address, May 22, 1964.
124 "extremism in the defense of liberty": Goldwater acceptance speech, July 16, 1964, American Presidency Project website, http://www.presidency.ucsb.edu.
124 "These are the stakes!": Lyndon Johnson's 1964 Presidential Campaign Spots website, at http://www.pbs.org/30secondcandidate/timeline/years/1964b.html.
125 "1. You have been elected . . . it was dealing with": Dallek, *Flawed Giant*, 190.
128 "Segregation now": Dan T. Carter, *The Politics of Rage: George Wallace, the Origins of the New Conservatism, and the Transformation of American Politics* (2000), 11.
128 "You and me, we'll be dead": Dallek, *Flawed Giant*, 217.
129 "Open your polling places": Johnson address, March 15, 1965.
130 "But only the individual Negro": Johnson signing remarks, August 6, 1965.

## Chapter 6. Paved with Good Intentions

133 "I knew from the start": Doris Kearns Goodwin, *Lyndon Johnson and the American Dream* (1991), 252–53.
134 "We went in there and killed them off": Robert David Johnson and Kent B. Germany, *The Presidential Recordings of Lyndon B. Johnson: Toward the Great Society, February 1, 1964–March 8, 1964* (2007), 68.
134 "On the contrary": Brands, *Wages of Globalism*, 222.
135 "Duty requires": Johnson message to Congress, May 18, 1964.
135 "An immediate and direct reaction": Brands, *Wages of Globalism*, 226.
136 "We are not about to send American boys": Johnson speech, October 21, 1964.
137 "If we should lose in South Vietnam": Brands, *Wages of Globalism*, 230.
137 "Stable government": Ibid., 232.

138 "We could have kept Diem": Ibid., 230.
138 "We must make clear . . . additional personnel": Ibid., 232–33.
141 "We must make no snap judgments . . . no one else": Ibid., 237–41.
143 "P.J., that was Lemmon . . . The Enemy": Philip Caputo, *A Rumor of War* (1996), 40–90.
146 "One sociologist": *Time*, July 7, 1967.
148 "Acid dealers *killing* each other?": Terry Anderson, *The Sixties* (1999), 98.
150 "We will not tolerate lawlessness": *New York Times*, July 25, 1967.
150 "It looks like Berlin": Ibid., July 25–27, 1967.
151 "Who ever heard": Alan Matusow, *The Unraveling of America: A History of Liberalism in the 1960s* (1984), 356.
151 "Violence is as American": Howard Sitkoff, *The Struggle for* Black Equality, 1954–1992 (1993), 203.
153 "We just don't belong there": Dallek, *Flawed Giant*, 369–70.
153 "We would replace power": Tom Hayden, *The Port Huron Statement* (2005), 43ff.
154 "The MP was trembling": Norman Mailer, *The Armies of the Night* (1968), 130.
155 "tremendous victory": *Washington Post*, October 23, 1967.
155 "sex, drugs, and treason": Terry Anderson, *The Movement and the Sixties* (1995), 142.
155 "Tip, what kind of a son of a bitch": Dallek, *Flawed Giant*, 485–86.
156 "steady progress . . . years in Vietnam": *New York Times*, November 16, 1967; Dallek, *Flawed Giant*, 491.
156 "What the hell is going on?": Patterson, *Grand Expectations*, 680.
157 "The enemy exposed himself": Ibid., 679.
157 "sinkhole . . . must begin to disengage": Brands, *Wages of Globalism*, 251–52.
158 "The United States is ready": Johnson address, March 31, 1968, Public Papers.

## Chapter 7. The Triumph of Cynicism

159 "I don't know what will happen now": *New York Times*, April 5, 1968.
160 "Those of you who are black": Ibid.
161 "If you keep talking like this": Matusow, *Unraveling of America*, 384–85.
161 "I was being forced over the edge": Goodwin, *Johnson and American Dream*, 342–43.
162 "Just think how much": *Los Angeles Times*, November 8, 1962.
163 "You know, the kids": http://www.americanrhetoric.com/speeches/richardnixon checkers.html (October 10, 2007).
163 "As we look at America": *New York Times*, August 9, 1968.
164 "My God . . . Democrats are finished": Matusow, *Unraveling of America*, 415–20.
165 "Left-wingers are incapable . . . agree on lunch": Frank Kusch, *Battleground Chicago: The Police and the 1968 Democratic National Convention* (2004), 134.
165 "I've never made a racist speech . . . in front of": Ibid., 424–25.
166 "That's one small step": *New York Times*, July 21, 1969.
167 "If we are to win": Kennedy special message to Congress, May 25, 1961.
167 "Why, some say, the moon?": Kennedy address, September 12, 1962.
168 "Houston, Tranquility Base here": *New York Times*, July 21, 1969.
168 "I wanted to be an activist president": Richard Nixon, *RN: The Memoirs of Richard Nixon* (1978), 353.
169 "the central paradox of the Nixon administration": Joan Hoff, *Nixon Reconsidered* (1994), 67.
169 "In a flat choice . . . destroying the system": William Safire, *Before the Fall: An Inside View of the Pre-Watergate White House* (1975), 592; Tom Wicker, *One of Us: Richard Nixon and the American Dream* (1995), 515.
171 "We've got those liberal bastards": Richard Reeves, *President Nixon: Alone in the White House* (2001), 145.

172 "the most significant foreign policy achievement . . . around the world": Robert Dallek, *Nixon and Kissinger: Partners in Power* (2007), 293.
172 "secret collusion . . . Nixon shokku": H. W. Brands, *The United States in the World: A History of American Foreign Policy* (1994), 2:328.
173 "It exceeds all expectations": Nixon exchange with reporters, February 24, 1972.
173 "Seize the day, seize the hour": Nixon toast, February 21, 1972.
175 "The problem lay buried . . . contemporary American culture": Betty Friedan, *The Feminine Mystique* (1963), 11.
178 "Ratification by mid-1973": Bruce J. Schulman, *The Seventies: The Great Shift in American Culture, Society, and Politics* (2002), 169.
179 "a big grab for vast federal power": Ibid.
180 "Five men": *Washington Post*, June 18, 1972.
181 "Under *no circumstances*": Bruce Oudes, ed., *From: The President: Richard Nixon's Secret Files* (1990), 271–72.
182 "I did not care": Nixon, *Memoirs*, 513.
182 "If you cover up": Stanley I. Kutler, ed., *Abuse of Power* (1997), 93.
182 "Play it tough": Leon Jaworski, *The Right and the Power: The Prosecution of Watergate* (1976), 214.
182 "third-rate burglary attempt": Stanley Kutler, *The Wars of Watergate: The Last Crisis of Richard Nixon* (1990), 189.
183 "Peace is at hand": *New York Times*, October 27, 1972.
184 "The president is very history-oriented": Kutler, *Wars of Watergate*, 368.
184 "I am not a crook": Nixon press conference, November 17, 1973.
185 "The president has nothing to hide": Nixon address, April 29, 1974.
185 "I just don't see how . . . this afternoon": Kutler, *Wars of Watergate*, 532, 539.
185 "I have never been a quitter": Nixon address, August 8, 1974.
185 "My fellow Americans": Ford address, August 9, 1974.
186 "full, free, and absolute pardon": Ford proclamation, September 8, 1974.
186 "During this long period": Ford address, September 8, 1974.

## Chapter 8. Days of Malaise

188 "Target has not left building": U.S. Senate, Select Committee to Study Government Operations with Respect to Intelligence Operations, *Alleged Assassination Plots* (1975), 33.
188 "Thanks for Patrice": Ibid., 51.
189 "the most dangerous Negro . . . bared to the nation": Brands, *Devil We Knew*, 112–14.
190 "This is an area": U.S. Senate, Select Committee to Study Government Operations with Respect to Intelligence Operations, *Final Report* (1976), 2:101.
191 "The Government has often undertaken": Ibid., 2:5–6.
194 "We feel this to be an historic occasion": Daniel Yergin, *The Prize: The Epic Quest for Oil, Money, and Power* (1991), 567.
195 "The possibility of an embargo . . . broken loose": Ibid., 609.
197 "The party is over": Ibid., 616.
197 "At the end of three months": Douglas Brinkley, *Gerald R. Ford* (2007), 113.
198 "Mr. Chevy Chase": Don Van Natta and Don Van Natta, Jr., *First Off the Tee: Presidential Hackers, Duffers and Cheaters from Taft to Bush* (2004), 97.
199 "The American dream endures": Carter inaugural address, January 20, 1977.
200 "I believe we can have a foreign policy": Carter address, May 22, 1977.
200 "You may rest assured": Gaddis Smith, *Morality, Reason, and Power: American Diplomacy in the Carter Years* (1986), 67.
201 "We need not fear change": U.S. Department of State, *American Foreign Policy: Basic Documents 1977–1980* (1983), 432–33.

203 "But as I was preparing to speak": Carter address, July 15, 1979.
206 "It's a mistake for Americans": Carter press conference, July 25, 1979.
207 "It was a salesman's dream": Brands, *United States in the World*, 2:348.
208 "unbreakable ties of friendship": Carter toast, November 15, 1977.
209 "making the world safe for communism": *Commentary*, April 1976.
210 "In each country": *Commentary*, November 1979.
211 "My opinion of the Russians": State Department, *American Foreign Policy: Basic Documents*, 811–12.
211 "Let our position be absolutely clear": Carter State of the Union address, January 23, 1980.

## Chapter 9. South by Southwest

215 "I have spent most of my life": Ronald Reagan, *An American Life* (1990), 141–42.
216 "the Goliath that is the federal government": Reagan speech, May 6, 1967, Reagan Presidential Library, http://www.reagan.utexas.edu/archives/speeches/govspeech/05061967a.htm (October 25, 2007).
216 "at 65 years of age": *New York Times*, August 20, 1976.
217 "Are you better off": *New York Times*, October 29, 1980.
218 "I hope you're a Republican": Richard Reeves, *President Reagan: The Triumph of Imagination* (2005), 38.
218 "I am in control here": Lou Cannon, *President Reagan: The Role of a Lifetime* (1991), 199.
218 "Under one such marker": Reagan inaugural address, January 20, 1981.
219 "Just what was needed": Reagan news conference, January 20, 1981.
219 "evil empire . . . modern world": Reagan address, March 8, 1983.
220 "For defense contractors across America . . . fish-feeding frenzy": *Wall Street Journal*, May 21, 1985.
220 "There will be many": Brands, *Devil We Knew*, 177.
221 "I never heard anyone": Cannon, *President Reagan*, 291.
222 "I was wondering . . . have swallowed it": Ibid., 268.
225 "She was forthright and convincing": Reagan, *American Life*, 280.
226 "Our government has the right": Michael Lienesch, *Redeeming America: Piety and Politics in the New Christian Right* (1993), 228.
226 "Denies the existence of God": Steve Bruce, *The Rise and Fall of the New Christian Right: Conservative Protestant Politics in America 1978–1988* (1988), 77.
227 "courage to speak out regarding liberals . . . forced to surrender": Richard A. Viguerie, *The New Right: We're Ready to Lead* (1981), unpaginated introduction and 109–10, 119–22.
228 "The apostle John predicts": Hal Lindsey with Carole C. Carlson, *The Late Great Planet Earth* (1974), 154–56.
228 "She turned out to be": Reagan, *American Life*, 280.
228 "If you would like to know": James T. Patterson, *Restless Giant: The United States from Watergate to Bush vs. Gore* (2005), 139.
232 "Defense is not a budget item": Michael Schaller, *Reckoning with Reagan: America and Its President in the 1980s* (1992), 47.
234 "If they do not report": Reagan statement, August 3, 1981.
234 "It struck me as singular . . . the controllers' strike": Gil Troy, *Morning in America: How Ronald Reagan Invented the 1980s* (2005), 78.
234 "A tree is a tree . . . will grow forever": Cannon, *President Reagan*, 529.
235 "liberals and Americans . . . cut more timber": Ibid., 531.
235 "exercises in failed socialism . . . to invent one": Kim McQuaid, *Uneasy Partners: Big Business in American Politics, 1945–1990* (1994), 177–78.
236 by 40 percent between 1977 and 1993: Andrew Busch, *Ronald Reagan and the Politics of Freedom* (2001), 88.

## Chapter 10. Fire or Iceland

238 "We view the current situation": Reagan news conference, December 17, 1981.
238 "this murder of innocent civilians": Reagan news conference, September 3, 1983.
239 "Support for freedom fighters": Reagan State of the Union address, February 6, 1985.
240 "Mr. President, have you approved": Reagan news conference, February 18, 1982.
241 "The Soviets are, you might say . . . of that kind": Reagan interview, March 3, 1981.
242 "Could you tell us, Mr. President": Reagan exchange with reporters, February 12, 1982.
242 "Can you envision": Reagan news conference, February 18, 1982.
242 "Terrorism is the antithesis": Reagan letter to Duarte, August 29, 1985.
242 "In El Salvador we've worked": Reagan radio address, June 8, 1985.
244 "We're not bugging out": Reagan news conference, February 22, 1984.
245 "Reagan always knows . . . Showing His Age?": Cannon, *President Reagan*, 543.
245 "You already are the oldest president": Reagan-Mondale debate, October 21, 1984.
247 "Who is it intended for": Reagan address, March 23, 1983.
248 "The United States gives terrorists no rewards": Reagan statement, June 30, 1985.
249 "contrary to our interests . . . too absurd to comment on": H. W. Brands, *Into the Labyrinth: The U.S. and the Middle East 1945–1993* (1994), 185.
249 "H-hour": Stephen Engelberg, *Report of the Congressional Committees Investigating the Iran-Contra Affair* (1987), 194.
250 "The charge has been made": Reagan address, November 13, 1986.
250 "Then our press took it up": Reagan, *American Life*, 528–29.
251 "No direct evidence was developed": Lawrence E. Walsh, *Iran-Contra: The Final Report* (1994), 446.
251 "I feel like number one . . . wasting time like this?": *Los Angeles Times*, October 3, 1985.
254 "AIDS is God's judgment . . . an awful retribution": John Clifford Purdy, *God with a Human Face* (1993), 38; Randy Shilts, *And the Band Played On: Politics, People, and the AIDS Epidemic* (2000), 311.
255 "I am not happy . . . God rest his soul": *Los Angeles Times*, October 3, 1985.
255 "This is a top priority with us": Reagan press conference, September 17, 1985.
256 "Today we are witnessing": *New York Times*, August 18, 1989.
256 "Burst some eighty-five hundred feet": Jonathan Schell, *The Fate of the Earth* (1982), 47–49.
259 "It is time to recognize": *Foreign Affairs*, Spring 1982.
259 "A freeze now": Reagan address, March 23, 1983.
261 "There is no way": Jonathan Aiken, *Nixon: A Life* (1993), 562.
261 "It would be fine with me . . . Let's go, George": Cannon, *President Reagan*, 768–69.

## Chapter 11. History Without End

265 "Wall Street's October Massacre": *Time*, October 26, 1987.
265 "Down five-oh-eight": Alan Greenspan, *The Age of Turbulence: Adventures in a New World* (2007), 105.
266 "the nearest thing to a meltdown . . . doesn't own a share": *New York Times*, October 20, 1987.
266 "I went straight to the hotel . . . financial system": Greenspan, *Age of Turbulence*, 105–8.
267 "I confess": Reagan, *American Life*, 693.
268 "He is definitely aware of it": *Washington Post*, May 3, 1988.
268 "The next ten days . . . I worried about": Reagan, *American Life*, 694–95.
268 "Not only can it tear down": Nancy Reagan, letter to anti–drug abuse conference, October 21, 1985, Ronald Reagan Presidential Foundation website, http://www.reaganfoundation.org/reagan/nancy/just_say_no.asp (November 15, 2007).
269 A 1995 survey of fifty thousand: *Philadelphia Inquirer*, December 16, 1995.

269 "A profound reversal": *New York Times,* February 20, 1996.
269 "In 1997 we seized 400,000 pills": New York *Daily News,* February 7, 2001.
269 Government statistics for 2005: *Los Angeles Times,* December 18, 2006.
270 "This treaty represents": Reagan address, December 10, 1987.
270 "We will research it . . . historic achievement": Reagan address, December 12, 1987.
271 "I want a kinder, gentler nation . . . no new taxes'": *Washington Post,* August 19, 1988.
271 "vision thing": *Time,* January 1, 1990.
272 "A new relationship": Bush address, May 12, 1989.
272 "no moral or political right . . . their way": *Newsweek,* November 6, 1989.
273 "Mr. Gorbachev, open this gate!": Reagan remarks, June 12, 1987.
273 "We've Done It! . . . happiest people on earth": *New York Times,* November 11, 1989.
274 "I was at my desk": George Bush and Brent Scowcroft, *A World Transformed* (1998), 148–49.
274 "I welcome the decision . . . very good about it": Bush question-and-answer session, November 9, 1989.
276 "Today begins a new chapter": Bush statement, October 2, 1990.
277 "It was over": Bush and Scowcroft, *World Transformed,* 563.
278 "The end of history": Francis Fukuyama, "The End of History," *National Interest,* Summer 1989.
278 "I was quite sure": Caspar Weinberger, *Fighting for Peace: Seven Critical Years in the Pentagon* (1990), 389–90.
280 "I was sitting . . . invade Kuwait": Bush and Scowcroft, *World Transformed,* 302.
281 "If Iraq wins": Ibid., 319–20.
281 "This will not stand": Bush exchange with reporters, August 5, 1990.
283 "To bring it down": *USA Today,* November 1990.
283 "I'm willing to use force": Bush and Scowcroft, *World Transformed,* 439.
283 "I felt the heavy weight": Ibid., 446.
285 "We would have been forced": Ibid., 489.
285 "No one country can claim this victory": Bush address, February 27, 1991.
286 "I was sitting in my office": Bush and Scowcroft, *World Transformed,* 451.
288 "Ted Turner is without doubt": Brands, *Masters of Enterprise,* 276.
288 "I think the people of America": Ibid., 281.
289 "The live CNN pictures are stark": Bush and Scowcroft, *World Transformed,* 523.
289 "I could go through": Ibid., 174.
290 "The Iraqis went to great lengths": Ibid., 457.
290 "Is Mr. Arnett": *New York Times,* January 29, 1991.
290 "But CNN has had": Brands, *Masters of Enterprise,* 275.

## Chapter 12. The Good Old Bad Old Days

292 "Read my lips: I lied": *New York Times,* June 29, 1990.
293 "giant sucking sound": *Washington Times,* October 16, 1992.
294 "The presence of homosexuals": *New York Times,* January 27, 1993.
295 "With free access for homosexuals": *Washington Post,* February 20, 1993.
295 "That seems ridiculous now": *Washington Post,* June 10, 1993.
296 "It is not a perfect solution": Clinton statement, July 19, 1993.
296 "I got the worst of both worlds": Bill Clinton, *My Life* (2004), 486.
296 "If you're going to keep staring": Ibid., 181–82.
297 "This health care system . . . never be taken away": Clinton address, September 22, 1993.
298 "A lot of the students": Clinton, *My Life,* 183.
299 "We are going to keep up this fight": Clinton statement, September 26, 1994.
300 "On September 15": Brands, *Masters of Enterprise,* 263.

301 "It was a disgrace . . . it was great": Ibid., 265.
302 $78 million: *Christian Science Monitor*, November 13, 1998.
303 "When the people responsible . . . or the Middle East": *Time*, March 8, 1993.
305 "Language: A Key Mechanism of Control": *New York Times*, September 9, 1990.
305 "We got the living daylights": Clinton, *My Life*, 629–31.
306 "If we agree on nothing else": Clinton State of the Union address, January 24, 1995.
307 "Armey was a big man": Clinton, *My Life*, 682.
308 "Just dead—dead": *Philadelphia Inquirer*, December 30, 1995.
308 "Enough is enough": New York *Daily News*, January 3, 1996.
308 "If he wants to cave": *New York Times*, January 4, 1996.
309 "He's a forty-nine-year-old Vietnam veteran . . . smaller every day": Clinton State of the Union address, January 23, 1996.
312 "America cannot and must not": Clinton address, November 27, 1995.
313 "Americans by the dozens . . . leaves Somalia for good": *New York Times*, October 5, 1993.
314 "We started this mission": Clinton address, October 7, 1993.
314 "I was sick about the loss . . . than the UN had": Clinton, *My Life*, 552.
314 "I couldn't tell . . . miss the Cold War": Ibid., 554.

## Chapter 13. Culture Clash

316 "See no evil": Jake H. Thompson, *Bob Dole* (1994), 223.
317 "People on welfare": Clinton remarks, January 28, 1995.
317 "ending welfare as we know it": Clinton signing remarks, August 22, 1996.
317 "Farmers will be free": Clinton signing remarks, April 4, 1996.
317 "Tonight let us proclaim": Clinton acceptance speech, August 29, 1996.
318 "I think one of the great problems": Larry Sabato and Glenn R. Simpson, *Dirty Little Secrets: The Persistence of Corruption in American Politics* (1996), 46.
318 "enemy of normal Americans": Thomas Frank, *What's the Matter with Kansas? How Conservatives Won the Heart of America* (2004), 13.
319 "The public understood": Clinton, *My Life*, 386.
319 "This story seems ridiculous": *Washington Post*, January 21, 1998.
320 "My initial instinct": Sidney Blumenthal, *The Clinton Wars* (2003), 324.
320 "I didn't want to . . . it wasn't true": Clinton, *My Life*, 769.
320 "Did you have an extramarital sexual affair . . . an affair with her": WashingtonPost.com Special Report, "President Clinton's Deposition," released March 13, 1998: http://www.washingtonpost.com/wp-srv/politics/special/clinton/stories/clintondep031398.htm (November 24, 2007).
321 "During the government shutdown . . . had been a setup": Clinton, *My Life*, 773–74.
321 "Is there any truth": Clinton interview by NPR, January 21, 1998.
321 "no improper relationship": Clinton interview by Jim Lehrer, January 21, 1998.
322 "I want to say": Clinton statement, January 26, 1998.
322 "Mr. President, were you physically intimate . . . completely true statement": Clinton testimony, August 17, 1998, released September 21, 1998, *Jurist*, http://jurist.law.pitt.edu/transcr.htm (November 26, 2007).
323 "This afternoon in this room": Clinton statement, August 17, 1998.
324 "a notorious example . . . kept the faith'": *New York Times*, January 17, 1999.
325 "The President has said . . . cannot convict him": Bumpers closing argument, January 21, 1999, *American Rhetoric Online Speech Bank*, http://www.americanrhetoric.com/speeches/dalebumpersdefenseofclinton.htm (November 25, 2007).
326 73 percent: "Poll: Clinton's Approval Rating Up in Wake of Impeachment," December 20, 1998, CNN.com: http://www.cnn.com/ALLPOLITICS/stories/1998/12/20/impeachment.poll/ (November 25, 2007).
327 "He was a hell of a good programmer": Brands, *Masters of Enterprise*, 317–18.

329 "vein of gold . . . history of the planet": David A. Kaplan, *The Silicon Boys and Their Valley of Dreams* (1999), 16–18.
330 "Winning Internet browser share . . . the English language": *Infoworld*, November 17, 1998 on CNN.com: http://www.cnn.com/TECH/computing/9811/17/judgelaugh.ms.idg/ (November 23, 2007).
332 "Three-Ring Circus": Montreal *Gazette*, December 6, 1999.
332 "Robocops Face Down Protesters": London *Guardian*, December 1, 1999.
332 "New Luddites at the Gates": *Japan Times*, November 24, 1999.
332 "Ugly from Start to Finish": *South China Morning Post*, December 2, 1999.
332 "Violent Protesters Disrupt WTO Meeting": *New Straits Times*, December 5, 1999.
332 "Seattle Feels World's Anger": Melbourne *Age*, December 2, 1999.
336 "The challenge before us": Clinton remarks, January 26, 1995.
336 "We live in a global economy": Clinton telephone interview by *Seattle Post-Intelligencer*, November 30, 1999.
336 "No one in this room": Clinton address, December 1, 1999.
336 "This administration has people . . . what I'm seeing": *New York Times*, December 2, 1999.
338 "We act to protect": Clinton address, March 24, 1999.
338 "I felt an enormous sense of relief": Clinton, *My Life*, 860.
339 "The whole world will be watching . . . serious for Rabin": Ibid., 543.
340 "colossal mistake . . . made me one": Ibid., 938, 944.

## Chapter 14. Blowback

343 "compassionate conservatism . . . encouraging the inspired": Bush acceptance speech, August 3, 2000.
344 "Today we affirm": Bush inaugural address, January 20, 2001.
345 "Across the board tax relief": Bush signing remarks, June 7, 2001.
346 At six o'clock on the morning . . . time was 10:03: *The 9/11 Commission Report*, http://www.9-11commission.gov/report/911Report_Ch1.htm (November 30, 2007).
351 "When you make a joke . . . 'Don't Kill' Rule'": "May We Laugh Yet? Onion Says Yes," *Media Life*, October 1, 2001, at http://www.medialifemagazine.com/news2001/oct01/oct01/1_mon/news4monday.html (November 30, 2007).
351 "We're going to rebuild": *New York Times*, September 13, 2001.
352 "Today our fellow citizens": Bush address, September 11, 2001.
352 "U.S.A.! U.S.A.! . . . all of us soon": Bush remarks, September 14, 2001.
352 More than 90 percent of Americans . . . "it won't last": Knight-Ridder Washington Bureau, September 25, 2001.
352 "the continuing and immediate threat": Bush message to Congress, September 14, 2001.
353 "war on terror . . . not neutral between them": Bush address to Congress, September 20, 2001.
354 "They will hand over the terrorists": Ibid.
355 "dangerously inadequate . . . regime from power": Micah L. Sifry and Christopher Cerf, eds., *The Iraq War Reader: History, Documents, Opinions* (2007), 199–201.
355 "It may be that the Iraqi government": John Davis, ed., *Presidential Policies and the Road to the Second Iraq War: From Forty-one to Forty-three* (2006), 51.
355 "Given the goals of rogue states": *The National Security Strategy of the United States of America*, http://www.whitehouse.gov/nsc/nss/2002/nss.pdf (November 30, 2007).
356 "He has broken every pledge": Bush statement, September 14, 2002.
357 "Some ask why Iraq": Bush address, October 7, 2002.
357 "We know that Iraq . . . mushroom cloud": Ibid.
358 "We have been more than patient": Bush address at UN, September 12, 2002.
358 "There can be no doubt . . . to acquire nuclear weapons": Powell address to Security

Council, February 5, 2003, U.S. Department of State website, http://www.state.gov/secretary/former/powell/remarks/2003/17300.htm (December 1, 2007).
359 "The United Nations Security Council": Bush address, March 17, 2003.
360 "But it had been worth the effort": General Tommy Franks, *American Soldier* (2004), 463.
360 "The Iraqis had prepared themselves": Ibid., 515.
361 "The goals of our coalition": Bush videotaped message, April 10, 2003.
361 "Major combat operations": Bush address, May 1, 2003.
363 "The United States and its coalition partners": Bush statement, May 22, 2003.
363 "The creation of a strong and stable": Bush news conference, July 17, 2003.
363 "Iraqi democracy will succeed": Bush remarks, November 6, 2003.
364 "a few who have betrayed . . . will be proud": London *Independent*, May 14, 2004.
364 "I want to tell the people": Bush interview, May 5, 2004.
365 42 percent in June 2004: *New York Times*, June 29, 2004.
365 "I'm John Kerry . . . our firepower": Kerry acceptance speech, July 29, 2004.

## Chapter 15. Still Dreaming

368 "I oppose the Kyoto Protocol": Bush letter, March 13, 2001.
369 "Bush Puts U.S. Above the Globe": London *Daily Telegraph*, March 30, 2001.
369 "Bush Defies World": *Weekend Australian*, March 31, 2001.
369 "Le coup de poignard américain": *Le Temps*, March 30, 2001.
369 "Rendezvous mit Klimastörungen": *Süddeutsche Zeitung*, March 31, 2001.
370 "to build up and disseminate": Nobelprize.org, at http://nobelprize.org/nobel_prizes/peace/laureates/2007/index.html (December 4, 2007).
380 "Senator Obama has achieved": Associated Press, November 4, 2008.

# INDEX